THE
Superhistorians
MAKERS OF OUR PAST

THE
Superhistorians
MAKERS OF OUR PAST

BY JOHN BARKER

CHARLES SCRIBNER'S SONS

NEW YORK

Copyright © 1982 John Barker

Library of Congress Cataloging in Publication Data

Barker, John, 1934-
   The superhistorians.

   Bibliography: p.
   Includes index.
   1. Historians—Biography.   2. Historiography.
I. Title.
D14.B33   907'.2   82-5461
ISBN 0-684-18050-2   AACR2

PARENTIBUS FILIISQUE MEIS

CONTENTS

time and cyclical time—God's intervention in history to achieve man's eternal salvation—the Jewish origins of Christian historiography—the early Church's rejection of classical history—the setbacks to historical thinking, and the constructive effects—Augustine's lasting influence on Western man.

PREFACE

Historical study, in its most creative form, has always been a vigorous inquiry of a Socratic kind in which the historian draws upon contemporary experience to ask imaginative questions about the past. He proceeds to eliminate old, comfortable questions and answers, and pursues fresh, positive conclusions; and, to be effective, his inquiry demands critics as well as an audience. But some historians stand apart from the rest. They are men who, when old versions of the past ceased to fit new realities, put fundamental questions to the human record and developed new interpretations. The most prominent of these I call "superhistorians": Herodotus, Thucydides, Augustine, Petrarch, Machiavelli, Voltaire, Scott, Ranke, Marx, Nietzsche, Du Bois, Toynbee, and Wells. Beginning with the question, "Who am I?", each eventually shifted his inquiry into an investigation of the past, answering a leading historical problem other historians had been unable, or unwilling, to solve. Each in turn enlarged society's sense of itself, giving it a different perspective. To the extent that each changed beliefs about the past, he became a "maker" of that past.

History's own history is its best introduction, and the lives and achievements of the "superhistorians" constitute a history of history in the West. These figures understood that history's primary subject is human beings as they grow and as they change; to a greater extent than other historians they fulfilled the historian's function of explaining the human condition within a particular period of time. Realizing that to study the past is also to study what we are now and what we hope to become, each decisively, if sometimes controversially, interpreted the past as he speculated on human nature and destiny. They influence our own beliefs in ways we cannot avoid; and to understand our history and its effects on us, we must examine their accomplishments.

Because historical knowledge affects our ideas of our world and ourselves, we need to assess the historians who hand us this knowledge but who often differ. Most of us have to take the historian on trust, since he is the one who assembles information about the past (often himself depending on the testimony of others) and publishes it. Although in modern Western culture accurate knowledge of the past has greatly increased, research is, nonetheless, still ruled by interpretation of evidence. Ask a group of people what the basis of history is, and most will reply, "Facts." Historical facts are events that have really occurred, but such facts have no life or meaning apart from some connection the historian applies; and even the clearest "fact" may be viewed in several ways. History is what the historian chooses from the facts to include and emphasize in his work, and his findings reflect the questions of the era in which he lives as well as his personal convictions. History is thus a constant argument among historians, and accounts of the past constantly change—the result of new questions and of differing purposes of historical knowledge as much as of new evidence. The "superhistorians" conspicuously exemplify this process of change and argument.

The most striking feature of history in the West is that it is endlessly rewritten. The historian reopens the inquiry and sometimes finds new evidence, sets the scope of his analysis, realigns events and figures in importance (and even dismisses some), reaches conclusions, and may move the course of history itself. The authority he exerts is far larger than the public imagines. Those histories that are biased, yet comprehensive and founded on solid evidence, are often among the best designed and executed and can wield tremendous influence; nowhere is the historian more powerful than in his textbooks. But history received uncritically by the public can soon become history wholly governed by opinion, and in present times ideology often overshadows evidence. Ideas of history divide mankind socially and internationally, and in an age when most of the world's peoples commonly obtain what passes as their history from television or radio, historical study can be used deliberately to transform the past into a vehicle for propaganda. We need to discriminate among history's rival versions; and to do this we must test historians and "superhistorians" for their knowledge and their accurate use of historical information.

The study of history prompts us to study those beliefs *about* history which touch everyone; and the leading beliefs today, the varied forms historical truth in the West has taken, derive from the "superhistorians." Our thirteen "superhistorians" differ greatly among themselves, in their style of delivery as well as in the answers they found. In ancient Greece, Herodotus and Thucydides saw the story of men and states as a recurring cycle; when Rome fell, Augustine held that history moves foward under God, ending in His final judgment on us all. In Renaissance Italy, Petrarch and Machiavelli studied Rome's achievements and tried to revive them; Voltaire, in the French Enlightenment, insisted that man had advanced by using his powers of reason and urged him to continue. Scott, a Romantic, preserved his nation's colorful past, and wrote novels to show how people lived through historical crises; but, in Germany, Ranke believed the historian should only search the archives for facts, while Marx argued from economic evidence that history's theme is class conflict, leading to a final workers' revolution. Nietzsche attacked late nineteenth-century "decadence,"and spoke discordantly of history's proper place in a new and more creative life for man; the American black, DuBois, rejecting the past as the tale of white supremacy, endowed his disinherited people with a history of their own. After the First World War, Toynbee analyzed the rise and fall of civilizations while Wells saw history as "more and more a race between education and catastrophe."

Each "superhistorian" explored and explained man's past in light of the truth as he could best conceive it in his time. Each answered a fundamental question by investigating the human record; and each, by imaginatively organizing the facts at his disposal and by means of his methods, facilitated further historical study. Their widespread influence also makes clear that the discipline of history in the West exists primarily to teach the public and draws its lifeblood from contemporary questions the historian and public share. This is especially noteworthy in considering the West today, where many people, though they have some interest in the past, may object that history as a whole is often inaccurate or irrelevant. We live in an essentially ahistorical age that is much concerned with the present and only superficially attracted to the past. Yet many historical events which may have continuing consequences, and not least family histories, do arouse our curiosity; and intelligent men and women have always tried to understand past human experience. If historians are to restore history as an intellectually satisfactory source of knowledge in Western daily life, they must be in touch with a general audience. Such involvement, and the ability to write well and to state his case forcefully, will surely be marks of a future "superhistorian."

The beliefs the "superhistorians" held have themselves become part of history. Their work should now encourage Western man to define anew his own questions and to find his own answers from the past. We study that past most keenly when links between past and present apparently break, as was notably true after the fall of Rome, and again during the Scientific Revolution. Current signs of disunity between past and present, in America and in the West, are promising for new historical thinking. In a world we find full of exceptional change, it is the historian's major task once more to challenge the human record with fundamental questions, thereby providing for us the opportunity for self-discovery. His efforts will shape our future as well as "make" our past.

The idea of this book began at Rice University, Texas, and developed at Trent University, Canada. I appreciate the stimulus of students and colleagues at both institutions. My thanks also goes to Grace Dyer for typing the manuscript; and I am very grateful to Jacques Barzun and Alex Holzman of Charles Scribner's Sons for their courteous professional advice. Our conversations must have touched on every topic of historiography.

The book's style and scope do not allow for full documentation of sources. In my research I encountered the ideas of literally hundreds of authors, who, I hope, will now accept my general acknowledgement of indebtedness. Any errors in the book are, of course, my own responsibility; spelling in quotations has been made to conform to modern American English. The bibliography is not meant to be exhaustive but to suggest further reading.

This book is dedicated to my parents and my three sons, who are my links to the past and future; but my respect for that past, and my future hopes, are equally my wife's.

JOHN BARKER
Lakefield, Ontario
May, 1982

THE
Superhistorians
MAKERS OF OUR PAST

CHAPTER ONE

HERODOTUS AND THUCYDIDES

I

As the story of man, history begins with the obscurity surrounding the first members of the human species, who appeared at least 2 million years ago, it seems, in eastern Africa. Those distant expanses of time have been called prehistoric because no accounts of them exist; but history is incomplete without them, for the achievements of early man —his toolmaking and mastery of fire, his acquisition of language, his extensive migrations, and the social patterns which he formed—are clearly crucial to the whole of human development and affect us still, as do his flaws and failures. What happened before, from the origins of the universe to the emergence of the primates, provides a background of extraordinary grandeur and interest; more exactly, it shows the biological and behavioral inheritance. But to describe the story of the earth as *history* is to use the term too freely. History is concerned primarily with human phenomena, not with natural; and history is doubly human because, as an idea, it is man's creation, challenging him to transcend the limits of information about himself and to discover what he is by finding meaning in what he has done. In short, it is man's commentary on man.

History's other beginning then—the history which will concern us most—is with man's self-awareness and his unique communication of thought. The first cultures were oral, transmitting their knowledge from one generation to the next and giving all knowledge the character of respected lore of the past; and, if surviving primitive cultures offer a comparison, tales and songs narrating events in the life of the tribe, the village, or the family were vital parts of early man's tradition. Once he recognized he had a past, early man evidently moved to turn it to his use, and we in an ahistorical age should appreciate his genius better. The anonymous human who first conceived how the preservation of memory might benefit a people, who feared its absence, who spoke a reason for recollecting at all, should by all rights stand foremost in this study. Civilization, let alone every kind of historian, is in his debt; for, by a process he can hardly have understood, he started shaping what history has been fundamentally ever since—a particular implement designed to serve the present.

But this new type of knowledge was potentially dangerous. Memory exhibits our belief in something we have learned, encouraging us to act in a certain way under certain circumstances. A communal memory, certified and upheld, should therefore promote social stability; but, when left free to organize experience as it chooses, it can release a chaos, and strenuous efforts were soon made by authorities to head off such risks and exercise control. Australian aborigines guard the past of their ancestors, for it legitimizes the customs of the present that will continue unbroken into the future; and at the other extreme the Inca, most ordered of preliterate cultures, had four versions of history, from secret to popular, transmitted separately and all under the state's strict censorship. Once memory was roughly fashioned as a particular implement for the present, it gained an official function, which greatly influences to this day history's composition and content. In a world of the spoken word, of course—as we see when conditions recreate it— history's impact is amplified; for there memory comes stamped with an individual's personality, with his gestures, and most of all with his tone of voice. Language heard is very different in its effects from language read; and the broad mass of people can still be moved only by the power of speech.

Two advances were necessary, however, for history to continue its evolution—the mastery of writing, which preserved ancient traditions but simultaneously stole most of the wonder from their words, and a more precise computation of time; for oral history's major weakness remains uncertain chronology. This progress was uneven, as a quick glance across the world will show.

The civilizations of Mexico and Peru kept their heritage alive with little or no written assistance, though they were strongly conscious of the past and each devised an elaborate calendar. Deciphered Maya glyphs sometimes tell of dates, places, and people's names, and the Aztecs learned of their special destiny from illustrated chronicles; but mostly this embryonic writing, like the Inca knotted strings, recorded lists of numbers. The Spanish conquest badly damaged the sequence of oral tradition and its place in society, and for these reasons our knowledge of the pre-Columbian centuries largely derives from what was set down soon afterward and from archaeology.

In several lands of the Middle East a more refined historical interest is conspicuous. To the Egyptians every detail of life depended on their gods, whose will was inscrutable; but that did not stop them from taking intense pride in their past as a nation. Lists of kings and genealogies were kept during three thousand years of changing dynasties, and rulers and private citizens alike noted their deeds on the stone of temples, tombs, and monuments, confident posterity would read them. In this context the Great Pyramid becomes the supreme statement of history's public importance in Egypt—or in any culture, come to that. Time flowed reliably like the Nile itself, it did not unfold at intervals; but to us such an uncritical static view of past, present, and future, marked by the absence of theorizing, is inadequate.

In Mesopotamia, where genuine writing first appeared, the past was a living reality, too; but it served a more practical purpose, to define relations once established with the deities and to guide the present in maintaining them. Legal codes and countless legal documents attest to this belief, which, in the seventh century B.C., caused the Assyrian king Ashurbanipal to assemble a vast library of earlier records useful and propitious for government. Other materials out of Babylonia and Assyria include royal annals, accounts of wars, lists of kings and officials, and semihistorical folklore. Self-glorification was a feature of Assyrian writing, whereas in Babylon a more impartial attitude eventually developed; the ancient world's chronologies, however, remained local and inefficient. Astronomical calendars were kept chiefly for accurate religious observance, not to date events of a secular kind or to enumerate years in succession. Lists of rulers had a certain regional value, and in late Egypt and Babylon separate collections were made by priests to synchronize them. The Greeks tried to reckon by the quadrennial occurrence of the Olympic Games, the Romans by their annual consuls; but an improved system did not arrive until the Christian chronology was widely adopted.

In India the Hindu scriptures are collections of hymns, prayers, and instructions for ritual, devoid of historical instinct. The vast majority of inscriptions register gifts to the gods or ownership of property; the edicts of Ashoka in the third century B.C. are unusual for providing an impression of the time. In China, though, history was the record of events, and the most notable works are invariably marked by intellectual and literary distinction. The Chinese historian came to his task as registrar rather than author, to synthesize not to analyze, and the huge dynastic histories written as an act of state became models for lesser types of compilation. Sources were classified and texts authenticated, but the resulting official versions of the past were bound by the convention that only what was worthy should be remembered; and they reflected accordingly Confucian doctrine and the current pressures at court. A complex chronology, distortion of events to save face, compliance with approved literary forms—and the pervasive anonymity— further obscure in Western eyes the strengths of Chinese historiography.

Every endeavor to preserve the past has an interest; but the history of man, conceived as an inquiry into the available information on man himself, set forth in a narrative, and, above all, explaining his actions, originated in two places which still deserve recognition as the fountainheads of Western civilization—Greece and Palestine. The Jewish achievement, important in itself, will be explored in the chapter on Augustine's Christian version of history. The Greeks were the first to develop history as we recognize it today, and to their spirit of rational investigation and their standards of historical scholarship Western historiography has repeatedly returned. Their initiative was but one aspect of their ambitious attempt on all fronts to apply their intelligence to the measurement and comprehension of man; and their historical revolution was principally the work of two men, Herodotus and Thucydides.

II

There exists in the National Archaeological Museum in Naples a double bust of Herodotus and Thucydides, portraying the founders of the two main schools of ancient history joined back to back, Janus-like —unfinished bookends, as it were, waiting to hold so much of subsequent history writing. Commemorated thus in a *herma*—a boundary post, used also in Roman times for garden decoration—the two acknowledged masters, one of social and cultural, the other of political and military history, dwell inseparably together. But, new and unusual though the contributions of both men were, neither created history entirely by himself. Herodotus's *Histories* of the Greek and Persian wars put history in the ranks of substantive knowledge; but to spend a few moments on the predecessors of Herodotus would reveal his indebtedness, and also help us see better his own originality.

To us it may seem that history, a long-standing fixture in the educational syllabus, would be a fairly easy discipline to define. Actually, a great amount of wrestling was needed to dissociate it from myth, and the struggle to keep that division clear has been constant and arduous ever since. An oddity of the Greek past is that, after early written beginnings—the so-called Linear B inscriptions, again mainly recording lists—Greek civilization moved into an oral period when events were enshrined in poetic form and given the character of myth. The truth about the past resided in the spoken word in all its inexactitude and power, and there was one "word" or version for every major event. Once one epic poet had treated a subject, some filling in of detail might be done by others, but no reworking of the topic was deemed necessary. The inspiration, not the strict facts, was what mattered most.

Homer, of course, is the outstanding example of this tradition. To deny this legendary singer—who lived some time between the tenth and the eighth century B.C.—a few of the historian's attributes would be absurd. In the *Iliad* especially he shows an attention to events, and even to fixed numbers of days and years, and he tries to render the past intelligible by selection; but his epic of the Trojan War was essentially myth, not history, telling to a company of lesser men a tale of heroes in a past that was remote, fashioned for the purpose of teaching religion, culture, conduct, and politics together. The mortal figures neither develop nor deteriorate, and the gods come and go, as real as the fighting kings and warriors. For instance, when Achilles prepares to face his Trojan adversary Hector, he dons a splendid suit of armor forged in a night for him by Hephaestus, god of fire. All Greek culture may descend from Homer, and he seeks out and finds many motives in his tale in secular, psychological terms; but an entirely rational understanding of phenomena is absent. Much of the historical information, as opposed to myth and story, in the *Iliad* reflects Homer's knowledge of later ages and of his own time rather than of the Trojan War. Nonetheless we should remember that all Greeks, even Thucydides, believed the *Iliad* to contain a nucleus of fact; and Herodotus, for all his advances, is clearly the great Ionian poet's disciple in the breadth and detail of his work, his sense of dramatic movement, his human sympathy, and his choice of subject.

An important forerunner of another kind was Hesiod, whose poem *Works and Days*, composed to offer his fellow farmers advice about morals and agriculture, provided Greeks and Romans with elements of a historical plan. Hesiod's was a pessimistic outlook, gazing backward with regret from the social distress of life in the eighth century. The golden or patriarchal age, the silver or voluptuous, the bronze or warlike, the heroic age of the Trojan War, all had summarily departed and mankind was now pitifully struggling in the present age of iron. Of interest too as history seen by the ordinary laborer (causing Hesiod once to be called the first Marxist historian), this gloomy view was brightened by men of a later epoch with the belief that degeneration would be ended by the age of gold's return. Obviously this cyclical scheme—whose consummation the Roman poet Virgil would celebrate in lines taken to mean the triumph of Augustus—was very different from the linear prophetic concept of time the Jews were developing simultaneously.

As a clearly identifiable means of recalling the past, history originated in the Greek settlements along the Aegean coast of Asia Minor and on the islands close by. This region, Ionia, was particularly susceptible to foreign influences, and in the sixth and fifth centuries B.C. an intellectual revolution occurred there whose significance may never have been exceeded. In this "Ionian Enlightenment" men began for the first time to put critical questions to all fields of human interest, rejecting time-honored religious and poetic explanations as unsatisfactory, intent to know what was knowable. Thales and Anaximander, both of Miletus, tried to discover the facts of the nature of the universe, and Hippocrates of Cos set superstition aside when he treated the sick by observing their symptoms and applying remedies drawn from experience and common sense. There was also the philosopher Heraclitus who was perhaps the most radical spirit of all. "Homer deserves to be thrown out of the contests and flogged," he says in one of his fragments.

The characteristic Ionian mind did not feel inhibited by the gods from asking what the Ionians' neighbors and occasional overlords, the Lydians and Persians, were like; and it came to regard them objectively in a manner not far different from a present-day anthropologist's. Indeed, the gods were thought to favor curiosity as it led to their acts becoming better known. With Hecataeus of Miletus an interest in local differences broadened into interest in peoples as a whole; and in his *Tour Round the World*, which was half geography and half rudimentary history, that extensive traveler described the eastern Mediterranean, Egypt, and Persia, commenting on the appearance, customs, and past of the inhabitants from a spectator's perspective. As the Ionians moved from mythical to rational explanations, the world became their province, a world one could start exploring anywhere. Reason, a sense of order, and a desire for skillful presentation inspired this energetic search for a better understanding of phenomena; and, regardless of the prevailing religious and Homeric beliefs, it began to seem natural that the observable truth should be candidly discussed and judged against the poetic.

For history proper to appear, it had to break from the form of its ancestors, emancipate itself from early philosophy as well as from myth, and, as an idea, literally be invented. The scientific thrust of the Ionian revolution paved the way, but Herodotus was history's creator and he gave it shape and integrity. There was, it has been well said, no Herodotus before him. In the *Iliad* a *histor* is an arbitrator between litigants; but by the fifth century B.C. the word *historia* had come to mean an inquest. Herodotus lost no time in announcing his fundamental aims, opening his *Histories* (really his *Inquiries*) with the statement that he hoped to do two things: "to preserve the memory of the past by putting on record the astonishing achievements both of our own and of other peoples; and more particularly, to show how they came into conflict." To record and celebrate—but especially to explain. Let us look at what little we know of this remarkable man.

When he was born about 484 B.C. in Halicarnassus, that Greek city in Asia Minor was reluctantly part of the Persian empire. The child Herodotus has been pictured standing on the city quay as the defeated ships returned from the battle of Salamis and asking, "Mother, what did they fight each other for?" Answering that question became his life's work. What Herodotus looked like as a young man would be interesting to know. The portrait busts we have are later artists' impressions of what he should have been, contrived according to current taste and transposed from the character of his writing. Suitably they show the Father of History (the title was conferred by Cicero) in old age; but when—perhaps with a touch of the spirit of a backpacking student—he first set out on the travels that would make him famous, he must have appeared exceptionally ready to learn from new experience. He suggests too the young Marco Polo, for Herodotus was possibly a merchant, like the Venetian, and his *Histories* frequently mention matters of commerce—cassia and cinnamon, salt fish from southern Russia, methods of transport, strange forms of trade and calculation. Journeying on land and sea—he knew, for instance, what Cape Sunium looked like when one rounded it—he traveled, sometimes in Hecataeus's footsteps, back and forth across the known world a century before Alexander's conquests forced it into a Hellenistic unity. A Persian order had been imposed, but bandits and pirates, not to mention other hazards, would have made the dangers of passage considerable.

His writing is full of the evidences of travel, with an occasional phrase like "I have observed for myself" to emphasize that his testimony is true; for Herodotus's career took him practically everywhere—as far east as Babylon, south in Egypt to Aswan, west to Cyrene on the North African coast, and north to the mouth of the Danube and to the Crimea. From the last, incidentally, he has provided us with the earliest information on Russia and its Scythians, as important a birth certificate as Tacitus's description of Germany. Herodotus knew in detail his homeland of Asia Minor, the Aegean islands and mainland Greece, and, indeed, he seems to have thought he had seen almost everything. "Eastward of India lies a desert of sand," he once wrote; beyond that the world stopped on the shore of the surrounding ocean.

The result of his journeys was that he became very cosmopolitan, with an unusual ability to comprehend other people's points of view. He observed that man's behavior conformed to his habitat, and that as a result each regional variety of man possessed its own process of growth—one reason why the *Histories* pay so much attention to geography and climate. This was an important notion for history's development, and the Ionian background must have fostered such an attitude in him. To the Greeks all other peoples were merely foreigners. Herodotus, however, allowed his native outlook to be modified by his very diverse experience, and saw those peoples with objectivity and tolerance. Throughout his work he is firmly on the Greek side; but he does not let patriotism distort his opinions, and he is magnanimous to the Persians when he believes their conduct deserves it. Xerxes, the Persian king, is shown to be capable of generosity and good faith; some individual Athenians, in contrast, are shown as traitors to their country.

For most of his life Herodotus was the sort of figure the twentieth century has become familiar with—a political refugee. Seeking liberty, he eventually moved to Athens, where he settled for a while, becoming friendly with the tragedian Sophocles, and where he delivered a series of lectures for which he was paid a handsome sum. His residence in Athens no doubt heightened his awareness of the city's leadership and unique values, which had turned the Persian tide, and he praised Athens in his *Histories*; but he was never granted citizenship, perhaps because, as the friend of foreigners, he was considered too liberal in that center of the Greek coalition. Finally he went to live in the colony of Thurii then being founded under Athenian protection in southern Italy, an area which was to Greece as America was to Europe a hundred years ago. Broad and fertile, it was the New World, and shiploads of settlers migrated there to build Greek cities. Whatever the circumstances of his going, the challenge of joining such an enterprise and testing Greek ideas and institutions afresh in the practical setting of a frontier would have gripped Herodotus's imagination. Though he may have returned briefly to Athens, he probably expanded and revised the *Histories* in his new surroundings, dying at Thurii about the year 430, after the Peloponnesian War had begun. Tradition says he was buried there in the marketplace.

Herodotus could hardly have set out to write a history, for no such thing existed until he created it. His work came out of a lifetime spent storing up information and ceaselessly asking questions; and the history came inherently from the questions. Perhaps the great conflict in his childhood set forever the broad pattern of his inquiry; or it might have slowly become for him the central episode around which all past events fell into place, as the idea of the covenant served the Jews. At any rate his finished *Histories* unfolded the grand theme of the Persian Wars and drew the story of the world together as the scenes moved toward their climax.

The Alexandrian librarian, who later divided the *Histories* into nine books and gave them the names of the nine Muses (starting with Clio, the inspirer of history), cleverly revealed the chain of argument and the symmetry of Herodotus's master plan. The first book describes the heritage of conflicts between Europe and Asia that culminated in the Persian invasion, and the next two concentrate on Africa, the conquest of Egypt by the Persians, and the repercussions of that event within the Persian Empire. The fourth relates the Persian expeditions into Scythia and Libya which laid the basis for King Xerxes's scheme of world domination. In the fifth and sixth books Herodotus drew attention to the affairs of the semioriental states of Asia Minor, his native area, where Greek and Persian interests increasingly clashed. Although the first Persian invasion of the Greek mainland by Darius met with defeat at Marathon in 490, Xerxes, who succeeded his father in 485, was bent on vengeance and prepared for the famous war described in books seven through nine—the war to which all events, Herodotus believed, had been building since Helen, the most beautiful woman in Greece, had been carried off to Troy. In this last section the progress of Xerxes's huge army, the construction of a bridge of boats across the Hellespont, the devastation of Greece itself, the campaign at Thermopylae, and the brilliant Greek victories at Salamis and Plataea are all told in detail. The story stops amid the skirmishes following the Persian defeat, the last episode catching the threads and leaving the audience to think further on its own.

The first aim of Herodotus was to perpetuate in the public memory deeds which should not be forgotten. The Persian Wars were just receding sufficiently for him to be comparable to a British author of the 1980s sitting down to write of his country's finest hour, Churchill's leadership and the checking of a German invasion being still very clear in the minds of the older generation. In that way the war lived on; Herodotus would have found plenty of survivors who remembered their participation and audiences with a keen interest. He believed the war had been a most important event—in magnitude and in its effect on Greek self-confidence—and he was most anxious that its memory should not die with the passing generation. Herodotus's intention was Homeric when he sought to make his story immortal; but in doing so he boldly broke local and racial prejudices by directing his work toward not just Greek communities everywhere but all mankind. He urged all men to marvel at the glorious deeds performed on both sides and to identify with them.

His second aim, though, was even less conventional—to show how the two peoples came into conflict; and in his performance of this we witness the breakthrough. The myths of the Greeks had related and interpreted the past before, but Herodotus now approached the past with the new principle of critical inquiry. He chose to ask why the war had happened, and in doing so he found he could not hope to answer his question adequately unless he investigated all that was taking place in the world at that time. A comprehensive history of the Second World War would similarly need to begin, as Churchill's did, with the origins of the First World War and the Treaty of Versailles—or with the unification of Germany, or even with the French Revolution. The war with Persia was an event of universal significance too in the world of Herodotus's day. If we draw a map of the eastern Mediterranean and divide it into four—Scythia, Persia, North Africa, and Greece—we may see how he and the Greeks could believe the Persian invasion was the last phase of a military plan executed in the other areas. To commemorate, yes, but his driving purpose was to show why the conflict had arisen after making as certain as he could what had occurred before and during the fighting. This was decisive for historiography; for, by and large, the search for reasons why things have happened—for the causes of events—has ever since been considered the superior part of the historian's calling, as opposed to mere recording or description.

But in spite of the great theme Herodotus was pursuing he was constantly drawn away from it—or so it would seem on first reading. There is an extraordinary mixing into his history of all sorts of anecdotes and departures from the main topic. Talking of livestock in Scythia, he suddenly says "a remarkable fact occurs to me (I need not apologize for the digression—it has been my plan throughout this work)," and off he goes to puzzle over why it is that mules cannot be bred in the Greek state of Elis. To Herodotus everything, it seems, is like one of the Egyptian oracles, "sufficiently interesting to warrant further notice"—the dimensions of the walls of Babylon, how the pyramids were built, burial customs the world over, the habits of crocodiles, the sorts of cables Xerxes used to hold his bridge of boats together. It is items like these that play a large part in making the *Histories* enjoyable reading. Never at a loss for a good story, Herodotus's first rule of inquiry was satirized by the playwright Aristophanes as "look for the woman." Some of the best of his respectable anecdotes have stayed in Western folklore: Arion and the dolphin, Polycrates's ring found in a fish, the Spartan Dieneces remarking when faced with immense numbers of Persian archers "we shall have our battle in the shade," Xerxes lashing the sea. He had an ear for a good phrase, too. Egypt was "the gift of the Nile," Persian boys were taught "to ride, to use the bow, and to speak the truth"; and the brave words on the General Post Office building in New York, "neither snow, nor rain, nor heat, nor gloom of night stays these couriers from the swift completion of their appointed rounds," are adapted from his description of the Persian messenger service.

One reason for Herodotus's digressions is that the *Histories* were designed to be read aloud; and, if Herodotus or any other public speaker can interrupt his serious subject with an odd fact or an intriguing yarn, he stands a better chance of keeping his audience—and presumably of being paid. Tales were occasions for vivid delivery, and, being usually about individuals, they encouraged the crowd to draw nearer; even in print they capture an oral setting. We are told the *Histories* won Herodotus a prize at Olympia, though a proverb has also come down to the effect that he lectured too long. Aristotle later dismissed him as a mere storyteller; but a closer look at the *Histories* reveals with what superb craftsmanship the stories accompany the theme. By including them Herodotus was able to offer a virtually total picture of Greece and all that affected it from the sixth century to his own time. The anecdotes are not incidental like the little scenes of Aesop's fables or of medieval husbandry in the margins of the Bayeux Tapestry; they have a role in building up the world portrait besides adding import to the life described. Not just concerned with political and military matters, Herodotus wished to tell what man everywhere was like, because an inquiry into a world war unavoidably became an investigation into the entire world's state and story. All that existed, all that was done, all that was thought, he believed, was relevant.

His achievement is all the more striking when we consider the difficulty of writing something similar today. Individuals certainly produce histories of recent wars and epochs, but such projects are now frequently undertaken by teams of experts, who give their books a committee's outlook and a committee's personality. A truly comprehensive study of the Second World War would have to have American, British, French, Russian, German, and Japanese contributors, among others. In contrast, Herodotus's *Histories* are the work of one extremely intelligent man. Perhaps there are only two good ways to grasp the themes and movement of history—traveling on foot, or seeing the world from aloft—and Herodotus gives the impression of taking his perspective from both. His *Histories* are simultaneously tightly detailed, all-surveying, and personal; the well-planned major parts resemble statues in a frieze taking their place around the sculptor's centerpiece. The finished product is a long and elaborate narrative, certainly not a string of stories casually put together; and not the least of Herodotus's distinctions is that, though his language was poetic, he was the first major Greek writer to use prose. This was a vital step in defining what history is, and perhaps no historian has ever had a greater effect on literature.

It is no wonder Herodotus was proclaimed as Father of History. His work had the essential features now assigned to that discipline—critical inquiry, prose narrative, popular presentation, and cultural significance—and its success inspired a stream of followers. But the *Histories* have other notable characteristics; we may take an obvious one first. Like Homer, but less romantically, Herodotus chose to write about a war. War, he believed, supremely tested a society's beliefs, called forth the ultimate in human conduct, and provided man's greatest dramatic situations. Ever since, historians have tended to see wars as the major subjects and the major punctuation marks in history, and modern experience seems to confirm that no topic is more important to peoples. The conflict of man against man, with the prospect of violence, still has the greatest appeal, for, as the English author Thomas Hardy once said, "War makes rattling good history; but Peace is poor reading."

Like Protagoras, his compatriot at Thurii, Herodotus believed man was the measure of all things. As Herodotus indicated in Themistocles's speech before the battle of Salamis, a man who laid his plans with due regard to common sense would enlist divine support. The pattern of the past showed a tension between human success and human fate, and the career of Xerxes proved yet again that immoderate success tempts divine intervention. Nature loves harmony, and lightning always strikes at great buildings and tall trees; but within the divine scheme there is, nonetheless, a great deal of latitude for human beings to take the initiative and act out their own affairs. Xerxes's decisions before and during the invasion illustrated this, and in each stage of Greek and Persian history personal choices, not divine whims, had set events in motion and brought reward or calamity. Man was by no means the plaything of the gods. Self-initiative was a part of his singular destiny, and one to be welcomed in the pursuit of the Greek ideal of being fully alive and fully human.

In this view Herodotus was uncommon. To his contemporaries the gods were still active, and all incidents of life were governed by their perpetual interference; but, without attacking religious belief, he set it on one side. Chance entered into the turn of events—the weather, disease, or, as Pascal was to say much later, the length of Cleopatra's nose. With his love of stories, Herodotus would surely have delighted in such recent examples of chance as the discovery of the Watergate burglars or Hitler's escape from assassination in July 1944. But he had reached the conclusion that men could largely determine their futures by their decisions, a key element of historical analysis. "One is surely right in saying that Greece was saved by the Athenians," he wrote. "It was the Athenians who—after God—drove back the Persian king."

Now the conduct of rational inquiry demands precise evidence on which to proceed; and in collecting and adjudicating his sources Herodotus set new and lasting standards. Not only was he the first person to write an ordered, human-centered account, he was the first to accumulate materials systematically and evaluate them for factual truth, and he remains exceptional. He seems to have had some familiarity with official records, even the Persian army list, and he took advantage of information gathered in temples, which in those days were also museums and public depositories; but, aside from borrowing from Hecataeus for his descriptions of Egypt and perhaps of Babylon, Herodotus hardly used written chronicles, partly because of the working difficulties they presented, partly because he was still a native of a largely oral culture. Monuments and the stories connected with them interested him especially; and most of his evidence was collected as he traveled around the ancient world using his eyes, his ears, and his talent for persistent critical questioning. If anyone is exempt from the English historian R. H. Tawney's censure that "what historians need is better boots, not better books," it would be he.

Herodotus regarded first-hand evidence as the best kind, and valued clear identification. Exact names were important, also measurements, both for accuracy's sake and because an audience would listen more attentively if he said that Hippias, son of Pisistratus, did this at Marathon—not some anonymous soldier at an uncertain place. For similar reasons as well as for sheer personal interest, he was indefatigable in trying to establish links between the deities of Greece and the gods of other countries. He was sometimes unobservant or credulous where animals were concerned (though he flatly rejected the fantastic story of the phoenix); but on the life and customs of the ancient world—for which, in many respects, he is our principal source and therefore deserves the title of Father of Anthropology, too—he has been proved remarkably truthful, ever since nineteenth-century archaeological expeditions set off with the *Histories* in hand. They found accurate his descriptions of round boats on the Euphrates, of Mesopotamian irrigation systems, and of the Phoenicians circumnavigating Africa—stories which caused Cicero to call him a liar. Herodotus had many detractors in antiquity, and the expeditions of Alexander revealed gaps in his reports; but he was a born verifier and had an instinct for rejecting the fabulous—like other travelers' tales of races of one-eyed men, or of Indians with feet so big they used them as sunshades. Nor was he fooled by tall stories from nearer home. Relating that Scyllias, a famous diver, was said to have swum ten miles underwater when deserting to the Greeks, he gave his frank opinion that the journey had been made by boat.

Yet another important feature of Herodotus's type of inquiry is his refusal, when confronted with several plausible accounts of a phenomenon or an event, either to soar off on a Homeric flight of imagination or to compress the versions into a single answer; he instead would say he had probed as far as he could, and would ask the listener to make a choice between the two or more statements most likely to be true. Such open-mindedness is in a way very modern, as we recognize afresh the impossibility of obtaining final versions of history: there will always be on every issue a Greek and a Persian side. A leading example occurs when Herodotus describes his attempts to establish the source of the Nile. One puzzling but quite acceptable theory he heard was that the mighty river began in the torrid south from melting snow, which was actually close to what the explorers Burton and Speke found in the nineteenth century; but, having traveled up the Nile as far as he could to see for himself, he had to be satisfied with the contradictory statements he had been given. "My business," he wrote about a Greek parley with Xerxes, "is to record what people say, but I am by no means bound to believe it—and that may be taken to apply to this book as a whole." Critical of miraculous explanations, he was obviously happier when he could make the past intelligible in human terms. Oracles were chiefly important for their consequences; but, aware of the dangers in frankly disputing religion, his attitude was generally respectful, and he usually tried to quote alternative opinions rather than supply them himself.

All these qualities cannot conceal the fact that the *Histories* have certain faults. Unlike Thucydides Herodotus never commanded an army, and he has often been charged with being inexpert in depicting military campaigns. His accounts of battles have a narrator's omnipresence about them, not a general's, and they depend on the reports of individuals who remembered the fighting themselves—no doubt veteran soldiers and sailors from both sides. Basically like Stendhal's description of Waterloo or Tolstoy's of Borodino, this kind of overview came from pieces of personal experience. Also he shares the common failing of the ancients in exaggerating numbers. His estimate of Xerxes's army was 1.8 million, not counting the attendants—literally every man he thought the king could muster; and when he considered the pack animals, too, he was not surprised the rivers were drunk dry. Today that army is thought to have contained between 150,000 and 200,000 combat troops. But, any dramatic inclinations aside, Herodotus had no modern way of estimating numbers, and probably his sources—like most of us trying to give the size of a crowd—proceeded largely by guesswork. The size of Xerxes's army had in any case become a folktale.

In one aspect of his work, however, his handling of time, he demonstrates both his advance on his predecessors and the limits of his own situation. In the *Iliad* Hector and Achilles had been heroic beings untouched by the normal passage of the years. In contrast, Xerxes, the Athenian leader Themistocles, and the other men and women in the *Histories* are entirely human characters, acting rationally in support of intelligible policies and moving in a calculable process. Hesiod had defined the dimensions of the present era; but Herodotus's ability to comprehend time within it was restricted. He had firm conceptions of antiquity and of the recent past, but little grasp of the intervening centuries. He could describe with some conviction personalities like Solon and Cyrus in the early distance, but people and events beyond approximately 625 B.C. become indistinguishably ancient, especially in Egypt and Babylon. But a limit of about 150 years (an old person remembering what his grandparents had told him as a child) is still one of oral history's characteristics, and, given Herodotus's circumstances, this fault could hardly have been overcome. It should in no way detract from his great accomplishment of disengaging the past from the eternity of myth and investigating it, as far as he was able, within his scale of time.

To ask why the war was fought was clearly Herodotus's main purpose, and his methods of inquiry and the form in which he delivered his answer made him famous. But, central though that question was to him, another is discernible. The Persians had withdrawn, but the threat of a renewed invasion was ever-present. Could the two peoples ever live in harmony? To this Herodotus, whose Ionian background placed him halfway between Athens and the Orient, whose native city had under compulsion fought on the Persian side at Salamis, replied emphatically "Never!" He believed the two cultures were incompatible, and thereupon addressed himself in his work to what emerges as perhaps the most fundamental of all his questions—What is a Greek? To be a Greek, Herodotus saw, was to be free; to be a Persian, no matter how great, was to be enslaved. Freedom gave the individual the chance to express himself, to aspire to excellence, and to frame his city's laws so as to protect his liberty. Slavery might bring wealth and ease as it had to the Persians and Lydians, but it made all men subject to the interests of a monarch who laid down laws dictatorially. In spite of their poverty and internal discord, the Greeks considered freedom's benefits to be so obvious that, as the Spartan Demaratus told Xerxes, it was unthinkable his countrymen would listen to conditions that would bring slavery to their land. Freedom was an ideal, but, Demaratus said, the Greeks would fight for that ideal whatever the odds; and Herodotus had no doubt whatever that this spirit in the war had given the Greeks an incalculable advantage over their physically much superior enemy.

This difference set the seal for Herodotus on all the lesser differences, and the Greek victory became for him, as it has become for us, victory for the idea of Europe, of the West, of a Western civilization that is special. He was perhaps the first of a long line of figures, including Augustine, who have been intrigued by the East and have communicated their enthusiasm for its marvels and its arcane wisdom; but he was not the last to pull back in the final analysis and defend the values of the culture from which he came. Herodotus's *Histories* perpetuated a personal conclusion of irreconcilability which still profoundly affects politics and life among nations. The deeds this first Western history commemorated fired the ambition of Alexander when, a century later, at the age of twenty-two, he set out for Asia to crush the Persian menace completely once and for all.

III

When Herodotus lectured at Olympia, according to an ancient biographer, the young Thucydides was in the audience, and the *Histories* moved him to tears. Herodotus, talking afterward with the boy's father, construed this response as a burning desire to follow his own example. If from an early age that was all Thucydides had been inclined to do, he might have become one of Herodotus's numerous copiers and his work very possibly would not have survived. Herodotus had written about the past as it had once occurred, and with genius and industry had inaugurated history as an independent branch of knowledge;

Thucydides instead chose to diagnose events as they happened around him. His invention was contemporary history, and, from his work's first appearance to the present, historians have been intensely affected by his purpose and by the techniques he used to accomplish it. That two such strides in historiography should have succeeded one another so rapidly remains almost beyond belief.

Far more than in the case of Herodotus, who lived and wrote in the afterglow of a heroic struggle, the story of Thucydides's life is the story of his subject. Here is a man whose career was smashed by the course of the events he recorded. Born about 455 B.C. into a leading Athenian family with gold mines in half-barbaric Thrace, he resembles a twentieth-century English schoolboy educated to govern India, only to find at early maturity that no such profession exists. By birth and connections Thucydides could have expected to rise in his beloved city and help sustain the commanding position it had acquired. Following the victory over Persia, Athens ruled a sea-borne league of Greek cities and islands pledged to collaborate against further attacks. Under Pericles Athens's wealth and power gained immortal expression in its democratic government, its philosophical and dramatic brilliance, and in the rebuilding of the Acropolis, crowned with the great temple to Athena. "As a city," Pericles declared, "we are the school of Greece"; but Thucydides found his own education put to other uses as a great civil war, now hot, now cold, ground its way from its outbreak in 431 to Athens's humiliation and Sparta's final victory. His own failure as commander of an expedition to relieve Amphipolis, a Thracian town and Athens's shipbuilding center, led to his exile for twenty years. He did not return to Athens until the war's end in 404, and he died a few years later, a dignified and embittered man, from what we can tell. In portraits his features, like his view of the past, have the look of a noble tragedy.

The most striking of all Thucydides's statements in his *History of the Peloponnesian War* is his opening remark, "I began my history at the very outbreak of the war"; for he is saying he deliberately chose to start his project as the events he would describe occurred—to write a history as the history was being made. The war could not yet be seen as a whole, and detachment—a virtue historians have come to cherish— would be more than usually impossible; but, as we read his subsequent work and reflect back on that sentence, his words suggest a decision he had felt compelled to take. It is as if a very perceptive young European, hearing on August 4, 1914, that Germany had invaded Belgium, had decided that this was no ordinary war, that the lamps indeed were going out, and had resolved to record its unfolding drama to his utmost ability, come what may. Thucydides said as much when he went on to explain that he had been persuaded by his belief "that it was going to be a great war and more worth writing about than any of those which had taken place in the past." To represent this war accurately—perhaps because he had seen how easily and quickly events could be transformed into myths—became his desire. The Greek word he used for "writing about" (*xunegraphein*) meant in the classical period the composition of arguments and technical memoranda as well as historical narratives, but not poetry, plays, or fiction. The breach had widened between history and Homer, and rigorous standards of precision and clarity are not the least of the attractions that made Thucydides's work famous.

But in the Greek audiences many would have heard Herodotus and would have wondered why Thucydides should now claim foremost place for the war he was describing. Thucydides accordingly took pains to vindicate his claim, occasionally implying criticism of his predecessor. In a remarkable prelude to his *History* known as his "archaeology," he sketched briefly but very effectively the story of Greece from the early Hellenic invasions to the eve of the war. The dualism in the Greek character, exemplified by the opposites of Athens and Sparta, went back to the beginning of time. Submerged when confronting Darius and Xerxes, this ineradicable rivalry had divided Greece into two systems of alliance in the years after Salamis, one supreme on sea, the other on land. "The greatest war in the past," Thucydides wrote, "was the Persian War; yet in this war the decision was reached quickly as a result of two naval battles and two battles on land. The Peloponnesian War, on the other hand, not only lasted for a long time, but throughout its course brought with it unprecedented suffering for Hellas"—destruction, refugees, loss of life in warfare and internal revolutions, earthquakes, droughts, and the plague, "which did more harm and destroyed more life than almost any other factor." "All these calamities," he continued, "fell together upon the Hellenes after the outbreak of the war." Every Greek state had been committed, and the destiny of all Greek history was fulfilled in the catastrophe. The tale, in Thucydides's hands, was not just history as chronicle, narrative, and analysis, it was elegiac history, a chord frequently struck by later historians and notably in the twentieth century by Spengler and Toynbee.

Like Herodotus, Thucydides wished to inquire into the war's origins, and to distinguish precipitating from underlying causes. What really made the war inevitable, he said, was "the growth of Athenian power and the fear which this caused in Sparta"; but, true though this seemed to him, his chief interest lay in the separate events and human actions which had built up the conflict and in the reasons expressed at the time. Again, if he had lived during the First World War, he would surely have investigated closely the assassination of the Austrian archduke at Sarajevo and the ultimatums that ensued—Austria to Serbia, Germany to Russia, Germany to France, Britain to Germany—rather than letting the matter rest at the armaments race or imperial rivalries. The sequence of events viewed from either side promised for him the plainest evidence and the most reasonable conclusions; and his *History* took to a large extent the form of an answer, found under great difficulty, to the question "What actually happened?" in the Peloponnesian War.

A short account of the war—for which, incidentally, Thucydides is practically our only source—might be helpful. In 431 Sparta declared war on Athens for interfering in the affairs of Corinth, a Spartan ally. For the defense of Athens Pericles relied on the fleet and fortifications, but the surrounding country was ravaged by the Spartan army, and in 430 the overcrowded city was devastated by typhus, Pericles himself falling a victim. No comparable leader emerged and Athenian policy became indecisive, the faction of Nicias wanting peace, that of the demagogue Cleon trying to fight on. Though Cleon gained some success, later Athenian losses led to a peace treaty in 421. But that brief calm only allowed a regrouping of forces, and warfare of a more ruthless kind was renewed two years later. Alcibiades, recklessly ambitious, applied a new Athenian strategy—to capture Greek colonies in Italy, of which the chief was Syracuse, and thereby cut off the trade and resources which sustained the Spartans and their allies; but, though exhaustively planned, the Syracusan expedition (like the daring Gallipoli campaign in 1915) was a disaster, the Athenian loss of ships, equipment, and men being nearly total. Experimenting with emergency forms of government, rebuilding its navy, Athens struggled on; but when Sparta allied with Persia and developed a fleet of its own, the end was in sight. In 404 the prostrate city surrendered, its empire lost, its ships confiscated, its walls razed, and its status reduced to Spartan vassalage.

To write a contemporary history is always difficult. It would seem prerequisite to be a native of the society one is describing; but, even with that advantage, evidence is either too scarce or too plentiful, evaluating it is difficult and very laborious, and there is the personal risk, as the Elizabethan Sir Walter Raleigh noted in his *History of the World*, that "whosoever, in writing a modern history, shall follow truth too near the heels, it may haply strike out his teeth." There is also the nagging suspicion that the verdict properly belongs to posterity, truth being, as Francis Bacon recalled, the daughter of time. On the other hand, encouragements do exist. The atmosphere is still distinct, there is no need to reconstruct it from documents alone, actors may be consulted, and the emerging manuscript is assured of a hearing. Moreover, no historian can avoid being in another sense a contemporary historian. Human intelligence alone gives life to the past, perfect objectivity can never be reached, and a history of current affairs differs from other sorts of history writing only in that events and perspective are more than usually intertwined. When done well—and Thucydides's *History* is a conspicuous example—the result can be a unique record both of the events and of the perceptions, hopes, and illusions of a particular moment in time. To achieve this as Thucydides did, with elementary resources amid disruptive circumstances, ceaselessly writing, deleting, and rewriting as the picture gradually took shape, is astounding.

Collecting materials for his *History*, he set his standards by his best opportunities. He made it his principle, he says, "not to write down the first story that came my way, and not even to be guided by my own general impressions; either I was present myself at the events which I have described or else I heard of them from eyewitnesses whose reports I have checked with as much thoroughness as possible." He knew eyewitnesses could differ depending on what side they had taken, or on their powers of recollection, and he tried to be the impartial assessor. He seems to have used much of his time in exile to travel and learn of the war from other positions. As the war unfolded he probably kept notes of events as they occurred, wrote up a narrative when he thought his information was sufficient, and then later filled out his narrative with greater detail. Indeed, the inferior condition of the eighth and final book of the *History*, which trails off in the winter of 411, may indicate a lack of time to bring it to the quality of earlier sections. His technique in essence resembles a journalist's; but the sweep of his vision, the severity of his style, and above all his unsurpassed depiction of man as a political creature, raise his performance into an altogether different sphere.

Aware that even the best evidence was defective for his use without an exact order of events, Thucydides was careful to establish a reliable chronology. The war's beginning was dated according to the calendars of Athens, Sparta, and Argos, and he often expressed time as the number of summers and winters that had passed since some episode took place. Our knowledge of eclipses confirms his accuracy. Regarding all enumeration Thucydides has a far better record than Herodotus —which leads to other comparisons. Herodotus drew from other writers,

Thucydides depended solely on his own research. Herodotus thought it fair and honest to give rival versions of the truth as he had discovered it; Thucydides held to the narrower conception that the historian must inquire until he can support one testimony against others. In Thucydides's *History* there are no digressions of the sort that delighted Herodotus and his audience, and we are hardly conscious of the author; for, while Herodotus the traveler guides us everywhere, when Thucydides enters his *History* as a general he describes himself in the third person —and proceeds to give a professional's account of his mission.

Each man's work, of course, was shaped by the purpose that drove him to start it. Writing on the Persian Wars, Herodotus found he had to write on the world in all its aspects. Thucydides restricted his subject to the Peloponnesian War in its political and military particulars, and everything—even the part played by individuals—was subordinated to it. We are told very little about Pericles, though he is close to being the hero; only in the case of Alcibiades, whose career Thucydides believed could not be understood without mention of his depravities, are personal details given. Geography, so fascinating to Herodotus, was only valuable to Thucydides to clarify military activity—except in the "archaeology" where he described the broad geographical setting. The absence of references to the Athenian empire's brilliant civilization and economic life has been seen by some as seriously negligent, denying that he was fully objective in the modern sense; but very likely he took for granted his listeners' knowledge of such things and pared away all that in his view was not central to his obsessive story. Lean and masculine, his literary style carries no superfluous words and demands unusual concentration. This is history cut to the bone; but by its very restraint the compressed emotion serves to convey with great realism the terror of the plague and the clash of arms and cries of combatants as the Athenians are utterly beaten at Syracuse, the centerpiece of the drama.

In one area, however, Thucydides departed from his usual high standards of accuracy—in the reporting of speeches, which amount to approximately one quarter of the *History*'s contents. Of these, the oration by Pericles at the mass funeral of the war's first casualties has become famous, with its stirring defense of Athenian democracy and its declaration that "heroes have the whole earth for their tomb." The excuse Thucydides gives for his speechwriting is understandable: "I have found it difficult to remember the precise words used in the speeches which I listened to myself and my various informants have experienced the same difficulty; so my method has been, while keeping as closely as possible to the general sense of the words that were actually used, to make the speeches say what, in my opinion, was called for by each situation." The problem could not be solved by omission, as speeches in debate were to the Greeks the essential determinants of political decisions; presenting them in pairs Thucydides gave rival arguments on each issue. Modern opinion on the whole agrees that these speeches do not violate credibility. Moreover, like the stories Herodotus told, they perform the function of psychologically reconstructing the mind and self-image of men and communities. As such, they help develop the account of the war.

Thucydides attempted to answer the question, "Exactly what happened?" and he gave as accurate a statement as was in his power to do. As listeners the general public might deplore its lack of obvious color, but, unlike Herodotus, he does not seem to have had a miscellaneous Athenian crowd primarily in mind. Thucydides's preferred audience was a small group of intelligent men in a position to know about political and military matters and to act on them responsibly. All the features of his work were calculated to win a hearing in those circles first—not least the speeches, which reflected the logical forms of Sophist rhetoric and later became models of it. "It will be enough for me," he wrote, "if these words of mine are judged useful by those who want to understand clearly the events which happened in the past and which (human nature being what it is) will, at some time or other and in much the same ways, be repeated in the future." Boldly he added, "my work is not a piece of writing designed to meet the taste of an immediate public, but was done to last forever."

For Thucydides, then, assembling his *History* was a necessary preliminary to asking a second question, a question being raised by himself and his Athenian listeners in desperation: "What lessons can history teach?" Much more specifically than Herodotus, he took the assumed constants of time and human nature to make the war serve an essentially didactic purpose. Within the fixed dimension of the present—the fifth of Hesiod's ages—events flowed, he believed, in cycles, and man's behavior was his response to the opportunities or pressures facing him at any given stage. As he observed in one of the speeches, "all things are born to decay." In broad outline, therefore, the Peloponnesian War with all its attendant horrors could be expected to recur; and in that situation Thucydides's *History* might instruct and warn future Greeks how once before a great war had crept up on their forefathers, how disastrous it had been, and how demoralized human nature had proven capable of becoming. Similar mistakes could then be averted while there was yet a chance—or their impact at least be lessened. In particular, the war could teach a great deal to a later generation of leaders born, like Thucydides's own, in a period when a city-state at its peak begins its inevitable plunge downward.

To meet future challenges, what was needed was a thorough education in all the manifestations of politics; and, while seeking to answer his two questions, "Exactly what happened?" and, "What can we learn?" Thucydides was visibly grappling with what was to him perhaps the largest problem of all: "What is the nature of power?" The gods do not preside over men's acts in the *History*. There is only a terrible destiny working itself out in the manner of an Aeschylean tragedy. Human decisions had brought Athens from imperial power to chaotic defeat, and Thucydides described the sequence in terms which imply a descent from laws of democracy to the law of the jungle. The Athenians had shown themselves unequal to the demands of empire, prosperity, and democracy, and they had failed to exploit their opportunities during the war itself. Thucydides could see Athenian power had depended in part on coercion, and that to some of the subject peoples Sparta came as a liberator; but he himself was dominated by a fierce nostalgia for Periclean Athens and horrified by the faults of human nature, which, given free exercise, especially in the cases of both Cleon and Alcibiades, had finally brought utter ruin. To him, an empire governed by a democracy of the Athenian type was absolutely superior to any Spartan alternative. But a kind of malaise had overtaken his city, partly the result of the plague, but mostly caused by the misuse of power for immoral or destructive ends.

Thucydides did not doubt that authority was necessary, and he was deeply interested in observing and evaluating forms of leadership and the class warfare they often entailed—matters discussed intently by all intelligent Athenians of the day. The demands of total war left no room for neutrality, and only pragmatic leadership, not a strictly interpreted constitution, could give a society a chance of surmounting extraordinary crises. Cleon had been a rabble-rouser and Alcibiades an adventurer on the make; but, even though Thucydides was an aristocrat, he distrusted the oligarchical government installed at Athens in 411. His attraction to Periclean democracy, however, did not prevent him from approving the subsequent Council of Five Thousand, a reasonable blending of the few and the many, which provided Athens, he believed, with a better government than ever before. The new emergency conditions had made a revised form of government entirely defensible as a practical alternative. His message was clear, that politics was in every way a harsh proving ground—an opinion with which one of Thucydides's first English translators, Thomas Hobbes, agreed. As the

English civil war approached, Hobbes called Thucydides "the most politic historiographer that ever writ." It is a tribute that is true and worth keeping.

IV

Several figures stand out among the later Greek historians: notably Xenophon, who tried to continue Thucydides's work in his *Greek History* and also wrote his better-known story of the heroic march of a Greek expeditionary force from Babylon to the Black Sea; Polybius, who showed how and why Rome, in just over a century, had risen to conquer every Mediterranean state, which gave their affairs an unprecedented unity; and Arrian, the most trustworthy biographer of Alexander. But there was no outstanding innovator after Thucydides in either Greece or Rome. Fundamentally, classical historiography rested at the bounds of Thucydides's great achievement. His *History of the Peloponnesian War* elevated contemporary history into the most worthy of the historian's pursuits. It portrayed and analyzed so well what seemed to be the causes of events and the laws of human behavior that, given the limits within which the ancient world discussed these matters, no further advance seemed possible. New stories were told, new heroes were celebrated, and *historia* acquired a further meaning, "knowledge." No radically new treatment of history's themes or materials was attempted, however, and often style of exposition was rated more highly than accuracy or strength of inquiry, leading Cicero to define history as a branch of rhetoric. The formal ending, summarizing what has been discovered or reflecting on its place in an eternal plan, was alien to the Greeks. The past, like the cosmos, was to be understood through its separate parts. Not until about seven hundred years later, when Christianity began to make inroads upon traditional historical thinking, was the concept of history that Thucydides developed challenged to any significant extent.

In other respects, too, Thucydides became the ideal historian for antiquity, for he epitomized the growing opinion that to have been a man of action, preferably in a position of leadership, was indispensable. Indeed, not to have been a general, proconsul, or senator practically disqualified you. Such a man should also have the opportunity, enforced or otherwise, to write up his life's experiences from memory and reflection; and here Thucydides in exile set the model again. The sight becomes a familiar one. Machiavelli, his fellow Florentine Guicciardini, the Earl of Clarendon after the English civil war, T. E. Lawrence and his *Seven Pillars of Wisdom*, Churchill, and de Gaulle—all were men who turned to the writing of history after engaging in politics, telling the story of their times and giving a personal defense as well. Caesar's *Commentaries on the Gallic Wars,* clear and accurate, were memoirs of another kind, written to move the tide of personal fortune forward while their author's popularity as a successful commander was still high. War at any time offers the historian his greatest chance for prejudice, and in Thucydides's *History,* for all its attempted objectivity, we see the beginnings of a tradition of contemporary political history being written by a participant not only as record but also as propaganda.

Established now as a form of inquiry with an area of its own, history had gained its independence; and its attributes and purpose were nowhere more clearly defined, albeit in a subordinate place, than by Aristotle in his fourth-century *Poetics.*

> The poet and the historian [he wrote] differ not by writing in verse or in prose. The work of Herodotus might be put into verse, and it would still be a species of history, with meter no less than without it. The true difference is that one relates what has happened, the other what may happen. Poetry, therefore, is a more philosophical and a higher thing than history; for poetry tends to express the universal, history the particular. By the universal I mean how a person of a certain type will on occasion speak or act, according to the law of probability or necessity; and it is this universality at which poetry aims in the names she attaches to the personages. The particular is—for example—what Alcibiades did or suffered.

Not only does Aristotle insist that history and poetry are separate; in his mind, poetry is still superior to history because it erects general truths from those facts which history merely registers.

How have Thucydides and Herodotus fared more recently? In the Renaissance Machiavelli revived Thucydides's mode of dissecting power; in Victorian England Macaulay acclaimed the *History* for the fine detail of its story; and to the late nineteenth century Thucydides was undoubtedly the greatest historian of old because he had researched so thoroughly and had no competitor to dispute him or show him false. Political, military, diplomatic, and little else, his *History* seemed to illustrate perfectly the latter period's narrow dictum that history is past politics, and that present politics is future history. But the twentieth century has misgivings. Was he really as objective as he has been called? Or was he perhaps too pro-Athenian and too aristocratic, his definite bias contrasting unfavorably with Herodotus's open-mindedness? Was the war really as important as he claimed it to have been? Did he oversimplify human motivations by being too rational in an epoch when myths and oracles as well as speeches produced action? Are politics really the chief content of history—or are economics, or ideas? Thucydides has his limitations. He omits things we would like to hear about, he may concentrate on great men too much, his outlook may be restricted, and his support for Athens too strong. But the twentieth century nonetheless has good reason to value him in one respect, for it has seen a prolonged repetition of the Peloponnesian War, on a far larger scale, with similar intervals of insecure peace, and it knows for itself how people can deteriorate under conditions of crisis.

Successive ages have seen Herodotus in more conflicting ways. Later antiquity called him a vulgar and inaccurate storyteller; but to the besieged Byzantines he was a fellow combatant against Islam, and sixteenth-century Europe—rediscovering the *Histories* at about the same time as it found the New World—came to see his descriptions of distant lands and tribes as not so far-fetched after all. The cosmopolitan eighteenth century embraced him, and Voltaire very much favored Herodotus's approach when he set out to write his own history of mankind. Today he sometimes seems more our contemporary than Thucydides. Politics is in his history, but like our age he emphasizes intellectual differences, cultural life, and the history of international relations. His account of the whole world's past from a secular and universal point of view (what the Germans term *Weltgeschichte*) appeals to us, since taking events from far and wide and placing them in a large or global context becomes daily more necessary. He was aware that human beings are a mixture of sense and credulity and was probably, by today's standards, the better psychologist; his own personality has increasingly been seen as one of the most attractive parts of his *Histories*. Commenting continuously as he conducted his personal tour of the past, he had an eye for the odder associations of past and present, noting each sight and moving on. Yet he always held fast to his greater purpose and ultimately transformed his materials into a work of genius. He is the universal historian in every sense, his history of the world offering pleasure to all groups and all ages among his audiences. By championing Greek freedom, he also fashioned history as the struggle for liberty.

But it could be argued that the time is now ripe for a new importance to be given Thucydides. The realities of today indicate that we are living less in a world of seemingly infinite wonders and more in a small community of states on whose order and stability depend our continuing lives and livelihood. History will always be in part the story of man's mind, of the heroic past, of society's segments—rich and poor, native and foreign, primitive and advanced; but our greater need now may be for a new understanding of history as politics, aided by the research of newer disciplines but concentrating on the words, acts, and behavior of political leaders and institutions under whatever system they have existed. Thucydides in fifth-century Athens believed politics was the essence of history and contrasted the rule of law with the anarchy arising from its absence. As we contemplate the assorted machineries of government today, the vast new population to be absorbed into world society, and the options and constraints inherent in the exercise of leadership, we find these and other problems become a function of the overriding problem concerning the nature of power. Thucydides can inform us on such matters and their tendencies.

Besides, though readers have found Herodotus fascinating, he lacks the mental breadth of Thucydides in grasping the significance of events. Perhaps no historian has ever penetrated the motives of men more relentlessly or with such telling effect; and the *History*, "done to last forever," seems full of valuable lessons waiting to be noticed. It also sparks the imagination to think what could have happened if Athens had won. But Thucydides could distinguish hard reality from dreams and knew the danger of confusing the two. Each age sees in a major historian's work something it wants for itself; Thucydides may now be more fitted than Herodotus to speak to our current predicament, by his accuracy, by his practical intelligence, and, not least, by his humane qualities.

CHAPTER TWO

AUGUSTINE

I

History is the creation of historians, and the bold inquiries of the Greeks into their past led to outstanding advances in historical thinking and skills. Man was seen clearly to be largely responsible for his destiny; but it was equally plain he could not control it altogether, and, in the last analysis, the human mind and will often seemed powerless to exert any real influence. As Thucydides had shown, even the ablest of men might be crushed by the turn of events. The belief that the deities presided over mankind from offstage continued to be handed down through the generations; but the panoply of gods gradually became less credible and, as the search for a primary explanation continued, a new principle for understanding the phenomenon of change came to be needed to take their place.

For the Greeks, change in all its forms was the greatest of mysteries. How can something which is become something which it is not; and how can that which is not become that which is? If the world is all that is, then how can it change and become something else? Questions like these challenged and stimulated Greek philosophy, but with no definite conclusions for history or any other branch of knowledge. Polybius tried to see in the incalculable forces behind changing events the workings of divine providence; but instead of an orderly alternative, this was only like the god brought in by the machinery in the plays of the time to resolve complicated plots. It was not until the fifth century A.D. that Augustine's great treatise, the *City of God*, solved the problem of change by invoking a radical new definition of man and of the whole purpose of human affairs. Admirable though some earlier attempts to comprehend history had been, to Augustine the best of them did no more than come near the knowledge triumphantly revealed in Christ.

As late as the seventeenth century in Europe and the eighteenth in New England, the *City of God* was regarded almost exclusively as the authoritative guide to history's total content and meaning. Only after the Scientific Revolution had forced another massive revision of beliefs about history and human nature was Augustine's statement reduced to being one of several possible interpretations of the past—if any scheme is tenable—one linked predominantly with religion. But Augustine's influence survives vigorously to this day; for wherever Christianity is upheld, in St. Peter's basilica or a Pentecostal mission, its doctrine of history comes strengthened by the resources the *City of God* provides. Augustine's history has an appeal that is universal, for it arises out of the story of his search for himself—which is recognizably each individual's struggle for self-unity. More than that, as theologian, philosopher, political theorist—perhaps most of all as the living person we encounter in his *Confessions*—Augustine shaped numerous ideas and attitudes which ever since have contributed to Western man's spiritual and intellectual environment. Even now our understanding of history often starts unconsciously along paths he laid down. And we can scarcely read the *City of God* today without reflecting that our own problems may be very much like those of the age in which Augustine wrote.

Although the *City of God* is very lengthy and diffuse, steeped as it is in the world of classical and early Christian disputation, its noble design is immediately obvious—and so is its author's character. By instinct and training he was a master of words and persuasion; he never undertook any formal course of philosophy or theology, nor was abstract thinking his foremost talent. He was a personality; and that is fundamental. All his life he was a seeker after a vision of God, and often his changes of mind are more significant than the positions he finally reached, positions others built into systems. Every one of his works conveys a sense of tensions impatiently striving to be satisfied; and the *City of God* was his most ambitious attempt to apply every power he had to facing a topic which challenged him—in this case the enormous and intractable problem of causation.

If the examples of Herodotus and Thucydides suggest how much a historian and his history are shaped by his experience, the evidence Augustine offers is of a far more dramatic kind. Probably no interpretation of history has ever come more wrenchingly out of a man. His view of past, present, and future grew out of the agonizing conflict within him between a Roman heritage and a Christian faith; but it did not find full expression until his correspondents and North African congregation sought his advice on how to act in the troubled times they faced. The questions they raised demanded the most fundamental, universal sort of answer and taxed all his qualities of spirit, and the task was to occupy Augustine on and off for nearly twenty years. Drawing on previous work by both Christian and non-Christian writers, stamping what he selected with the mark of his own insights, sometimes rethinking the whole complex of his ideas about God, man, and grace when some single point struck him with new force, he was able in the end to break with the deadlocked schemes of classical antiquity and to carry a widening audience with him. Out of the great number of his ideas we shall restrict ourselves to the questions he worked out in the *City of God*, and to that book's effect upon later historical thinking. We shall first study his life and the era in which he lived, for these factors illuminate the answers he reached.

Aurelius Augustinus was born in 354 in the small provincial town of Thagaste, now Souk Ahras, in present-day Algeria, the son of a pagan father and a Christian mother. The family's opposing religious beliefs, the division in the local population, and the whole disunited fabric of the Mediterranean world at the time all helped make him into what he has come to typify—the man who bridges two ages and cultures. From his earliest days, Augustine habitually lived as a citizen of two worlds. Beginning with Constantine's reign earlier in the fourth century, the Roman empire had been officially Christian; but the old religions remained active (under the emperor Julian they had even briefly returned to power), and Augustine's parents were examples of the uneasy truce still existing between Christianity and paganism. In child-hood he spoke Latin and wept over the story of Dido and Aeneas, a local legend Virgil had gilded; around Augustine's North African home, however, in the villages with their forests of olive trees, he saw a rural people scarcely touched by Roman influence and still speaking Carthaginian dialects. He himself was proud to be a native of a Roman city, one of the many to be found from England to Egypt, with schools and law courts, theaters, baths and arenas; but he was also an African, delighting in sounds, bright colors, vivid language, and enthusiastically conscious of both his cultures. We can see now that the world he knew was being transformed, so that Augustine may be equally well described as an outstanding figure of late antiquity or as a forerunner of the Middle Ages.

Surprisingly to us, it never seems to have impressed Augustine greatly that he might be living on the critical boundary between the Roman era and whatever state of affairs might follow it. His thoughts centered upon the eternal contrasts: between ignorance and wisdom, evil and good, darkness and light, and finally, gathering all together, between earth and that other country of heaven. He was heir, nonetheless, to an accumulated feeling of exhaustion that pervaded classical culture, a sense that events were bringing an age to its natural conclusion. All sorts of religion and sorcery flourished, changes in social life were widespread and accepted, and new forms of government were experimented with; even a century before, Cyprian, the bishop of Carthage, had deplored this disarray. The seasons had grown irregular, Cyprian wrote, the harvests less plentiful, supplies of gold and marble were dwindling, "the farmer is vanishing and disappearing in the fields, the sailor on the sea, the soldier in the camp, innocence in the market, justice in the courts, harmony among friendships, skill among the arts, discipline in morals." He grieved that all things which come into existence must die, that the strong must become weak, the great small; and that it is God's law that finally the world itself should come to an end.

But when Augustine looked back on his youth he remembered most his inner turbulence; and in his *Confessions,* an intensely personal document as interesting to the psychologist as the later *Confessions* of Rousseau, we can read of his development and his anguished preoccupation with sensual pleasures. His parents, who were not wealthy, were determined that their son should rise through education. His local schooling was pagan, literary, and narrow, aiming to produce the orator; and, since he was a gifted student, Augustine proceeded from Thagaste to Carthage to study law. By his own testimony, he lived an immoral life in that big city, or "cauldron" as he thought of it, enamored with the theater and fathering a son by the girl he lived with. He had received strong Christian instruction from his mother; but he lacked the will to change his life and clung to sins which humiliated him. As part of his legal training he took instruction in rhetoric, which led him to discover philosophy through the reading of Cicero and to the desire for ideal wisdom. His nature, however, craved more than an intellectual opinion he could respect. It wanted a belief he could love to his utmost. At length he was drawn to a group of Manichaeans, an Eastern sect which believed in a universe where Light and Darkness were joined in cosmic battle, and which professed its ability to free men from evil while leaving the good part of human nature essentially unharmed. He remained an adherent for several years; but, when Faustus, a Manichaean authority on doctrine, arrived in Carthage and could not answer all his questions, he defected.

By now Augustine had become no ordinary seeker—if, indeed, there has ever been one. He was sensitive, serious, and singularly intelligent, and he was desperate to know real truth wherever it might be found. He might have drawn what he could from some competing belief and resigned himself to that; but instead his experiences only pushed him to look further for the deeper religious satisfaction he needed. His mind, however, possessed an unusual ability to profit from comparisons, and he used in his search the discoveries he made—about the world and about himself—to develop his own position. His keenness of intellect, however, confused for a time by the conflicting answers it received, delayed his finding that position. He had to find his own way, like Luther, Pascal, and Kierkegaard were to do after him; but, as so often happens, the hurdles he had to surmount contributed in no small measure to the making of the man.

Disillusioned with Manichaeism, Augustine took the route many North Africans believed led to success and voyaged to Rome, where, after a disappointing start as a teacher, he soon was fortunate in being chosen professor of rhetoric at Milan, the current capital of the empire's western half. Once there he became deeply impressed by Ambrose, the city's great bishop, whose preachings offered Augustine fresh insights into the Bible. Augustine had ridiculed Scripture as crude and unintelligible, but Ambrose showed how it might have a spiritual as well as a literal meaning—a notion supported by the Neoplatonic writings Augustine had also begun to read. The Manichaeans and the Stoic philosophers he had admired had been decidedly materialistic in outlook; he was now being persuaded that the insubstantial was the real.

This gradual intellectual conversion prepared him for his spiritual conversion in 386. The story, although well known, is worth repeating. Augustine had been talking with two friends in his Milan lodging about St. Paul and about St. Anthony, the desert monk of Egypt, who, by renouncing the world, had stormed the gates of heaven. Finally, unable to bear the conversation any longer, Augustine left, flinging himself beneath a fig tree in the garden, where he wept unrestrainedly. His years of spiritual torment flashed through his mind, and he could not see how to continue living as the captive of his sins. But from where could he ever get the strength to make a new beginning? At that moment he heard the sing-song voice of a child in a nearby house calling again and again "Take it and read! Take it and read!" Here, a passage from his *Confessions* movingly relates his spiritual rebirth:

I looked up, thinking hard whether there was any kind of game in which children used to chant words like these, but I could not remember ever hearing them before. I stemmed my flood of tears and stood up, telling myself that this could only be a divine command to open my book of Scripture and read the first passage on which my eyes should fall. . . .

So, I hurried back to the place where Alypius was sitting, for when I stood up to move away I had put down the book containing Paul's Epistles. I seized it and opened it, and in silence I read the first passage on which my eyes fell: "Not in revelling and drunkenness, not in lust and wantonness, not in quarrels and rivalries. Rather, arm yourselves with the Lord Jesus Christ, spend no more thought on nature and nature's appetites." I had no wish to read more and no need to do so. For in an instant, as I came to the end of the sentence, it was as though the light of confidence flooded into my heart and all the darkness of doubt was dispelled.

With this revelation an old life closed and a new future began to open. Illness too was ending Augustine's career as a public orator, and he decided to return to North Africa to found a small religious group on semimonastic lines—the classical ideal of a learned retreat. His mother, who had followed him to Italy and been overjoyed at his conversion, died at the port of Rome while they waited for the lifting of a naval blockade. Augustine's quiet existence at Thagaste, however, before long seemed empty of purpose, devoid of the opportunities for growing that he hoped his new faith would bring him. But he was known locally as a man of ability, and in 391 he was visiting the nearby coastal town of Hippo when, as he told his congregation thirty-five years later, "I was grabbed. I was made a priest . . . and from there, I became your bishop." He remained Bishop of Hippo until he died; and the problems of governing his diocese and the perils of sea travel prevented him ever leaving his native area again.

At last his restless nature had found a calling where his talents could be used to advantage. His responsibilities were akin to those formerly carried out by Roman officials, and demanded the utmost of his broad knowledge, his maturity, and his spiritual commitment; but he also managed to write a great many theological works, carried on an extensive correspondence (for Hippo was a major port, in contact with the world beyond), and expounded the Bible in his sermons with every orator's trick he could summon up. Self-expression in words was for him compulsive. "I am the sort of man who writes because he has made progress," he once said, "and who makes progress—by writing." His fame spread far beyond his province; but, at the time of his death in 430, Vandal invaders were destroying the Christian community he had built up, and a year later Hippo itself was evacuated and partly burnt. His life, it seemed, had been lived in vain.

His writings, however, survived, and they remain an encyclopaedic monument to his intellect and character. They show us too how he gradually formed his opinions, not just by refining on the thoughts of others, but by letting the day-to-day problems he faced as a bishop mold his thinking. All played a part in enlarging his vision of Christian truth. A particular set of circumstances led him to write the *City of God*; but the groundwork was laid when he was forced to make up his mind on certain preliminary issues, chief of which was the question "What is the Church?"

Familiar with the Church's endurance of Roman persecution and its rise to sudden prominence, Augustine the bishop saw it as still a small, fledgling body liable to further oppression. He believed, nonetheless, that it should stand by the claims it was making and assert their importance to all men. This conviction was certainly sharpened during the early years of the fifth century when he confronted the challenge of Donatism in his diocese. The Donatists were a puritanical sect of North African Christians who held that only those who had stayed loyal in times of persecution were in a state of grace. Members of the Church and clergy who had in some way compromised their faith should be rebaptized or reordained. Donatism was strong among the rural population which distrusted the Romanized cities, and local resentments were therefore added to disputes over doctrine with the Church at large. Several efforts to heal the schism had failed, and rival churches and rival bishops competed throughout the area.

Against the Donatists Augustine maintained that baptism and ordination once received had an indelible effect upon a person; but to bring out the best in the gifts they conferred it was necessary for the proper atmosphere to exist in Christian communities. He held that the Donatist churches fell short in this regard, being more distinguished for fanaticism than for piety and love. Their Christianity also seemed static, unreceptive to new experience, as he had found the Manichaeans. The true Catholic Church was renewing itself and reaching out beyond itself constantly, as Ambrose had taught that its nature required. Its claim to authority rested on divine foundation, not absolute purity, and that claim was substantiated by the Church's growth and its universal character. Its members were found in all parts of the empire among all social classes, and it alone had sufficient power to master society and raise it to a higher plane. On every count the Catholic Church was the one genuine church. If all efforts at persuasion failed, Augustine considered the words of Christ in a parable, "Go out into the highways and hedges, and compel them to come in, that my house may be filled," justified constraint to bring individual adherents back from their errors. For his insistence on that text, Augustine has sometimes been called the originator of the Inquisition.

After the synod of Carthage in 411 the Donatists' strength declined, and the *City of God* is noticeably free from conflicts with heretical groups. The Donatist challenge, however, greatly increased Augustine's practical understanding of the Church's nature and its place in the world. It also gave him a specific opportunity to analyze amid heated controversy and to reach his own conclusions under the pressure of current alternative beliefs. This ability to see essential principles at stake in local issues was soon being tested again, when Christian fears that paganism might be invincible after all led him to define his thought on the meaning of history. The work that resulted, far larger than even he could have expected, proved to be his masterpiece.

II

The event that precipitated the writing of the *City of God* was the capture of Rome by the Goths under their leader Alaric. Constantinople was now the chief imperial capital, and Rome was sometimes not even the seat of the empire in the West; but its fall—which still stirs the imagination—sent a profound shock throughout the ancient world, for it was seen as far more than the fall of a mighty city. It signified the end of a civilization; and that, it was feared, meant the end of civilization altogether. Today, civilization is often complacently thought of as a state of affairs capable of infinite development; but in classical culture it was regarded as almost unnatural when it appeared, a hard-won clearing in a forest full of untamed forces always intent on destroying it. Its existence depended on a series of remarkably gifted rulers and on the kindness of fate. To maintain it, let alone expand its area, was considered a peculiarly difficult task; but Rome, to her credit and despite all her shortcomings, had been able to ward off those forces from without and within that threatened destruction. Her rulers and her institutions of government had secured the fundamental conditions required for a civilized society.

The Roman Empire had maintained its supremacy over the Mediterranean world for so long and with so large a measure of success that, to many of its inhabitants, its permanence was taken for granted.

The struggles for power in the old Roman republic had been resolved by Augustus, whose authoritarian type of government had restored peace, increased prosperity, and, it seemed, safeguarded civilization's continuance. After the second century A.D. major adjustments to the system were periodically made to preserve this unique creation, a sign in itself of vitality; but the fabric of Roman institutions decayed, the fiber which had won an empire and learned to rule it weakened, and barbarians in large numbers were allowed to settle within the empire's borders in the mistaken hope that, as citizens and soldiers, they would act in Rome's defense. Invasions grew harder to restrain, and the city of Rome was ominously refortified. When Constantine adopted Christianity in 312 the imperial government gained a new basis of support; but his policy only partly led to the desired reinvigoration of Roman life.

Attacks upon the western half of the empire in particular increased, and in 410 the Goths took Rome itself. What happened does not appear nearly so catastrophic now. Though the invaders sacked the city, they held it for only three days, and spared church buildings and people seeking refuge inside them. Indeed, Rome had become something of a liability to the imperial government seated nearer the frontier at Constantinople. But this was the first time in eight hundred years that the all-conquering city had been conquered itself, the city which was thought—as Virgil had once written—to enjoy attributes of eternity; and it was widely believed that Rome's fall doomed the world to revert to total barbarism. The cycle which had claimed all other empires could be cheated no longer; and no successor to Rome was waiting, ready to take up the torch from her hands.

In the general inquest that followed, the obvious scapegoat for the calamity was the Christian Church, which not long before had gained imperial favor and officially displaced the time-honored guardian gods. Now, the pagans charged, the old gods who had raised Rome to power were taking revenge on the city for abandoning them; and near the end of his life Augustine recalled that, burning with zeal, he had decided to write the *City of God* against the blasphemies and errors he heard. Replying to the Church's adversaries was not his only concern; he also had to give ready answers to Christians around him, bracing themselves for a new wave of severe persecution and wondering why Rome had fallen only after accepting Christianity. Alaric had succeeded where Hannibal had failed; did this mean that God was unwilling—or unable —to save His people after all? Many Christians saw the event involving momentous consequences. A belief born out of pagan and Jewish tradition had taken root that Rome was the last of the great empires, and that its disintegration would signal the end of the world. The demise of all things seemed imminent, and it was anticipated with far more dread than hope. "The whole world perished in one city," wrote Augustine's great contemporary, the monk and scholar Jerome, who poured out his lamentations from his cell at Bethlehem.

Augustine, though deeply affected, saw the situation differently. Whether correcting false charges among the populace or encountering a stream of wealthy refugees, he found in his position that the fall of Rome reduced itself to smaller, practical problems; and it was again a local issue that brought the larger perspective into focus. He had been corresponding with the Roman proconsul in North Africa who wished to know more about Christian teachings. His letters were passed among a circle of readers, one of whom, a lawyer named Marcellinus, wrote back describing their effect and telling of other questions troubling the group—especially that of how Christians should conduct themselves in such critical days. Injunctions found in the Gospels, such as "if anyone strikes you on the right cheek turn to him the other also," were hard to practice when one's city was being attacked and civilized life was breaking down. It was bewildering that these afflictions had occurred under emperors observing for the most part the Christian religion; and Marcellinus asked for a "full, thorough, and luminous reply."

Augustine's advice epitomized the opinions he would later develop so fully. The central history for the Church, he claimed, was the tradition of divine revelation, not the epic story of Rome; and Christians should see in the events around them the fulfillment of prophecy— which should lead them to trust God's other promises with increased confidence. "When the world's day is drawing to its close," he wrote, "and the approaching consummation is heralded by the calamities which exhaust its energies," Christians should watch and pray, patient in the knowledge that theirs is the final victory. As for Rome and its fall, no state was perfectly established and preserved unless it was founded on Christ's commandments; and the breakdown of morality had been Rome's ruin. But Rome had shown how great a city might be through civic virtues alone, and God's purpose there was to teach by comparison; for, when true religion was added, "men are made citizens of another commonwealth, of which the king is truth, the law is love, and the duration is eternity."

Thus, before he wrote the *City of God*, Augustine had begun to bring into mutual relation such basic elements of his doctrine of history as the authority of Scripture, the two cities, and the separation of men by their loves. He had himself searched them out, and he had tested their truth in action; but now he was being required to set down his thoughts in full in an atmosphere more than usually charged with the drama of foreshortening time. Christ and his living experience of Him was his starting point for understanding Rome's fall, not the city and empire of Rome itself; and his faith was fixed upon Christ's promise to return. When that might be, he warned, was known only to God, and Rome still stood in spite of the disaster; but nothing interpreted better the events of the present, and of times past and to come, than the "approaching consummation," which drew together the whole retrospect of history. He discarded whatever ideas he had of writing a tract for a particular crisis, or a conventional history—a task he gave to his subordinate Orosius. He determined to produce the work he had long been wanting to write, a work which would permanently defeat pagan philosophy by sheer intellectual weight as well as by vigorously affirming central Christian beliefs. As bishop of Hippo he was constantly pitting his strength against the pagan world and its great heritage, in which he himself had been educated. Only a thin brick wall separated the baptistery of his basilica from a luxurious house on whose mosaic pavement were set the old culture's symbols, medallions of the nine Muses. Rome's downfall brought the project to a head; his choice of title set the theme. This would be history as argument.

Augustine also needed to write the work for himself, to reconcile the tensions from his past between pagan and Christian teaching that increasingly obsessed him; but, convert though he was, he was too educated a man to be as radical as Jerome, who condemned classical civilization outright. Augustine admired Rome's immense achievements and valued its intellectual tradition. For instance, although he may have taken his immediate scheme of two cities from a Donatist commentator on the Book of Revelation, his own concept of "city"—essentially a group of people bound together by a common interest—drew upon Roman political thought, a phrase of Marcus Aurelius, and, of course, Plato's portrayal of an ideal republic. Augustine scattered throughout his work ideas and quotations from Greek and Roman authors, making points and enticing the scholarly reader; the style of writing in the *City of God*, however, was Augustine's own. Grounded in rhetoric and Roman literature, it had been shaped and polished in sermons which were more like conversations expounding and encouraging his listeners at a few yards' distance than formal statements to be chiseled on stone. Like everything Augustine wrote, the Latin was unusually sensitive and vivid. Written between 413 and 426 and dedicated to Marcellinus, the *City of God* had as its apparent motive answering the question "Why did Rome fall?" But it soon moves far beyond that earth-shaking event and seeks to explain the origins and the primary purpose of history as a whole; for, to Augustine, the importance of the great causal question "Why?" so constantly asked in his sermons, lay in its opening up the question "What is the meaning?"

The *City of God* is composed of twenty-two books and falls into two divisions, as Augustine explained on its completion. The aim of the first ten books is destructive—to defeat the militant pagan belief that worship of traditional deities had been the guarantee of Rome's prolonged good fortune, and to refute the supporting views put forward by even the most admirable non-Christian philosophies. Judging the past by the pagans' record, Augustine argued that the old gods had repeatedly proved themselves ineffectual, no more able to save Rome than Troy; and each increase of Roman power—the early Italian and the Punic wars, the wars of Marius and Sulla—had been accompanied by far greater misery than that recently experienced. Had Rome remained peaceful by nature as she was in the days when the legendary king Numa reigned, her history would have developed differently. As it was, she had won an empire partly by force of character, partly because she had acted energetically in self-defense; but that empire was really not of her own making. It was conferred by God, who alone had power to give all earthly kingdoms and determine their destinies.

The story of Rome was nonetheless inspiring, and her republican qualities deserved to be copied; but the honesty of Cincinnatus, who left his plow when his country needed him and returned when his task was over, the courage of Regulus keeping his word and going back to his death in Carthage—these and other examples like them were a challenge to Christians to surpass. Roman life had been directed to earthly ends; when Constantine guided it to a higher sphere the superiority of a Christian Rome was immediately plain. In the same manner, Constantine was greater than any previous emperor, and the Christian martyr finer than the self-sacrificing Roman.

Turning to the religions of classical times, Augustine noted that the Roman antiquary Varro had compiled an immense catalogue of divine visitations in Roman history; but, after studying it in detail, Augustine had to conclude that the pagan deities could neither help in temporal affairs nor give convincingly the reward of eternal life—both of which Christianity had been shown to do. However much the more enlightened side of paganism had benefited mankind, the accompanying vice and wickedness could not be separated from it. Plato's doctrine of God, Augustine thought, reached the closest approximation of truth among all the ancient philosophies; but it, too, was tarnished because it tolerated the worship of immoral deities. By argument and illustration Augustine eliminated the pagan gods as factors in the rise and fall of Rome. As interpreters of past, present, and future—and of man and God—the worst of philosophies was a deceit, the best inferior to Christianity.

In the twelve books that follow, Augustine moves into his full-scale exposition. His aim is constructive—to teach both pagans and Christians that God presides over history, and that, like everything else He has made, God's purpose in it is good. History's theme is the origin, progress, and consummation of two cities—the heavenly city of God, and the earthly city of man. God, who is eternal, has created the universe and finite time together; and the city of God, to which Scripture and human testimony alike bear witness, began with the creation of light. The earthly city, making its own gods, was born in darkness with Lucifer's fall. Both will run until time is swept up into eternity again. Time, therefore, is a phase in eternity, coming from it and closing into it, moving in a linear direction. The common opinion that events in time recur in cycles is incompatible with essential Christian beliefs.

> On the basis of this cyclic theory [he wrote] it is argued, for example, that, just as in a certain age the philosopher Plato taught his students in the city of Athens and in the school called the Academy, so during countless past ages, at very prolonged yet definite intervals, the same Plato, the same city, and the same school with the same students had existed again and again, and during countless ages to come will exist again and again. Heaven forbid, I repeat, that we should believe that. For Christ died once for our sins, but "rising from the dead he dies no more, and death shall no longer have dominion over him"; and after the resurrection "we shall always be with the Lord."

Earlier Christian thinkers had seen that, if history moves cyclically, then the actions of Adam and Eve, or Moses, or Judas, would be repeated; but Augustine offered a clear challenge, with immense and far-reaching consequences.

When God created man He endowed him with free will; but Adam chose to sin, with sin came death, and "thus from the abuse of free will has come the linked sequence of our disaster." Some, however, by God's grace, were acquitted from a second, eternal death by choosing to live according to the spirit instead of the flesh; and this difference between two sorts of men, far more fundamental than distinctions of language or dress, made Augustine speak of them as two cities. The nature and state of these two cities were quite opposite, though the objective of each was peace:

The two cities then were created by two kinds of love: the earthly city by a love of self carried even to the point of contempt for God, the heavenly city by a love of God carried even to the point of contempt for self. Consequently, the earthly city glories in itself while the other glories in the Lord. For the former seeks glory from men, but the latter finds its greatest glory in God, the witness of our conscience. The earthly city lifts up its head in its own glory; the heavenly city says to its God: "My glory and the lifter of my head." In the one, the lust for dominion has dominion over its princes as well as over the nations that it subdues; in the other, both those put in charge and those placed under them serve one another in love, the former by their counsel, the latter by their óbedience. The earthly city loves its own strength as revealed in its men of power; the heavenly city says to its God: "I will love thee, O Lord, my strength."

The human race has therefore taken two contrary courses from the beginning; and the Bible, the record of the Christian God's dealings with man, shows how history bore out the case Augustine was making. Cain, guilty like Romulus of fratricide, had been of the flesh, Abel of the spirit. Indeed, Augustine noted, it was said that Cain built a city, "but Abel, being a sojourner, founded none"—a clear indication that the heavenly city, existing in both present and future, does not need a material presence. The chronology and apparent inconsistencies in early Scripture are explained in many digressions; but Augustine keeps to his argument, proceeding to the story of Noah, a just and perfect man, whose ark was both historical and an allegory of the safety of Christ's Church. After the flood, the city of God was found among the descendants of Noah's son Shem, who came to be called the Hebrews. The rest of mankind, in contrast, chose to worship other gods, and the building of the Tower of Babel was an outstanding example of human pride. In His covenant with Abraham—who had left the city of Ur— God chose the Jews to witness to His plan for mankind in history, and the story then became a stirring testimony of promises fulfilled. The two cities were repeatedly in opposition—Jacob and Esau, Moses and Pharaoh, the prophets and the idolators among the Jews themselves; but during the era of David and Solomon the city of God had assumed some features of an earthly kingdom at Jerusalem which lasted until the time of Christ. Augustine interpreted the prophecies of a Messiah, but considered that those promising peace to the Jewish nation more properly referred to the greater heavenly city of the future; as the Roman world had learned, peace had no permanence on earth.

The earthly city, meanwhile, was represented by Babylon, Assyria, and later the empires of Greece and Rome—all of which, unwittingly, had helped prepare the way for God's final revelation of Himself in Christ. Ancient oracles and Jewish prophecies might be made compatible, chronologies could be related, and Greek philosophy made the pagan intellect ready. Further, the later Jewish prophets broadened their message and made a place in it for the Gentile nations, and the translation of the Hebrew scriptures into Greek was an outstanding example of God's hand at work. The coming of Christ, the savior of the world, was history's focal point; and on His death, and on the dispersion of the Jews and the destruction of their Temple, Christ's followers in the Church became witnesses of God's new covenant with man. Not all in the Church, however, were members of the heavenly city. As the Church's numbers increased—partly through its new official status—it had come to include many who were still sinners, gathered in with the good as in a dragnet. These would be separated at the end, like chaff from wheat on the threshing-floor; but when that end and the final persecution would be was for neither Christian nor pagan to know.

Having traced the two cities in his account of history, Augustine in the nineteenth book discusses much more fully the goals to which the cities' energies were directed. His thought turns to the organization of society, necessary and desirable in the conduct of human affairs. Peace is for both cities their highest aim; but, though earthly peace may be temporarily secured by the earthly city, the enjoyment of a perfect peace—of orderly obedience to God's eternal law—is the privilege of the heavenly. In addition to the faithful angels, God's servants of the Old Testament, and the saints, the city of God contains the faithful members of the Church, living and to come. Since, however, this group of elect (and Augustine never precisely defined the mechanics of election) is bound up in the earthly city's affairs and shares in the peace of earth while also enjoying the peace of heaven, a spirit of concord may unite both cities when each pursues the same temporal ends on their different levels. At its finest, Roman government had given the blessing of peace on earth to both good and wicked together within its all-embracing citizenship.

But, when the Lord shall come, the purpose of all history will be achieved, and the good alone will know peace without sin for eternity. With many references to Old Testament prophecies, the teachings of Jesus, and the Book of Revelation, Augustine firmly upholds the certainty of a final divine judgment—the last great prophecy to be fulfilled—although, of course, God is also judging men every day. The devil, the fallen angel responsible for the earthly city, will be loosed and will subject the Church to savage persecution before being struck down and cast into a lake of fire and brimstone. Time will vanish into eternity, the dead will be raised and the book of life opened, that book in which the commissions and omissions of every man on earth are recorded. The wicked, the unfaithful in the Church, all those in all ages who have chosen the world, will be sentenced to a second death in everlasting damnation. Augustine colorfully describes the torments of hell, grappling too with some intricate questions about who may and may not expect to receive punishment. The reward of the righteous is life eternal and happiness in heaven as victorious citizens of the new Jerusalem, the perfect manifestation of the city of God. They will no longer have discord between body and spirit, and will live in a state of perpetual sabbath, continually enjoying God's face from the steps of His throne. "Behold what shall be in the end without end!" Augustine cries out, bringing his huge work to a conclusion. "For what else is our end, except to reach the kingdom which has no end?"

III

Clearly the *City of God*, this spacious exposition of the Christian view of history, is not akin to the histories of Herodotus, Thucydides, or what we call history today. It is Michelangelo's history, stretching across the ceiling and far wall of the Sistine Chapel as the world's story from God the Creator to Christ the Judge. It is the history from which Dante devised his *Divine Comedy*, the history in Handel's *Messiah*. To us it may seem strange and predominantly visionary, but to Augustine its argument was absolutely rational, a simple line of reasoning from its fundamental premise: since God in His love has created the world, how can He have left its history outside His care? With very great learning and an expert's skill in debate, Augustine argued that the fall of Rome was neither as abnormal nor as catastrophic as the enemies of Christianity were saying. It resulted from a division in the whole order of existence going back to the world's beginning, and was only the latest episode in God's masterplan for the entire human race. The Bible revealed and verified that plan. Its record showed that earthly empires flourished but always passed away; it showed too that the people of God—often an oppressed minority—always survived and had been proved indestructible. As history moved rapidly to its finish Christians should take heart: it was proceeding as God intended. In the midst of disaster they were called to witness to the truth, to give forth light like olives crushed in the press. The pagans had analyzed history, like all experience, incorrectly.

History to Augustine was therefore teleological, its developments

[margin note: Romes fall not as catastrophic merely latest episode in Gods plan.]

[margin note: Earthly empires flourish + pass away Christ survive]

[bottom margin note: └ natural processes, of being directed toward an end, shaped by purpose] due to the purpose served by them. And Augustine's general thesis is that God has designed history to reconcile the two conflicting forces in the world. Dualisms abound in Augustine's life and writings; and in the human story every man was a citizen of one city or the other. Augustine's readers would be aware that this was no casual distribution, for in the Graeco-Roman world the concept of citizenship was a powerful one, giving a man a basic definition and marking him off from others. It was also an ideal, and the possession of citizenship was for long an unusual privilege. The two cities, so opposite in nature, so different in the allegiance they demanded, were not, however, quite exclusive. Members of the city of God on earth were subject to the claims of an earthly city, and were sinners still; but they were in effect resident aliens—like Herodotus in Athens—and, if faithful, would secure their full heavenly citizenship after the final separation.

At the heart of Augustine's interpretation of history was his belief that each man would be held responsible for choosing between the two cities entangled here on earth. The first man had been given free will; and ever since, he and his descendants had lived out their lives according to their choice. In the end, all would be judged in a scene of eternal dimensions. There would be no second opportunity, no cyclical recurrence, and at stake was God's offer of immortal life; and, besides attempting to answer "What is the nature of the Church?" and "Why did Rome fall?" the *City of God* was also Augustine's studied response to what to him was, beyond any doubt whatever, the most important question asked of each human being—the call of God searching for Adam in the garden, which echoes throughout the rest of Scripture: "Where are you?"

The specific purpose of history to Augustine was thus the salvation of individual men and women. History was not the record of man's perpetual defiance and estrangement—which would exclude God from the world He had created. It told of men seeking peace and happiness and finding it through God's mercy. Augustine admitted that the relation between free will and predestination (another dualism) was a paradox; but few authors have exalted more highly the liberty of man. He argued with all his learning and inspiration that each man had the choice to be restored to his natural state of righteousness. By making the right response, a man could be a citizen not just of Athens or Rome, but of something far greater. There was a price for him to pay, renouncing his self-mastery and yielding to Christ, who had died for his sins. But he could then rejoice in knowing that no matter how many Romes might tumble, he had gained his place in the "most glorious city of God."

We have stressed earlier that Augustine's character and teaching are inseparable; throughout his life he thought of knowing God as having a personal connection with a being in whom man's only real satisfaction can be found. Of the truth of the Christian analysis of human nature Augustine himself had had direct and unforgettable experience. When reflecting on history, what he surely did was to project his own spiritual drama onto the universal drama of human affairs and transfer the insights he had obtained about himself onto mankind as a whole. He would not be the last to do so. In this respect, his interpretation of history becomes in the last resort no academic or rhetorical exercise alone, nor a matter of coordinating the biblical record with events in the world around him. It was an extraordinary personal testimony, a confession from the heart; for, as he knew from the miracle of his conversion, the most important person in history in the eyes of God was not Alexander, or Caesar, or even Constantine—but oneself.

By giving history this great yet intimate purpose, the *City of God* delivered a destructive blow to the sense of futility pervading the ancient world. It solved, too, the outstanding problem of causation, which, in its old context, had baffled historians and philosophers and confused the teachings of the early Church. The classical theory, exemplified in Thucydides's *History*, was that time recurred in cyclical fashion, that men could not totally control their destinies, and that the ultimate reasons of history were unknown. It is often asked why the Greeks and Romans did not develop a linear progressive view, like that held in the modern West. To some extent they did, the Romans especially, as we shall see; but the evidence overwhelmingly seemed to them to point the other way. Cities, empires, and the fortunes of individuals visibly rose and fell, generations lived and died, and, in the world of nature, the tides, the seasons, and the heavenly bodies went through their rhythmic mutations. Technological advances, which are the great underpinning of the modern Western idea of progress, were relatively few and far between.

Augustine, however, saw individual events, not repeatable sequences, as forming the contents of history, each event having its unique significance. He said nothing about Herodotus and Thucydides by name; but he condemned all cyclical theories by implication, and even took the meaning of a verse in the Psalms to be, "the wicked shall walk around in circles." Time was finite, but it existed within eternity— a notion the precise Greek mind had not readily grasped, always wanting to close the circle. Time was a process with a beginning, with a focal point in Christ, and with what was expected to be a brief aftermath before a triumphant conclusion. It was directed by God, all was pervaded by God's progressive revelation, and God's providence gave history its total meaning. History's supreme events were therefore not the founding of Rome or the fall of Rome, but Eden and Calvary. Within this scheme, the working of the spirit of God on the one hand and the diversity of human response on the other made a massive and intelligible pattern.

The phenomenon of change in human affairs could therefore be a mystery no longer. With God established as the center of the universe, as the creator of time and man, and with the universe seen as a continuous, active whole, nothing had come out of nothing to become something else. All history proceeded from God and moved back to Him in accordance with His plan of divine salvation. On the small scale, Augustine could understand the radical and permanent change in his own life in no other manner. Evil, which also baffled the classical world, became no longer meaningless, nor, as later generations have seen it, a human trait to be educated or explained away. It ran right through man's character and the whole order of things from beginning to end—a solution which remains one of the strongest claims to importance the Christian interpretation of history can put forward. The course of history might sometimes seem fragmented and inconclusive, and an event might not gain its full import until centuries later; but this was because man's vision was limited. In God's great plan each event has a definite place, each change serves to fulfill His purpose a little further, and, when all things are under God, the true unity of history appears. Meanwhile, the Christian can live knowing that the passage of history is not the dreary, impersonal cycle from which men have been vainly seeking a release as victims of their time and place; he should set aside, too, Cyprian's pessimistic reservations. He can live in a spirit of hope, knowing that history's and all creation's outcome is assured—a spirit as bright as the light of confidence that once suddenly flooded into Augustine's own heart. For those who love God, all things work together for good; and, in the present, each man may work with God too for the extension of His heavenly kingdom.

Though challenged periodically by revivals of the cyclical theory, this linear view of history has dominated in the West ever since; and by choosing it as his projection Augustine designed the historiography of the future. Yet he was really a consolidator, not an innovator, and his history was an inspired amalgam of certain earlier views. An idea which has had so many consequences demands to be traced to its origin; and for that we turn first to the other parent of Western civilization—the Jews. While Greek and Roman conceptions of history spread throughout the classical Mediterranean world, the Jewish idea of history had been largely confined to the Jews themselves. In the early Christian era, however, it began to produce as profound an effect upon Western thought as the Greek achievement had done—but of a very different kind.

Among the Jews the belief that Yahweh, the one god they came to recognize, had presided over mankind since creation—and, since Abraham left Ur, over the children of Israel in particular—had steadily grown in acceptance. The myth of Genesis had shown how a primeval deity had determined contemporary world order, an order maintained in the end by the actualization of the myth into the cult. To early Israel, however, time had not yet become linear, but was inseparable from a specific event—for example, the time to give birth, the time when kings go forth to battle, the time to build the Temple, the tree yielding its fruit in its appointed time. Like the latter-day preacher in Ecclesiastes, Israel spoke rather of "times"; and important feasts commemorating times of old, such as the deliverance from Egypt and the building of tabernacles, enabled the community to relive and participate in those unique events. The seemingly endless existence of the earth could only be conceived at this stage by putting together a sequence of "times." Finally, the faith of Israel grew to base itself not on any one event or particular chain of events, but on a sense of historical development in which certain cultic features—Jacob building an altar at Bethel, for instance—were set in order in a common frame. Israel therefore did not come to a linear concept of history philosophically but through grasping that Yahweh pursued a plan, for which He had traveled a long road with Israel's forefathers and had marked their descendants— singled them out in His covenant with Abraham. A whole nation would be the keeper of God's awesome history.

Once this scheme was defined, Israel sought restlessly, not to enlarge the historical period, but to elaborate the action of Yahweh in history and man's obligations. The prophets undertook this task with great seriousness and extraordinary alertness to new historical phenomena. Gradually they reached the conclusion that Yahweh would make a new beginning with His people, seal a second covenant, in which the purpose of history would be fulfilled. Their eschatological message— concerning the last things—was thus an extension of Israel's thinking. Jeremiah was no longer interested in old covenants, and the second Isaiah looked forward to a new reign of peace, justice, and holiness, realized in the form of a saving action of God. From then on, Israel's life was determined by what was coming. The prophets each took a certain position regarding God and Israel, imagining themselves to be placed at a juncture where history was starting to move forward again after nearly stopping. They had in common a belief that the past had a predicting significance, but their gaze was fixed ahead; and, in lessening the value of the old acts of Yahweh, they turned their faces toward an encounter with the Messiah they proclaimed. In the Book of Daniel these prophecies give way to visions of apocalypse, the world undergoing a complete destruction and renovation. Jewish writers also produced some exceptional historical narrative in the age of David and Solomon, describing the deeds of those kings from first-hand knowledge and glorifying them for posterity. In the second century B.C. the author of the First Book of Maccabees actually departed from past rules of interpretation by ascribing Jewish victories to the personal talents of their military leaders. This tradition of Jewish historiography, however, was rejected by Christian historians in favor of more conventional Jewish interpretations. These saw the course of events in history as displaying the hand of a holy, fierce, but loving God, and as recognizably unfolding His purposes alone.

As the Christian Church grew into prominence, the ideas, content, and chronology of Jewish history began to affect the practice of historiography more widely; for the early Christians confronted through experience the fact that it was to any religious group's great advantage to be able to point to a historical background. If that background were verifiable, it would be a priceless asset in winning converts, for many competing religions were ultimately vouched for only by legend. The Church's message, of course, stood or fell on the truth of a historical event; and as the Gospels and the Acts of the Apostles show, the Church strained both to document the lives of Christ and His followers and to make use of Jewish scriptures to give itself a convincing historical and theological lineage. The humanization of God in Jesus—born of an earthly mother, part of a human family, preaching in human terms to all who would listen, forming human friends of mostly humble origins, dying a human death, and appearing as God in the form of a risen man —lent itself in certain respects to making these attempts credible. Their success firmly established Christianity for centuries to come as a religion rooted in history, whose central events, enshrined in the Apostles' creed, were authenticated by their having actually happened. Though the first Christian accounts of history were mostly credulous, interpreting by way of allegory or symbolism, the origins and fortunes of Christianity were competently chronicled; and, after the final collapse of the ancient Jewish state, the Romano-Jewish historian Josephus boldly asserted that Jewish history was as important as that of the Jews' Roman conqueror.

The Jewish version of history shared certain features with the Greek, for Jewish history recognized that the Jews' religious faith waxed and waned; and the Greeks acknowledged that events move forward within the cycle. Thus the two theories of history were not totally incompatible. The Jewish conception of history with its Christian supplement nonetheless provided Augustine the basic model for his linear view. There were, however, other strengths he could draw upon to make that view of history persuasive; and one of these was the time-honored story of life as a journey. Take a hero, with a mixed set of companions perhaps, send him on a quest, the issue of which hangs on unforeseen events, and bring him at last to safety—this was the story of Odysseus, of Jason and the golden fleece, of Xenophon's tale of the march of ten thousand Greek soldiers from Babylon to the Black Sea, and of Virgil's great poem on the founding of Rome, the *Aeneid* (which Augustine frequently quoted). History in that style was assured a popular reception, and the biblical story, in whole or in its parts, was cast by its authors for that sort of presentation. Then, too, history had also begun to appear as biography, in the work of Arrian and of Plutarch, whose parallel lives of famous Greeks and Romans were accompanied by moral reflections. Familiar with that tradition of writing, audiences were prepared for a history that told of a succession of God's servants—Abraham, Moses, Elijah, and a host of others—culminating, of course, in the life of Christ Himself.

And what could be more suited to Augustine's needs than the great epic of Rome? Rome might be failing at the end of its cycle, but its long history had already been portrayed in linear terms by Livy, whose quiet career as a scholar provides one leading exception to the classical standards of what a historian should be. In 142 books, Livy had chronicled the growth of an Italian village to nationhood and then to mastery of a universal empire of peace and justice. His research had errors and deficiencies, but his tale, *The Annals of the Roman People*, was unequalled—a lesson for the whole human race. It was packed with dramatic episodes, infused with patriotic feeling, and it immediately became a classic. Under Roman rule, it implied, mankind and civilization had strikingly advanced—an idealizing opinion Augustine rejected, for though some material progress had occurred, Rome was not improving itself into the city of God on earth even after the adoption of Christianity. But he himself was proud to be a Roman, Rome had had an interest in keeping its past alive, and every reader, almost every citizen, would be familiar with the outline. As an eternal Rome became a lost vision, an eternal Jerusalem could be a satisfying alternative; and Augustine's linear, Christian view of history slipped into place at an appropriate moment.

The total philosophy of history contained in the *City of God* was nonetheless unprecedented, and it produced an effect none of its tributaries had accomplished separately. Taking the Christian view of man's personality and seeing men within the all-enveloping plan of God, it discarded antiquity's exhausted answers to the problem of causation and offered its thorough solution in the author's strongest affirmative. Through Christ the process and ends of history could now be understood; and Augustine's masterpiece, respectful of the classical heritage but simultaneously demoting it from supremacy, completed the change of outlook. For the depth and force of his teachings, the Western Church in the Middle Ages was accustomed to rank Augustine first after the Apostles.

IV

In many ways the effect of the *City of God* on the idea of history was devastating. Already the Greek and Roman method and purpose of investigating the past had been challenged; and Augustine's achievement, by establishing the Christian historiographical revolution, encouraged men to abandon the earlier kind of inquiries. Producing political and military studies of history in the classical tradition or accomplished works of literature held little attraction for the new school of ecclesiastics—by and large the only literate class—and such aims were mostly forgotten or lost until the Renaissance. The Christian past—principally its Old Testament period—was the one history necessary for men to know. Moses (the supposed author of the first five books of the Bible) was now the first historian—and geologist. The whole purpose of studying history had become different. While for Thucydides history might teach what decisions to take in certain situations, for Augustine it taught man how God intended him to live, and why he should expect still greater things from God in the future.

After Augustine, therefore, history became essentially the story, not of man, but of God. It was *Heilsgeschichte*—the recital of God's mighty acts of salvation. As transmitted through the Church it was primarily the accessory of theology, and little or nothing separated a historical fact from a theological truth. The Jews had tended to compress all knowledge and interpretation of the past with which they were familiar into their divinely sanctioned scheme. The Christians followed that practice and saw Egypt, Babylon, Greece, and even Rome, not as great or interesting in themselves, but of importance only when their affairs happened to brush against the history first of the Jews, then of the Church. As a result Pericles vanished before Solomon; Emperor Augustus was more fortunate and survived thanks to his decree that all the world should be taxed, ensuring that Christ's birth would be at Bethlehem. The history of the world which Orosius prepared for Augustine ignored the pagan empires' cultural distinctions and showed them as wicked and visited by almost incessant disasters. Since the rise of Christianity, in contrast, it showed that the horrors of war, crime, famine, and earthquake had decreased—clear evidence, Orosius claimed, that the charges against Christians were unjustified. His work became the basic manual of universal history for the Middle Ages. It was not until the eighteenth century that historians in any number, partly copying the Greeks and Romans, began to take God out of history again and concentrated on the actions of men alone.

Bede's *History of the English Church and People,* written in the early eighth century, illustrates what Christian historiography could attain. Living in the far north of his country, the monk, who is often called the father of English history, compiled a notable account of the conversion of England by missionaries Pope Gregory the Great sent over a hundred years before. Bede used with discernment the best sources available to him, and his work is of very high quality—a splendid start for English history writing; but his story has an intensely Christian bias which is not always easy to accept. It is the story of the English Church first, of the English people second. From Bede's perspective, no greater event had happened to England than the coming of Christianity; his *History* was a late sequel to the glorious deeds of Christ's apostles, and every episode showed God's guidance and protection. It told of God's city on earth bringing the gospel to a distant part of the city of man—the idol-worshipping English—until, after much heroism and bloodshed, the Christian faith in its Roman form had spread throughout the land. It is decisively a history from the Christian side, allowing few chances to hear the heathen version—unlike Herodotus's mode of treatment; and Bede's habit of dating events before or after the birth of Christ greatly furthered the usage. Miracles frequently occur—but then to Bede the whole story of his people's conversion against all odds was miraculous. No other interpretation was possible. It would offend reason as well as faith; and Bede wrote to praise God, and to inspire succeeding generations in the time remaining.

To most readers in the modern West such a view of history is a travesty; but some of its consequences were constructive for the idea of history's development. History now had a grandeur about it which widened man's imaginative horizons; and, by stressing actual events, Christian historiography increased Western man's awareness of precise historical facts. It further emphasized in its details—as Bede's example indicates—the necessity of an orderly pattern. Augustine's personal compulsiveness to know about history, since history was in part a means to understand himself, brought a new resolve to the study of the past that did not exist in more abstract inquiries. Augustine also set himself to persuade the ancient world to give up old concepts of man and the cyclical scheme; and he succeeded so well that his optimistic explanation of all temporal events is one of the great historical theories. It helped build the civilization of the Middle Ages— which, according to Arnold Toynbee, is Western man's finest creation. It eventually came to exercise a still more powerful effect, in cruder secularized form, on the modern idea of progress.

Augustine's life and thought show so much of the progressive attitude that it is hardly surprising he fostered it in others. Even to have the pursuit of growth, knowledge, and light as an objective was, he believed, a promising start. We may find advantages in nonlinear thinking, and the mind's potential for this has been underestimated; but in one Western ideology after another the world has been seen as working for a cumulative purpose which human agents can assist. Generating optimism and activism, linear schemes have moved human affairs and set a value on time at the daily level—every hour and, later, every minute of it. The West's sustained dynamism would surely have been inconceivable if man's hopes and energies had been confined within a cyclical system.

The success of any history may also be measured in other ways of no less importance: the *City of God* is an outstanding example of a history which met and still meets an explicit human need. It was written amid crisis; and a crisis reminds us the historical process is not as straightforward as we once took it to be. Marcellinus called for convincing reassurance. Augustine in his reply provided his friend and his fellow Africans—and with them the Christian world—with a rock of faith, which served as stronghold and hiding-place in the spreading disorder. Whoever sought security here below was distorting his love and judgment; he who recognized security in God alone could view earthly chaos, even the fall of Rome, with equanimity. No wonder his message appealed to people cowering in ruined cities or fleeing into the desert, as the safety of life and possessions disappeared. Rome, the city, at its peak had close to 1 million inhabitants; under Pope Gregory, at the end of the sixth century, the population had dwindled to fifty thousand, a town scattered through an immense masonry yard. Whenever conditions of catastrophe emerge, Augustine's analysis of history can immediately become valid; it makes the earthly secondary to the eternal, stresses God's unalterability, and reminds man that God can act most powerfully when man expects it least.

Of course a Christian history, by taking an extratemporal perspective, is more than an interpretation of history. It invites men to stand outside history altogether; and so, as Hegel charged in the nineteenth century, it is essentially antihistorical. But for the Christian this escape is from unreality to reality. The facts are not the same for him as they are for the agnostic or the atheist; the moral ambiguity of history has been taken away, and Jesus Christ reigns as Lord. The Christian sees himself primarily as one with men of faith of all the ages and only secondarily as a man of the present. History is nonetheless still unfinished, and man lives in a world that is still a world of possibilities. The present therefore is an age which challenges the Christian to serve the promised future. Sustained by what Kierkegaard called a fighting certainty, he sows in hope and acts in self-surrender; for he knows that, though he stands in sight of that future, life is to be risked if it is to be won.

Jesus never outlined a version of history and the Christian view is accordingly deduced from Scripture and supplemented by interpretation. It thus reflects the currents of historical research and religious experience. One hundred years ago, under pressure from rationalism and positivism, there was a widespread belief that the kingdom of God Jesus had in mind would gradually permeate society by man's cooperation; and, influenced by the research of Ranke, scholars sought the historical Jesus. Today the liberal theology is less prominent than the theology of the Christ of faith, proclaimed by the Gospels and the Church as God's word addressed to man; and current Christian thinking has again moved closer to Augustine's vision. Scholars now reluctantly concede that we do not possess the kind of sources which can fully document the life of Christ as He was, for in the Gospels His representation underwent an irreversible metamorphosis; and, after the First World War, the crises of the secular age could no longer be easily resolved by the idea of progress and trust in human reason. In a catastrophe seemingly as great as the fall of Rome, Christians began to be reminded that time had a destination as well as a direction, that mankind was actually living between the "times" of Christ's ascension and His absolute victory. All other conditions for that final event have been met; only a residue of God's great plan remains.

A responsible expositor of Christian history is aware that today the subject itself is between "times." The Church's traditional teaching is largely medieval; and modern man is unlikely to be wholly satisfied with the elaborate providential designs of Augustine and his successors, many of whom perhaps knew more answers than questions. Nor is he inclined to want the Church to be linked with the state; he may regret that Rome's acceptance of Christianity destroyed much of Christianity's early vitality. The Christian community holds that the divine scheme of history does not change as earthly philosophies are liable to do; but Christianity has generally, though often reluctantly, allowed its claims to be examined on all levels of inquiry. The present era has a new understanding of what history is and what it is about, the work mostly of historians and philosophers, not of theologians; and, as man continues to probe the sky, questions are raised again of his place in the cosmos and of the personal characteristics of God. New and divergent Christian thought addresses issues concerning the nature of the whole historical process, urgent now that scientific certainty is no longer assured, as well as restoring the individual's importance.

In today's greater intellectual freedom, any single reformulation of the Christian doctrine of history will hardly enjoy the authority Augustine's once had; but the search for historical certainty is again ready to be less exclusively rational, often shows a new religious feeling for the earth and for life, and may work more closely in hand with Christian teaching about man. Christianity still demands faith as the price of its acceptance, a faith centered around the nucleus of a historical event which, as in the years closest to its occurrence, can sometimes only be worshipped. For the Christian the Incarnation which the prophets foretold and the angels announced establishes history. In return for his faith, history for him becomes no longer finite, frustrating, and reduced to human limitations. Quoting H. G. Wells, who was himself no believer, to take Christ seriously is "to enter upon a strange and alarming life, to abandon habits, to control instincts and impulses, to essay an incredible happiness."

But men live more typically on the mundane level. What has been the effect of Augustine's thought on the city of man, and on that city's aspirations to its own earthly peace? To the ancient world history was mainly the story of wars, but, with the *City of God*, men were systematically challenged to make it instead the story of reconciliation. To act for justice in the present, and to strive for a common future of concord and freedom, became the aim of all who sought the well-being and completeness of society and everyone in it. All his life Augustine sought to bring opposites together, first in himself, then in those around him; and he knew the peacemaker's effort called for greater talents and dedication than did the pursuit of violence and personal fame. The new history, far from being poor reading, would be stirring in every chapter, its tale the advancement of the individual from the best that Roman citizenship offered to a nobler commonwealth of brotherhood and peace. The *City of God* raised men's expectations for the community in which they lived. It was apparently the favorite book of Charlemagne, the warrior who, unable to read himself, had it read aloud, and is still revered as the architect of an early united Europe. Though a "Popish" book, it inspired the Puritan settlement of Massachusetts Bay; for Governor Winthrop spoke in the accents of Augustine when he likened in hope the tiny colony to "a city upon a hill" on whom the eyes of all people were set. And its spirit has not been absent from the League of Nations, the United Nations, and other experiments in international cooperation, and has spread to wherever on the globe peace in its best reality is sought. For many reasons, it is impossible not to admire the thoughts and actions Augustine's history has brought forth.

CHAPTER THREE

PETRARCH AND MACHIAVELLI

I

Western man accepted Augustine's argument for a thousand years because it satisfied him. It satisfied his intellect, and it satisfied his search for peace of mind and for self-understanding. The *City of God* formalized for him the Christian view of history, although it had no more validity than the weight of Augustine's name behind it. In the West, however, that was considerable. The characteristic medieval work of history in consequence explained events with much interpretation but little further analysis—for none was really necessary. The meaning of events was implicit in God's great scheme. Medieval historians lost few chances to moralize; events and individuals were chiefly important for what they represented as symbols, not as the cause of what next took place.

In a culture changing slowly until its final period, the need to look at the past afresh was in any case reduced; and medieval man, seeking guidance from the next world, not from the last, lacked a historical perspective. Figures of the past were projected out of the present with absurd anachronisms, Moses and Alexander for instance being depicted in art wearing the current style of armor. Ruins, although marvels, were otherwise part of the landscape, not objects for much investigation; and, when written evidence of the past was available, the general rule was the greater the authority, the more reliable his story. Few historians tried, like Bede, to compare their sources critically. Legends achieved

58

the status of fact and were readily invented to justify pretensions or existing situations. For example, according to Geoffrey of Monmouth, Britain was first settled by a band of Trojans under their leader Brutus. Again, certain documents were forged, like the Donation of Constantine, which supposedly made the pope the emperor's heir in Italy. The intent was not criminal, but rather to show that such a reasonable transferal must have taken place. World histories were attempted which often divided time by the four empires or the six ages described in the Book of Daniel. Of greater interest to us, however, is the chronicle, which, beginning as notes in the margin of the Church's annual calendar, emerged as a record of happenings in the life of the chronicler's community.

The chronicle of chivalry became medieval historiography's finest achievement. It flourished during the Crusades and afterwards, enthralling audiences with the actors, deeds, and ideals of the age. Like the Crusades themselves—"the acts of God through the Franks"—it was largely a French performance. Geoffroi de Villehardouin, a leader in the Fourth Crusade, left a spirited account of the conquest of Constantinople, the first work of history in the vernacular; but the supreme author of this form of contemporary history was Jean Froissart, a minor cleric born in Flanders in 1338. Something of a medieval Herodotus, Froissart traveled repeatedly through much of western Europe, winning friends at one court after another with his verses and tales, and developing his *Chronicles of England, France and Spain*. The life and splendor of chivalry in the era of the Hundred Years' War delighted him; he wanted to know all sides to every encounter, and he had an extraordinary gift for making people tell him what they could remember. It is in Froissart that we find the famous stories of the Black Prince winning his spurs at Crécy, the blind king of Bohemia's heroism in battle—and many others. Written in French, the *Chronicles* was exclusively about nobles and for nobles (his benefactors), and it derived from noble sources. The work praised knightly manners and feats of arms without probing too closely into their causes or the intrigues behind them—a subject explored much more by the later writer, Philippe de Commines. Froissart tried merely to record his times —which he did splendidly for his circle—and not to judge them. Gallantry was his real theme, and it rose above considerations of motive or nationality. Like Herodotus, he said his aim was "to encourage all valorous hearts, and to show them honorable examples." He hoped, too, that his work might give pleasure when he was gone; and there can hardly be a reader since who has not owed him gratitude.

In Froissart's day the pattern of society was divinely ordained, and all questions of history were decided finally by Christian teaching. Nonetheless, the *Chronicles* put forward human values—idealized, perhaps, and of religious origin, but still human. The new interest in man for what he was, not just for what he could be, led in time by various means to the Renaissance discovery of man as an individual. The history of history is at bottom the story of man reappraising himself, and it often proceeds not steadily but by sharp and sudden turns. New evidence from the past, new experiences in the present, force changes in the story itself, of course; but, whenever man the central subject sees himself in a different light, all the human past comes up again for reevaluation—thereby altering ideas on the present and future, too. The transition from the Middle Ages to the Renaissance may not have been as marked as some historians, such as Jacob Burckhardt, once claimed; rather the Renaissance followed late medieval tendencies, it never broke entirely with the Christian faith, and the modern era is now often said to begin with the Scientific Revolution. But we can look forward and see Machiavelli taking a very different view of history from Augustine's—a view which sprang from a new confidence in man's ability for self-knowledge and self-improvement. As this attitude grew common, two views of man's past and prospects started to assail one another. I will shortly sketch Machiavelli's new kind of history and, more briefly, the resulting confusion over history's aim and practice, which is well illustrated by the state of history writing in Shakespeare's England.

If, however, the Renaissance and its discovery of man had an originator—and contemporaries were sure it did—the choice is Francesco Petrarca, whose name has been anglicized to Petrarch. A fourteenth-century Florentine, Petrarch reflects the transitional period in which he lived. He never doubted the higher truths of Christian revelation; but he was first in the movement to set the intellect free from religion. The humanist outlook he proposed was pursued so keenly after his death that eventually the close union between speculative thought and the Christian faith was broken—as Machiavelli's type of history shows. Petrarch is now a neglected figure, unfairly so, for the Renaissance concept of history—indeed the Renaissance as a whole—cannot be properly understood without him. He did write a history of Rome, *Lives of Illustrious Men,* from Romulus to the emperor Titus; but he was more a man inspired by a new vision of the past, and by a belief in its importance. His influence on the form and the direction of historical thinking was profound.

II

You make an orator of me, a historian, philosopher, and poet, and finally even a theologian [wrote Petrarch in 1362 to the papal secretary in Avignon]. You would certainly not do so if you were not persuaded by one whom it is impossible to disbelieve; I mean Love. Perhaps you might be excused if you did not extol me with titles so overwhelmingly great: I do not deserve to have them heaped on me. But let me tell you, my friend, how far I fall short of your estimation. It is not my opinion only; it is a fact: I am nothing of what you attribute to me. What am I then? I am a fellow who never quits school, and not even that, but a backwoodsman who is roaming around through the lofty beech trees all alone, humming to himself some silly little tune, and—the very peak of presumption and assurance —dipping his shaky pen into his inkstand while sitting under a bitter laurel tree. I am not so fortunate in what I achieve as passionate in my work, being much more a lover of learning than a man who has got much of it. I am not so very eager to belong to a definite school of thought; I am striving for truth.

In these words with a modern, even a Thoreau-like ring, the man credited with giving impetus to the Renaissance in Italy offers a charming and modest self-portrait. But for all his inquiring spirit and sensitivity to nature, this is not yet an altogether modern man; for, though Petrarch went on to say "I do not believe in my faculties, do not affirm anything, and doubt every single thing," he admitted he was held back by "the single exception of what I believe is a sacrilege to doubt." Elsewhere he summed himself up best, more frankly than Augustine ever did, when he wrote "I am as if on the frontiers of two peoples, looking forward and backward."

The usual reaction ever since to so perceptive a remark has been to stress the looking forward. By self-admission, it seems, Petrarch cast himself as our ancestor, as the pioneer whose striving for truth would lead to the brilliant cultures of Florence, Milan, Rome, and other cities of the Renaissance—and eventually to the civilization of today. But the remark in its context gives a different meaning. Petrarch's two worlds of which he spoke were the ancient—with which he identified— and the centuries which follow it, the age we call medieval; and light for him lay only in the classical past. We have, then, a man paradoxically encouraging his audience, not to make what they have in the present into their future, but to aim at recovering a past they had lost. The future for Petrarch had to be Rome restored, Rome for its own merits; and his enthusiasm governed most of his activity and drew men's ambitions away from the new Jerusalem and down to thoughts of earthly glories and rewards. His remark also implies that the two sides of his mind and life were often at odds with one another.

As a poet writing in Italian Petrarch was Dante's successor and Boccaccio's master; and, as a poet and writer in Latin, he retrieved the vigor of classical style and substituted Roman concepts of life and its opportunities for those the Church had offered. In the century before printing—his library contained only about two hundred books—he gained fame as a classical philologist and devised procedures of textual criticism. In fact, he became the first great man of letters in Europe, a position only a few such as Erasmus, Voltaire, and Goethe have filled after him. Part of Petrarch's success undoubtedly came from his boundless capacity for friendship. Cardinals and an emperor sought his conversation; and his personal correspondence, each piece a literary exercise, was treasured by its recipients and sent on to others—thereby spreading the new learning. Few authors have ever been more popular with the public at large. It is recorded how, when traveling to Padua in 1368, he crossed freely the battlelines between warring Italian states, where anyone else would have been robbed or slain. Indeed, he was overwhelmed with gifts of fruit, wine, and game by the soldiers. The story recalls a similar incident centuries later, the regiment of Scots Greys breaking ranks to let Sir Walter Scott pass through the crowd at the coronation of George IV. Petrarch involved himself in politics and wrote as an Italian patriot; and his works—like Scott's—could reach humble people, and sometimes were about them.

Macaulay tells us that once, while searching in an attic for some apples, the young Samuel Johnson found a large folio volume of Petrarch's works. The name arousing his curiosity, he eagerly read hundreds of pages. In approaching Petrarch today, we are more likely to be faced with barriers. Not least of these is what to Johnson in the eighteenth century was Petrarch's chief attraction—his fame as rediscoverer of the classics. It is astonishing by what slender threads the Greek and Roman authors survived to the modern era. The earliest of the few extant manuscripts of Herodotus and Thucydides date from the tenth and eleventh centuries. But, since the classics are now so readily available—and also less influential—it is hard to recapture the excitement men of the Renaissance and for three centuries afterwards felt. Petrarch's own discoveries and the quotations he was first to make seem like very old news. In literature his development of the sonnet and of a new Italian poetic diction, though vital at the time, can appear of only academic concern. Then, in the nineteenth century especially, he became celebrated as the sighing lover of Laura, the Avignonese lady on whom his affections were fixed for twenty years, writing over three hundred poems in her honor (but mostly about himself), and ever planting laurel bushes when she was dead. The passion was, it seems, real enough, but prolonged expressions of unrequited ardor no longer suit our taste. Much of Petrarch is plainly out of fashion, but his qualities as innovator and experimental scholar persist.

We know a great deal about Petrarch's life and character. He was proud to call himself a Florentine; but he was all his life a political exile, born fifty miles away in Arezzo in 1304 and only seeing the city he called his home on two brief visits. His notary father, who had left Florence when his party had lost in one of the frequent internal struggles, eventually made his way to southern France, where, in 1309, the papal court under Clement V had become established at Avignon. The effect of the Papacy's arrival in that small riverside city may be likened to what would happen if the United Nations relocated itself in Annapolis, Maryland. Suddenly Avignon was a boom town, offering unlimited prospects to lawyers and speculators, and buildings and provisions were needed on a large scale to maintain the papal adminis- tration. In the winter of 1312 the father sent for his wife and two sons; and many years later Petrarch could still recall vividly the beauty of the Italian coast and the horrors of the sea journey from Genoa to Marseilles. Although, if any place could be called his home it would be Avignon, he possessed to the end feelings of a displaced Italian, and, more specifically, came to see both himself and his Church as displaced Romans. Avignon to him was always a place to get away from, and Rome, the lost ideal; that ideal fascinated him and led to a deepening conviction that history was something to be rectified.

In later years Petrarch became famous for his censures of the Church's "Babylonian captivity"—although he received plenty of favors from his association with it; but the principal reason why the popes settled in Avignon, permanently it seemed, was the insecurity of life in Italy. Relations with France were better and Avignon was desirably peaceful, remote from Italian and imperial problems. It was much closer than Rome to the rest of Europe and well suited for perfecting the machinery of papal government, especially, in a new money econ- omy, the tax operations. As a portrait in greed, luxury, and complacency, the Avignonese Papacy has come to form a backdrop to the Reforma- tion, but, given the situation, the move can be defended as a firm attempt to make claims of papal authority a working reality, which succeeded, perhaps, too well. Since Italy remained turbulent, any return to Rome came to mean waging a war of reconquest at huge expense—causing the stay at Avignon to be rationalized still further.

It was not until after 1360, when bands of mercenary soldiers released from the Hundred Years' War started to attack Avignon, compelling the popes to buy ransom year after year and fortify the city, that a return to Rome began to offer some advantages.

As a boy Petrarch flourished in Avignon's cosmopolitan society; and at school he discovered the writer whom he would prize above all others for the rest of his life. When other boys were studying Aesop, he tells us, "I gave myself wholly to Cicero." Everything else he read seemed graceless and discordant. Intrigued by what he could understand, he made the extraordinary effort to absorb Roman thought, instead of seeing it as a phenomenon external to himself. He grew to love the style of the great Latin authors still more—Virgil, Horace, and Seneca, as well as Cicero—and to detest the legal and theological Latin of his day, barbarized and delighting in obscurities. Compared to the learned around him, the Romans seemed men of a higher breed, who had dignified individualism and defined excellence. To increase the meager supply of Roman literature available to him, Petrarch soon started his lifelong search for manuscripts, procuring what he discovered or tediously making copies, extending further his knowledge and his sense of his real identity.

Sent by his father to study civil law at Bologna, Petrarch returned to Avignon and for awhile led the life of a young man about town. He gained a local reputation for poetry written in Italian in the courtly tradition of Provençal troubadours; but, probably because his family was defrauded of his father's estate, he took minor ecclesiastical orders, which insured some constant means of support. Shortly after, he had the good fortune to gain the friendship of Bishop Giacomo Colonna, of the eminent Roman family, and soon the patronage of the bishop's brother, the cardinal. Admittance to the Colonna household not only gave Petrarch time and leisure to pursue his scholarship; in 1333 he was dispatched by Cardinal Colonna to Paris, the Low Countries, and the Rhineland, where he took every opportunity to sightsee (he has been called the first tourist) and to search monastery libraries for manuscripts. On his return he was depressed by the worldliness of Avignon; but, receiving a copy of Augustine's *Confessions*—a Latin as well as a Christian classic—he read it and immediately applied its story to himself. Avignon became his Carthage, and he, like Augustine, was seeking release from it in struggles for self-understanding and self-mastery. His search led him in 1336 to take an action, which, more than anything else he did, draws a modern audience to him. As if to symbolize his eternal curiosity, yet also compelled by some need for self-purification, he climbed a mountain—Mont Ventoux, thirty miles away from Avignon, but clearly visible at over six thousand feet high.

In today's terms this was no great feat, but until the nineteenth century the impulse to climb was most uncommon. Mountains were traditionally shunned as the abode of dangerous forces naturally hostile to man; to climb what seemed merely a larger rock in the landscape "because it was there" was quite alien to the medieval mind. For Petrarch, however, the stimulus—as it often did with him—came from classical precedent. He had read in Livy that King Philip of Macedon had climbed Mount Hemus in the Balkans to discover if the Black Sea and the Adriatic could both be seen. Petrarch's report of his own journey with his brother, written immediately afterward, ranks as one of his best compositions.

Meeting an old shepherd who tried to discourage him, Petrarch nonetheless pressed on, feeling with each step he was leaving his past behind and raising his life to a loftier plane. Reaching the summit he was thrilled, like all mountain climbers since, by the air and the wide unbroken view. He looked toward Italy "for which my mind is so fervently yearning," at the sea beyond Marseilles, and he tried to discern the Pyrenees. Tales of Mount Olympus seemed less incredible, and he revelled in his physical accomplishment. He had with him Augustine's *Confessions,* to read whatever might strike his spirit as he stood where earth meets heaven.

> I happened to hit upon the tenth book of the work [he relates]. My brother stood beside me intently expecting to hear something from Augustine on my mouth. I ask God to be my witness, and my brother who was with me: Where I fixed my eyes first, it was written: "And men go to admire the high mountains, the vast floods of the sea, the huge streams of the rivers, the circumference of the ocean, and the revolutions of the stars—and desert themselves."

This, for some, spoils the story—the new man of the Renaissance lapsing into pious introspection at one of the highpoints of his forward-looking career. But, for the period in which Petrarch lived, religion was still the natural medium for sublime expression—as his poems to Laura show, too. His account of his ascent—neither a celebration of the deeds of the first Alpinist, nor the diary of a scientific expedition—is in fact a masterly blending of the literal and the allegorical, and, with its similarity to Augustine's conversion experience, no doubt partly contrived. But this is not to say the Renaissance spirit in Petrarch was absent. In the first place, he *had* climbed the mountain. And although he had closed the book in a mood of self-rebuke, he found himself, he says, remembering what even pagan philosophers had taught about the soul and, during his descent, thinking of man's nobility in spite of his errors and vain purposes. If the two sides of his exultation were not quite reconciled, they were not for that age inconsistent.

The following year Petrarch made his first visit to Rome, the city on which his thoughts had been set since he was a schoolboy. He probably went on business for Cardinal Colonna; but, in contrast to his minute descriptions of cities in France and Germany, he recorded few impressions. Like Edward Gibbon in 1764 he was overwhelmed by what he saw, in spite of the squalor and systematic destruction, and he needed time to articulate his emotions properly. "You used to think I should write something 'in the grand style' when I had reached Rome," he told the cardinal in a brief note dated "The Ides of March on the Capitol." "I have found, it is true, a vast subject for future writing; at present there is nothing that I dare attempt, for I sink under the weight of so many marvels around me. . . . In truth Rome was greater, and its remains are greater, than I had imagined." Back at Avignon again, he retreated to the country, purchasing a cottage at Vaucluse, a half-day's ride away. He laid out a garden, where he enjoyed the nightingale's song, and became a fisherman, as always writing at his best when out of doors. At Vaucluse he began work on *Lives of Illustrious Men* (modeled on Plutarch's *Lives*), started his poetic sequence the *Triumphs*, and in 1338 decided in a flash of inspiration to write a great poem on Scipio Africanus, the conqueror of Hannibal and the embodiment of all the old Roman virtues. This epic, *Africa*, would be written in Latin and, he fervently hoped, be a worthy successor to its model, Virgil's *Aeneid*. Posterity—and Petrarch too when honest—have in that respect found it wanting; but few of his works reveal so well as *Africa* the substance and the dreams of his thoughts on history.

Perfect though his refuge seemed, Petrarch nonetheless still craved the world's recognition; and he conceived the idea of being publicly awarded the laureateship as Rome's great poets had once been honored. One or two recent precedents existed in other cities, but the custom had lapsed in Rome for over a thousand years; and there were other obstacles in the way. His poems in Italian were not particularly admired by men of learning, although he had an excellent reputation as a bibliophile and a Latin stylist. He let it be known, however, that he was writing a Latin epic on Rome's greatness; and aggressively seeking earthly glory, in 1340 he wrangled an invitation from the Roman Senate to be crowned with the wreath of laurel. Visiting Naples first, he was pronounced worthy after examination by the king, and Petrarch then traveled on to Rome for the greatest event in his life. In the senatorial palace on the Capitoline Hill he made his coronation speech to the sound of trumpets, concluding with a request for the crown of poetry and shouting three times, "Long live the Roman people and the Senator, and God maintain them in liberty!" The presiding senator placed the wreath on his head, and the now-honored Petrarch was declared a Roman citizen and given the right to discourse on all poetic and historical subjects in any place and at any time.

Like the failed epic *Africa*, the coronation shows how Petrarch's reverence for the classical past could degenerate into worship and antiquarian revival. But for all its air of fantasy, it should be taken seriously. The honor was a recognition of secular, not religious, literature; and, after years of self-identification with the great Latin authors, Petrarch officially became one of them himself. The coronation established his fame, and he noticeably grew in assurance. Deeply impressed once more by the mighty ruins of pagan Rome, but shocked by present Roman ignorance about them, it was then, it seems, he asked the question that summarized his whole approach to the past. "Who can doubt that Rome would rise up again," he exclaimed, "if she but began to know herself?" Recalling his wanderings around the sights with his friend Giovanni Colonna, he wrote:

> After the fatigue of walking over the immense circuit of the city, we used often to stop at the Baths of Diocletian; sometimes we even climbed upon the vaulted roof of that once magnificent building, for nowhere is there a healthier air, a wider prospect, or more silence and desirable solitude. There we did not talk of business nor of private or public affairs on which we had shed tears enough. As we walked over the walls of the shattered city or sat there, the fragments of the ruins were often under our very eyes. Our conversation often turned on history, which we appeared to have divided up between us in such a fashion that in modern history you, in ancient history I, seemed to be more expert; and ancient were called those events which took place before the name of Christ was celebrated in Rome and adored by Roman emperors, modern, however, the events from that time to the present.

What is most remarkable about these reminiscences is not just Petrarch's clear preference for pagan Rome over Christian, but the new division of history he was now prepared to make. The *City of God* had been an interpretation designed for fifth-century Christians when Rome and civilization itself seemed tragically doomed. Augustine had respected Rome's achievements where respect was due, but they were inferior to

life in a Christian commonwealth, and transient too compared with
the heavenly city. Time was linear and unrepeatable, and Christ was the
hinge on which history turned. Before His birth, there stretched an age
of darkness, the only ray of light coming through the Jews; but since
Christ's sacrifice men could live forever in the new clear light of God's
saving grace, to which the Church bore witness.

It was Petrarch's fundamental contribution to historiography to
alter this verdict and divide up time afresh—without a direct challenge
to Christianity's essential teaching. In every sphere but that of man's
salvation, antiquity was the age of light, a light unparalleled in brilliance.
Rome, viewed panoramically from the roof of Diocletian's massively
imposing edifice, or judged from the boundaries of its walls, was a
sepulcher, but still the ultimate in human civilization. The Christian
buildings Petrarch saw were in decay, neglected for Avignon. The
broken monuments of ancient Rome, however, still had a majestic
quality about them, an air of unconquerable permanence. "What else,
then," he asked, "is all history, if not the praise of Rome?" The
boundary-line in history as a whole therefore became not the birth of
Christ but Rome's acceptance of Christianity, which changed its spirit.
When Petrarch's medieval predecessors had not used the ruins as
building materials for their own houses, they had marveled at them, too;
but they took them for granted within the context of eternity. His own
notions of the past were much more acute. With his extensive knowledge of Roman history and literature, he could place Rome's remains
precisely within human time instead. The builders of this stupendous
city—more than a city, a sublime idea—had been mortal men, not a
vanished race of superior or godlike beings; and, though they had been
pagan, the world had not seen their equal since.

Rome thus meant to Petrarch every sort of ideal greatness of which
man is capable. But, if Rome represented light, what else could the
succeeding centuries be but an age of darkness? In the end he actually
came to use the Latin word for darkness, *tenebrae*, to describe the
centuries following the era of Augustus. In his epic *Africa*, when the
father of Scipio Africanus prophesies Rome's future, he breaks off with
the first-century emperors Vespasian and Titus. "I cannot bear to
proceed," the austerely virtuous Roman says to his son, "for strangers
of Spanish and African extraction will steal the scepter and the glory of
the Empire founded by us with great effort. Who can endure the
thought of the seizure of supreme control by these dregs of the people,
these contemptible remnants, passed over by our sword?" Elsewhere, in
language anticipating that which Voltaire would use, Petrarch dismissed
a host of later emperors as men "whose names were always obscure and

are now entirely obliterated because of the long lapse of time." Christian though he was, he saw in the past the greatness of antiquity perishing, to be followed by the pedantry of the Schools, and still later, by the gaudiness and corruption of Avignon. Among his claims to originality must be included the invention of the "Dark Ages" as a derogatory term.

To the end of his days, Petrarch's letters reveal his despair that his own times fell so far short of the Augustan age, the period in which no doubt he would have chosen to live. The fourteenth century seemed particularly full of misfortunes. Widespread warfare (practically constant in Italy), fanciful scholarship and speculation, a cowardly Papacy pursuing its own interests—and in 1348 the Black Death, which claimed Laura among its victims—filled him with misery. But Rome had risen out of similar chaos and degradation. He voiced his yearnings for the future in the concluding lines of *Africa*, when, addressing his own poem, he wrote: "My fate is to live among varied and confusing storms. But for you perhaps, if as I hope and wish you will live long after me, there will follow a better age. This sleep of forgetfulness will not last for ever. When the darkness has been dispersed, our descendants can come again in the former pure radiance." Petrarch had altered Augustine's scheme of history by choosing other values, without discarding Christianity completely; but here he went further, hinting at history moving in cycles, bringing the idea back to brighten the prospect of seemingly endless decline and unrestrained conflict. Rome had not fallen once and for all, as Gibbon would later believe. It could be restored, and continuity with the ruling ideas of civilization would then be reestablished.

So that men might know Rome for what she once had been, Petrarch energetically tried to acquaint his contemporaries from wherever he was living—Vaucluse, Milan, Venice, Pavia, Padua—with the history of Italy under Roman rule and the light he himself had gained from the classics. The task was urgent. "Pliny's *History of the Roman Wars* disappeared in our own times," he wrote; "our descendants will have no knowledge of the past." Greek was not known to him, except in Latin translation, but toward the end of his life he sought Greek manuscripts, too. Every fragment of classical writing, every inscription, every coin was a treasure, and he infected his friends with similar enthusiasm. He was primarily a scholar; but on occasion his hopes rose that the return of the golden age could actually be accomplished. After all, he had himself helped to revive Latin literature, and his coronation as a Roman was a reminder of the ancient Roman's proudest boast—*Civis Romanus sum*! Could not Rome return in other ways as well?

The wish to make this dream a reality dominated his interest in public affairs, which began in 1345 with the discovery of Cicero's letters to Atticus—again an example of classical precedent spurring him on. These letters revealed not the cultivated man of letters Petrarch had known before, but a scheming unscrupulous politician. Surviving the disillusionment, Petrarch decided to follow his master and engage in politics too, and he began to urge the Papacy to return to the city that had traditionally led the world. His desire to see Rome rise again was so strong that he would support anyone who seemed capable of recovering the city's greatness. In 1347 he found a hero in the erratic and low-born Cola di Rienzi, who, with the backing of the Roman populace, overthrew the nobles—the Colonna among them—set himself up as a people's tribune, and summoned an Italian national parliament. In an enthusiastic letter Petrarch described Rienzi to the Romans as a man sent from heaven, and he called on the leader himself to follow the great examples from Roman history. But though the Pope recognized the new republic, Rienzi's success was short-lived, and in 1354 he was killed by his opponents.

On Rienzi's failure, Petrarch turned to the newly elected Holy Roman Emperor, Charles IV, pressing him to come to Rome and establish the empire anew. The title of "Roman emperor" in western Europe had been revived by Charlemagne in 800; but the new line of Roman rulers seldom exercised any effective authority outside the boundaries of Germany, where most of them had their origin. Charles, with whom Petrarch had a most cordial relationship, visited Rome to be crowned in 1355, but for that purpose only. He made no attempt to enforce order in the city or in Italy and returned to his capital at Prague. Before Petrarch's death Pope Urban V had spent three years in Rome; but he yielded to his cardinals and left it again for Avignon.

In practical terms, Petrarch's efforts had achieved little. Basically he disliked Avignon because it was French, and no country compared to Italy, his homeland, which he saluted in fervent poems as the glory of the world. But his dream continued long after he died in 1374, pen in hand, it is said, over his *Life of Caesar*. His summons to action went out to every Italian patriot, his emotions at the sight of Rome itself came to be shared by countless visitors; and the popes—who finally returned in 1378—would themselves choose to rebuild Rome magnificently and thus affirm its enduring strength in the face of Protestantism. Italian unity was not won until 1870, but the hope for a rebirth of greatness became part of the national spirit and inspired in time the patriot Garibaldi and the would-be Caesar, Mussolini. As a discernible set of republican ideals, the vision would also appear in revolutionary France and in the America of Thomas Jefferson.

Petrarch's innovative spirit blew clean winds into almost every area of historical thinking. It brought the past down to earth, made Rome and its heroes the models for men to copy, and suggested history might have another pattern—after decline, renewal. In general, Petrarch set the tone for a new secular interpretation of history, without, for awhile, endangering Christian authority. His ideas could be accommodated. And there is much more to his achievement than nostalgia. We can now see that the problems of the age had become suffocating, demanding bold solutions; and Petrarch's search for Rome is surely part of a larger reaching out for a different idea of man and of the world in which he is placed. Human history too was familiar yet unknown, and Petrarch looked outside current opinion for a new and clearer perspective on it, just as he had climbed Mont Ventoux to see Avignon better and up on the roof of the Baths of Diocletian to gain the best view he could of Rome. In Venice, he tells us, his imagination was gripped by ships casting off, perhaps with passengers bound for the Caucasus, the Ganges, the Indies, and the Eastern Ocean; he rediscovered Rome with the same enterprise that would mark the voyages of Columbus. His many followers, looking around them in the fifteenth century, came to believe that the rebirth of learning and greatness, the Renaissance, had actually begun. This, they thought, seemed to close the era which had stretched for a thousand years from Rome's first adoption of the Christian faith; those centuries now appeared to be the middle section of the human story, the Middle Ages. It was a seventeenth-century German historian, Christian Cellarius, who in the end put into common usage through his textbooks the practice of dividing the past into ancient, medieval, and what we call modern; and, though as inadequate and misleading as it has often been shown to be, it survives as a handy outline of Western man's development.

For Petrarch Rome could only be great again if she knew herself correctly; and that kind of knowledge could only come from close study. This scrutiny could have highly practical as well as intellectual uses. Petrarch's experience with documents once led Charles IV to consult him on a decree, supposedly coming from Caesar and Nero, which, the Duke of Austria claimed, exempted his territory from the emperor's jurisdiction. After examining it point by point and finding anachronisms, Petrarch denounced it as a modern fake. "The whole thing," he wrote, "is so different from what the forger aimed at, so remote from antiquity and the style of Caesar, that a credulous old woman or a mountain peasant might perhaps be taken in, but certainly not a man of intelligence." Forgeries, he seemed to imply, no matter what intentions lay behind them, were unacceptable in the search for truth; history should stand on no other foundation than the careful judgment of genuine evidence. On another occasion, Petrarch expressed bewilderment that Cicero could ever, in the same breath, have called Herodotus both father of history and a liar. Petrarch knew little of Herodotus, but what shocked him was Cicero's association of history with falsehood. A historian should seek to eliminate all that was mythical or seemingly dubious in the record, even if this research led him, as it did Lorenzo Valla in 1439, to disprove the authenticity of the Donation of Constantine, on which the popes had based their claims to power throughout the Middle Ages. On these grounds Petrarch saw his epic *Africa* as history, every detail of the Roman world he pictured being as accurate as he could make it; and, in a definite way, Petrarch thus anticipates hundreds of future scholars, among them Leopold von Ranke, who, in his nineteenth-century setting, was likewise impelled to found his own inquiries into the past on the methods he had acquired in the field of textual criticism.

III

The scene moves next to late fifteenth-century Florence, a city of enormous vitality and equally great brutality. Like Venice, Milan, and other city-states of northern Italy, Florence acknowledged no immediate overlord. Aggressively pursuing its interests, it lived precariously, in conflict with its rivals and often torn by struggles within. The key to power was violence, and blood in the streets was common. Italy had nonetheless prospered in her halfway position between Europe and the East; and, never having really experienced feudalism, it had become a land of merchants and self-made men. As such they welcomed humanism and its emphasis on independence and individual human qualities. Men with cultured tastes and the leisure wealth afforded them patronized the arts and spent time talking or writing about intellectual things, delighting in a heritage they could call their own. The arrival of scholars and manuscripts after the fall of Constantinople in 1453 increased their activity, though to a lesser extent than once imagined.

The Renaissance has been given many faces: a complete cycle of human achievement in itself according to the biographer of the artists, Vasari; a major step in progress according to Voltaire; as an age of titanic individuals it attracted the Romantics; and, for the twentieth century, it is a laboratory for finding the creative society's special chemistry. However, its chief feature has remained its intense preoccupation with man and man's capabilities, which affected every part of its life—but notably painting and sculpture—and caused the people of the era to differentiate themselves consciously from their predecessors. To employ one's talents to the full became the new ideal. This is illustrated not only in the careers of Leonardo da Vinci and Michaelangelo but in the adventures of numerous men and women caught for a moment in Benvenuto Cellini's autobiography. Circumstances aided the transition. The miseries of plague and famine began to recede; in France, Spain, and England the nation-state imposed order where before there had been civil war; and, significantly, clocks began to be given two hands, so that precious time might be used to still better advantage. Nowhere did Western man face the world with greater self-confidence than in Italy. From Petrarch's ascent of Mont Ventoux until Galileo's discoveries in astronomy three hundred years later, we find an extraordinary flowering of the inquiring, adventurous human spirit; of this achievement Machiavelli is an outstanding representative.

Machiavelli's fame as a political scientist has overshadowed his work as a historian, which extends far beyond the official history he wrote of Florence. Like all humanists, he regarded history, whose composition gave opportunities for style, as a form of literature. It might also celebrate effectively the glories of the state, its subject, and it was of great value for the moral and political lessons it could teach. Such were Petrarch's insights. It was Machiavelli's distinction to carry the last of these forward and see in the knowledge of history an essential implement for dealing with contemporary problems. He admired antiquity but the purpose of studying the past was to manipulate the present; Machiavelli's treatise on government, *The Prince*, conveys a particular sense of urgency which is lacking in Petrarch's works. Others would develop the materials for his theory of history but his own blunt, practical statements launched the first frontal attack on Augustine's scheme and jeopardized its long supremacy.

Born in Florence in 1469, Niccolò Machiavelli was the son of a lawyer with republican sympathies, who obtained his copy of Livy for having produced an index to that great Roman history. Machiavelli's education included training in the Latin and Italian classics, and he seems to have made men and affairs his chief study. For that, the world around him offered the best instruction possible. The Florence of his youth was ruled by Lorenzo de' Medici, "the Magnificent." It was a very brilliant society indeed, and more self-observant, perhaps, than any other; Machiavelli witnessed there the rise, beginning in 1491, of Savonarola, the Dominican friar who denounced the new paganism and the corruption of Florence in his fiery sermons. When the Medici were driven out in 1494, Machiavelli entered public life as a clerk in the second chancery of Savonarola's new republic.

The expulsion of the Medici resulted in part from the invasion of Italy that year by Charles VIII of France, an event that shook the life and thought of every Italian. Italians had long considered their land separate from the rest of Europe, walled off by the Alps as if by divine planning, and favored above all others. Their civilization had no equal, and their affairs were their own to resolve. Machiavelli's fellow-historian Guicciardini believed Italy had just reached a peace and prosperity unknown since the days of the Roman Empire; but the easy French conquest—"with a piece of chalk," it was said, as the soldiers marked the doors of houses requisitioned as their quarters—changed that happy picture. Other states intervened; and Italy, rich, clever, but disunited, became the prey of stronger foreign forces, who chose its soil to further their quarrels and ambitions. The situation was to last nearly four hundred years; and the disaster—for such it was quickly seen to be —was a sharp stimulus to asking new questions about politics and history.

Savonarola's experiment in government ended in 1498 with his savage execution; and Machiavelli, enjoying the chief magistrate's protection, was made secretary and second chancellor of the reconstituted republic. Most official business passed through his hands, and he learned much from a critical distance about politics, contingencies, and the causes of failure and success. Serving on missions to other states, he obtained first-hand knowledge of the subtleties of Italian diplomacy and the nature of foreigners. Maxims of political conduct, later to be laid down in The Prince, began to take shape in his head. A war with Pisa convinced him that mercenary troops could not be depended upon; and, coldly observing the conduct and fate of Caterina Sforza, ruler of Milan, he concluded it was better to rely on the love of one's subjects than on fortresses. Louis XII of France, he noted, had committed fundamental blunders when he too had invaded Italy; he destroyed the minor powers while strengthening a major one, he did not settle in the country, and he did not found colonies. All these mistakes the Romans had scrupulously avoided. When in time Machiavelli visited Rome, he was less interested in its visible past than in what Roman history could teach the present. An embassy to France in 1500 was particularly formative for his thought, for it opened his eyes to the people and customs of a strong nation united under a single ruler, in contrast to the Italy he had left.

For several years, however, Machiavelli's attention was fixed on the threat to Florence presented by Cesare Borgia. Borgia, the handsome, brilliant son of Pope Alexander VI, had great talents as a soldier and diplomat, and, with his father's support, was attempting to carve out a principality for himself in central Italy. Watching the great *condottiere* in his camp in the Romagna, Machiavelli came to admire Borgia's self-reliance, his clever use of cruelty and deceit, his just but firm administration of conquered provinces, and his use of native troops. Returning to Florence, Machiavelli pressed for a citizen militia. No usurper, he believed, could be more astute than this adventurer in all he was doing to create and establish a new state; but Borgia's hopes were suddenly dashed by the election of a new pope, Julius II, his sworn enemy—whom Machiavelli also accompanied on campaigns. Nonetheless, Borgia remained in many respects Machiavelli's ideal prince; he was also the leading example of the man who rises on the fortunes of others, who is prepared for every event but the one which happens (in Borgia's case his father's death and his own simultaneous illness), and who falls not through his faults but through what he cannot control.

The Medici were restored to Florence in 1512, the city's troops failing to protect it against a Spanish army. As a leading figure of the republic, Machiavelli was soon arrested and, after being tortured, released to live in near poverty in the country. There on his farm, from which he could see the dome and campanile of Florence seven miles away, he returned to his books. In a very famous letter he describes his country life: how the day was spent in various practical pursuits; then, in the evening, he would change from peasant clothes to his noble court dress and enter his study to enjoy the beloved company of his friends and masters, the classical authors. In their company he wrote, "I forget every trouble, I do not dread poverty, I am not frightened by death; entirely I give myself over to them."

To regain his lost position became his all-consuming goal. Politics had been his life, not trade or business; and unable to drive it from his mind, he now wrote about it in the hope his work would win him self-advancement. He first took up his commentary on Livy, a project his father may once have suggested. Preparation of these *Discourses on the First Ten Books of Titus Livius* was continued for several years, though, by the end of 1513, in the same frame of mind, he had written *The Prince,* now his most famous work. The manuscript circulated but was not published until 1532. The story goes that in 1516 a copy was submitted to the Medici ruler, to whom it was hopefully dedicated, at the same time that somebody else was offering two greyhounds. The ruler showed more interest in the dogs. Repeatedly seeking office, Machiavelli at last received a commission from the Medici in 1520 to write a history of Florence. He also wrote the *Art of War,* arguing again for a strong Florentine army, and some satirical comedies, one of which, *Mandragola,* still holds the stage. He died in 1527, a few weeks after the Medici had once more been expelled but before he had secured any appointment in the new republic. He never did return to the world of secrets and negotiations for which he longed.

Throughout his life and works Machiavelli was fascinated with power; and nothing concerning him has attracted more interest than his sheer realism about it. No subject raised such burning questions for Florence, or for Italy. For himself, he wanted to know passionately "what a princedom is," he wrote, "of what kinds they are, how they are gained, how they are kept, why they are lost." Medieval theory had its answers, which Machiavelli found his learning and experience leading him to reject entirely. "I have determined to enter upon a path not yet trodden by anyone," he claimed in the *Discourses*. His conclusions had been forged in his time of action as secretary and diplomat; we can see him in his dispatches growing from caution to assertiveness, having in the end no fears about assessing situations and recommending policy. He had also, he tells us, communed with the great minds of the past. It could not be plainer to him that politics and government were quite obviously not guided by philosophic first principles. If there were rules for behavior at all, they could only be deduced from the actual conduct of men, evidenced in history.

History's chief importance to Machiavelli was thus to provide political examples. Both contemporary and classical history (which he knew mostly it seems from Herodotus, Plutarch, and Livy) gave him abundant illustrations. His use of the past is seen in the *Discourses* and *The Prince*. The *Discourses* was the more solid achievement, drawing a vast number of lessons out of Livy's account of the Roman republic; *The Prince*, written down quickly in the clear light of certainty, summarized what he had found to be true and could not wait to explain more fully. Clothed in the words of a court adviser, it was short enough for a busy ruler to read, and it dealt tactfully and unidealistically with Machiavelli's obsessive question—how to gain power and keep it. The answer is notorious: "A prince who wants to keep his post must learn how not to be good"; "a prudent prince cannot and should not keep his word when to do so would go against his interest"; "you must be a great liar and hypocrite"—from these and other maxims Machiavelli gets his popular reputation. His exact intentions in writing *The Prince* will always be a matter for debate, but one may be sure his remarks were not cynical; they reflected the normal practice of Italian politics. Still, the opinion early took root and has held ever since that he was an unscrupulous opportunist who preached that "in the actions of all men, and especially of princes, where there is no court of appeal, one judges by the result." His remarks give offense by their naked honesty; but, as he said, they were only what he had found from studying the deeds of great men.

It is easiest to give Machiavelli's view of politics and history by quoting his conclusions, which rest on his conviction that human nature is base. "Whoever desires to found a state and give it laws," he wrote, "must start with assuming that all men are bad." Man's nature was constant; wherever Machiavelli looked, he saw the same desires and vices present, the only change being the shifting possession of power. The visible cause of events was not God but the human will, directed toward a goal of its choosing; the men in history Machiavelli most admired were those who had pursued their destiny through action. All men had potentialities they hoped to realize. Each man worked with a certain given material, and each should learn as much as possible about it to succeed. A sculptor should learn about stone, a soldier about arms, a murderer about poisons. A would-be ruler should study human nature by surveying the scene around him—the day-to-day politics of Florence, for instance—and by absorbing the past, without illusions. The prince advanced by ruthlessness, but of all goals his was the most desirable to attain; for, to develop other men's highest potential, some human agency was required to promote harmony and peace as well as the fame and splendor of the state.

According to medieval thought, the conditions for harmony and peace were provided by the Church and the Holy Roman Empire, the twin pivots around which European politics should revolve. The royal power came from God, through Church and pope. To Machiavelli this assumption flew in the face of stark facts. History refuted old ideas of ideal princes and showed that power was seized by men determined to seize it. As Machiavelli had himself seen in Rome, Julius II had secured his election as pope with the help of promises and bribes. Moreover, the builders of great and glorious societies—Theseus, Romulus, Moses—had succeeded through personal qualities such as energy, self-discipline, a talent for organization, and singleness of purpose; and they had all been skilled in war. They had achieved by ruthlessness what Christian obedience never could create—as the fiasco of Savonarola's experiment proved. In each case there had been handicaps—humble birth perhaps, physical or psychological flaws, lack of resources, or defeats; but the man had taken these into account and pressed toward his goal, as Michaelangelo (for instance) would later make allowance for the irregular block of marble from which he wrested his David.

A ruler, Machiavelli wrote, should be strong as a lion and shrewd as a fox; but again and again the record showed that the primary quality he needed was *virtù*. This favorite word of Machiavelli's may be best translated not as "virtue" (which we noticed a prince has to learn to get rid of), but as ingenuity. With *virtù* a ruler might turn events to his advantage, particularly those directed by *fortuna* or chance—the unpredictable element which governs half our actions, though still leaving "the other half, more or less, in our power to control." In the twenty-fifth chapter of *The Prince* Machiavelli compared *fortuna* to a raging river sweeping all before it, which men must tame or learn to resist as best they can. The successful ruler, like Borgia for a time, or Julius II, his antagonist, acts, not from preconceived ideas, but according to auspicious circumstances. He survives setbacks with fortitude and cunning; and when chance offers opportunity, he is ready for it. *Fortuna* was changeable, and Pope Julius II too would have come to ruin, because his nature preferred certain policies. Like a woman, *fortuna* favored the bold; one caught her as she came near or one lost her completely. Surely Shakespeare expressed a similar view in *Julius Caesar*, when the assassins are encamped waiting to fight with Antony and Octavian. The evening before the battle Brutus is made to say:

> Our legions are brim-full, our cause is ripe:
> The enemy increaseth every day;
> We, at the height, are ready to decline.
> There is a tide in the affairs of men,
> Which, taken at the flood, leads on to fortune;
> Omitted, all the voyage of their life
> Is bound in shallows and in miseries.
> On such a full sea are we now afloat;
> And we must take the current when it serves,
> Or lose our ventures.

The pattern of history to Machiavelli was cyclical and repetitious, being the rise and fall of states and individuals, and occasionally their resurgence. Nothing including mankind is stable; but because change happens with some regularity (how could Machiavelli's experience persuade him otherwise?), a ruler may learn from examples whether his own cycle is ascending or descending, and how to keep his state for himself from prosperity through adversity—and back. "Wise men say, and not without reason," Machiavelli wrote in the *Discourses*, "that whoever wishes to foresee the future must consult the past; for human events ever resemble those of preceding times." Such a view of history is not necessarily fatalistic; but it assumes that the past contains no mysteries. This is Petrarch's cyclical plan refined and put at the service of practical politics.

When, however, a state has become corrupted, its greatness can still be restored by a ruler comparable in stature to its original founder. Thus, Machiavelli ended *The Prince* with an exhortation to liberate Italy from the barbarians. Petrarch 150 years earlier had been roused by the idea of reviving Rome's grandeur and had written moving poems deploring Italy's distress and urging Italian unity. Machiavelli may have been writing for Florentines or Italians, for the Medici or for a nameless ruler yet to appear; but his call for a patriotic reawakening is clear and so is the conviction that the Italians held their destiny in their hands. The French invasion had humiliated Italy and plunged it into misery again; but the bottom of the cycle was in many ways not a bad place to be, for all history's lessons are there to be learned and applied. With boldness and *virtù* events could be molded in one's favor. Disregard my advice, says Machiavelli, and you will only prolong the present agony. As he saw it, the time was suited to action. Italy could hardly sink lower; and, if Italians, armed and bent on success, rose up under strong leadership, the foreigners would be driven back across the Alps, and a new Italian state—perhaps the ideal republic of the *Discourses*—would compete effectively with the nation-states that had ravaged the divided peninsula. Anyone could lead in that flexible society—bankers like the Medici, an adventurer like Borgia, a foundling like Lucca's Castruccio Castracani, whose life Machiavelli wrote, or a washerwoman's son like Rienzi. "Under your banner," Machiavelli insisted, "our country may become noble again and, with your guidance, those words of Petrarch's may come true:

'Ingenuity against rage
Will take up arms and make the battle short,
For the ancient valor
In Italian hearts is not yet dead.' "

In Machiavelli's uncompromising view of history we witness the abandonment of the Augustinian scheme. Men were now seen not as potential citizens of the city of God, but as Italians, Frenchmen, or Germans. Machiavelli took them not as they should be but as he found them—fickle, cowardly, greedy, swayed by opportunity, and even on occasion by Christian teachings. History was about their everyday affairs. The break with tradition went deeper still—it proposed a new way of life. For a thousand years Western man had been urged to seek the unique truth which came from God's revelation; having found it he could begin to try living the perfect life. Politics too should follow that truth. But after Machiavelli, Christian ethics and political behavior were split into two. Secular and sacred history alike showed that expedient action brought success, and staying in power is a ruler's ultimate goal. To Machiavelli, the individual is confronted with a choice. Either he can develop his potential on earth, and so lead a life very likely incompatible with Christianity; or he can forgo his advantages, ignore the actual, and very probably—as Machiavelli predicted—suffer unpleasant consequences. Men's eyes should be on the present, not on the future; the best possible eventuality was for the level of civilization once achieved by Greece and Rome to be reached again. Machiavelli's concentration on his practical theme of success and regeneration was so great that he paid little attention to other aspects of Italian life, and scarcely noticed the New World's discovery.

The force behind the shock that *The Prince* sent through western Europe was its explicit advocacy of what is essentially a pagan view of life. A prince, Machiavelli wrote, "must not flinch from being blamed for vices which are necessary for safeguarding the state." In this indifference to Christian duty, history as a whole ceases to be the unquestioned story of God's purpose working itself out. Rather, history is a casebook of political techniques, to be put to use on the right occasions. Indeed, religion is simply a card like the rest, to be played at the right time. A strong state is the highest human good; the model for men's conduct is not Jesus Christ, nor even Petrarch's virtuous Scipio, but the cruel and treacherous Cesare Borgia.

In 1559 the entire works of Machiavelli were placed on the Index of prohibited books compiled by the Inquisition; but, no matter how often his teachings have been condemned, he has never lacked readers. One after another European ruler has used the advice Machiavelli gave. In France, the massacre of St. Bartholomew's Eve in 1572 was attributed to Machiavelli's influence on Queen Catherine de' Medici; and in 1593 Henry of Navarre chose to change his religion, and thereby gained both Paris and the French crown. Elizabeth I of England, with every show of reluctance, executed her cousin, Mary Queen of Scots, and kept her throne. To Englishmen of the period he was "Matchevil," "Match-a-villain," "Hatch-evil," a name synonymous with the devil, but Francis Bacon clearly noted the reason for his lasting appeal: "We are much beholden to Machiavel and others, that write what men do, and not what they ought to do." The list of Machiavelli's admirers and followers is inexhaustible.

The Prince is a book that no doubt almost wrote itself, and

Machiavelli's enforced seclusion in the country created exactly the right environment for its production. His major literary purpose afterward became to demonstrate by more extensive argument and examples the validity of his rules. The *Discourses* was an attempt to provide this background through a work of political philosophy. Assisted by conversations with like-minded Florentine friends in the Oricellari gardens, when his offenses were less infamous, Machiavelli set down his reflections on what makes a state strong and united, taking Roman history especially as his source of reference. Livy's precepts were tested by the "new path" of analysis from life; and by impressive reasoning Machiavelli stressed the Roman constitution's superiority to any other. He used Roman history, not as a subject for antiquarian enthusiasm nor for genealogical self-congratulation, but as an incentive to find the best working solutions to contemporary problems.

If the *Discourses* gave substance to Machiavelli's interpretation of the past, the *History of Florence* enabled him to apply his ideas in a work of history itself. Written in Italian too, his study spanned the centuries from Roman times to 1492, ending just before the Medici were deposed. Like other Renaissance official historians he imitated Livy for his guide, to the extent of including orations (like Thucydides). Florentine history lent itself to being seen along the lines of an ancient city-state. But much of the work dealt with the recent period, for which Machiavelli relied considerably on papers with which he had been familiar as the republic's secretary. As might be expected, he saw Florentine man as a political creature, not as a child of God; he saw human opportunism at work in events; and he evaluated success and failure with detachment. Believing his career had qualified him, he wished to give guidance for future action, to teach lessons in advance of situations. At the beginning of the fifth book, he put forward a cyclical view of time and history, reviving the concept that had last received notable expression in Thucydides and Virgil. Rome was the measure against which Florence should compare itself; and, if Rome was what Florence might once have risen to equal, Rome was perhaps what Florence might still become.

From a modern standpoint, Machiavelli's history clearly has faults. It is very much a history of individuals (the people, to him, were wild beasts and only a means to power). Even complex events seem only to have one cause, and he is little aware of economic forces. His faith was no doubt excessive that what worked for the Romans—such as a citizen army—was bound to work again. But the chief criticism has always been that his examples from the past are predetermined by his rules.

Actions are fitted to results too logically, their uniqueness is obscured. Machiavelli's interpretation of history thus becomes a series of black and white generalizations. What is left of each event is the residue of a particular rule or law in operation. His maxims can often be refuted by equally sound contrary evidence; and his limited evidence—to say nothing of the central place he gives to chance—restricts the validity of his deductions. It equally has been plausibly argued from history that human nature is basically good and improvable.

Comparisons are often drawn between Machiavelli's treatment of history and the histories of Florence and Italy by his younger contemporary, Francesco Guicciardini. The two men exchanged letters, but Guicciardini's work grew out of the local tradition of family histories, and he retained an aristocratic outlook. His research was wider and more critical than Machiavelli's, and his conclusions more imaginative; for, examining the functions and effects of various types of government, he found that human nature differed more than Machiavelli had perceived. "How wrong it is to cite the Romans at every turn," he wrote, adding that Machiavelli had put things "too absolutely." For that reason (and for others relating to his competence) Guicciardini is sometimes rated more highly as a historian. Both men, however, broke decisively with the other main types of history writing existing in Italy—the keeping of chronicles and the compilation of histories on the classical model that sacrificed content to form. Both were in advance of their times in their methods and their capacity for rational analysis. It is interesting to reflect that it was a comparative study of their works which launched Ranke on his career as a historian.

The Prince, of course, outshines all of Machiavelli's other writings. His supreme distinction in it was his new paganism. And he expressed as well the spirit of the age, the cult of the individual. Running behind his thoughts on power and the cut-and-thrust of politics, moreover, is a distinct notion of human greatness. What makes a ruler great is his ability to assess the situation, adapt to it, and move on toward his goal. He may have other talents, but this one is vital, and the study of history can develop it in him. The prudent prince, Machiavelli writes, ought to read histories and keep some famous figure before him as his model—"as they say Alexander the Great imitated Achilles, Caesar Alexander, and Scipio Cyrus." Power and knowledge have not always gone together, but it is desirable that they should. We realize today that Rome can never be restored; the elements that made it have been transformed into something else; but out of Machiavelli's maxims comes the clear impression that the examples of history serve a purpose still. History is more than a subject for princes. A knowledge of history implies intelligence and a capacity for decision and action; and that is one of the marks of a man.

IV

In 1520 Machiavelli had been commissioned to write his *History of Florence*. That same year a papal bull was issued condemning Martin Luther in Germany. Luther promptly burned it, and as the spread of his teachings began the Reformation, Augustine's style of history strongly revived in some circles, especially among followers of Calvin. Protestants looked back to the early Church for authority, Catholics to tradition, and both parties energetically searched the records of the past to prove their cases against each other and among themselves. The Lutheran authors of the *Magdeburg Centuries* surveyed all Church history in one-hundred year periods to show Catholic deviance from Apostolic Christianity, and thus promoted a new method of dividing time. Protestants also enlisted the past to stir passions and win the support of the papacy's enemies; and in Elizabethan England John Foxe's *Acts and Monuments of the Christian Martyrs* was an instant success, portraying first the victims of Mary's persecution as heroes against popery, and later the martyrs of all centuries as champions against the anti-Christ. To English reformers this history's credit was sealed with blood; and the movement of current events, though fraught with dangers, seemed a further sign of God's care of His faithful people. No examples of this could be clearer than the Spanish Armada's defeat and the failure of the Gunpowder Plot. Every occurrence—not least the voyage of Columbus—was part of God's providential plan; and this philosophically comprehensive, eschatological view was carried forward in the first noteworthy American history, Governor William Bradford's simple but eloquent account of the Pilgrim fathers, *Of Plymouth Plantation*.

Bradford, like other Puritan historians, had a high regard for accuracy as well as a sense of religious destiny; and English historiography of the sixteenth and seventeenth centuries illustrates the dilemmas that can occur when rival concepts of historical truth exist. Protestant or Catholic, the historian was still bound to respect the Bible as the supreme historical document; but new evidence was making old positions harder to maintain. The pivotal problem of universal history was to synchronize the events reported in Egyptian, Assyrian, Babylonian, Persian, Greek, and Roman annals, as they were rediscovered in the West, with biblical history—and the sharpest arguments concerned the origins of the four great empires. One of the most influential attempts to resolve these divergent accounts was made as late as the 1650s by the Irish archbishop, James Ussher. Upholding biblical genealogy as the axis of world chronology, Ussher established a continuous series of dates going back to the week of Creation, which, he reckoned, started on October 23, 4004 B.C. Printed in the margin of many Bible editions, his system—especially his dating of Creation—was increasingly criticized.

The historian of this era found further confusion in the state of ancient history; and Sir Walter Raleigh's argument when writing his *History of the World* typifies how the medieval and the humanist outlooks could be reconciled. New evidence, Raleigh believed, should be used only when it seemed Scripture was insufficient; but the former's quality differed from that of revealed knowledge and should be evaluated skeptically. Where the Bible conflicted with other ancient accounts— regarding Nebuchadnezzar's reign, for instance—he followed the Bible. Raleigh distinguished between first and second causes of events, the first being the will of God, the second, of men; all history, sacred and secular, nonetheless affirmed the divine intention. Nonscriptural history therefore had a moral purpose, but that was a matter for conjecture; and Raleigh saw the Persian kings in Herodotus as instruments of God's power, and the Athenian disaster at Syracuse (described by Thucydides) as a lesson that, when God punishes a people, He first destroys their rulers' ability to make judgments.

Other difficulties facing the historian were political in nature. Partly owing to the effect of Machiavelli's *The Prince*, every ruler took a personal interest in history. Roman or recent, the past was full of rebellions, coups, and murders, of sudden rises and violent reversals, and the public might draw dangerous conclusions from them. The English chronicles available to Shakespeare were largely the work of native Renaissance writers, officially approved for supporting political doctrines the Tudors favored. These chronicles showed how political discord had begun under Richard II, continued under Henry IV, but had triumphantly ended with the victories of Henry V. But troubles had begun again under Henry VI, developing into the Wars of the Roses. It was the achievement of the first Tudor monarch, Henry VII, to defeat the tyrannical Richard III and restore health to the state under a new dynasty. The pattern was therefore one of decline and recovery twice over.

Materials from these histories lent themselves to drama; but the writing of history in any form was a hazardous business. It was out of prudence, it seems, that Shakespeare changed Sir John Oldcastle, leader of a popular revolt, into the genial Falstaff. Since Elizabeth I was displeased with the popularity of *Richard II*, the king's deposition scene was cut from all editions published in her lifetime; and eventually Elizabeth handed down instructions that no more works of history were to be printed without her consent. Doubts persist over the Tudor representation of Richard III. Was he in fact the monstrously wicked uncle Shakespeare gave to posterity, following Sir Thomas More's portrait of him? Or was he a white knight, progressive and enlightened, unfairly victimized by a new regime anxious to blacken its counter-revolutionary predecessor? Very few historians were allowed access to state records, and Shakespeare's history plays served ends his audiences considered to be legitimate purposes of history—among them to promote order and unity in the realm, to teach political and moral lessons for the present, and to warm English blood. Dedicated with the force of poetry to England's greater glory, this sequence of plays about the struggle for the Crown has instructed, and inspired, generations of English men and women.

In general, then, humanist historiography won a victory for its values that was incomplete. History was written again in the classical style and spirit, but the Christian concept of the past persisted, sometimes in harmony with humanist standards, though it was now a maze of rival versions. Truth had become more than usually relative to the particular historian's, or reader's, beliefs; and historians were commonly identified in public as Catholic or heretic. It was not until the Enlightenment and the emergence of the modern idea of progress that the insights and methods of Petrarch, Machiavelli, and their followers began to be applied to the history of man more unequivocally.

CHAPTER FOUR

VOLTAIRE

I

In 1784, looking back at a century which had seen an unparalleled growth of knowledge and an ambitious program to coordinate and use that knowledge for the betterment of mankind, the philosopher Immanuel Kant concluded that an appropriate motto for the era would be *Sapere aude*—"Dare to be wise!" Perhaps only the burst of intellectual activity in Greece over two thousand years before has claims to the same description; for the seventeenth and eighteenth centuries in Europe saw the emergence of a bold, exhilarating new civilization that looked quite different from its predecessors. Certainly no landmark in history since the rise of Christianity compares with the Scientific Revolution. Its immediate origins lay in the world of the Renaissance; but it was also born from acute disillusionment with the disruptions of the Reformation. Instead of the golden age returning, Catholics and Protestants fought each other ferociously with guns on the battlefield. But by the early eighteenth century, what has been called the "crisis of European consciousness" had been passed, when old, predominantly religious ideas inherited from the Middle Ages yielded in the minds of most intelligent literate men to ideas derived from reasoning about objects. The patron saints of the dawning Enlightenment were two Englishmen, Sir Isaac Newton and John Locke; but its most characteristic and energetic protagonist by far was the Frenchman, François Marie Arouet de Voltaire.

French Benedictine monks were the first to practice "scientific" historical research; they collected sources on Church and national history, edited them, and published them with scrupulous concern for authenticity and accuracy. But, because the Scientific Revolution inaugurates the theory of modern historiography, it is worth describing in a few words its general character. Astronomy and physics were early important fields in the evolution of modern scientific method, and Galileo was one of the chief practitioners. He observed the heavens with the newly invented telescope and defended Copernicus's theory of a heliocentric universe against the ancient astronomers upheld by the Church. In his work in the physical sciences he was one of the first individuals to use mathematics as a precise method for description.

In late Elizabethan England, Francis Bacon could not urge too strongly the need to reexamine all knowledge in light of recent discoveries. Experiment, observation, and common sense—the empirical approach—were what he recommended to his readers. He proposed methods they and future "natural philosophers" should apply in their investigations, yet Bacon's greater talent was for instilling and justifying a spirit of confidence in the whole cooperative enterprise, so men might rise above what Bishop Sprat, the Royal Society's apologist, would later call "the passions and madness of that dismal age." "By far the greatest obstacle to the progress of science," Bacon wrote, "and to the undertaking of new tasks and provinces therein is found in this—that men despair and think things impossible." To give hope, he said, was "no unimportant part" of his purpose, and to make hope in his conjectures reasonable—"just as Columbus did, before that wonderful voyage of his across the Atlantic, when he gave the reasons for his convictions that new lands and continents might be discovered besides those which were known before." Dismissed at first, those reasons "were afterwards made good by experience, and were the causes and beginnings of great events."

With a novel grasp of historical perspective Bacon argued that men should not be held back by a reverence for antiquity. "The old age of the world," he wrote, "is to be accounted the true antiquity; and this is the attribute of our own times, not of that earlier age of the world in which the ancients lived, and which, though in respect of us it was the elder, yet in respect of the world it was the younger." If the present only knew its own strength and chose to exert it, "much more might fairly be expected than from the ancient times, inasmuch as it is a more advanced age of the world, and stored and stocked with infinite experiments and observations." It would be disgraceful, he continued, "if, while the regions of the material globe—that is of the earth, of the sea, and of the stars—have been in our own times laid widely open and revealed, the intellectual globe should remain shut up within the narrow limits of old discoveries."

The work of medieval logicians and of contemporary craftsmen facilitated the Scientific Revolution; but there can be no denying the unusual role played by individual genius. In 1619, while a soldier in the Thirty Years' War, and discontented with what he had learned from his education and from the world, René Descartes had the first inkling that the mind should accept only what it can know from its own resources. Much later he published a discourse on his new philosophic method, explaining by rules how the mind should start with the simplest problems, move forward to the more complex, and throughout the procedure approximate its standards of truth to those of mathematics. The conclusions, he believed, would be indisputable to all men, whatever their language, homeland, or religion. Mostly testing his principles in Holland, he sought in the field of natural science to develop a practical philosophy in place of the speculative scholastic teachings. Its benefits could be immeasurable; for, through knowing "the force and actions of fire, water, air, of the stars, of the heavens and of all the bodies that surround us," we might render ourselves, he wrote, "the masters and possessors of nature"—a magnificently confident, or ominous, prophecy.

Under the influence of these and other pioneers, new and different standards for truthful knowledge were adopted, placing exceptional value on accurate measurement, exact computation, and the ability to repeat an experiment. Though scientists feuded over primacy and correctness of discoveries, sometimes placing national honor at stake, they aspired to a detachment which contrasted with those passions, religious and political, that Sprat so deplored. In England's Royal Society, chartered in 1662, the rule was, take nothing on trust; and academies of science in correspondence with each other were founded under royal patronage in most European countries. Eventually, one was established in Philadelphia by Benjamin Franklin and his friends in 1743. In England especially, the *virtuosi* rejected religion sharing in their activity, but they did not initially see their work as conflicting with Christianity; rather, science increased understanding of God's revelation, since His purpose in the natural world might thus be shown more clearly.

In England the various strands of the new philosophy were united in 1687, when Newton published his *Principia Mathematica*, demonstrating the regular movement of the universe in accordance with the force of gravity. Newton convincingly combined mathematics and observation in his great treatise. When it was reworked in popular forms over the following decades, its effect went far beyond that of a scientific law receiving definition; for, if science could comprehend the universe accurately, many readers reflected—and it was not until the twentieth century that Einstein made the first serious modification in Newton's theory—what else might it not be capable of doing? At practically the same time, in 1690, Locke's *An Essay Concerning Human Understanding* appeared, which studied how the mind acquires and expresses ideas. Locke proved from examples that the traditional belief that God had implanted certain innate ideas in the human mind was untenable, and he gave his opinion that a child's mind at birth was as white paper, waiting to be written upon. The sensations and experiences to which we are exposed produce knowledge, and the abstracted composites of this knowledge form into ideas. Expose a child to the right knowledge originating from the new philosophy, Locke inferred, and the child would avoid false and harmful ideas and develop more satisfactorily. In other words, mankind was capable of making its own future free from divine constraints, a better future if the rational aspects of human nature were cultivated and the emotions disciplined.

By 1715, in Holland and England especially, the results of the new learning had begun to be evident. For the first time the center of European intellectual activity had moved north, across the Alps, to the region that was the center both of commercial activity and of Protestantism. Where Newton's formula was approved, the universe was not to be understood as a living organism whose actions are intent upon the achievement of goals. The universe was to be regarded as a beautiful, even if not precise, machine whose cogs God has to repair every once in a while. Since, however, the natural order was no longer thought liable to be upset any moment by divine whim, miracles were fast becoming the weakest of Christian defenses. And where nature could not be depended upon, it could at least be controlled—marshes drained, canals dug, crops and livestock improved, diseases checked or cured. In the Renaissance the dissection of a corpse was still rare, needing special religious and legal permission; but by 1632, a group of Dutch gentlemen had already chosen to be recorded for posterity by Rembrandt in a painting that depicts them watching a prominent physician conduct an anatomy lesson with a corpse on the table. A freethinking attitude came to indicate the cultivated man, who, by expressing himself in words that were simple and precise, hoped to avoid the sorts of dissension which so frequently arose from the obscurities of theologians. The practice testified to Bacon's belief that the new truth should be shared with as many other men as possible, not remain the property of a special priesthood. Success in understanding the natural world encouraged the wish that reason and common sense might be beneficially applied to the improvement of society as well.

In and out of the discussion carried on in academies, *salons*, coffeehouses, very rarely at universities, can be sensed the suspicion—and the hope—that, behind the mass of information being collected and communicated in so many fields, there must lie other natural laws similar to those Newton had discovered in physics and astronomy. Find these laws, the argument went, and man would have the right handle for grasping every area of knowledge. In consequence, several men tried, each in his own way, to be Newtons in other fields of endeavor—Montesquieu in jurisprudence, Adam Smith in economics. Voltaire aimed to be the Newton of history. The challenge he chose was not without precedent, but the prize was; for, if man could remake his life by his intelligence alone—like Robinson Crusoe on his deserted island—the history he would need had to be reliable and fitting to his new status. The challenge was a history on which a new world could be built. The prize was securing the future.

But the Age of Reason, in which Voltaire lived, cannot really be described properly by such a straightforward name. It was the view held by the Enlightenment about itself; but, until the great encyclopaedia of the French *philosophes* appeared in the mid-eighteenth century, and even later, the age was still seeking to escape from older propositions and define its own. Meanwhile, doubts that reason was all-sufficient for truth sparked in the case of some men a religious revival. The fundamental question for Voltaire's generation was the one announced in 1749 by the provincial Academy of Dijon for a prize essay contest: "Has the restoration of the arts and sciences done more to corrupt civilized life or improve it?" In his works of history, the most important of which would appear soon afterwards, Voltaire saw the recent advances in knowledge suggesting and promoting a new organizing principle of great power, with which all of mankind's past, present, and future could be understood—the idea of progress; and, although he did not submit an entry, his answer to the question was already widely known, vigorously affirming the benefits of this progress to society.

II

Voltaire was a man of many careers, whose writings were by no means restricted to history. Preeminently, he was a literary figure, a writer of plays, poems, and stories, and on these he always considered his reputation essentially rested. Born in 1694 as François Marie Arouet into a Paris bourgeois family, he was in fact a child prodigy at poetry; and, when at the age of twenty-four his tragedy *Oedipe* was performed, he was hailed as the successor to Sophocles and Corneille. More plays, and later philosophical tales such as *Zadig, Micromégas,* and, above all, *Candide,* sustained and enlarged this fame. He was also a prolific letter writer—twenty thousand of his letters exist—who throve on the challenge of enemies, and for half a century conducted a relentless guerrilla war against the Church, against superstition, bigotry, and inhumanity in any form, against anything that, in his opinion, held man back from a happier future. *Écrasez l'infâme!*—'crush the wicked thing!'—was the slogan with which he ended so much of his correspondence. His intellectual gifts were not profound, but few men have ever had a sharper, more destructive wit. He wrote in 1767: "I never made but one prayer to God, a very short one, 'O Lord, make my enemies ridiculous.' And God granted it."

This campaign caused him on occasion to take up the cudgel of an active social reformer, seeking to rectify notorious miscarriages of justice—such as the Calas affair, in which a Huguenot had been barbarously executed for the supposed murder of his son after a trial that was a spectacle of perverted religious zeal. Voltaire's ideas were naturally considered subversive by the government of Louis XV, and he spent much of his life in exile, for a few years being the guest of Frederick the Great of Prussia. When their friendship deteriorated, he fled from Potsdam and settled at Ferney, near Geneva, where, having become rich partly from his writings and considerably from his business speculations, he ruled in effect a miniature state, making the manor he owned into a model community. There, from his study, with a portrait of Confucius on the wall, he corresponded with kings, an empress, people of all kinds, even a pope, and advised his followers in France. At the age of eighty-four he was allowed to return to Paris, and he was welcomed in the academies and theaters by fellow men of letters and in the streets by rapturous crowds as defender of the oppressed. This success literally killed him; when his remains were reinterred in an impressive ceremony at the height of the Revolution, he was recognized as its intellectual progenitor. "Poet, philosopher and historian," ran the inscription on his bier, "he gave a mighty impetus to the human mind: he made us ready for freedom." For much of the nineteenth century he had the reputation of a dangerously clever atheist (he was in fact a deist): but few figures have seemed so enduringly topical to the twentieth, which has seen *l'infâme* reappear in new and unimagined forms and has sought in its turn effective powers of indignation and irreverence to check them.

Like Petrarch in the early Renaissance, Voltaire is the central figure in the Enlightenment and is the most outstanding of that group of thinkers and reformers in eighteenth-century France known as the *philosophes*. Today many of them would probably be crusading journalists, for they were not simply thinkers but men who in the main held a few ideas very strongly and were convinced the world would be a better place if those ideas were followed. They used their writings, their friends, whatever means they could, to try to persuade the society of their day to move in a progressive direction. Though there was a loose movement of opposition in France dating back to the centralizing policies and the wars of Louis XIV, their stimulus came mostly from the skeptical tradition of Montaigne and Descartes—also from the voluminous writings of a Huguenot refugee in Holland, Pierre Bayle, who showed how unreliable and absurd most accepted versions of religion and history were. "Does not a factual truth destroy a hundred volumes of speculative reasoning?" Bayle rhetorically asked. But much of their activity was stirred up by Voltaire himself.

What was Voltaire's conception of "progress," that source of energy which provided the mainspring of his life and animated his historical analysis? Western history, perhaps world history since the eighteenth century, can be reduced to a graph of fluctuations in the belief in progress, and the consequent surge or contraction of forces. The term in its fullest expression has proclaimed the forward and onward movement of all human enterprise, affecting human nature itself; but it has been qualified at different periods and in different places by reservations, small or large, and the often harsh standards of success and failure it applies have been rejected as well as upheld. Moreover, today it is often used carelessly as little more than a synonym for change. To understand Voltaire the man and Voltaire the historian, we need to recapture the particular vision of progress he maintained, unencumbered by later views and criticisms.

Although some French scholars have disagreed, there seems little doubt that the crucial event in Voltaire's life was his three-year visit to England, which led to his writing the *Philosophical Letters*—sometimes called the *Letters on England*. The circumstances of his going had a great deal to do with making him receptive to his experiences there. He had already been imprisoned in the Bastille for a satirical poem, which, though regulations had been relaxed after the death of Louis XIV, had attracted the censor's notice; but, in 1725, the successful young dramatist quarrelled in public, first at the Opéra, then at the Comédie Française, with a prominent young nobleman who ridiculed him for having taken the aristocratic name "de Voltaire." For his impudent reply to his better, the upstart bourgeois was beaten in the street by the nobleman's servants and arrested. Given permission to spend a period of exile in England, he left the caste-ridden, impoverished, Catholic France of his day for the country which, for the rest of his life, came to symbolize many of the qualities he would look on as utopian.

Arriving in London on a fine spring day in 1726, Voltaire witnessed a royal pageant on the Thames and was immediately struck by the air of prosperity around him. A little later he was a spectator of Newton's funeral, the coffin being carried into Westminster Abbey by peers of the realm. Lord Bolingbroke, whom he had known in France, introduced him to Pope, Swift, and other men of letters, and his presentation at court was arranged. Voltaire, however, chose to stay mostly at the home of a merchant, Everard Falkener, whose subsequent career—being knighted, made ambassador to Turkey, and later becoming postmaster-general—Voltaire watched with admiration. He learned English, wrote essays, and sketched his play *Brutus* in that language; and, at the very end of his life, he would insist on conversing in it with Franklin. It even seems that at one stage he considered remaining a resident. "In this country," he wrote to a friend, "it is possible to use one's mind freely and nobly without fear and cringing. If I followed my own inclinations, I should stay here, if only to learn how to think." He was allowed to return to France in 1729, but in many respects England never ceased to be his spiritual home. His sense of right and wrong was confirmed by his stay, and, most important, he perceived that an alternative society, preferable on most counts to the France he knew, could exist not just in theory; it had been realized across the Channel. It is especially useful to a reformer to be able to point beyond a set of ideas to a place where those ideas are already being successfully practiced.

The *Philosophical Letters*, written on his return, is not a travel account or an exhaustive study of England and its institutions. It is a slight, suggestive, witty work, comparing England mostly to France's disadvantage, with Voltaire constantly reining in his sympathies to avoid offending the censors. In brief, it depicts a free, thriving, and rational society, and nowhere else does Voltaire describe so clearly his conception of progress. The forces which shaped his interpretation of history leap from its pages. His first impressions remained some of his most durable—that a country with a fraction of France's population, and quite unequal in terms of natural wealth, had nonetheless achieved an enviable prosperity and strength enough to defeat Louis XIV. "Commerce," he wrote, "which has enriched English citizens, has helped to make them free, and this freedom in its turn has extended commerce, and that has made the greatness of the nation." The bond struck in Voltaire's mind between freedom and riches would have economic and political repercussions for the next two hundred years and more; the ideas and practice of *laissez-faire* economy and free trade became cornerstones of progress to Victorian liberals, and of heartless capitalism to Marx. Voltaire also noted the respect in which trade was held even among the nobility; in France, with its centralized, controlled economy, noblemen were disdainful of commerce when not actually barred from pursuing it.

If freedom to do business had been attained in England, so, to a remarkable extent, had freedom in government—though not without some difficulty. In other less fortunate countries, however, blood shed for liberty had only increased bondage; for Englishmen, the execution of Charles I had established the power of Parliament. The House of Lords and the House of Commons now governed, and the king was the umpire—a balance the Romans had lacked; but the Commons's power had grown, and the initiative in financial matters rested with them alone. The impact on Voltaire, of course, was to see that the class to which he himself belonged—the bourgeoisie—in effect ruled England through the Commons, whereas in France it was denied any such participation. Moreover, in England there was no distinction between nobility, merchants, and poorer classes regarding the administration of justice and the payment of taxes. "Everyone gives, not according to his rank (which is absurd) but according to his income. . . . nobody is downtrodden and nobody complains." The country was run by those who contributed most to its wealth and had the largest stake in its retaining the advantages it presently enjoyed—the men of substance of the middle class.

English literature provided Voltaire with the chance to discuss an area in which he was a professional. He found Shakespeare's plays too uneven for his taste—he called them barbaric—and felt more at home with English comedy; but he was particularly struck by the public respect the English gave their men of letters. "The portrait of the Prime Minister is over the mantelpiece of his room," he recalled, "but I have seen Mr. Pope's in a score of houses." In France actresses were refused religious burial, but a famous one in England had, like Newton, been buried in the Abbey. His own experience, the rejection of his talents in France, rankled in Voltaire's mind. As for the place of scientists in society, there was no comparison between the two countries. The Académie des Sciences might be better organized, but the great

Descartes had chosen to live in Holland and had died in Sweden. Newton, on the other hand, had the great good fortune to have been born not only in a free land but in a time when reason was cultivated there. If he had lived in Spain, Voltaire wrote, he would have been burned by the Inquisition; but in England he was honored "like a king who had done well by his subjects." No other country was so receptive to new and enlightening ideas and allowed them to change its thinking so fundamentally. The growth of inoculation against smallpox was a prime example of the practical way in which the English reaped the benefits of scientific discovery. "Perhaps in ten years' time we shall adopt this English method, if the priests and doctors permit," Voltaire commented.

The *Philosophical Letters*, however, is especially famous for its description of English religion in its multitudinous forms. "This," Voltaire wrote, "is the land of sects. An Englishman, as a free man, goes to Heaven by whatever route he likes." No group was more calculated to interest his readers than the Quakers, who in Catholic Europe had the reputation of being the wildest Protestants of all. A few years earlier, for instance, an Italian artist, picturing an imagined Quaker meeting, had painted a scene similar to the madhouse of Bedlam. But Voltaire chose to begin his work by describing the personal acquaintance he had made with Quakers and how he had found their unassuming manners attractive, their lack of a priesthood and their absence of sacraments sensible, and their dislike of oaths and their love of peace praiseworthy. He had attended a Quaker meeting, which he described with some amusement; but the memory stayed with him that here was a "natural" Christianity he could immediately sympathize with. In general, the case for religious liberty against state-enforced Catholicism was overwhelming. "If there were only one religion in England there would be danger of despotism," he concluded; "if there were two they would cut each other's throats, but there are thirty, and they live in peace and happiness."

A mere glance at Hogarth's engravings of London's Gin Lane or of a farcical English election are enough to see that the England of those days fell far short of our conception of a perfect society; but to Voltaire the country had strikingly advanced where France was failing. And its advances had not remained at a mental or spiritual level—they had caused men and women to be better housed, better clothed, and better fed. Throughout the *Philosophical Letters* there runs Voltaire's implicit suggestion that this is what human reason can accomplish when unobstructed. His notion of progress is not the confused understanding of the term to which the twentieth century has become accustomed. Voltaire is convinced that certain elementary needs of mind and body demand to be satisfied, and that the result will be for the good of all. In today's world that could be by fighting every epidemic disease, by teaching African peasant farmers how to cross-breed cattle and develop new strains of corn, by spreading literacy in South America, by ensuring freedom from torture anywhere, or freedom of the press, or freedom to have one's name on the voters' list—and by countless other examples. Progress to the eighteenth century meant the growth of a humanitarian spirit and the beginnings of philanthropy, besides discoveries in science and political reform—as many of Hogarth's pictures in fact illustrate too.

England to Voltaire seemed good, and, indeed, he later said he might have called his great history, *The Age of Louis XIV*, "the English Century." But there are signs he conceived that a country even better than England might exist—a country where a Quaker had become a sovereign. He described in the *Philosophical Letters* William Penn's settlement of Pennsylvania and the foundation of Philadelphia, the treaty with the Indians being "the only treaty between these people and Christians which has never been sworn to and never broken." All religions were welcomed there, all citizens (except magistrates) were equal, the government was without priests, one spoke to the ruler with one's hat on, and no weapons were carried; and it had prospered. In Benjamin West's later painting of the treaty signing, solid-looking houses are being constructed in the background. "William Penn," Voltaire wrote, "could congratulate himself on having established on earth the golden age so often talked about, and which has probably only ever existed in Pennsylvania." Until about 1760, progress to intelligent, forward-looking Frenchmen signified the English model; but, after that date, its location began to move to that descendant of Voltaire's earlier, idealized society, the emerging United States.

III

In his satirical tale *L'Ingénu*, written in 1767 when he was seventy-three, Voltaire related the fictional adventures of a Huron Indian in France. This New World child of nature encountered European civilization from a fresh viewpoint and made some perceptive observations, which were, of course, the thinly veiled opinions of Voltaire himself. At one point in the story, the Huron is imprisoned and finds himself in the same cell as a Jansenist—an austerely pious Catholic—who instructs him in various branches of knowledge. After studying mathematics and

metaphysics, the Huron turns his attention to history; and this is how
Voltaire described his reactions:

> He read history and was saddened by it, for the world seemed to him
> altogether too wicked and miserable. After all, history is but a chroni-
> cle of crime and misery. The host of innocent and peaceloving people
> always disappears from view in this vast theater, while the chief actors
> are nothing but evil and ambitious men. There seems to be no pleasure
> in History any more than in Tragedy, which languishes unless it is
> enlivened by passion, crime, and great misfortune. Clio as well as
> Melpomene must be armed with a dagger.

> The history of France is as full of horrors as the rest. But there was
> so much to displease him in the early stages, so much that was dry
> in the middle period, so much that was petty even in the days of
> Henri IV—no sign of the great monuments and the bold discoveries
> which have done honor to other nations—that he was obliged to
> struggle with boredom in reading all the details of minor calamities
> confined to a corner of the world.

> [The Jansenist] felt the same. They laughed with pity when the people
> concerned were the sovereigns of Fezensac, Fesansaguet, and Astarac,
> those tiny tracts in Armagnac, a subject for study which would interest
> only their descendants, if they had any.

> The splendid centuries of the Roman republic made him indifferent
> for a time to the rest of the world, and his whole mind was engrossed
> in the spectacle of victorious Rome as lawgiver of the nations. He grew
> excited at the idea of a people who for seven hundred years were gov-
> erned by enthusiasm for liberty and glory.

One of Voltaire's purposes in this episode was to show that the
mind of a child of nature—as perfect and unspoiled as some might
consider it to be—could still profit from education in Europe's finest
achievements. But, more immediately, we may discern in the Huron's
revulsion Voltaire's verdict on the state of historical writing in his time;
and in the Huron's respect for Rome we catch a glimpse of the criteria
Voltaire used when he chose his themes and made his judgments as
a historian himself. The Huron, a man of outstanding common sense,
goes on to give further opinions on ancient history. He expresses
astonishment at the way in which the histories of most nations solemnly
begin with fabulous origins; and he declares himself most satisfied by
the accounts of ancient China, because "nearly everything in it is
credible and natural." If we must have fables, the Huron exclaims,

"for heaven's sake let them at least be emblems of truth. I love philosophers' fables, but I laugh at children's, and I hate those that are foisted upon us by priests."

We may gather from the Huron's comments, then, that Voltaire demanded that history be accurate, probable, relevant to a reader's needs, and illuminating; and he selected the material for his own histories accordingly. He also was sure that evidence was actually available to make his analysis of the past more informed and exact. These characteristics have a modern air about them; and his major works displayed a new approach to the methods of historical research. But—unlike the Huron—Voltaire did not arrive at his positions in a matter of days. It took him many years to define for himself the historian's task, how he should use his materials, and what was the nature of history's content; to follow Voltaire's path, we must go with him as he worked his way into history from literature. Simultaneously, the point must clearly be made that, for Voltaire, history never ceased to be a branch of literature, the benefits of that association being traceable back to Herodotus. Nothing less than the truth should be told, but the truth gained immeasurably if expressed in the most attractive form of which a writer was capable.

An epic poem, *The Henriade*, begun while he was a prisoner in the Bastille, was Voltaire's first excursion into history. Celebrating Henri IV, the French king who had ended years of religious warfare, it was written in verse, and considerable research went into it. The *History of Charles XII, King of Sweden*, written in England and published in 1731, marks a long stride in his evolution as a historian. Voltaire had chosen the Swedish monarch for the vivid memory of him as a military genius—he had been killed only a few years before, in 1718—and because his character and life had immense potential for drama. The energetic rise of the soldier-king, his extraordinary adventures in Russia and Turkey, his losses, and his sudden death were complemented in theatrical fashion by the equally heroic career of his antagonist Peter the Great. The *History of Charles XII* was really an extended pamphlet; but although Voltaire did not go beyond military affairs and explained issues mainly by reference to rulers, he paid close attention to documents and interviewed eyewitnesses, and his narrative was very readable. It also delivered a clear moral message of a kind that would remain typical. Charles XII had been, perhaps, another Alexander, but his ambitions had ruined his country. He had carried heroism well beyond its merits, and his life, Voltaire wrote, "may be a lesson to kings and teach them that a peaceful and happy reign is more desirable than so much glory." Voltaire's manner of presentation was justified by the

History's instant success. Soon after, he started upon the study which would contribute most to his reputation as historian—his *Age of Louis XIV*. The task would take him twenty years to complete.

The reign of Louis XIV had acquired an aura for eighteenth-century Frenchmen comparable to that which the Victorian era may possess for the British today. Voltaire had been twenty-one when the great king died in 1715; and, though the last years of Louis's reign had fallen short of its potential, and though Voltaire himself was one of the government's severest critics, he could not deny that the epoch was one of extraordinary national greatness. France had exerted unique power and prestige, its achievements in many spheres had been outstanding, and, not least, the French language had reached its highest level of perfection—or so Voltaire believed. But, brilliant as the age had been, the historian held that there was one overpowering reason why its history should be written, and why it should be written according to a distinctive plan. He stated his argument forcefully in the introduction to the work when it appeared in 1751:

> It is not merely the life of Louis XIV that we propose to write; we have a wider aim in view. We shall endeavor to depict for posterity, not the actions of a single man, but the spirit of men in the most enlightened age the world has ever seen.

> Every age has produced its heroes and statesmen; every nation has experienced revolutions; every history is the same to one who wishes merely to remember facts. But the thinking man, and what is still rarer, the man of taste, numbers only four ages in the history of the world; four happy ages when the arts were brought to perfection and which, marking an era of the greatness of the human mind, are an example to posterity.

> The first of these ages, to which true glory belongs, is that of Philip and Alexander, or rather of Pericles, Demosthenes, Aristotle, Plato, Apelles, Phidias, Praxiteles; and this honor was confined within the limits of Greece, the rest of the known world being in a barbarous state.

> The second age is that of Caesar and Augustus, distinguished moreover by the names of Lucretius, Cicero, Livy, Virgil, Horace, Ovid, Varro and Vitruvius.

> The third is that which followed the taking of Constantinople by Mahomet II. The reader may remember that the spectacle was then witnessed of a family of mere citizens in Italy accomplishing what

should have been undertaken by the kings of Europe. The scholars whom the Turks had driven from Greece were summoned by the Medici to Florence; it was the hour of Italy's glory. . . .

The fourth age is that which we call the century of Louis XIV; and it is perhaps of the four the one which most nearly approaches perfection. Enriched with the discoveries of the other three it accomplished in certain departments more than the three together. All the arts, it is true, did not progress further than they did under the Medici, under Augustus or under Alexander; but human reason in general was brought to perfection.

Rational philosophy only came to light in this period; and it is true to say that from the last years of Cardinal Richelieu to those which followed the death of Louis XIV, a general revolution took place in our arts, minds and customs, as in our government, which will serve as an eternal token of the true glory of our country.

With these words a transformation of European historiography was begun. Gone were the memoirs of the court, the chronicles of the deeds of petty lords of ancient times, the old stories of miracles—all the misplaced interest in the past of which the Huron complained; gone too was a religious or a narrowly political framework within which all events were set. Voltaire proclaimed that his *Age of Louis XIV* would be an intellectual history, a portrait of the mind of an era. The idea was not new: Bacon, for instance, once observed that, without representation of the state of learning, "the history of the world seems to me as the statue of Polyphemus without the eye, that very feature being left out which most marks the spirit and life of the person"; but Voltaire's was the first attempt to follow it through in a comprehensive and purposeful form. The century of Louis XIV was well suited to his intentions, he thought—not because it had been free from crimes and misfortunes, but because it was an age of genius and the only one of its competitors to have profited from accurate knowledge and "rational philosophy."

Seeing Louis XIV's reign as an entity rather than a chronological process, Voltaire arranged his materials according to what has been called the "chest-of-drawers method." Instead of plodding through the period year by year in the customary manner, he placed, as it were, each piece of evidence he selected into a drawer labeled with a topic, and made each drawer a chapter. France was put first in its European context, and two-thirds of the book dealt with war and diplomacy; but the remaining section in particular shows how far his ideas had grown since his *History of Charles XII.* Voltaire explored such general subjects as justice, trade, finance, and ecclesiastical affairs with a breadth of analysis, and he devoted four chapters to the sciences and arts—to him the century's chief distinction. The reader should not expect minute details of wars, he warned, for "every event that occurs is not worth recording." His history would confine itself to "that which deserves the attention of all time," and, in a letter of 1735, he set his standards. One hundred battles contributed nothing to the human race: and "a sluice in a canal joining two seas, a painting by Poussin, a fine tragedy, a truth discovered are things one thousand times more valuable than all the records of life at court, than all the tales of military exploits." His intention led him to include such details as Louis XIV's suppression of dueling, and the installation of street lights in Paris.

Voltaire surprisingly ended his study with a chapter entitled "Disputes Concerning Chinese Ceremonies," which described the quarrels between the Dominican and Jesuit missionaries in China. Because toleration there was only extended to religions which tolerated each other, the Chinese emperors had concluded that Christianity should be proscribed. But Voltaire's purpose in finishing on a tangent was calculated. The reign of Louis XIV had indeed had its triumphs, but it also possessed conspicuous defects; and religious bigotry—at its worst in the persecution of the Huguenots—was one of them. Meanwhile, China had increasingly come to represent to Voltaire an empire admirably governed by reason and tolerance, an expanded version of England perhaps, or the nearest existing equivalent to imperial Rome. To draw his readers' attention abruptly from Louis XIV to the emperors K'ang Hsi and Yung Cheng paid a compliment to the French king's stature; but it also implied, by the examples of those enlightened monarchs, that there were heights which not even the Sun King had reached. There was a similar lesson in the eventual dedication of the work not to Louis XV—who made slight effort to rectify his predecessor's errors—but to Frederick the Great of Prussia, whom Voltaire considered the most promising ruler to lead humanity forward.

While laboring on the *Age of Louis XIV*, Voltaire came to see it not as an isolated project but as the final installment of a great history of mankind—an enlargement of his theme which he planned during his liaison with the Marquise du Châtelet. The Marquise once complained that history bored her, on grounds resembling those of the Huron Indian; and to engage her interest, Voltaire began to write the book known briefly as the *Essai sur les Moeurs,* or *Essay on the Manners and Spirit of the Nations.* Portions of the *Essai* were published in 1745 and 1751, though the complete work did not appear until 1757. Once

again stating his guiding principles at the outset, he sharpened the
remarks he had made in the *Age of Louis XIV*. Addressing Mme. du
Châtelet, Voltaire declared:

> You wish in short to overcome your distaste for modern history, since
> the decay of the Roman empire, and to form a broad idea of the
> nations which inhabit and devastate the earth. In this immense field
> you seek only what deserves to be known; the genius, the manners,
> the customs of the leading nations, supported by facts impermissible
> to ignore. The aim of this work is not to know the precise year in
> which a prince unworthy of our attention succeeded a barbarous
> prince in a brutal country. If we had the misfortune of remembering
> the chronological order of all the dynasties, they would only be words
> to us. Just as we ought to know the great deeds of rulers who have
> made their peoples better or happier, we can pass over the common
> run of kings who only burden the memory. What good will it do you
> to know the details of so many petty interests which no longer exist,
> of so many extinct families who fought over provinces since absorbed
> in great kingdoms? Today practically every city has its history true
> or false, ampler, more detailed than that of Alexander. The mere
> annals of a monastic order contain more volumes than those of the
> Roman empire.
>
> In all these huge collections exceeding our grasp, we must pick and
> choose. History is a vast storehouse from which you take what you
> find useful.

The *Essai* became primarily a history of the world from
Charlemagne to Louis XIII, but it contained a lengthy preamble
summarizing the centuries before. It is a storehouse in itself from
which any number of examples may be taken to illustrate Voltaire's
leading merits and defects as a historian and his special place in the
Enlightenment as *roi des philosophes*. Although Voltaire was most
interested in European civilization, he surveyed the histories of other
countries on a generous scale, from Japan to Peru; and he was quite
prepared on occasion to praise their cultural successes and deflate
European claims to unique excellence. Classical Greece was passed
over quickly as one of the much-lauded four great ages; and the Jews,
who had received preferential treatment from historians for so long,
were relegated to the position of one of the weaker Syrian tribes.
Constantly asking if stories were probable, he destroyed, often with
merciless wit, a number of time-honored versions of the past, both
sacred and secular; and he brought antiquity to life by novel comparisons
—for instance, between the Stoic teachers and Confucius, and the early

Christians and the Quakers. Muhammad received a fair appraisal for the first time in Western historiography, and the blood-thirsting, pillaging Crusaders were contrasted with the exemplary character of the Arab general Saladin. Since Voltaire was a cosmopolitan man, he was determined to give history a cosmopolitan nature, too. Besides, a scientific inquiry should not stop at artificial limits but should explore its subject in its entirety to find the truths it seeks. His reading for the *Essai*, though very largely in secondary sources, was extensive, but he did not lose his sense of direction. In order to set down only "what deserves to be known," he selected according to his chosen code—until, as we shall see, his virtues became his major weakness, harming his considerable reputation as an objective historian.

A mention should be made of some of Voltaire's other historical studies—his *Age of Louis XV*, *Annals of the Empire*, *History of Russia*, and (most ambitious, perhaps, in view of the difficulties involved) his *Historical Fragments on India*. These have some interest; but Voltaire's development as a historian reached its peak in the *Age of Louis XIV* and the *Essai*. We shall therefore concentrate upon these two works in summarizing what he contributed to the understanding of history.

IV

"He has invented history," remarked the Marquise du Deffand in her *salon*, and opinion since has largely agreed in seeing in Voltaire the first recognizably modern historian. Broadly speaking, historical writing before the *Age of Louis XIV* was dominated by the presuppositions that history was the record of either the religious or the political life of man. The former thesis, which had been perfected by Augustine, saw the biblical story providing the theme of all history, and it received a major exposition in 1681 when Bishop Bossuet wrote his *Discourse on Universal History*, to instruct the Dauphin. Though Bossuet was learned and aware of evidence from other sources, he nonetheless emphasized the events of the Bible and followed classic Augustinian doctrine. Although he took note of geographical and economic factors and of the traits of particular men, he saw divine providence governing human affairs through first and secondary causes. At the same time, since the Renaissance, history had been valued as a record of past politics, in which the Greeks and Romans especially held a leading place. Works of this second type had been written to teach lessons in statecraft—as well as for general interest—and emphasized human explanations of events instead of the supernatural. There also existed a vast and miscellaneous agglomeration of chronicles, memoirs, biographies, tales of chivalry (of the sort that filled Don Quixote's brain), legends and genealogies, in which events were often haphazardly strung together, and which displayed several levels of veracity.

The new history Voltaire produced from this chaos which the eighteenth century had inherited had four major characteristics. First, it brought to the study of the past certain rules of methodology and organization which have led to his being called a scientific historian. Revolutions in history and the social sciences have often occurred when the forms of data gathering and data evaluation are changed; and, when Voltaire carried out his historical research, he purposely made use of methods and mental habits which had proved so profitable for scientific inquiry. It should not be forgotten that, during his years with Mme. du Châtelet, when he was writing his best works of history, he also tried to make a reputation as a physicist. The scientist approached the information available to him with skepticism, examined it with care, and rejected conclusions he found to be foreign to his experiment and unwarranted. His evidence guided him, not he his evidence, and his goal was a truth from nature, verifiable by reason. Voltaire believed the historian should try to do likewise. Facts, comparable to mathematical axioms or chemical elements, were to him the historian's essentials in the search for valid laws regarding man and his life in society; and, to obtain them the historian should try to establish the contents of the past as accurately as possible. When in doubt of his proof he should settle for the most likely explanation, seek more evidence—like a scientist—and still press for results. With the ideal of scientific investigation before him, Voltaire proceeded with his task.

Painstakingly reading books and documents, critically listening to reminiscences, Voltaire raised research techniques to a higher and more efficient level. He was greatly helped in the preparation for the *Age of Louis XIV* by his appointment for a while as Historiographer Royal; no French historian was to have access to government papers in a similar way until Jules Michelet a hundred years later. Comparing descriptions of events from one source with another, Voltaire invariably preferred a commonsense account to one which seemed improbable or fabulous. Semimythical stories, of the kind the Huron had immediately distrusted, were either omitted completely or explained away; and, by a selective process, Voltaire's mind was always thinning his materials, whittling whole volumes down to a few pages or sentences, exhaustively trying to separate what had happened from all its dubious accretions. He did not achieve faultless accuracy, of course; but his work demands to be seen in light of what it moved away from, not of its shortcomings.

In brief, he pioneered the modern scientific examination of history, which has been of the utmost significance ever since.

Secondly, Voltaire's efforts to be a scientific as well as a literary historian led his work to treat the past on a scale that was universal. Bossuet, who had included histories of other peoples in his *Discourse*, was nonetheless imprisoned by his heritage. Voltaire, however, turned his back on such a European, Christian-centered outlook and strove to see history in global terms according to a common standard—the level of enlightenment attained. Mankind, not individuals, was its subject, and Voltaire enlarged the bounds of history for his age to include the whole human race. The Huron had observed that other nations seemed definitely superior to the Europeans, and Voltaire, especially in the *Essai*, pursued this theme with relish. He found frequent opportunities to commend the Chinese Empire. He approved the selection of mandarins on grounds of merit instead of birth, and preferred the ethical precepts of Confucianism to the superstitious character of so many Christian beliefs. Cultivating this breadth of inquiry because he believed that only in this way would true and applicable laws be forthcoming, his knowledge was naturally restricted, and he sometimes made comparisons and deductions too quickly; but he should be credited with opening the way.

Voltaire's wide-ranging approach was reflected in other features of his histories. His ability to grasp a historical problem from many sides made him see the Reformation, for instance, as a social and political as well as a religious phenomenon; and, like a good journalist, he welcomed help from new disciplines—such as archaeology, palaeography, and textual analysis—for better investigation, and to make his books better reading. He also restored to historiography the importance of a civilization as a whole, giving it a place it perhaps had not received since Herodotus, whom he admired. He by no means wished political and military affairs to be overlooked, but he strongly believed they were secondary to cultural and social matters in the history of nations or of humanity—and that the flowering of human genius was the most important thing. Previous historians had often dwelt endlessly on such subjects as the antiquity and dimensions of the Egyptian pyramids, but Voltaire dismissed their interests as concerned with trivia; "I only examine the history of the human mind."

But, when Mme. du Deffand credited Voltaire with inventing history, she likely meant not only the achievements just mentioned but also that he was a "philosophical" historian; and by this was meant that he had used history to express certain opinions and beliefs held dear by the *philosophe* movement. Voltaire the innovator in scientific method and in universal outlook was one and the same with a third Voltaire, the apostle of enlightenment, who saw in history a ready-made vehicle for his liberal, reforming message. Few of his writings communicated this message more successfully than his histories and perhaps none stated it more forcefully—that mankind could improve its condition dramatically if only it used its intelligence and powers to free itself from *l'infâme*.

The skeptical attitude, fostered in France by Montaigne, Descartes, and Bayle, became in Voltaire a splendid weapon for persuasion, particularly in the *Essai*, where there was ample opportunity to accompany it with wit. The past as conventionally understood was often more than a collection of errors, he argued; it was a tissue of lies, ingrained by tradition and upheld by authority, designed to mislead man and stifle him. His militant purpose was to clear away the misconceptions and let the reasonable reader judge for himself. He rudely challenged the fundamental assumptions on which laws and customs justified their existence, found heroes had feet of clay, and delighted in showing kings and emperors without their clothes. How could John II of France be called "the Good," he asked, when he started his reign with an assassination? Oracles were shown to be as fallible as almanacs, and papal power to rest on fabrication. The Bible, too, was full of misinformation. Drawing up an interesting statistical table, Voltaire laughed at the number of Jews recorded as having been killed in the entry to Canaan; and, rather than try to reconcile the inconsistencies of the Gospels, he mischievously cut the knot by saying one had to believe the Holy Ghost had written them to explain the mess they were in. He told the story of Joan of Arc—he had already written a licentious mock-epic about her—and called her "miracle" a sham; yet he still thought Joan a heroine. Her trial and burning as a heretic and witch illustrated "that fanaticism composed of superstition and ignorance, which has been the sickness of nearly all centuries."

In place of God's judgment on history, Voltaire gave the final verdict to posterity. It is "the only defense we have against successful tyranny," he wrote with respect to Philip II of Spain. Men were to be judged on their actions, which were produced by their characters; and the thought of a shameful reputation among more enlightened future generations would, he hoped, serve as a stronger deterrent. Not surprisingly, religion in general was the most frequent target of his sarcasm and wit, in particular those religious myths which had hindered the desire of the human race for truth. As a deist, Voltaire owned in the *Essai* that he believed "the knowledge of a God, maker, rewarder and avenger, is the fruit of cultivated reason." What he detested most was the religious bigotry so prominent in the human record—innumerable examples of which were to be found in the period the *Essai* covered.

One result of this tendency, however, was that at times Voltaire's opposition to the Christian religion, especially in its Catholic form, practically canceled out his attempts to be objective. The *Essai* has been called a reform pamphlet, every page reverberating with a passionate war cry; and Voltaire had a constant tendency in it to distort and caricature, a tendency bound to become most pronounced when the man of reason found himself writing on the Middle Ages. Medieval society to him had been barbaric, and its civilization, dominated by unscrupulous priests, had largely created the bad laws and institutions from which he and his circle were trying to liberate themselves. If in his best historical writing Voltaire typified Kant's dictum, "Dare to be wise," in the *Essai* he was determined his readers should be wise after his own fashion.

In Voltaire's eyes the medieval period was an enormous morass between two peaks, marvelously ended by the Renaissance; it was the night of the human race, whose darkness was finally broken by the rays of the Enlightenment. The human mind had been denied its natural expression, the human will crippled by self-serving religious interests; and he took every chance to contrast the few shining examples of human intelligence bravely struggling against the prevailing black of the cassock. His antireligious prejudices could overwhelm him; he treated the humanist Sir Thomas More with disgust, for to Voltaire More's steadfast allegiance to Rome quite outweighed his qualities of intellect and spirit. In the twentieth century Arnold Toynbee saw the Middle Ages as the height of Western civilization, a time when faith, thought, art, and government were singularly unified, an age, too, from which parliaments and universities emerged; but his interpretation met stiff resistance. With Petrarch's influence in the background, Voltaire seems to have fixed enduringly the popular picture of the Middle Ages as superstitious and backward, and the word "medieval" itself has become a term of rejection and abuse. The epoch is broadly labeled the "Dark Ages"—a term now only used of the early centuries; and it is sometimes hard to think of its image ever recovering.

The fourth characteristic of Voltaire's history was his belief in gradual human progress—progress as conceived from his English experience, tested in his warfare against *l'infâme*, and held as a "philosophical" conviction. In the *Age of Louis XIV* he had identified four eras in the world's history as models for posterity—Periclean Athens, Augustan Rome, Renaissance Italy, and the France of Louis XIV itself. The later ages had built on their predecessors' achievements, but all had been great because they showed the human mind stretching itself and advancing. But they were of crucial interest too because they revealed in themselves the conditions for progress and, indeed, it seemed, the secret of history as a whole. Voltaire had studied the past as far as he could to produce a reliable, universal, man-centered history; but he hoped at the end to establish a fundamental law of a Newtonian kind, to explain the historical process and benefit the human race. The four great ages—and their reverse, the medieval period—provided him with the conclusive evidence he needed.

This was the law he found: that mankind had never progressed at any time without the guidance of strong enlightened persons in positions of authority; and, if a truly enlightened society were ever to come into existence, it would be largely through the efforts of rulers of that sort. The four most brilliant ages in history were proof of his theory's correctness. Periclean Athens, he argued, could not have happened without Pericles, nor Augustan Rome without Augustus; in the modern era, what did Pennsylvania's life not owe to Penn? Among the few men he admired in the Middle Ages were Alfred the Great, Prince Henry the Navigator, and—a late example, perhaps—Henri IV. Alfred the Great had been the father of England's government and learning; Prince Henry the Navigator had used the position into which he was born for planning a series of great Portuguese explorations; and Henri IV, by his sensible resolution of the religious wars and his sympathy for the common people, had been the best ruler France had ever had. Charles XII of Sweden, though a hero, had brought his country to ruin. Only through the exertions of wise and dedicated rulers, and of the men—like the great French minister, Colbert—they had placed in office, had mankind advanced at all; and Voltaire was heartened by the appearance in so many countries of "enlightened despots"— Frederick the Great, and Catherine the Great of Russia, in particular. They seemed to promise further progress was in the making.

Voltaire delivered his law of history in numerous forms in his writings, and it became practically as repetitious and routine for him as its corollary—that ignorance and superstition had held men back. But, novel though the idea of progress seemed to his contemporaries, in shape it was not entirely original; for, with a Christian theme and destination, it had existed since Augustine's *City of God*. It was the Enlightenment's distinction, as the American historian Carl Becker pointed out, to take the Christian theory of time moving in a linear direction and secularize it, to substitute for God's unfolding revelation the ascent of human intelligence from the savage to Isaac Newton—

and beyond. The end of history was sketched with broad strokes as the triumph of reason over *l'infâme* and the establishment of an earthly utopia, instead of the coming of the Kingdom of God. Like many an increasingly confident scientist, Voltaire took God out of history; it could, like the universe, be explained satisfactorily without Him. But much of the old interpretive structure remained. The possibility of human progress had been raised before in the ancient world, as we noted; but Voltaire was the first to build a comprehensive version of past, present, and future upon it, and, like Augustine in his day, to win the prize of acceptance.

Yet, at the center of Voltaire's idea of human progress, we see tensions of a most fundamental sort threatening to pull it down. From his wide research and critical investigation, Voltaire was convinced his law of history rested on solid ground; but, although he could point to certain ages which stood out like mountains, he was at a loss to explain why they were so few and why the triumph of reason was coming about so slowly—or, indeed, whether there could be total assurance that further progress would come about at all. Civilization was cumulative, its present benefits had been laboriously won, and now, at last, rational philosophy had just started to mature. It was vital for mankind, therefore, that civilization be guarded by those who could protect it, because, all too easily, the achievements of the four great ages, and of the handful of authentic heroes, could be wiped out by an unleashed mob. Ignorance and superstition were bad enough simply because they were irrational; but ignorance, superstition, and weak government was the worst catastrophe of all. Man collectively was unreasonable, and, if allowed to gain control as a mass, could wreck everything that enlightened rulers might accomplish. There was no guarantee this catastrophe could not happen, for history showed there had always been crimes, wars, and misfortunes. Obviously, Voltaire would have been appalled by the French Revolution.

If man was to continue his recent extraordinary advance, believed Voltaire, he should emulate the four great ages. Other parts of the past should be studied only as the soberest of warnings. "Abolish the study of history," Voltaire once wrote, "and you will probably see a new St. Bartholomew in France and a new Cromwell in England." His prescription for the future was therefore a highly selective continuity. But the nagging pessimistic fears remained. What if the enlightened ruling class failed in their duty, or separated themselves from society— as Voltaire noticed had happened in China? Suppose rational philosophy withered from unexpected causes, or the will for improvement failed, and mankind fell back into darkness once again—perhaps for another millennium, perhaps this time forever? "Philosophical" though he was, Voltaire at such moments found no more in history than a record of meaningless change, and he fell into the habit of explaining events by accidents and coincidences. Ultimately it seems we are at the mercy of powers we cannot control.

Like Augustine and every great historian, Voltaire put the truth as he had personally found it into his history; but the absolute faith in a victory already won, which had made Augustine's interpretation so compelling, was lacking. Man's advance might only become permanent if reason was rightly used by government; failing that, it was a matter of hoping for the best. Despite his running battle with Christian piety, Voltaire and the *philosophes* were never able to formulate an alternative explanation of human nature which could satisfy equally. Superstition, backwardness, they said, would all be eliminated in the end, given the right combination of circumstances. Today, from twentieth-century experience and modern psychology's certainty that human behavior may never be made entirely reasonable, this hopeful view may seem naive. The sacred, too, has come to be seen as an element in the structure of consciousness rather than merely as a stage in its history; and Voltaire's proclamation of progress, in the face of opposing elements and the great bulk of the historical record, can seem like so much frivolous insouciance.

Nothing haunted the Age of Reason more than the possibility of a return to the Dark Ages from which it had gained release. In the last century man had advanced without precedent; but how could this uniquely powerful upward trajectory possibly be maintained when the pattern of history was against it? The answer might lie in understanding more clearly why past failures had happened; and none of the three previous great ages had been more successful or had a more calamitous downfall than the Roman. The Enlightenment saw imperial Rome as the closest parallel in the past to the civilization it now hoped to build for the whole world. Under able and virtuous rulers the Roman empire had united mankind under common laws; within its borders peace and prosperity had been preserved for centuries; it had been generally tolerant of competing religions; and its philosophy and ethics had been admirably secular. So the *philosophes* rejoiced that they too professed paganism, the new paganism of science. But even Rome was not secure, and its fall had ushered in a thousand years of night. Machiavelli had studied Rome's history to ensure success again; but now Montesquieu and Edward Gibbon studied it to prolong current successes—to find the causes of Rome's decay, so any comparable symptoms in the new Western civilization might be checked in time.

Gibbon first thought of writing on the end of classical civilization when he sat musing amid the ruins of the Capitol, listening to monks chanting their Christian liturgy. In his *Decline and Fall of the Roman Empire*, published between 1776 and 1788, he found that Rome had succumbed to "the natural and inevitable effect of immoderate greatness." "Prosperity ripened the principle of decay; the causes of destruction multiplied with the extent of conquest; and as soon as time or accident had removed the artificial supports, the stupendous fabric yielded to the pressure of its own weight." The fall of Rome marked, for Gibbon, "the triumph of barbarism and religion"—two evils, with little to choose between them. "We may inquire, with anxious curiosity," he continued, "whether Europe is still threatened with a repetition of those calamities"; but he thought it probable that the Dark Ages could never now return. "The region of independent barbarism is now contracted to a narrow span," he wrote; "the abuses of tyranny are restrained by the mutual influence of fear and shame." Technology had given the West unique military advantages, and, even if Europe were reconquered by a new horde out of Asia, it would revive and flourish in the American world. But perhaps the most hopeful sign of all, from four thousand years of experience, was that, "unless the face of nature is changed," no people were likely to relapse into their original barbarism. Once savages had received the gifts of civilization, even its techniques of war, they had ceased to be barbarians. "We may therefore acquiesce," Gibbon concluded, "that every age of the world has increased and still increases the real wealth, the happiness, the knowledge, and perhaps the virtue, of the human race."

Armed with such weighty reassurances, the conception of history as progress captured first an influential and then a general audience; and Voltaire's histories, like his other writings, became powerful engines in the battle for reform and change. Counseling, urging, encouraging, Voltaire saw man no longer as the helpless victim of his past but as history's agent, patiently building to bring to fruition his hopes for a better life on earth now, not in a heavenly future. When he secularized Augustine's theme, Voltaire brought men into a new constructive relationship with the historical process, and they boldly took more risks as knowledge expanded and man's mastery over nature steadily grew. Progress, Voltaire believed, was a constant struggle with temporary respites; but his distinguished disciple, the Marquis de Condorcet, argued even as an outlawed fugitive that the French Revolution and modern science had already brought mankind to the threshold of a tenth and final stage of civilization, a stage happier, freer, and more ideal than any known before. Progress in fact could be endless, the mind could assign no limits to what it could achieve in knowledge, virtue, even in adding years to human life. Popular education was the means to ensure this future; and Napoleon ordered Condorcet's summary of the great epochs of history to be taught in French schools as the approved story of the past and the vision of what was to be.

If we look still further ahead, "the history of England is emphatically the history of progress," the future Lord Macaulay wrote in 1835; and nowhere did he express his conviction better than in the famous third chapter of his *History of England from the Accession of James II*. If by magic the England of 1685 could be set before the reader's eyes, said Macaulay, he would hardly know a single landscape or building. "The country gentleman would not recognize his own fields. The inhabitant of the town would not recognize his own street." Everything had been changed except the great features of nature and a few massive castles and cathedrals; and the whole transformation of England and English life for the better was a tribute to the principles of parliamentary power and steady change with moderation. Without a shot being fired, the Glorious Revolution of 1688—a Whig achievement—had inaugurated an era of unbroken stable government. Crown and Parliament had been brought into harmony, and, while other countries continued to struggle through wars and violence, England had enviably moved forward and enjoyed in peace the fruits of her freedom and industry. The strengths Voltaire had noticed only marked the beginning; science had flourished and been applied to practical purposes "on a scale never known before," and further improvements were currently proceeding with ever-increasing speed. The Great Exhibition of London in 1851 displayed beyond all doubt the triumph of modern liberalism and the beneficial results of science and technology. "A most gorgeous sight," Macaulay wrote, on having visited the Crystal Palace; "vast; graceful; beyond the dreams of the Arabian romances. I cannot think that the Caesars ever exhibited a more splendid spectacle. I was quite dazzled, and I felt as I did on entering St. Peter's." By the mid-nineteenth century it seemed irrefutable to Macaulay and his great following of readers that the restoration of the arts and sciences had purified and advanced mankind.

But, as the world knows, the Dijon Academy's essay contest of 1749 was not won by a fellow traveler of Voltaire's, but by a footloose, Swiss-born musician, Jean-Jacques Rousseau, who, in a flash of inspiration, argued quite to the contrary—and on startling new social grounds. In his *Discourse on the Sciences and the Arts*, he bypassed issues of science and religion and passionately asserted that history showed culture had always depleted a people's goodness and vitality, fostered inequalities, and caused political and military decay. At a time when the luxury of the *ancien régime* was becoming the object of criticism even among aristocrats, Rousseau extolled the virtues of simple living, whether exemplified by Sparta, republican Rome, or the Swiss cantons. This was a better goal for man to advance toward than the refined version of the gentleman urged by Voltaire, who, to put it bluntly, had admired the age of Louis XIV too much. The natural goodness of man should be released rather than false cultural values be preserved and further developed. They were garlands that merely concealed the iron chains holding mankind down. To guide mankind to a new beginning, Rousseau in 1762 wrote an educational treatise, *Émile*, in which he imagined a boy learning from manual projects and field trips instead of from books—excepting *Robinson Crusoe*. The study of history is delayed until Émile is eighteen years old, and then it only gives finishing touches to his knowledge of human nature gained by direct experience.

Under the impact of the American Revolution—the birth, it seemed, of a new republic of citizen-farmers—the mood in France moved closer to Rousseau's; and, in 1789, the aim of many resolute Frenchmen became to leave their past behind, "to make," that perceptive analyst Tocqueville later wrote, "a scission in their lifeline and to create an unbridgeable gulf between all they had hitherto been and all they now aspired to be." The perfection of human happiness was now imminent, near enough to be marked by a new chronology, and the triumph of reason over *l'infâme* came to be seen, almost literally, as strangling the last king with the entrails of the last priest. "Soldiers, forty centuries look down upon you," Bonaparte in Egypt reputedly told his troops before the Battle of the Pyramids, reminding them that they could simultaneously make history and break with it there at the foot of the oldest monuments known to man. The future had no need of the past, it would be built from noble abstractions, not from what the past had shown to be humanly possible. As the French Revolution's critics were quick to charge, its leaders evidently saw men as abstractions, too.

Today, conflict continues between those who, like Voltaire, think of progress as the constant cultivation of social values that are reasoned and humane, who see merit in past successes, and who by and large view man's mastery over nature with favor—and those who take Rousseau's position to support their argument that progress means liberating man to be himself again, freeing him from technology's burdens and interference perhaps, setting him right to live in a minimally organized society or even as a noble savage. But beyond controversy over definitions, the modern West also has difficulties with the fundamental idea of progress itself, which was born out of eighteenth-century optimism and developed in nineteenth-century confidence. The twentieth century's experience has been so different from what either of its predecessors anticipated that the notion itself is in doubt; and a leading problem for historians—and for everyone else—has been to find a firm alternative to the belief Voltaire defined in England that once amounted to a faith.

In consequence, twentieth-century man has experimented with other organizing principles and long-term perspectives. Alternative claims to explain history scientifically draw his attention, among them the scheme of Voltaire's Italian contemporary, Giambattista Vico, who discerned a three-stage rhythm in the life of all civilizations, clearly marked in their mental and cultural growth. From time to time we hear the essential soundness of the very idea of progress being reaffirmed; but the debate to resolve what in fact constitutes progress appears interminable—not least because we now see primitive societies are often deceptively complex. Voltaire and Rousseau together have changed the face of the world, in many respects for the better; but it often seems the Academy's question—whether the new arts and sciences had done more to corrupt or improve mankind—still awaits a satisfactory answer.

CHAPTER FIVE

SCOTT

I

The Scientific Revolution shattered the already disintegrating unity of Western civilization and set science and religion on a divided course in which science steadily drew ahead. Although the Christian conception of history continues today to have a considerable following, beginning in the eighteenth century Western man increasingly chose the idea of progress as the principle by which he explained himself and made his decisions. He found the new implement served his needs better and commanded his respect. But it was really an adaptation of the old; and we might pause here for a moment to recall how much the linear view of time—which Voltaire and Augustine shared, despite their differences—has meant to Western history and has precipitated human activity within it.

The ability to see time moving from a beginning to an end instead of in repeated cycles was the achievement principally of the Jews; and, if we start by looking at the biblical story as it is told, we notice that, ever since Abraham heeded God's call to leave Ur of the Chaldees to establish a people, the linear concept has stirred their imagination. The migration of the children of Israel out of Egyptian bondage to the promised land—a land, incidentally, where they would not only be free, but a land flowing with milk and honey—set the pattern for seeing history as a journey; and, under the prophets' influence, Jerusalem was gradually transformed in the Jewish mind from a fortress to a temple to the symbolic goal of history itself, the perfect community realized.

The idea of a new covenant sealing God's promise afresh prepared for the birth of Christ, and the Church in turn looked forward to the consummation of all things at His second coming. In the fifth century Augustine raised the Jewish and Christian beliefs into a systematic exposition of the whole of history, arguing that time was unique and unrepeatable, and affirming that each man and woman was responsibly engaged in an earthly pilgrimage to a destination in eternity. He also made use of the popular impression that Rome too had had a destiny, which opened as Rome grew.

To Petrarch, and more urgently to Machiavelli, classical Rome restored represented an advance; and, though the Enlightenment was often bitterly antireligious, it did not reject the notion of the linear movement of the Christian heritage. It used it for its purposes. History as God's unfolding revelation was abandoned; it was now about man climbing out of ignorance toward knowledge. Man would gain his freedom by his intelligence, not by his faith; and his prospects, whether they were defined by Voltaire or Rousseau, came to be seen as limitless. The British peoples everywhere for many years took from Macaulay their chief conclusion about their own recent history—that England had found the secret of good government and gone on to thrive while other countries stagnated. Indeed, it seemed to Macaulay that England in the foreseeable future would always be improving and becoming wealthier, as long as it maintained the Whig tradition. At the same time George Bancroft's *History of the United States* was bringing a comparable message to Americans, celebrating their Revolution and the Republic's success as the epic of democracy.

In nineteenth-century Germany, Ranke believed each European nation developed along lines determined by its essential character; and Marx forecast inevitable change from economic inequality to the utopia of a classless paradise. Constant scientific and technological discoveries meanwhile increased the public's sense of time as moving and forceful; and, after Darwin's evolutionary theory appeared, historians and biologists became co-workers exploring man's development. To Toynbee, writing in England after the First World War, history showed the rise and fall of civilizations, but in every instance man had gone forward to a higher level of spiritual understanding. Wells, who was trained as a biologist, saw nations evolving into a world state and believed the real human adventure was about to begin—if only men would renounce their destructive habits. We can see too that whenever other peoples have been touched by Western influence their idea of history soon reflects the linear way of thinking. American slaves, singing of their hope for deliverance, used biblical imagery; *Up from Slavery* was the title of

Booker T. Washington's famous autobiography; and, while the Civil Rights movement in America organized freedom marches, Asians and Africans looked upon independence as the climax to a long colonial struggle. Every scheme of history has an assumption about man behind it; and, in the case of the linear theory in all its forms, the assumption is that man will continue to grow and that this is good. "I could make no progress in it," Augustine wrote about his life with the Manichaeans; with Christianity he found that growth was possible. No matter how much the linear view of time has been challenged by other beliefs—cyclical, harmonized, or the denial of any pattern—it has remained a vital, perhaps inextinguishable part of Western man's outlook, perhaps the greatest difference between his own and other cultures; for, besides being a basis of reasoning on which structures of thought have been erected, its invariable invitation to man to be a participant in the historical process has unleashed dynamic energies and bred an obstinate disposition to optimism.

Although much of Western historiography may be described as a set of variations on the linear theme, its story is of course more complicated. The constant tension between linear and cyclical beliefs gives the story much of its interest; and, as we have seen, even within the linear tradition, views of history often develop in reaction to one another. Since Voltaire and his associates spread the idea of progress, however, no one scheme of history has had the field largely to itself. Western civilization is no longer united by common agreement on the process or the purpose of history, and no single historian or historical thinker straddles it as an unchallenged colossus. With Voltaire we begin to approach modern times, and the unprecedented explosion of knowledge and information which has characterized the nineteenth and twentieth centuries—knowledge to be grasped and information to be absorbed. Instead of being somewhat isolated figures as they have been so far, innovators in historical thinking now begin to follow one another thick and fast as ideas of history are adjusted to new situations. The sequence of schemes speeds up, and competition to lay hold to the precious historical implement becomes more strenuous. All the men we shall review in the remaining chapters of this study have decisively influenced the way we look at history today—which is not to say the earlier figures are less important, only less immediate. Historians from Herodotus to Voltaire continue to be valuable for us as explorers of many essential issues; but from Scott to Wells, the questions more closely approach today's questions.

To include Walter Scott in our list of great historians may surprise some; for, although he wrote a life of Napoleon and a history of Scotland for his grandson, Scott was primarily a poet and a novelist who, furthermore, has been criticized for altering the facts of history for the sake of narrative effect. Moreover, the Romantic approach to history—being a source of a certain measure of vivid perception, and giving rise to a particular form of expression which his "Waverley" novels came to typify—has not survived as a comprehensive interpretation of the past. But, if only because the bulk of professional historical scholarship since Scott is an apparent repudiation of his kind of history, he demands our serious consideration; and in one respect his achievement has never been surpassed. History as a rational inquiry begins in the modern era with Voltaire, but history as the story of living people—history in which we for the first time may recognize ourselves—begins with Scott. The Scientific Revolution had made history man-centered, but it remained for Scott to portray the men and women in it as creatures of flesh and blood. Between the works of Gibbon and Macaulay we can see man being redefined, and the whole concept of history with it; and perhaps no figure in our study more than Scott has altered the historical outlook of his contemporaries more quickly and effectively.

Few men of whom we know so much have guarded their privacy so well. "The Great Unknown"—as the anonymous author of *Waverley*, theoretically a mystery to the general public until 1827, was once termed—is still elusive and complex, and today his books are seldom read. But, of the individuals considered in our survey, it is hard to think of another more relevant to everyone; for, in an age of upheaval, when change—political, social, economic, and intellectual—was affecting every branch of life, Scott's historical interest led him to ask how earlier people had reacted to change and survived in times when old loyalties had conflicted with new. He has been called the last minstrel and the first best seller, and Mark Twain once claimed that Scott's picturesque account of the days of chivalry so shaped the Southern character that he was in large measure responsible for the Civil War. But Scott's novels, more than we often appreciate, investigated how men and women in all their variety functioned under historical conditions of strain. His imaginative reconstruction of the past as earlier societies lived through it gave him the answers he wanted.

II

In order to explain Scott's extraordinary hold upon a whole generation's idea of itself and its past—affecting its literature, art, architecture, even its fashion—and upon his own country's sense of its history, we should bear in mind two primary factors. They are the spirit of the Romantic

Scott
Hst
as story
of living
people

era during which he lived and wrote, and the condition of Scotland itself in the late eighteenth century.

To speak in the most general terms, the Romantic movement arose in opposition to Newton's view of the world and Locke's view of the mind. In the years following the publication of Newton's *Principia* the universe came to be regarded as a marvelous machine, whose processes rolled on in regular fashion, repeating themselves again and again; and the machine seemed so perfectly planned and executed that, to Newton's adherents, Nature and Reason became synonymous. Meanwhile, Locke had argued in his *Essay* that the mind was limited to the passive perception of physical objects and had exalted rational thinking as the only way to dependable knowledge. The Enlightenment built its beliefs on these discoveries; but, after 1760, these accepted beliefs were challenged from France by Rousseau, who had formed from his own personal experiences striking new opinions of what was natural in man and the world.

For Rousseau, man was not the clear-headed thinker living in a self-complacent state of order, but a being of sensitivity and passion, who demanded that the world be adjusted to his freeborn needs. In his *Confessions* and in *Émile* (his treatise on education), Rousseau made plain that he found instinctive judgments and honest feelings better guides to living than a set of contemporary abstractions and clichés. Locke's teaching had robbed man of his mind's chief function— to know through the emotions, to create with the imagination. In consequence, as the eighteenth century draws to a close we see the signs appearing which we associate with the Romantic era: an emphasis on the emotions instead of on reason, on diversity instead of on uniformity, on individual men, not Man in general, on the unusual, not the average, on the birth and growth of things rather than on completion, on dejection and sadness as much as, if not more than, on happiness, and on the imponderable as opposed to what can be weighed and measured. The universe, it was said, resembled a poem more than a machine, and, not surprisingly, the Romantics chose to express themselves differently from their predecessors. The age of Voltaire aspired to precision in prose. The age of Scott preferred verse, or prose with the eloquence of poetry.

To a degree the Romantic movement saw its task as adding to gains of the Enlightenment and, except for a few extreme cases, it did not reject reason and science. It sought to correct the impressions they gave by employing the other nonrational faculties of man that the early scientific theorists had practically disowned. Since Nature was good, the Romantics argued, natural man must be good also, and all his parts equally valuable—not just his powers of reason. The crucial event which shaped the new era, however, was the French Revolution; for in that cataclysm, with its immense repercussions in every area of life, and in the waves of hope and gloom which accompanied it, were embodied the fulfillments and the failures of the age. The Revolution joined the dreams of young Romantics to the reforming aims of the *philosophes* and demonstrated in itself the widespread conviction that the times were ready for a change. Its effects were felt all over Europe and beyond, and Napoleon Bonaparte became the supreme contemporary example of the Romantic hero, the uniquely gifted individual carving his own pathway to the summit, absorbed too, it seemed, in the noblest of callings that existed—the reconstitution of government and society.

But, as first the excesses of the Revolution and then the dictatorship of Napoleon proved, the utopian future the progressive thinkers had wanted turned out in fact to be a delusion, and the four great ages of Voltaire or the simplified modern life idealized by Rousseau no longer held the same attractions. Some other model from the past was sought with which a more comfortable identification was possible. The France of Louis XIV could not serve the purpose as the abuses of the *ancien régime* were too strong a memory. The Roman republic suffered now from association with the deeds of revolutionaries, and imperial Rome had been corrupted by Napoleon's efficient copy. Suddenly the Middle Ages, which Voltaire had despised so much, hit the mood of the day exactly. As men looked back from the turmoil of the present, life in the Middle Ages seemed steadier and more fixed—simpler, purer, happier, and more honorable—under the partnership of monarchy and religion. The strongest human feelings, forbidden to modern civilization, had flourished, and the roughness of old literary styles had been well-fitted to put them into words—as the German language now enjoyed a certain vogue over French. The prime setting for history in the imagination ceased to be Athens, Rome, or Philadelphia, and became instead a brooding landscape where great buildings lay, now decayed and open to the sky.

In England the interest in the Middle Ages arose more gradually, out of the search for a new country of fantasy. By the mid-eighteenth century Horace Walpole was leading taste in a new direction, famously erecting—and reerecting—plaster battlements on his remodeled cottage of Strawberry Hill; and, in 1764, Walpole wrote *The Castle of Otranto*, a story of hopeless love amid supernatural scenes of trap doors, bleeding statues, and a gigantic helmet crushing a young knight to death. Like the Gothic novel it initiates, it was medieval in inspiration but non-historical; it was, however, in Scott's own opinion, "the first modern attempt to found a tale of amusing fiction upon the basis of the ancient romances of chivalry." Ballad literature—which had been regarded as uncouth—had already gained a following, and prompted James Macpherson in Scotland to announce his discovery of Gaelic legends, supposedly the work of the third-century bard Ossian. In *Fingal* and other epics, the misty glories of a remote past were summoned forth with an uplifting melancholy, which caused Napoleon to be among Ossian's admirers. Though the poems were mostly fabricated, their instant success—especially in Germany—gives them an importance on their own account, showing how much men of the time could delight in finding a new Homer who, they thought, sang in tones unspoilt by modern sophistication. Here was genuine poetic utterance at last; and it brought cold and barren Scotland with its Highlands and Hebrides to the forefront as a nation of artistic distinction.

As a Romantic writer, Scott reflected and in his own way strongly stimulated the spirit of the age; but Europe was simultaneously paying attention to Scotland for reasons other than those related to Ossian. As Scott observed in 1814 in a postscript to *Waverley*, "there is no European nation which, within the course of half a century or little more, has undergone so complete a change as this kingdom of Scotland." The failure of the Jacobite uprising of 1745, he noted, had led to the destruction of the clan system, and to the total disappearance of the Jacobite party (supporters of the deposed Stuart dynasty) that had prided itself on maintaining ancient Scottish manners and customs; and the influx of wealth and the growth of commerce in the years since had made the present Scottish people "as different from their grandfathers as the existing English are from those of Queen Elizabeth's time." The change, though rapid, had nonetheless been gradual; but those of his readers who could remember as far back as 1780 or 1775 would agree with his conclusion, especially if they had known men and women who still cherished the house of Stuart. "This race has now almost entirely vanished from the land," Scott wrote, "and with it, doubtless, much absurd political prejudice; but also many living examples of singular and disinterested attachment to the principles of loyalty which they received from their fathers, and of old Scottish faith, hospitality, worth, and honor."

Scott was right; Scotland had changed dramatically. In little more than a generation it had moved from being a constantly violent, impoverished backwater, its intellectual life governed by the Presbyterian Church, its economic life stifled by London, to being a peaceful and prosperous country whose capital, Edinburgh, was widely regarded as the modern Athens. Scotland's scholars—such as Adam Smith, the philosopher David Hume, and Hume and William Robertson as historians—were renowned wherever books were read; its new factories were in the lead of the Industrial Revolution; and its prominent men had begun to take over the running of England. There was some truth in Benjamin Franklin's witticism that Jonah was now swallowing the whale; and perhaps the only parallel of a country's emergence from relative isolation to instant importance is that of late nineteenth-century Japan. By the act of union with England in 1707, Scotland had surrendered the independence of its parliament, though keeping its legal and educational systems, its church, and its local government. In return the opportunity to share in English commercial activity was thrown open to it; but it was not until the Jacobites, led by Prince Charles Edward Stuart, were finally defeated at Culloden in 1746 that the long delayed benefits of the union began to be realized. Under Hanoverian rule the industrial activity of the Lowlands began to affect the agrarian Highlands, an area now properly controlled for the first time; and the city of Edinburgh, crowded defensively along a rib of hill from the Palace of Holyrood to the Castle, burst its ancient bounds when, in the 1760s, the New Town started to be built across the ravine. Symbolic of the securer life now possible, more rational and elegant in every respect, its plans demonstrate the belief in the harmony of man and nature; and it soon attracted the notables of the city, who moved from their crowded apartments in the narrow stinking wynds and closes of the Old Town to the order and cleanliness of the New, a place where, as a famous judge recalled long after, you could go to the northwest corner of Charlotte Square in the evening and listen to the ceaseless noise of birds in the fields beyond. The old and the new are still largely separate in Edinburgh, as one immediately sees standing on Princes Street, looking across its gardens to the Castle on its rock, or looking down from the Castle ramparts at the Georgian squares on the other side.

In this new Edinburgh society, the leaders of which saw each other regularly to a remarkable extent, time-honored values were reassessed in conversations carried on in English rather than in the Scottish dialect. New prosperity was creating new ways of living and new loyalties, and, in the process, Scotland was leaving its past behind and fast becoming "North Britain." How could the crumbling Old Town, the broken peasant society of the Highlands which Johnson observed with Boswell, the dirks and Highland dress—the "king" in exile—fail to be seen as anachronisms when the ideal city for the new era was rising before Scotland's eyes? Into this land of sharp transition, and into a larger European world of revolutionary upheaval came Scott, who was considered by his contemporaries to be a genius but by his countrymen to

‹
w
Sc
su(
the
But,
still,
twee(
two o

V
Edinbu
warmer
moved t
contracte
paternal
country, t
society, wl
polished wc
a well-know
until the righ
rebellions of

Other teachers insisted on
ambitious general systems. ... within the unifor
history, the variety of mankind ... and Sc
of an advanced state of civilization; and altered a
Scots law, its fabric patched and ... the wisdo
but still showing, he thought, the ... to mee
he was told, were expedients to ... of soci
and to secure the peace of ... imaginat
ciples. The strong ... compleme
strained and ... on the la
meditation on the ... law
The complement
The effect of
the one hand
ways ahead
he rebe
hood

..., as well
as songs and ... ...uch often celebrated
the deeds of h ...ers were devout and fairly prosperous folk, inc ...and proud of their heritage; and Scott, living
for long periods in that beautiful region whose past was so entwined
with England, absorbed there a mostly oral culture at a time when it
was beginning to pass away.

Left lame for life but now strong and active, Scott began his education at the Edinburgh High School. He explored the colorful Old Town, read every romance of knight errantry he could find, and never lacked listeners for the improvised stories he could tell. Proceeding to the University of Edinburgh to study law, he qualified for admission to the bar in 1792. The French Revolution was concentrating the influence of Scottish scholars within Scotland itself; and, though Scott is usually and properly described as a Romantic, we should remember that the teachers whose lectures he attended were by definition men of the Enlightenment, and that the Scottish bar was receptive to new philosophical currents. The broad view of history he obtained was essentially that of Voltaire—that man progressed by avoiding past mistakes and improving on improvements. But this conviction was qualified when he learned in other classes to be skeptical of rash generalizations and over-

the complexity of
nity, and the dangers
tt became fascinated by
housand times over the ages
n and skill of its founders. Laws,
the specific problems of situations,
ty; they were not a set of natural prin-
ve tendency of Scott's character was re-
ted by his education—and by a lifetime's

this background was to produce a man who was on
a sentimental loyalist, on the other a realist—in certain
of his time. Though Scott followed his father's profession,
ed against Presbyterian narrowness, liked the theater from boy-
, and refused to expurgate the works of famous authors when pre-
aring new editions; but he was a great antiquarian and collector of
relics, and never could forget, as his postscript to *Waverley* acknowledged, that the old Scotland had possessed some noble virtues. In a
letter he wrote shortly before *Waverley* appeared, he commented on a
conflict between the two sides of himself he saw very clearly: "Seriously
I am very glad I did not live in 1745; for though as a lawyer I could
not have pleaded Charles's right, and as a clergyman I could not have
prayed for him, yet as a soldier I would I am sure, against the convictions of my better reason, have fought for him even to the bottom of
the gallows."

Waiting hopefully for briefs in the old Parliament House, Scott
enjoyed the rich variety of character on show each day in the business
of the courts and improved his powers of storytelling among a group
of similar young lawyers; his dreary training in copying documents
would hold him in good stead later. His passion for poetry continued,
however, and he learned foreign languages to read their literatures.
Struck by the vigorous expression of the German *Sturm und Drang*
movement, he translated and published Bürger's *Lenore* and Goethe's
first play; but, while Wordsworth and Coleridge welcomed the French
Revolution and for a time embraced republicanism, Scott drilled with a
company of Edinburgh dragoons to repel an expected French invasion.
He was a conservative to the end of his days, though more flexible and
progressive than has often been said. His appointment as Sheriff of
Selkirkshire in 1799 gave him a permanent link with the Border, where
he increasingly made his home—though he retained a house in the
New Town. Unsuccessful in his first love affair, he married a young
Frenchwoman living in England. He seemed settled as a rising figure

in the legal world (he would be made Clerk of the Court of Session as well) and as a well-known member of Edinburgh's literary life.

It was out of the Border country that Scott's career as a historical writer began. He had collected its ballads since boyhood, although that kind of literature still met with ridicule in some quarters; during vacations, he had ridden through the valleys finding many more, sometimes with friends who shared his enthusiasm. In 1802 he brought together his researches in *The Minstrelsy of the Scottish Border*, which, as his son-in-law and biographer Lockhart said, hinted at all his later work as a poet and novelist; for in it he discovered his gifts as a recorder and expositor of Scottish history and tradition. Scott saw the ballads he had learned first at his grandfather's farm as a direct expression of a society that had vanished or was nearly gone, but which had left behind in its songs the captivating means for its recreation. Publication of them was a tribute to that ancestral past. "By such efforts, feeble as they are," Scott wrote, "I may contribute somewhat to the history of my native country; the peculiar features of whose manners and character are daily melting and dissolving into those of her sister and ally. And, trivial as may appear such an offering, to the *manes* of a kingdom, once proud and independent, I hang it upon her altar with a mixture of feelings, which I shall not attempt to describe."

Scott believed the ballads were far better proof than Macpherson's Ossian—poor stuff, in his opinion—that genius was present in untutored native verse. Burns had already added dignity and life to folksongs, and Scott sought to make the ballads pleasing to modern ears. Several times he admitted to rearranging texts—even inventing a few stanzas of his own when he assumed the originals had been completely lost. In this way he began altering the past, a practice which would remain with him; but that should not detract from his great feats in uncovering and preserving the past in the first place. He saved numerous fine poems from being lost; and for the rest of his life he continued to collect manuscripts and papers energetically, publishing an impressive series that placed Scottish history on a solid documentary basis. The welcome given to the *Minstrelsy* by critical readers justified his editing; and through the ballads he began to reach a wider audience, who, like himself, had no illusions about the turmoil and barbarism of not-so-distant times but were ready to reassess them too.

The *Minstrelsy*'s warm reception persuaded Scott to write poems himself in extended ballad form that would bring the ancient Border past to life more dramatically. He knew that region's martial past, its families and its feuds, in minutest detail; and he had astonishing success with *The Lay of the Last Minstrel, Marmion,* and *The Lady of the Lake,* all imitations of medieval romances. People liked the strongly rhythmic verse and enjoyed Scott's stories about individual men and women living through stirring events. His poetry seemed exhilarating after the formal style ánd abstract themes the eighteenth century had chosen. Crowds began to visit the scenes Scott had depicted, and his patriotism struck a universal chord. "Breathes there the man, with soul so dead, Who never to himself hath said, This is my own, my native land!" he wrote in the *Last Minstrel.* His popularity, however, made him write too quickly, which turned into a habit. With publishers and the public encouraging him on, rather than rewrite something that did not entirely satisfy him, he would send it out to the clattering printing press with the intention of doing better next time. Exploring new territory in *Rokeby,* a tale of the English civil war, he found himself out of his depth and his sales went down. Moreover, Byron's poems like *Childe Harold,* far more passionate and set in more exotic surroundings than the Scottish Border, were beginning to appeal to current taste. It became necessary for Scott to find a new line of writing or lose a triumphant literary reputation.

The difficulty was resolved in a remarkable way by the composition and publication of *Waverley.* The story circulated when the anonymous novel appeared in 1814 was that the author had begun the work several years before and then mislaid it. He had discovered it again accidentally in its unfinished state among other waste papers in an old cabinet, "the drawers of which I was rummaging in order to accommodate a friend with some fishing-tackle." As we shall return to *Waverley* later, it is enough to say here that the three-volume novel launched Scott on a new tide of success, which made him far and away the highest paid author to that date. One best seller on the Scottish past followed another—*Guy Mannering, Rob Roy, Old Mortality, The Heart of Midlothian,* and many others. He ventured further afield in *Ivanhoe* (the England of Richard Coeur de Lion) and *Quentin Durward* (fifteenth-century France); and his fame expanded in England and throughout Europe as the great entertainer of the age.

With the profits from *Waverley* Scott purchased a farm on the river Tweed and sought to realize his dream of founding a landed family on a substantial estate. He remodeled and enlarged the small house into a castle, acquired hundreds of acres in the neighborhood (it was said that to be a rich man all one needed was land adjacent to Scott's property), and named the place Abbotsford, after a nearby spot where the monks of Melrose Abbey had made their crossing. The house was adorned with relics Scott had collected or had been presented as gifts—Rob Roy's gun, the sword of the great Marquis of Montrose, Prince Charles Edward's hunting knives, the keys of Lochleven Castle, found in the water after Mary Queen of Scots had escaped. His desk was made out of wood from a wrecked galleon of the Spanish Armada, and to one side of it stood the hero Wallace's chair.

At Abbotsford Scott could live as the exemplar of the new kind of Scotsman—a successful lawyer and man of business, his house fitted with modern conveniences (such as gas lighting)—but also as a staunch traditionalist surrounded by loyal retainers. As lord of his domain, he extended never-ending hospitality to fellow lawyers and antiquaries, London and Edinburgh society, and notable literary figures. No expense was spared in furnishing Abbotsford, and Scott proceeded on the assumption that it was an unbeatable investment. He had kept his legal career and was by no means incompetent in money matters; but his expenditure was always greater than his income. One last great novel, he believed, would pay off all his liabilities; but the complexity of his affairs necessitated a day-to-day management he had little chance to give, particularly where his books were concerned. In Abbotsford lay the seeds of his tragedy; for, by fulfilling Scott's ambitions, it also led to his downfall.

Believing authors were robbed of most of their rightful earnings by publishers, Scott had entered into a secret partnership with James Ballantyne of Edinburgh, who printed his books; but Scott could never obtain from Ballantyne a clear statement of profit and loss. Why he did not demand such statements is unclear, although Scott was known for his good-natured trust; at any rate, the company needed his novels, and Scott needed the publisher's commitment to be certain of funds for the building and upkeep of Abbotsford. In 1826 the Ballantyne press went bankrupt—a few months after Abbotsford had at last been completed—and the firm was found to have used Scott's name to obtain advances of credit. Although he was not legally bound, Scott considered himself morally obliged to pay off a debt of over one hundred thousand pounds. The story of how he declined all assistance and worked to redeem his interest has become familiar in literary history. The honor of his name and dwelling meant most to him; and the most famous living Scotsman—now a baronet—the rediscoverer of the Scottish crown jewels, drove himself mercilessly to write in the service of his creditors, crying out in his journal, "my poverty but not my will consents." The quality of the novels deteriorated, only *Chronicles of the Canongate* catching the spark of his earlier self. Illness and prolonged stress began to take their toll, and, in 1832, after a journey to Italy in

search of health again, Scott was carried back to Abbotsford to die.
The debt, however, had largely been cleared, and the house remained
in the family.

III

In his life at Abbotsford Scott tried to resolve for himself the tensions
between past and present which were also profoundly affecting the
Scotland of his day. He welcomed the peaceful progress the now solid
connection with England had brought; but he fervently wished Scotland
to remain distinct from its larger neighbor. The same theme of recon-
ciling progress and tradition dominates his greatest novels; and, of all
the twenty-five or so novels he wrote, two in particular, *Waverley* and
Redgauntlet, stand out as being Scott's interpretation of his own country's history, for himself and for his fellow countrymen. Both are tales
about the Jacobite party seeking to restore the exiled Stuarts—indeed,
Rob Roy should be added to make a trilogy; and they demonstrate some
of Scott's finest talents for historical writing. But they are not, of course,
proffered as works of history, restricted to authentic evidence and inquiring why events were caused. They are historical novels; when Scott
wrote *Waverley*, he invented a form of literature which flourishes to
this day.

The historical novel is a representation of life in the past inter-
woven with a fictitious plot. The novel itself in England had sought
first to copy society, and interpret it. The established form in Scott's
time was the novel of manners, in which the author as spectator described the varieties of contemporary human nature and commented
on them as he pleased. The public had also developed a strong appetite
for mystery and the sensational; but, when an author wanted a retrospective setting for his story—as Walpole did for his *Castle of Otranto*—
he chose the plot first and then put it into history. Scott chose the
setting first and then devised the plot; the unfolding of the plot was
attendant upon historical events. He had always found it exciting and
lucrative to exploit the wealth of ready-made stories from the past in
his works of poetry. The form of the historical novel enabled him both
to appeal to the public afresh and to illuminate the past on a scale
impossible for him before. Certainly the public was there, for cheaper
printing and spreading literacy had created a whole new market of
paying readers. In *Waverley* Scott was able to draw together brilliantly
the tastes of the day and to launch history and the novel forward into
a new phase as an enterprise of the imagination.

It may well be asked why, instead of *Waverley*, Scott did not write a conventional type of history of the 1745 rebellion, from the coming of the Young Pretender with only seven followers to the final defeat at Culloden. The answer is that the novel gave him far greater freedom for exploring what he had in mind—the rebellion's effect on different sorts of people rather than on the nation or society in general. Small events were indicative of the whole episode; and, by selecting a few individuals for his story who would take certain stances, he could display his deep knowledge of the actuality more clearly. He did not reach this decision suddenly. He had used the technique in his longer poems; and, at the beginning of *Waverley*, he reflected on his aims as they related to the book's second title. Scott debated and discarded several possibilities before the right one came to mind: "A Tale of Other Days," he believed, would suggest another *Castle of Otranto*; "A Romance from the German," a horror story; "A Sentimental Tale," the adventures of an auburn-haired heroine; "A Tale of the Times," a dashing sketch of the fashionable world. Ultimately he chose "'Tis Sixty Years Since," which he thought would indicate that the story was neither a romance of chivalry nor a tale of modern manners, and would imply that its object was the description of men and women. In this way the force of the narrative would be thrown upon the characters and passions of the actors, "those passions common to men in all stages of society, and which have alike agitated the human heart, whether it throbbed under the steel corslet of the fifteenth century, the brocaded coat of the eighteenth, or the blue frock and white dimity waistcoat of the present day."

By choosing among the subjects of his novels ordinary human beings who happened to live in earlier ages, Scott showed the connection between the past and present to his readers of the same class and tradition. The Gothic writers had deliberately made the past remote; Scott saw the advantage of bringing it close. He enlivened his tales by reproducing the color of uniforms, heraldic devices, landscapes, which played a role in creating an atmosphere. It was important in his opinion to be able to feel what a blood-soaked tournament or a castle dungeon was like. But it was also important to be sure the scenes were not fanciful, and a large measure of Scott's extraordinary reputation as a historical novelist came from his accuracy. His reading public, as heirs to the Enlightenment, rejected false statements on matters of fact; and they were increasingly well-informed about the past and the alien or exotic owing to improved means of travel. The settings and details for any stories had to pass the test of critical examination, and the acknowledged genuineness of Scott's backgrounds proved to be among the novels' greatest strengths.

Without knowing it, Scott, in his early forties, had been preparing for *Waverley* all his life. He knew more of Scottish history than any man before him, was widely read in several literatures, knew something of several careers himself, and was fascinated by every type of human character and occupation. His ability to recapture reality, past and present, in all its aspects and convincingly was far ahead of any competitor's. Perhaps the chief reason for his success, as the English historian G. M. Young has observed, was that he treated every document as the record of a conversation and went on reading until he could in imagination hear the people speaking. As all historical novelists since Scott have found, one must know a great deal about a portion of the past and immerse oneself thoroughly in it over a period of time to be able to "hear" the people who lived in it. Scott acquired this faculty, writing out of a mind abundantly stocked with precise information—one reason why he produced his books so quickly. He was able to convey to his public the feeling that they, too, were within earshot of long-forgotten, sometimes momentous conversations. His men and women put all of themselves into what they say to one another, and bringing effective dialogue into history was perhaps the most revolutionary thing Scott did.

But Scott's ability to reconstruct the original past was limited. Intelligent and well read though he was, when oral tradition played no part in the preparation of his works a vital quality went out of them. From his earliest childhood experiences on his grandparents' farm, he had heard people talking—and afterwards talking in his mind—about events, sometimes dating back as far as the late seventeenth century, with which some thread of association had been preserved; and those tenuous, older Scottish recollections represent a kind of limit to his fictional skills. But further back than that his grip is never firm, and the earlier ages tend to merge into one—as they did with Herodotus, who also came out of a largely oral culture. *Kenilworth*, set in the sixteenth century, seems closer in time to *Ivanhoe*, set in the twelfth, than to the late seventeenth-century Scotland of *Old Mortality*, one of Scott's finest books; and stories set in other lands, like *The Talisman*, a tale of the Crusades, also lack one element of the realism that is never missing from the Scottish novels.

Knowing far more about Scottish life and history than he could actually use in his novels, Scott not surprisingly won fame for describing the recent past of his own country—the history to which his instincts also most attracted him. He specialized in portraying the great social and political crises that swept all before them yet affected people at various levels of life differently, all in intensely personal ways. Every popular historical novelist after him has done the same, whether they have written A *Tale of Two Cities,* *War and Peace, Gone with the Wind,* or *Roots.* They are all followers of Scott with their tales of individuals caught in conflict, and our eyes are always fixed on the character who survives. He is the center of the story, he triumphs in the end; and, because our emotions become so bound up with him, the historical novel wins hands down over every other type of history in holding our attention.

If ever a writer threw himself completely into his work it was Scott with *Waverley,* finishing the last two volumes in the evenings of three summer weeks. The story is about the Jacobite rebellion of 1745, the conflict portrayed as one between the heart and the head. The Jacobites appeal to all the past loyalties of Scotsmen, the Hanoverians to reason and the future. The young Edward Waverley—the name itself suggests a certain ambiguity and unsettled nature in the hero—has been brought up in England by a strongly Tory uncle and tutor, from whom he has learned Jacobite ideals and observed their impotence. Traveling north to Scotland after a commission has been purchased for him in a regiment of dragoons, he leaves his regiment for a short time to pay his respects to his uncle's old friend, the Baron of Bradwardine, whose character and estate display Jacobitism in all its likable eccentricity and decay. Introduced there to Highland tribal life and in particular to the MacIvor clan, he falls in love with Flora MacIvor—Jacobite faith at its purest—whom he first sees singing by a waterfall, to the accompaniment of a harp. He makes the acquaintance, too, of her brother Fergus, a young man of wild courage who has been reared in France, the son of an exiled rebel. Prince Charles Edward meanwhile having landed to regain the throne of his ancestors, Waverley falls under suspicion because of his visit to Bradwardine and is charged by a Scottish magistrate with treason.

Having thus progressed from an intellectual to an emotional attachment to Jacobitism, the young man is soon confined by the Hanoverian authorities for his alleged fondness for the white Stuart cockade—though he claims that he is innocent. The stage is then set for his rescue by the rebels and his presentation to the prince in Edinburgh. There, for love of Flora MacIvor, out of enthusiasm for the loyalty to the Stuarts he found in the Highlands, and through force of circumstances, he enlists in the prince's service and takes part in the Jacobite victory at Prestonpans, where he rescues an English officer, Colonel Talbot. Accompanying the subsequent invasion of England, he loses touch with his own army during its ragged retreat and goes temporarily into hiding. With Talbot's assistance he obtains a pardon at the rebellion's end, witnesses the trial and execution of Fergus MacIvor—an incident his servant regards with indifference—and, after Flora has rejected him and entered a French convent, marries the Baron of Bradwardine's daughter and restores the baron's confiscated estates.

Edward Waverley reconciles himself to the new order by compromising with it; his settling down at the conclusion seems to prefigure the domestic life Scott himself secured at Abbotsford with a failed romance behind him. The turning-point in Waverley's life occurs during his period of hiding as the Highland army straggles back to Scotland. Then, Scott wrote

> . . . most devoutly did he hope, as the rarely occurring post brought news of skirmishes with various successes, that it might never again be his lot to draw his sword in civil conflict. . . . These reveries he was permitted to enjoy, undisturbed by queries or interruption; and it was in many a winter walk by the shores of Ullswater that he acquired a more complete mastery of a spirit tamed by adversity than his former experience had given him; and that he felt himself entitled to say firmly, though perhaps with a sigh, that the romance of his life was ended, and that its real history had now commenced. He was soon called upon to justify his pretensions by reason and philosophy.

Waverley survives by using his common sense; and Scott, for his part, came to recognize that he himself was not only a loyal subject of the Hanoverian kings, but that he was sure England had been fully justified in discarding the Stuarts. With his broad and strong sense of history he saw that far more than a choice between dynasties had been at stake—that in every important respect the conflict had involved future cultural and political development. But could the issue be left satisfactorily at quite such a compromise?

Scott came to the conclusion it could not; for in *Redgauntlet*—a story written around an event that may or may not be a historical fact, an abortive landing by the aging, debauched Prince Charles Edward many years after the 1745 rebellion—the utter folly of the Pretender's cause in the end is underlined. The story unfolds around two young men, Darsie Latimer and Alan Fairford, who, like Edward Waverley, are inexperienced figures drawn into dangerous events. A complex and intellectual novel set in the area of the Solway Firth, that no-man's-land between England and Scotland, *Redgauntlet* paints in the strongest colors the old Scotland and the new as they had diverged since Culloden.

Hugh Redgauntlet, an outlawed Jacobite whose name is assumed (and symbolic), first appears on horseback with his companions in a wild chase, spearing salmon—a sport of an earlier age. His violent character, ready to redress his grievance by force, is contrasted with the personality of the Whig lawyer Saunders Fairford (supposedly drawn from Scott's father), who holds that in the present age the preservation of order is more valuable to society than rising up in arms yet again, and with that of the Quaker Joshua Geddes. Geddes catches his fish by the less cruel and vastly more efficient means of setting nets; and an incident early in the book concerning fishing rights between himself and Redgauntlet illustrates how much the heroic feudal past and the unheroic but peaceful present are opposed.

Living in an anachronistic world of old loyalties and lost causes, striving to keep the dying Jacobite cause alive single-handed, Redgauntlet desperately plans to seize the city of Carlisle with five hundred men and proclaim Charles king; but the older men are dubious, and the younger more ready to seek their fortunes in legal practice than in the old turbulent Scotland resurrected. The end comes suddenly when, as the reluctant plotters assemble, the news is suddenly broken that the prince himself has arrived—but accompanied by his mistress whom he refuses to abandon, although the conspirators consider her untrustworthy.

No sooner has the rebels' figurehead been found tarnished than government troops arrive, the plot having been betrayed; and the novel ends in a memorable scene, perhaps the best conclusion of any of Scott's novels. Wearing a black cockade, General Campbell bows to the prince, and informs the group—including Charles—that they are without exception free to return to their homes quietly if they so choose, and the prince to his wanderings abroad. These are the King's specific instructions.

> "I speak the King's very words, from his very lips," replied the General. 'I will,' said his Majesty, 'deserve the confidence of my subjects by reposing my security in the fidelity of the millions who acknowledge my title—in the good sense and prudence of the few who continue, from the errors of education, to disown it.' His Majesty will not even believe that the most zealous Jacobites who yet remain can nourish a thought of exciting a civil war, which must be fatal to their families and themselves, besides spreading bloodshed and ruin through a peaceful land. He cannot even believe of his kinsman that he would engage brave and generous, though mistaken, men in an attempt which must ruin all who have escaped former calamities; and he is convinced that,

did curiosity or any other motive lead that person to visit this country, he would soon see it was his wisest course to return to the continent; and his Majesty compassionates his situation too much to offer any obstacle to his doing so."

"Is this real?" said Redgauntlet. "Can you mean this? Am I—are all—are any of these gentlemen at liberty, without interruption, to embark in yonder brig, which, I see, is now again approaching the shore?"

"You, sir—all—any of the gentlemen present," said the General—"all whom the vessel can contain, are at liberty to embark uninterrupted by me; but I advise none to go off who have not powerful reasons, unconnected with the present meeting, for this will be remembered against no one."

"Then, gentlemen," said Redgauntlet, clasping his hands together as the words burst from him, "the cause is lost for ever!"

The spirit of Jacobitism could endure martyrdom and defeat, but it could not endure the ignominy of dismissal. This ending Scott gives to *Redgauntlet* is heartbreaking: the vision of a young, handsome prince and the past he represented has faded, and the wish of the new generation is to curb the crime and bloodshed, so that the advantages of peace and prosperity may be enjoyed. Redgauntlet alone accompanies the prince into exile. His companions remain on the shore to make their peace with the Hanoverians at last. The assembly might have been for no more than a cock-fight.

Scott recognized the Jacobite movement had ended not in compromise but in futility. It had become totally incongruous in the Scotland of his day. His desire to seal the reconciliation, however, and bring a king for all Scotsmen back to Scotland was demonstrated at its best in 1822, when, as chairman of the organizing committee for the ceremonies, he did his utmost to make George IV's visit to Edinburgh an outstanding success. The direct Stuart line had died out some years previously; but no Hanoverian had come north of the Border since the "Butcher" Duke of Cumberland had conquered at Culloden, and no crowned king since Charles II. Scenes like that of Prince Charles's entry into Holyrood Palace, described in *Waverley*, filled Scott's head, and resulted in an extravaganza of historical sentiment and tartan color being paraded daily before applauding townsmen (though George IV excited some derision by wearing a kilt). In the public's eye Scott had created the modern Scottish nation, that paradoxical mixture of intense loyalty to the spirit of an ancient past and proved capability for leadership in the modern age, which in slightly bogus form has caused one-half the world to claim itself Scots and the other half to wish it was. Scotland had made peace with its history—at any rate until the mid-twentieth century; but, through Scott's wizardry, it had not lost itself in the process. It had survived with integrity and honor and was beginning its own renaissance.

IV

Whatever the opposition today to including Scott among the historians, there is no doubt that his contemporaries saw him as endowed with a historian's genius. No one had ever told Scotland's story with such skill against such an encyclopaedic background of fact; Scott had also uncovered the life of the Middle Ages, as marvelously, it seemed, as archaeologists had exposed ancient Rome to sight and touch from the ashes of Pompeii. His success caused other scholars and patriots across Europe to look for history in dusty papers and to find it in relics and scenes and songs; and their ambitions grew to write national histories, from national sources, especially if the author's native land—like Scotland—was in danger of disappearing. Scott himself had admired the brilliant pictures of courts and chivalry Froissart had given in his fourteenth-century chronicles, and he tried in his works to create the same sense of direct participation. "I thank God I can write ill enough for the present taste," he said; but the truth was, he brought the past to life as no historian had done before.

He also brought it within reach of large numbers of people who had lacked ready access. Since at that time little history was taught in schools, knowledge of it had to be gained through self-education; and, for most readers, the "Waverley" novels, with their accounts of battles and their royal portrait galleries, offered the most pleasurable and profitable way. Gibbon had been a gentleman writing for other gentlemen, but Scott—a gentleman too—wrote for everybody. Each book sold fast, and Scott's fame as the supreme narrator of history spread among all classes. Thomas Carlyle, a fellow Scotsman and a Romantic historian, identified Scott's special strength.

> These Historical Novels [he declared] have taught all men this truth, which looks like a truism, and yet was as good as unknown to writers of history and others, till so taught: that the bygone ages of the world were actually filled by living men, not by protocols, state-papers, con-

troversies, and abstractions of men. Not abstractions were they, not diagrams and theorems; but men, in buff or other coats and breeches, with color in their cheeks, with passions in their stomach, and the idioms, features and vitalities of very men.

The public also found it a revelation to see history through the eyes of ordinary men and women. During the Enlightenment historians had selected and stressed the few rulers who had helped civilization forward, and, in writing, had made them deliver formal speeches in classical fashion. Scott gave the leading place to common folk who talked freely in the vernacular—often, in Scotland, in a dialect almost unintelligible—and who were frequently more perceptive than their social betters. Shakespeare had similarly given parts in his plays to soldiers and servants, but such persons were often incidental to the main business of the drama. Scott put these sometimes lesser figures at center stage and let the history swirl around them—somewhat as in our day *Hamlet* has been rewritten as a play about Rosencrantz and Guildenstern. The people, he believed, were the enduring elements of history; they were his Border tenants and the members of his household, and he was ultimately more interested in them than in the famous and powerful. His readers found the horizons of the past suddenly broadening for them as they read about people like themselves; and Scott, by writing about the lower classes—the peasants and clansmen—introduced an approach to history which would be taken abstractly by Marx, and in a general sense by Wells.

"The most romantic region of every country," Scott observed, "is that where the mountains unite themselves with the plains or lowlands." It followed that the most picturesque part of history was where ancient customs clashed with new knowledge and thinking. By showing how men and women had lived in such tumultuous periods, he enlarged his readers' perspective on the past still further. It was impossible to read his novels without grasping what political issues actually meant in everyday life. Society for Scott was not a generalized entity but a collection of miscellaneous groups and individuals, who react to events in a diversified manner—an insight which makes him a social historian of enormous consequence. The various people in his stories are caught up in a situation whether they like it or not, and when the crisis comes everyone has to make a choice—to cling to the past, to reject it, or to try to work out some combination—or yet again, just to survive. By expressing past politics as ideas and interests, he made decisions taken long ago resemble those demanded in the present and helped the average person see himself as part of history. He let his large audience discover something of themselves and thus enhance their consciousness, as all historical knowledge is bound to do.

Scott was unmistakably a novelist, and to what extent the historical novel is a form of history is and must remain open to debate. The genuine past was the setting for his tales, but each plot was constructed from his imagination; and, though he had unusual talents for precisely describing the past, Scott would occasionally alter facts if the result would be a better story. He had begun this practice in one form when editing *The Minstrelsy of the Scottish Border*; and professional historians have never ceased to complain that the cast of *Ivanhoe* (which includes Robin Hood and Friar Tuck) could never have been assembled at any one date, that Charles II was never concealed at Woodstock, and that in *Quentin Durward* the Bishop of Beauvais is murdered thirty years too soon. They have also criticized his novels for always presenting a right side against a wrong side, a prejudice the reader's emotional involvement does not allow him to challenge; and, if the Middle Ages still reel from the onslaughts of Voltaire, neither have they recovered from Scott's portrayal of them as the age of knightly deeds and pageantry.

Scott defended his inventions and anachronisms, mostly found outside his Scottish tales. To reach an audience effectively, he argued, it was impossible to stay within the limits of the period of a story; for *Ivanhoe* to be really authentic, its dialogue would have to be in Anglo-Saxon or Norman-French, and the book printed with the type of Caxton. "It is necessary for exciting interest of any kind," he wrote, "that the subject assumed should be, as it were, translated into the manners, as well as the language, of the age we live in." As we are aware, there was little hope for him to verify all the particulars in any case. He wrote against deadlines to meet his soaring expenses, and seldom had a plot fully planned in his mind when he first put pen to paper; of *Woodstock* he casually commented there was one volume to go and he had not the faintest idea of how to resolve the story. Even when writing his nine-volume *Life of Napoleon* he did not change his habits. "What signify dates in a true story?" he asked himself in his journal; and he answered, "better a superficial work which brings well and strikingly together the known and acknowledged facts than a dull boring narrative." The detailed historian certainly gave useful information; but nothing was so tiresome as walking through a beautiful scene with a botanist or a geologist who was forever interrupting you to look at grasses or pebbles. Scott's admirers, though aware of his faults, accepted his excuses, and maintained that the vast new audience his books had won largely made good his shortcomings.

Scott's creation, the historical novel, surely stands between history and poetry according to the distinction Aristotle once made. It aims to present both particular and universal truths—and neither of them exclusively. However, it has lost esteem among twentieth-century readers, because we now like our serious history to be reliable; and we are inclined to believe a novelist's proper field is the life of his time—the life with which we presume he is most familiar. In Scott's case, the dialect in his books is an added impediment. To write a historical novel today is therefore to violate contemporary standards of truth on both sides; but it is often attempted nonetheless (there are still popular historical novelists and also writers of so-called nonfiction novels), and, within its limits, it can produce a truer account than anything strictly factual can be. We can understand the past only just so far with our reason; to complete the picture, to capture the life of the moment, we have to call in our imagination. We can then see beyond the mere written evidence, share in the things most important to the men and women of the time, and reexperience the motives which led people to think, feel, and act as they did. In short, by establishing empathy with the past we make new connections with it, and within it. We learn with the help of feeling—which was, of course, the Romantic movement's essential premise, from which the historical novel sprang. If the element of imagination is well defined, we should accept the resulting work for what it is. Far from distorting the past, an informed historical novel may illuminate it. *Waverley*, for instance, is probably still the best account of what life in the 1745 rebellion was actually like.

The "Waverley" novels also made the past enjoyable for its own sake, as historical novels have done ever since; and their success inspired a host of imitators, as well as a "drum and trumpet" school of history writers who to this day prefer above all the picturesque. Few authors, though, possessed Scott's powers of scholarship and artistry, and by the mid-nineteenth century many of them were mere storytellers, freely imaginative, and much less concerned with accuracy. Scott's language in the interests of atmosphere degenerated in other hands, too—such phrases as "Zounds!" or "Marry forsooth!" becoming ludicrous barriers between past and present, causing readers to wonder if the people speaking could ever have existed. But Thackeray's *Vanity Fair*, and, in America, James Fenimore Cooper's *The Last of the Mohicans* were among the genuine achievements; and Macaulay patterned his popular *Lays of Ancient Rome* on Scott's style of historical verse. Cooper—who called himself nothing more than a chip from Scott's block—really begins the American novel. And it is but a slight exaggeration to say that the European novel as well is practically of Scott's making. Scott extended the range of time and place suitable for fiction, took the lower classes seriously, and made regional peculiarities acceptable, all of which had a bracing effect on literary convention. Manzoni (*The Betrothed*), Pushkin (*The Captain's Daughter*), Alexandre Dumas (*The Three Musketeers*), and Victor Hugo (*Les Misérables* and *Ninety-Three*), are only a few of the famous writers who followed Scott's ideas and methods. Balzac explicitly acknowledged Scott in his more recent and contemporary "history," the *Comédie Humaine*. Indeed, for long it was almost impossible for novelists of any kind to escape Scott's influence—an influence which, in his own country, reappeared strongly in the historical tales of Robert Louis Stevenson.

Responsible historians, not just the creators of historical romances, were touched by Scott's spirit—and they too were able to reap the audience his books had developed. Macaulay read insatiably, and saw England as the story of progress along lines suggested by Voltaire; but, "a truly great historian," he wrote, "would reclaim those materials which the novelist has appropriated," and his *History of England* is full of local color and makes use of ballads and popular literature. Unlike Voltaire and Gibbon, who shut themselves up in their libraries, Macaulay visited the scenes he described to picture the past more intensely; and his famous third chapter is an exercise in social history that also bears Scott's imprint. Another notable historian of the nineteenth century was Jules Michelet, who wrote passionately—and realistically—on the great epic that was France. Michelet was a poor printer's son who, in his words, "had been born like a blade of grass without sun between two cobblestones of Paris." He saw that the common French people had survived the Revolution while the mighty had toppled; and he believed they were the solid France, the enduring France, the men and women who had repeatedly put France to rights—Joan of Arc having once been their splendid representative. Struggling upward, he became an extremely popular teacher and writer. He explored the national archives far more thoroughly than any previous historian had done, but the documents were only part of his research. He heard in the silence there, he said, "the whispers of the souls who had suffered so long ago and who were smothered now in the past," all the soldiers who had fallen in all the wars, beseeching him to tell their story too. Because Michelet's childhood was spent during the Revolution, he claimed he had experienced almost all the anguish of which he wrote; and that, he held, gave him a personal advantage over "scientific" historians. He remained loyal to his social class; and his republican history of the French Revolution emotionally described such incidents as the taking of the Bastille and the march of the women on Versailles. Here were the people, the principal actors in the drama, leading France forward; and, through them, France was leading and emancipating mankind—which was its exalted destiny.

Scott's appeal was broader yet. Composers found his stories promising for operas, children were dressed in Highland costume by their parents, and architects were guided by the spirit of his novels and by the nationalism the novels helped engender; between 1824 and 1828 Windsor Castle itself was completely restored in impressive Gothic style to George IV's commission, to make it a fitting residence for British monarchs. Later, Queen Victoria made a love for Scotland, as Scott had portrayed it, into a royal way of life at Balmoral. Lockhart's study of Scott proved to be one of the best half-dozen biographies in the English language; and Scott's reputation as a gentleman and as a man of honor (in contrast to tales of scandals in the careers of Byron and Shelley) commended his novels even to households with strict morals. He was often compared, usually favorably, with Shakespeare. No two authors had observed mankind so closely, seen it in such variety, and shown each figure in such exclusively human terms; none had excelled more at tragi-comedy, or at the power and language of their dramatic scenes. Even their faults—clumsy plots and writing with haste—were seen to be shared.

Quite obviously, we have in the "Waverley" novels a new conception of history with immense and complex consequences—as we shall increasingly see. Scott's contributions to our understanding of the past are so many and his influence is so vast that we cannot dismiss him as a writer of books for boys, or exclude him from the company of historians because of his inaccuracies or because he wrote fiction. So many other figures who have most stimulated historical thinking—Augustine, Machiavelli, Marx—have not been historians' historians either; but to omit them is to distort and impoverish the history of history badly. By bringing in their external perceptions, they met man's chief demand from the past—that it should serve the present. Scott's audience was enchanted by the romance of his novels and warmed to their human interest, but this response reflected a more substantial approval—an acceptance of this new analysis of history coming from outside the normal terms of discussion, and of the conclusions Scott offered.

The French Revolution and the Napoleonic Wars were the first events directly experienced by the great mass of Europe's inhabitants together. Previous events had been localized, often affecting only certain professional or social groups; but now revolutionary doctrines spread swiftly almost everywhere, everyone shared in war or the threat of war, bayonets passed by the garden hedge, and all of society was swept up in history's movement—sometimes summoned by its rulers as never before to take part in it actively. Living in an age rocked by upheavals and in a country already familiar with rapid transition, Scott wrote his novels as a commentary on the traumatic experience of change. The Enlightenment had given history a direction and a broad scheme of progress; the Romantics had preached that men could inaugurate a new era by breaking the antique bonds that held them back. Scott's distinction was to take the concept of social change that the great eighteenth-century writers had expressed and show what his audience had already discovered for themselves—that in actual life change did not happen that way. Historians and philosophers had talked about change and proposed change; but, as Scott and his generation had discovered, society could in fact change, and change drastically, and everyone responded to it differently. Change, and how it should be obeyed, fascinated the social theorists of the Scottish Enlightenment; change and its outcome filled each morning's newspapers; and, for Scott to write a history, as it were, of change was in the circumstances a natural and a very rational undertaking.

Scott challenged the foundations of the Enlightenment's theory of history—its assumptions of man and society—out of his personal knowledge. To imply that human nature was everywhere the same (as the *philosophes* had done) seemed to him absurd, from his study of characteristic people in both past and present and from his practice as a lawyer. The diversity within mankind was limitless. It was nonsense to think, as some idealists were saying, that all men were rational. They clearly were not, and Scott, with his interest in folklore, liked to illustrate in his novels how fear of the supernatural might determine men's actions. To take some figures from the past more seriously than others was therefore simply not valid; to select some ages of civilization for imitation and reject the rest further showed incomprehension of actual human society. Ideally, human society lived by principles of reason, but no society ever really developed in this way because, as the French Revolution showed so dramatically, human nature was recalcitrant. Each set of human laws was in fact based on expediency, and each form of culture flourished in temporary circumstances. History was now often taught as the story of progress, and Edinburgh itself was visibly a city where scenes of a violent past had been forsaken by many residents for the newly built squares of light and grace; but Scott argued that, when cultures clashed to produce historical change, men on both sides stood forth as being ruled essentially by passion, a truth which ballads also recognized. The only predictable element in history was human nature's permanent variety.

Consequently, Scott saw the past without fixed pattern or scheme; and there is no conviction in his writings that men will progress toward a utopian goal. In *Waverley* and *Redgauntlet,* for example, he welcomed the forsaking of violence for order and peace—drab though that future might be. But this progress was not inevitable; and though the old culture was barbarous, he did not entirely dismiss it. Each society deserved to be judged on its merits in light of its situation. At a time when Voltaire and Rousseau had each decided what was "truly" civilized and what was not, Scott stood independently and saw society in no such simple terms. A Borderer with a feeling for the outward features of the Highland world, a student in a Romantic era educated in a school of rationalism, a lawyer trained to see two sides to a case, he knew prejudice was involved in any appraisal of an alien phenomenon. He took the view, moreover, that one kind of society, or one sort of experience, does not necessarily refute another. Above all, he did not choose to apply a favored theory and make it fit. Each culture contributed something unique to mankind; and each man and woman, principal and insignificant, gave something to a society's composition.

The chief feature of history, Scott found, was not progress but conflict—conflict between opposing groups in society, a conclusion partly shaped by the events of the age in which he lived. He struck the theme in *Waverley,* and used it again and again—conflict between the old Scotland and the new, between Jacobites and Hanoverians, between honor-loving Highland clans and commerce-minded Lowlanders. "Four generations had not sufficed to blend the hostile blood of the Normans and Anglo-Saxons," he wrote in *Ivanhoe,* "or to unite, by common language and mutual interests, two hostile races, one of which still felt the elation of triumph, while the other groaned under all the consequences of defeat"—words which suggested another conflict, that between conquering England and defeated Scotland. Sometimes the differences were almost unbridgeable. The character and appearance of the Highlanders in 1745 surprised the Lowlands "as if an invasion of African Negroes or Esquimaux Indians had issued forth"; and, in *The Heart of Midlothian,* a story about the Porteous riots in Edinburgh in 1736, Jeanie Deans, a girl who walks to London to plead for her sister's life, needs the Duke of Argyll as interpreter for Queen Caroline to understand her. The historical novel from the start is therefore, almost by definition, a political novel. The tensions latent in society come to a head when forces of change surge in from the distance, like the racing tide of the Solway Firth—*Redgauntlet*'s basic motif; and, in the crisis, each individual struggles in his or her particular way. Some Marxists have commented that Scott's view of history supposes a dialectical process. He studies societies in a stage of complex economic dissolution, they say, sees classes set against each other (a thesis and antithesis), and moves them toward a synthesis—a pattern Marx took for his uses from the philosophy of Hegel.

The lesson from history Scott most wanted to teach was that, of the three alternatives of action in a crisis—to cling to the past, reject it, or compromise—the third way was the best. As his own life indicates, the outcome he preferred would be a society more traditional in character than modern—and Scott has been censured by radical opinion for this; but his concern to preserve Scotland from assimilation or extinction dominated his view of history. Once the opposing groups had been reconciled, however, society had advanced. Normans and Saxons had finally united to become English; Jacobite and Hanoverian supporters together had produced prosperity in Scotland; and now Scotsmen and Englishmen were joined in a new era as loyal subjects of George IV. One reason for *Waverley*'s success, surely, is that it appeared in 1814— the year of Napoleon's first defeat—when the public were ready to read about people like themselves who had also survived a prolonged crisis, and who had succeeded in finding the largely conservative solution for society they now also wanted. But, desirable though progress was, the peace of the present was temporary. At some point the tide would surge in again; and, in this repetitive history of change and turmoil, the most striking sight was the human will fighting the power of the current. Scott was more interested in human struggle than class struggle, and, with a fundamental fairness, he judged men by their ability to face new historical pressures, adjust to them, and survive with integrity.

It is often said that in Scott's novels there are no complete heroes, nor villains either; but, if any heroes do exist, they are not his time's customary kings. Scott set aside the enlightened despot and abandoned the Romantic notion that a hero was a man like Napoleon. Great men grew out of the age in which they lived, rather than created the age itself; and many so-called great men were rather mediocre human beings. Genuine heroes were men and women who, in eventful or uneventful careers, performed well in difficult situations. They could be found in any social class, upper or lower, but they were essentially uncommon "common" people. Once they had done their work, they did not go on to conquer the world. They stepped back into their normal lives, like Jeanie Deans when her sister's pardon was granted. They had, however, explored heroism's possibilities in an unheroic age; and they had gained an honored name.

Ultimately, history was about the people who reached the next stage. Because Fergus MacIvor in *Waverley* staked all on an unyielding retrogressive cause, he was doomed—though he would not be forgotten; Edward Waverley, on the other hand, adapted, and found happiness in a society which on the whole was an improvement. So many incidents in Scott's novels are concerned with arrangements for property to pass smoothly from one generation to another, with the wish for continuity in the thick of disorder. Having a will that was up-to-date and precise or a well-drafted land settlement was far better for a man than going to court, with all its risks, or physically overturning the law itself as Redgauntlet tried to do. The route to success, in this lawyer's approach to human affairs, was to build for the future efficiently. There is consequently no great ending in Scott's scheme of history—only personal endings to which we can relate. History does not move forward so much as simply move on—with or without us.

In the late twentieth century, when no single formula seems adequate to explain the historical process, Scott's effort to resolve the changes in the Scotland he knew has plenty to teach. A New Town of the future again opposes an Old Town of the past, challenging us to justify our pretensions by "reason and philosophy." Scott made his analysis by solid, hard-headed thinking; and, when we seek a clear understanding of who we are through what the past still has to offer, his type of history is invaluable. It not only redefines the people in history for us; it becomes a part of our attempt at our own redefinition. Scott's achievement as a historian is manifold, and, because his work demands such a multiperspective approach, he keeps his air of elusiveness. Yet, as was said at the outset, it is hard to name another historian who speaks with more immediacy to us today.

CHAPTER SIX

RANKE

I

Between 1827 and 1831, not long after his appointment to the faculty of the University of Berlin, Leopold Ranke enjoyed the privilege, extraordinary for those days, of subsidized travel to inspect the archives at Vienna, Venice, and Rome. His rigorous, methodical habits of research had already won him recognition, and he worked relentlessly and joyfully, feeling (he wrote) like a new Columbus as he explored the vast collections of decaying papers. Interesting archives, it has been said, meant more to him than all of St. Peter's—indicating some difference, at least, between Ranke and Macaulay. But such intense effort could only be sustained by a powerful inner confidence, and in 1829 he made some unreserved comments on his motivation in a letter to his brother:

> I have been here in Rome for a long time. All summer long, indefatigably I kept it up. There is something invigorating and refreshing in this searching and finding, in the uninterrupted pursuit of a greater universal purpose, although my universe is only a library. . . . You are always on a venture. You hope and strive, and come closer to your aim. You strike an obstacle; you can overcome it only by, shall I say, personal skill or a gift of combination. You find a broader field than you expected. From smaller interests you drift into larger ones. There is also a goal beyond which nobody can be urged. But you find other ways. In the end you must say: I was called to this, for this I was born, for this I exist: in this I find my joys and sorrows; my life and my destiny are included in it.

145

Labor ipse voluptas—"work itself is pleasure"—was the motto Ranke chose for his coat-of-arms when he was ennobled by the Prussian government in 1865; and the dedication he showed as a young man lasted the rest of his very long life. Year after year he maintained a rigid schedule of study and writing, broken only by short daily walks in the Tiergarten to collect his thoughts and occasional visits to foreign archives. Inaugurating with his own publications the nineteenth century's scientific approach to history, and consolidating it by the special training he gave his students in his seminars, he was hailed in 1885 by the American George Bancroft as "the greatest living historian," the scholar who had enabled men to see the past accurately—so they believed—for the first time. It was his success at getting the facts, the truth, of history out of the documents and offering them without dogma that gave him this high reputation among positivists. Indeed, to his many supporters Ranke was much more than a scientific historian: he was the father of historical science.

But today, though Ranke occupies a special place in discussions of the methods and whole intention of historical studies, his spirit is more often invoked than his name, which is little known outside of Germany, except among professional historians. Of all the leading figures in this book, it is fair to assume that he is the least familiar. This is remarkable, because the scientific, professional methods with which he is identified dominate the discipline of history at every Western university—though often in modified form. These characteristic methods may be instantly recognized. The Rankean scholar defines his task as exploring exhaustively the small area of the past in which he is an expert, asking limited questions, and then producing a reliable report for other historians to use, so that there will be no need for the evidence he has summarized to be inspected again. His business is to increase knowledge within the bounds of the scientific method of inquiry. He works on the principle that at the moment we may not know exactly what caused the Renaissance, or the Second World War, but one day we shall; meanwhile, we must try to find out. He never speculates as to any authoritative version of history as a whole; that will eventually take shape from the labor of all true historians together.

Yet Ranke was not the uncomplicated man he is widely considered to be. He founded modern historical professionalism, but—as his letter indicates—he had a vision far larger and more idealistic than objective analysis for its own sake. He himself awaits discovery in the archives, for a full modern biography of him has yet to be written; but what we know reveals a man of dreams as well as of technical abilities, who was guided by an almost mystical sense of vocation.

II

Ranke was born in 1795, in Wiehe, Saxony, in an area famous for its fertile landscape and its associations with medieval emperors and Martin Luther. He grew up in a Germany largely under the control of revolutionary France, where boys copied Napoleon's bulletins as lessons on their slates. His father was a lawyer, but there was a tradition in the family of entering the ministry, and the young Ranke was first expected to move toward that goal. What indications there were that he might become a historian were for a long time incidental. His childhood education included Homer's *Iliad* and *Odyssey,* and he recalled many years later having often played "Greeks and Trojans" as well as having read both books through in the original Greek three times. The Bible, with its history, also became part of his life; but it was without a career clearly in mind that he enrolled at the University of Leipzig in 1814 to study theology and classical philology.

It is essential to grasp how important philology had become as a learned discipline by that time. The classics and the Bible remained the foundation of education and still provided a guide for living; but, especially since the Enlightenment, the authenticity of texts and documents of all kinds had come under closer and closer scrutiny. If the original words of the *Iliad* or the Gospels, for example, could be discerned behind the errors and alterations of copyists, Homer and Jesus would be freed to speak in the pure form their first listeners heard—or conceivably be shown never to have existed. Simultaneously, if texts were established more precisely, many arguments would be made invalid and claims to authority finally settled. German scholars led the way in this effort, and at Leipzig Ranke studied under Gottfried Hermann, who, in a stimulating manner, taught that linguistics was the only road to understanding classical civilization.

As a student Ranke acquired the techniques of philology. He tried to reconcile the Psalms with events in the history of the Jewish kings; but history itself he found tedious, "a mass of undigested notes, indeed of facts not understood." Alone among contemporary historical works, the *Roman History* of Barthold Georg Niebuhr won his respect for completely revising conceptions of ancient Rome by the use of exact critical methods. Niebuhr's volume, Ranke declared long after, convinced him historians could exist in the modern world; and, after he had settled in Berlin, a bust of its author occupied the place of honor in his study. Classics, however, remained his chief subject; he chose to write his dissertation on Thucydides, applying textual criticism to the *History of the Peloponnesian War* and discussing its political teaching.

In 1818, having gained his degree, he became a master at the *Gymnasium* of Frankfurt-on-Oder, a Prussian town east of Berlin, and by taking that position entered the service of the Prussian government.

The seven years Ranke spent at Frankfurt were formative; it was there he developed from a philologist into a historian. But more should be said of other forces that affected him. The Lutheran religion of his childhood home proved an enduring influence. It gave him a deep personal faith in God, which survived exposure to the rationalized Christianity he heard at Leipzig, and this faith gradually transcended Protestantism. IIe came to see the reflection of God in all existence, and this serene belief, by lifting him above sectarian disputes, allowed him to write two of his finest works: the *History of the Popes* and *History of the Reformation in Germany*—topics bristling with antagonisms. As a student he had been stirred by the celebrations marking the tercentenary of Luther's Ninety-five Theses, and Ranke briefly attempted a life of the great reformer, attracted in part by the power of Luther's language—modern German at its source. The Reformation history, which became a national classic when it appeared between 1839 and 1847, saw Luther as a heroic figure, his spiritual struggle and his personality having been decisive in causing the upheaval so fateful for the politics and future character of the Fatherland. Though the book took the larger scene of European affairs within its scope, the religious aspects of the Reformation were its center; and Ranke expressed his convictions vigorously on the rightness of this decision. "History is religion," he wrote, "or at any rate there is the closest connection between them. As there is no human activity of intellectual importance which does not originate in some relation to God and divine things, so there is no nation whose political life is not continually raised and guided by religious ideas."

But, if Luther's example prompted Ranke's patriotism as well as reinforced his religious faith, the events of his youth had an impact almost as profound. The sudden burst of brilliance in the Germany of Kant, Goethe, and Schiller excited his generation, which was further roused to action by Fichte's *Addresses to the German Nation*. The new spirit of nationalism swept the fragmented country and led it to find intellectual justification for its hostility to the French invader in the teachings of Johann Gottfried von Herder. Herder opposed the universalizing philosophy of the French Enlightenment and, not unlike Rousseau, discovered the genius of each people in the early phases of its development. Each people had its distinctive culture, he argued, a culture rooted in its language; and each was slowly evolving along its own path. A nation should therefore not imitate others but be true to itself and grow out of itself. Every people had a unique and valuable contribution to make to the civilization of mankind. This is cultural nationalism. Though aloof from the political nationalism of the student movement, Ranke could not help being touched by the many social and intellectual pressures around him, and they played a part in turning his interest toward modern history. The main current of thought supported the rising German nation and the desire to make its frustrated aspirations into realities. Some of the most conclusive battles of the Wars of Liberation were fought on Saxon soil, and at the Congress of Vienna his native territory was annexed by the victorious Prussia. But Ranke long remained a reluctant Prussian and kept a sympathy for the alternative conception of a federal Germany which would include Austria.

In addition to Lutheranism and nationalism, the Romanticism of the age was clearly an influence molding the future historian, and it later provided Ranke with the intellectual structure which gave form to his studies. The second-generation Romantics, of which he was one, were aware to a disconcerting degree of the extraordinary evanescence of things. Their predecessors had established the importance of inspiration, the flash of insight or chance discovery which brings life and energy to the workings of unaided reason; the need was now felt to pin down experience, to give it permanence so it would not vanish like a momentary vision. In English literature the sonnets Keats wrote on reading Chapman's translation of Homer and seeing the Elgin marbles—and, of course, his *Ode on a Grecian Urn*—show delight in finding beauty preserved and holding the promise of never-ending pleasure. In the Germany of Ranke's youth a speculative, idealistic philosophy developed, which sought to invest knowledge acquired through the senses with intuitions and ideas of an infinite quality. The era of Goethe and Schiller was passing, the new leaders were emerging: Hegel, Schelling, and the von Humboldt brothers, Wilhelm and Alexander. The last named provides an excellent illustration of this new generation's aims; for Alexander von Humboldt became a well-known explorer of South America, a naturalist, who strove to label and classify all he found, so that in the end he would be able to write a long-planned great work entitled *Cosmology*. This project, moving upward from a scientific foundation, would bring all knowledge together in an overarching scheme, grander and more artistic than the simple catalogue of science.

At Frankfurt-on-Oder, Ranke's duties were to lecture on classical languages and literature, conducting sometimes as many as thirty-three exercises weekly. There he discovered that the textbooks habitually used depended almost totally on secondary sources; in reaction, he determined to teach only what he knew from his own study of the originals. His work at Leipzig had prepared him for such an attempt, and as his duties changed and his interests expanded he found himself moving from ancient to postclassical and then to medieval literature, history, and the reading of the medieval chronicles. His command of history thus developed through the critical study of primary sources, and as he grew increasingly familiar with conflicting historical documents he began to apply to them the same techniques he had used on the classics. In this way he came to discern his true calling—to apply to history the skills of textual criticism in which he had been trained and which had led him to make Niebuhr's history of Rome his model.

Since the older a classical text was, the more likely its authenticity, Ranke reasoned that the closer a witness had been to an event, the truer his story would probably be. As he had wished in his lectures to teach from the writings of the Latin and Greek authors themselves, so he now sought to obtain correct information about the past, and, no less than Voltaire, to eradicate the myths. Unsupported or dubious views had no place in historical truth. He would try like Thucydides, from whom he often confessed he had learned more than from any other historian, to be as accurate as his strength and circumstances permitted him. But his decision to change his career seems ultimately to have hinged on his breaking the spell the most popular novelist of the day had cast over him; and, in some fascinating words Ranke dictated when he was in his ninetieth year, he described the experience:

> In the twenties of the nineteenth century the conviction spread that only a deeper study of the foundations of states and empires would satisfy the needs of the future. The romantic historical writings of Walter Scott . . . contributed chiefly to awaken an interest in the actions and attitudes of past ages. I was myself sufficiently attracted by them and I read more than one of these works with lively interest, but I was also offended by them. Among other things I was hurt by the way in which Charles the Bold and Louis XI were treated in *Quentin Durward*, in full contradiction to the historical sources, even in the details. I studied Commines and the contemporary reports . . . and gained the conviction that Charles the Bold and Louis XI, as Scott depicts them, had never existed. The good and learned author probably knew that for himself. But I felt unable to pardon him for adding traits to his treatment which were entirely unhistorical and for presenting them as if he believed them. In comparing the two I gained the conviction that the historical reports themselves were more beauti-

ful and, in any case, more interesting than the romantic fiction. Thereafter, I turned away from it altogether and decided to avoid everything fictitious and fanciful and to cling strictly to the facts.

Deciding to enforce his resolutions further, Ranke began preparing a study of the history of the Renaissance, basing it on the collection in the *Gymnasium* library; and, in 1824, it appeared as the *History of the Latin and Teuton Nations, 1495–1514.* The work itself intended to show the origins of the modern system of nation-states and the interrelated paths which the two great European peoples had followed; for the universal outlook of Herodotus, as well as the painstaking research of Thucydides, had caught his imagination at Frankfurt. Men of action filled the center stage, populations and the conditions of the day being peripheral; and the *History* was moralistic in that Ranke blamed Italy's corruption for subjecting it to the control of foreign powers. But in this, Ranke's first historical production, it was the appendix which especially drew the attention of scholars, and it still deserves attention as the first example of Ranke's critical method. Until he reviewed the sources, the principal authority for that period had been Guicciardini's *History of Italy*; but Ranke now declared that Guicciardini was in many respects thoroughly unreliable, having misrepresented or altered the facts and having drawn heavily on secondary accounts. Discussing Machiavelli and certain other Florentine historians for comparison, Ranke opened the door for a far more professional evaluation of the materials traditionally used in Renaissance studies. Though Guicciardini's reputation has in the end been considerably restored, this rehabilitation in no way lessens the importance of Ranke's initiative.

At the outset Ranke had announced that his *History of the Latin and Teuton Nations* would use "memoirs, diaries, letters, diplomatic reports and original narratives of eyewitnesses; [and] other writings only when they were immediately derived from the former, or seemed equal to them by virtue of their information." The words which subsequently made him famous, however, which have been endlessly repeated, embodied a rule deduced from his manner of research, but they were delivered with unusual thrust and purpose. "History," Ranke wrote, "has been given the task of passing judgment on the past for the benefit of the present and the future. The present attempt does not aim at such a great responsibility. It merely wishes to show the actual past." The phrase "to show the actual past"—*wie es eigentlich gewesen*—still bears the stamp of the philologist; for that discipline sought no more than to perceive behind the intervening distortions and embellishments the text an author had written, the very words he alone had uttered. Translated and quoted in various forms—"to show how things actually were," "to tell how it actually happened," "to show what essentially took place"—it has come in its shades of meaning to epitomize the nineteenth century's scientific investigation of history in all its glory and limitations.

The time was right for such a goal to be proclaimed. Voltaire had tried to view the past objectively, to turn the study of history away from its religious associations into a definitely secular direction; but his crusade against *l'infâme* had tended to make his histories into works of propaganda. During the revolutionary period and afterwards, inevitably, history had been used to promote one social or political dogma after another. In Germany in the 1820s, Hegel was delivering to university students lectures which became his impressive and very influential *Philosophy of History*, a speculative work which saw the march of history as the progress of Freedom—an ideal most nearly realized in the reformed Prussian state. Trying to fill the void caused by the collapse of Christian consensus on the past, rival interpretations flourished and would continue to do so—as we shall see in the writings of Karl Marx, Ranke's younger contemporary.

At the same time a yearning had arisen for a more uniform, systematic impartiality than the early Romantics had offered—for thoroughly factual knowledge. Then the imagination might enjoy free play and practical philosophies and political programs be constructed at will, separate and distinct from the solid basis of truth. In their own way too, national enthusiasts searched for precise evidence of their country's particular development, eager to establish continuity with a self half-remembered, half-vanished. In brief, the scientific spirit began to be a common prerequisite; and, in a Europe dominated by *a priori* systems of history or colorful improvisations, the new generation was disposed to know what the past had actually been. Only with a satisfactory answer to their question could they consider, like Alexander von Humboldt with his botanical and zoological specimens in hand, any broader vision of knowledge or of national self-hood justified. It was Ranke's distinction, by demonstrating the sophistication and success of his techniques, to provide at the appropriate moment an acceptable means to that answer. By rejecting the kind of study which is influenced by present existence and future hopes, by disdaining any other interest than the wish to show the past as it was, he was able to restore links with the traditions of Voltaire at his most impartial and of Thucydides.

The promise of Ranke's first book was clear enough; but when the Prussian minister of education received a copy, what struck him was its freedom from dangerous political opinions. Within a week Ranke was promised a post at Berlin; three months later he was appointed assistant professor at the University. No position could have suited his talents more. The University of Berlin had been founded in 1809, largely through the initiative of Wilhelm von Humboldt, as an instrument for Prussia's revival. It would be a weapon of war as well as a nursery of learning; and to gain its purpose it expressly repudiated all attachment to any particular creed or school of thought and fostered instruction and research at the highest level. Each of its original teachers represented only himself and pursued the path of inquiry or the completed theory which he himself had propounded. With this emphasis on a new standard of excellence, it attracted many of the country's leading minds; and it quickly became one of the outstanding German universities.

At Berlin Ranke's teaching assignments were much lighter than at Frankfurt, and he mixed in a much more stimulating social and academic world. While writing his *History of the Latin and Teuton Nations,* he had been persistent in seeking to borrow books from the Royal Library; and it was jokingly said when he moved that the choice was either to bring Ranke to Berlin or send the Royal Library to Frankfurt. He now had ample time to explore the library more thoroughly, and soon he had made what would be the greatest discovery of his career— forty-seven folios containing the reports of the Venetian ambassadors to their government, commonly known as the "Venetian Relations."

Though Venice had succumbed to the army of Napoleon and was now under Austrian rule, its centuries of wealth, longevity as an independent republic, and extraordinarily clever diplomacy had made it the wonder of Europe. The Venetians had selected highly educated, well-trained men as ambassadors, to pursue a distinct career with its own promotional ladder. The reports these ambassadors sent back to the Senate of Venice were unusually accurate and to the point in their full descriptions of men and events. No scholar had used them before; Ranke immediately recognized the Venetian Relations as an unequalled account of the political history of Venice and Europe over several centuries, as close a record of what actually happened as one would ever be likely to obtain, written by onlookers who were also cultivated men of proved capability. Abandoning the idea of a continuation of his first book, he hurriedly wrote *The Ottoman and Spanish Empires in the Sixteenth and Seventeenth Centuries,* announcing the existence of the Venetian Relations, parts of which he believed were scattered in several European locales. The Prussian government saw possible gain for its own diplomacy in these important sources, and Ranke was commissioned to travel to Vienna and Italy to look for further records. "I am headed for the Venetian Archives," he wrote in August 1827; "here rests a still unknown history of Europe."

In Vienna he made more discoveries; and, becoming interested in the stirrings of Balkan peoples for independence, he took time to write a short *History of the Revolution in Serbia*. It was a case study of a nation reawakening, an account of the recent attempt by the Serbs to throw off the Turkish oppressor. A Serbian friend, the recreator of the Serbo-Croat language, helped him with materials; and Ranke, who had laid Scott's novels aside, included a chapter on the native ballads and stories his friend had told him. These were not fiction but the roots of a unique culture, the historian's key to the forces defining a people's character. Arriving in Venice, he was permitted on Metternich's recommendation to enter the archives and immediately tackled them, applying his skill to the hoard of documents and revising many long-standing assumptions about the Republic's past. He worked just as strenuously in Rome, where—though barred as a Protestant from the Vatican Library—he was more than satisfied with the quantity of information he found in the private collections of Roman families. Italy worked its enchantment even on this single-minded scholar; and Ranke returned to Berlin a fuller man as well as a more accomplished professor, certain now of his superiority in the field of political and diplomatic history.

His ambitions too had expanded during his travels. He would not now write, as he had planned, a history of Venice or of Europe in the period covered by the Venetian Relations. He would make his first work into a prelude to something far larger—a history of the growth of modern Europe. He would treat each leading state in turn. As Ranke saw it, Europe was still basically the Latin and German world. Within that world, and in the broader European context beyond, international politics was governed by the interplay and balance of the great powers. Yet the process was not wholly arbitrary. Each state acted according to its character, which had received its modern definition at a decisive stage of its development between the sixteenth and the eighteenth centuries. If that episode were isolated, Ranke reasoned, and the experience analyzed thoroughly and impersonally, then all the subsequent actions of that state could be explained—and projected—with greater certainty. The central cause would be known, and if he put these causes together, the forces operating the modern power system would for the first time be accurately understood. It was a task Ranke was confident he had the knowledge and training, and the incentive, to carry through particularly well.

The first product of this master plan was his *History of the Popes*, published between 1834 and 1836. The Protestant Reformation stood at the origin of modern Europe, dividing Europe into two camps and freeing the kings to build their nation-states unchecked. Since the Papacy was now in the sunset of its authority, Ranke believed a dispassionate evaluation of its former activities was at last possible. "What is there in the present day," he asked, "which can render the history of the papal power of importance to us? Not its relation to ourselves, for it no longer exercises any essential influence nor creates in us any apprehension." Its sole interest lay in the spectacle it offered of a great historical phenomenon and in the record of its role as one of the chief competing European powers. Looking at that record as if from a great height, Ranke searched for its inner structure. This would constitute the true form of papal history. By sympathetic understanding, Ranke was able to find in the documents a pattern to events and establish his conclusions in a work of magisterial excellence.

After writing with enthusiasm of the medieval popes who had welded the peoples of Europe into a Christian civilization, Ranke described how the popes of the Renaissance had become Italian princes; and he used his knowledge of Italian sources very effectively to reveal the opportunism of these men in their diplomacy, and to explain their management of papal government and finance. Faced with a Church preoccupied with wealth and political success and grown corrupt, Luther and Calvin had wished to construct it anew. But this new impulse to cleanse the Church from worldliness was not confined to Protestantism; and the heart of the book—strange for a Lutheran—was the Counter-Reformation, of which Ranke was the first authoritative interpreter. The Catholic Church too had felt the need of change and regeneration; and, in a recovery of its vigor and zeal, Paul III had summoned the Council of Trent to reform its doctrine and abuses, new religious orders had been founded—notably the Jesuits—and the Protestant advance in southern Germany had been turned back. A fresh decline had set in during the eighteenth century; but whatever power the Papacy retained was exercised in the spirit of its sixteenth-century decision to recreate its religious life and restore its universal domination. All the policies it had since pursued fell into place around this central motive, now clearly exposed to view. Men of action and great personalities had shaped the course of events—hence the title *History of the Popes*. Perhaps the most memorable portrait was that of Sixtus V, who in five years reorganized the government of the papal states, remade the curia, and beautified the city of Rome. Throughout the story the reader was led by demonstration from the evidence to perceive one proof after another; and Ranke also presented the results of his scholarship with a maturity of judgment and an artistic sense which made this the most celebrated of his productions.

The rest of Ranke's life may be told briefly. Elevated to a full professorship at Berlin, he gave himself wholly to his chosen goal, not marrying until comparatively late, and only discharging routine business when he held from time to time administrative posts at the University. Protestant criticism that his *History of the Popes* was too favorable to the Catholic Church was one reason for his writing his *History of the Reformation in Germany,* which profited from his researches in Italy but drew substantially on the reports of proceedings in the Imperial Diet and on a mass of correspondence of the Emperor Charles V he found in Brussels. A subsequent work, *Memoirs of the House of Brandenburg and History of Prussia during the Seventeenth and Eighteenth Centuries,* was less popular. Its preparation was as thorough as usual, and the project was aided by Ranke's appointment in 1841 as official historiographer of the Prussian state; but his ambivalent attitude to his adopted homeland could not be concealed. His emphasis on the efficient administration of Frederick William I overshadowed the heroic wars against the Hapsburgs of Austria waged by that king's more famous son, Frederick the Great, and did not satisfy current Prussian sentiments.

With his studies of the Papacy and the German powers behind him, Ranke turned to France and England, concentrating as before on the decisive stage in their recent past. Everywhere the archives were thrown open to him, and in Paris he was amazed at what previous scholars had neglected. Out of his labors came *The Civil Wars and Monarchy in France in the Sixteenth and Seventeenth Centuries,* in which he traced the French monarchy's evolution to the death of Louis XIV and identified its theme as the drive for strong, absolute government—a necessity both to restrain internal disorder and meet the threat of Hapsburg domination. More unremitting than Voltaire in his concern to find out the truth about the past, Ranke was acclaimed by French historians for setting his subject on its authentic foundations. The obvious success of his methods now prompted them to investigate state papers more fully, instead of leaving the task to foreigners.

In London, with an introduction from the king of Prussia, Ranke was welcomed by Prince Albert as a scholar widely known already.

Researching more extensively than perhaps for any of his other works, he sifted through collections in London, Dublin, and in private hands, and ultimately published his *History of England, Principally in the Seventeenth Century*. He had concluded that the French character was aggressive and excitable, the English orderly and deeply conservative; and the thrust of England's modern history was its struggle to maintain the liberties of Parliament first won in the Middle Ages. In contrast to Macaulay, Ranke was ill at ease with Parliament's victory since he disliked the similar aim currently pursued by German liberals; but, whereas Macaulay saw England mostly from within, Ranke recognized that, like France and Germany, it was a part of the European system. This was one of the book's great merits; it established with abundant new materials that the Glorious Revolution had a European character and argued that the change of rulers could not be properly understood without that larger reference—which was Macaulay's opinion also. England's history illuminated the history of its neighbors and vice versa, just as the Counter-Reformation threw light on Protestantism. In the end, all accurate analysis of the forces governing the states of Europe rested on unassailable facts, arduously pursued and strictly represented. In his manner of writing on both France and England Ranke fulfilled his own prediction: "I see a time coming when we shall build modern history no longer on the accounts even of contemporary historians, except where they possessed original knowledge, much less on derivative writers, but on the relations of eyewitnesses and the original documents."

Retiring from Berlin University in 1865 and reconciled to Prussian leadership in Germany by Bismarck's premiership, Ranke worked further on German and French history, including a study of the wars of the French Revolution. In 1880 he announced his intention of crowning his labors with a history of the world. Like Alexander von Humboldt's *Cosmology* this would be the climax to a life of dedication, an ending indeed that may always have been in view; for, while preparing his *History of the Popes*, he had said, "No history can be written but universal history. I am enchanted by the loftiness and logic of the development and, if I may say so, by the ways of God." Aged, infirm, and nearly blind, he went to work at a tremendous pace with the help of two secretaries, drawing on his decades of scholarship, making use of notes going back to his schooldays, and surveying the historical process from an Olympian summit. In the tradition of Herder nearly a century before Ranke held that finally the separate histories of nations join in the theme of the history of mankind; but Ranke's outlook was exclusively Western, and his aim was really to show the heritage of modern

European civilization. The first two volumes on the Greeks and Romans were out of touch with recent research, but beginning with the Middle Ages Ranke started treading ground he had practically made his own. The great project had reached the twelfth century when he died in 1886, but from the notes students had taken in his lectures it was completed down to 1453. Unintentionally, the career which had started at the Frankfurt *Gymnasium* with a study of the Renaissance had come nearly full circle.

III

If in 1900 a man had taken up reading history again after leaving it fifty years before, he would have found little to remind him of the subject he had once known. Its leading cast and its geography would be much the same, but he would immediately notice that its content had drastically altered; much of what he had thought was true had been discredited. Old landmarks like the Renaissance and the Reformation would seem more complex than he remembered and overgrown with politics; most of the historical novels he had once enjoyed would be condescendingly dismissed. Scholars had ceased on the whole to be gentlemen of independent means or retired men of action. They had become professionals who taught and wrote for a living; and the reader would see that they were far more numerous and that the practice of history was now centered at universities rather than in private libraries. These scholars worked with texts brought close to perfection, with manuals and bibliographies at hand to guide them; indeed, a college student in America or Australia could learn quickly and reliably from the latest book what a European specialist had spent years to establish. But perhaps the foremost impression of historiography would be of a subject still in transition, moving faster in some fields than in others, changing as each fresh discovery in the archives, each excavation, and each new auxiliary discipline made old knowledge suddenly obsolete.

This reflective man of 1900 might ask himself to what extent all these developments had led to better history being written; but he could hardly avoid crediting historians with a deluge of detailed, verified information. A new discipline had been constructed piece by piece, no longer Romantic, no longer what Carlyle called "the distillation of rumor"; and it was well on the way to being, it seemed, as precise and steadfast a body of data as chemistry or physics. The belief that, by rational analysis, the past might be reduced to an exact record of human phenomena was not of course new. Herodotus had conducted his inquiries with a purpose similar to that of Hippocrates in medicine; and

Voltaire had been fired by the same idea, though a large part of his intent was simply to rid history of religion. But with Ranke the effort to make history into a science had advanced immeasurably, and before long the "scientific" history he inaugurated was being called the third great historiographical revolution, equal in magnitude to those of Herodotus and Augustine.

The success of Ranke's attempts "to show the actual past"—words, incidentally, very similar to those in which Thucydides had announced his intentions—challenged other historians to copy his method, and they accepted his standards of accuracy and detachment with few qualifications. History was now to be drawn solely from original documents, critically examined and authenticated. The historian, in the late nineteenth century's view, was supposed to work like the scientist, who assembles his materials, performs his experiments, and publishes his results. The scientist's conceptualization of the word "fact" was imposed on the facts of history—with high expectations. If treated like a science, history would respond like a science; when all the evidence had been systematically examined, the facts would speak for themselves. There would no longer be any need for history to be rewritten. The most fleeting exposure to historical studies today will show that Ranke's aims and standards (though not his expectations) have ruled nearly all professional historians ever since; and, apart from such fundamental influences as Christianity or the idea of progress, his principles of research have given the modern West its most characteristic notion of what history is.

The secret of Ranke's influence is to be found not so much in his books, or in his lectures (which were poorly delivered), as in his seminars at Berlin, where he taught his better students. Training them as future professional historians, his manner was formal. Often papers were presented, and it was considered a special honor when Ranke himself assumed the criticizing of a paper. In 1837 his students started to publish a series of monographs, the *Annals of the German Empire under the House of Saxony*—with which a Ranke school of historiography may be said to have begun. His method of instruction spread further and was copied in other countries, sometimes to an extreme. Introducing it to America at Johns Hopkins University in 1880, the historian Herbert Baxter Adams designed and redesigned the "perfect" seminar room. Ranke's method was also enduring, as this description of classes in medieval history given by Theodor E. Mommsen at Cornell University in the 1950s illustrates. Mommsen (grandson of another Mommsen, the great historian of classical civilization) did not study under Ranke himself, but he closely followed Ranke's style of making the seminar a workshop for research, a technique he had learned in Germany:

> From term to term he chose a few documents—an early history, a biography, some letters—and led his students through a microscopic examination of them. They searched step by step, discussing here perhaps the phrases by which a pope described his authority or a king alluded to his powers, perhaps there a seemingly innocent word which suggested a new turn of thought in the relations of church and state. Together Mommsen and his students put before one another at these seminars the fruits of the studies each had made in preparation for the discussion, and in this exchange of knowledge and opinions they worked until, to use his phrase, they had "squeezed the sources dry." While the labor continued there was no time for rest. So intense was the concentration that all felt the effects, not least Mommsen. He had prepared as assiduously as his students; he had guided and stimulated the conversation from idea to idea and called into play the whole range of his knowledge. The end of the week's seminar—the weekly crucifixion, as one of his students called it—left all exhausted. Mommsen repaired the ravages of the afternoon by leading the group, or most of it, away to dinner at the Faculty Club. . . .

Ranke's new outlook on history, popular for several reasons, was moreover promoted in many European countries by deliberate official plan. Governments saw history as a valuable instrument for integrating society. Enthusiasm for a shared national history would bind the classes together, promote unity, and deflect revolutions. Professional research, it was hoped, would justify the claims and the policies of the centralized administration. Accordingly, chairs of history were founded at universities, now the capstone of the modern educational system meant to serve the state. Such an important subject could no longer be left to men of general experience or literary talent. To obtain the right results particular skills were required, the product of a rigorous apprenticeship. As positions were being created, Ranke's students, and their students in turn, supplied that need, emphasizing in their teaching the traditions of specialized source examination which they themselves had inherited. Their style of research and publication made them just what contemporary opinion expected perfect historians to be; and the doctorate of philosophy, a German degree widely adopted in the United States in the 1880s, began to be the historian's indispensable badge of competence.

On the heels of professionalism and specialization came bureaucracy, as national and regional historical societies assumed new functions. Projects were organized by committees and editorial boards, often at government initiative, and standards were debated and refined at conferences and in the book reviews of learned periodicals. In much of Europe and in the United States—to a lesser extent in Britain, where the older, more literary practice of history still continued to have many defenders—if a historian wished to be taken seriously it was desirable for him to be a frequent contributor, from a solid academic position, to the right scholarly journals, to publish less for posterity than for his contemporaries and successors in the field, who were chiefly his own countrymen. The social utility of history has always been recognized; but in France or Germany official sponsorship now caused a historian's performance to be judged by how much his work served the active national interest as well as by what he had added to the store of incontestible knowledge.

Beyond academic circles Ranke enjoyed an even grander prestige. By establishing history on a secure footing, he reinforced the nineteenth century's tendency to make all its inquiries into man and his world start with "the historical background." Ranke was seen as a figure of cultural eminence, the servant of mankind; his ninetieth birthday was a national holiday. But, though the long-term consequences of his influential scholarship demand an appraisal, Ranke's own words need to be read in their setting no less than the words of a classical text. It is not enough to parrot his famous phrase, *wie es eigentlich gewesen,* and ignore all else of note that he said, or to see him only as the forefather of today's monographer. Like all great historians he was his own man, and he defined his individual position in relation to his experiences and the world he knew. As hinted at earlier, this figure hailed as the exemplary scientific historian saw history as akin to religion and planned his life's work according to an essentially aesthetic design. The student who wrote on Thucydides was also the boy who read Homer and, before that, the child who learned prayers in a Lutheran household. He would soon be the young teacher who abandoned Scott but who never quite forgot him. In the scholar all these elements combined. Ranke on deeper scrutiny becomes more interesting than many of his superficial defenders or detractors have allowed.

To appreciate Ranke adequately we must be aware that he did not see his work as beginning and ending with the factual recreation of the past. He placed a larger purpose before him. In the footsteps of Wilhelm von Humboldt, the great educationalist and founder of the University of Berlin, Ranke conceived the historian's task to be the discovery of the leading ideas on which men based their actions—a task he undertook himself in his separate studies of the major European states. The mistake of both Hegel and the French *philosophes* had been to assume too readily the importance and intrinsic nature of certain ideas, and to explore history downward from them; their philosophy had confused and inflamed historical analysis. The better way, of which Niebuhr had been such a splendid pioneer, was to examine the records more thoroughly, to test and make certain the validity of these foundations of history. As history became "true," discussion would rise to a new realism, providing a clearer guide to ultimate values for individuals and peoples than before. The larger goal was therefore not eliminated; rather one could begin to move toward it with greater certainty.

Trained as a philologist, Ranke found himself unexpectedly well equipped to work with this scheme when he decided his vocation was to be a historian. The ideas that most attracted him, like other German intellectuals, dealt with religion and politics; and the clash of these two groups of ideas, he believed, had invariably marked each country at the crucial stage. For Ranke it was religion which provided by far the greater theme. The content of his books was actually very largely political, and scholars in the Ranke line came to look on politics as the stuff of which real history is made, the political being particularly amenable to the scientific method and clearly relevant to contemporary European affairs. But however great the curiosity Ranke felt about the state and about the balance of great powers within a European system, he saw behind all historical phenomena the movement of the divine spirit. The famous phrase *wie es eigentlich gewesen* should not be lifted out of context; for the preface to the *History of the Latin and Teuton Nations* confidently concluded with a different aspiration: "The main thing is always what we deal with . . . humanity as it is, comprehensible or inexplicable, the life of the individual, of generations, of nations, and at times the hand of God above them."

For Ranke the conviction that history displayed "the hand of God" complemented his aim "to show the actual past," both together being necessary to show us his celebrated objectivity in its proper context. The first quality of a true historian, he said, was to have "a feeling for and a joy in the particular in and by itself." But that was not all. "It is necessary that the historian keep his eyes open for the general," and, ultimately, observe "the spirit that manifests itself in the world." Every event and every human existence was touched by this infinite spirit; if its presence were not acknowledged, the particular lost most of its capacity for larger meaning. Behind the visible ideas which governed the acts of men and of nations lay an eternal idea; within the causal nexus an inner nexus lay concealed, the absolute explanation of historical change; but what these final truths of history, the Creator's thoughts and purposes, were could only be conjectured from a distance. "I consider it impossible to solve this problem entirely," Ranke wrote. "We can accomplish something only through exact research, through step-by-step understanding, and through the study of documents."

Ranke's creed concurred with his Lutheran upbringing as well as with Romantic philosophy. In another famous phrase, from his *History of the World*, he said he wished he could, as it were, extinguish himself from the history he was writing—words that have been taken repeatedly to indicate an ideal of scientific detachment. But this desire for self-effacement was not meant to let the facts speak unhindered for themselves; it was to allow God to be seen more clearly through them. In short, the philologist's love of the fully authenticated document was accompanied by exalted religious emotions. For Ranke, a historian at his noblest was someone who uncovered God's tracks in the human record; and he should not in his duties interpose his own personality between God and man. Earlier scientists had believed that examining nature more closely would lead to a clearer revelation of God's handiwork, and Ranke explored the Venetian Relations and other original sources in the same spirit. His sense of high calling sustained him in his ascetic daily life.

As Ranke's attempt to discover the facts of history was inspired by religious motives, so too was his evaluation of history as the story of progress. In a series of lectures delivered in 1854 to Maximilian II of Bavaria—who had tried to persuade him to take a position at Munich —he rejected current schemes of steady universal development and Hegel's doctrine which saw freedom driving forward through a series of phases. The first left men without a will of their own; in the second case, "men would have to be God or nothing at all." "I accept progress in material matters," Ranke told the king, "because here one thing proceeds from the other. It is different in moral affairs." Adapting words which had defined the equal relationship of states within the Holy Roman Empire to the emperor, he declared, "every epoch is immediate to God, and its worth is not at all based on what derives from it but rests in its own existence, in its own self." No period was better or worse than another—for all were equidistant from eternity. Consequently, each segment of time demanded to be reviewed by the historian regardless of what happened before or after, and not as a link in a chain. Thus each society should be investigated for what it alone produced. This statement held significance for the future, for it embodied the new scholar's attitude toward the past as opposed to the sweeping systematizer's and gave rise to the outlook known as "his-

toricism," that is, the study of the past as consisting of the identification and analysis of separate phenomena. Again, the method is akin to
a scientist's, but the language in which it is formulated is hardly
scientific.

Individuals made history, Ranke believed, but its movement was
guided by God. Wherever he looked beneath the surface of events he
detected the divine spirit. Particulars gained their importance in its
light; by the meaning of its signs all the past came together in the
most perfect pattern. The discovery of America he called "a gift of
God"; Cesare Borgia's devastation of Italy was "the judgment of God";
the history of the popes, he wrote, encourages us to scrutinize anxiously
"the plans of God in his government of the world"; and the mysterious
balance among the powers of Europe could only by interpreted as
God's intention. The critical techniques Ranke had developed to attain
the strictest accuracy were therefore tools to be laid on God's altar; and
perhaps at no time did he communicate better his abiding sense of
purpose than when he was beginning, as early as 1820, to think seriously about history. "God dwells, lives, is recognized in all history,"
he wrote to his brother. "Every act testifies of him, every moment
preaches his name, but most of all, it seems to me, the context of
history. Good cheer then. No matter how it goes, let us try to reveal
for our part the sacred hieroglyphics. In that too we serve God, in
that too we are priests, in that too teachers."

Ranke's dream of course was not unique; visionary historians like
Augustine had said as much before. The novelty of his conception of
history lay in his theory of God's immanence proceeding from a body
of acceptable fact. He never fully reconciled the two aspects of his
thoughts, the rational and the religious, in a great enterprise—not even in
the *History of the World*. And he recognized that such an effort would
be premature; there were archives yet unopened, hoards of documents
waiting to be read. For a traditionalist of the Ranke school there is as
yet no "final" history, only attempts which have a claim to be histories,
and no meaning in history except the meanings found so far. For Ranke
the professional investigation of the past had just begun, and the indispensable unit for study was the nation, its life fixed in laws and
institutions. But here again his thought rose upward, from the individual who can fulfill himself only in the nation, to the nation itself,
and then to mankind as a whole—like the unfolding themes of the
Greek poet Pindar, whose odes to victors in the Olympic Games had
delighted Ranke at Leipzig when the modern Greek struggle for independence was catching the imagination of European youth.

Indeed, the Olympic Games, revived in 1896, give a vivid idea of

Ranke's view of history in action. The nations march into the arena, each asserting a heritage stretching behind it and a future true to its soul. The athletes parade their identity, wearing distinguishing uniforms, carrying their national flags; and national anthems are played and dances performed. Old nations make their expected reentry, new nations join the procession, some speaking languages still lacking a vocabulary of modern government, but each supposedly having passed a crucial stage in its growth: all have become states, all are sure on this day at least of their individual character. They present themselves to the crowd as distinct entities, and are recognized for what they are. The sight is inspiring, for according to Olympic ideals this is a festival of human unity, not diversity; all men are temporarily brothers, all compete for the glory of sport as well as for their country's honor, a manifestation of indomitable optimism. Ranke's history has this same quality which ascends from the local to the sublime. When his writings are seen in relation to their era and their author's true character, they no longer appear to be dry scientific reports but as much a statement of German Romanticism of the 1820s as Beethoven's setting of Schiller's *Ode to Joy* in his Ninth Symphony—a rhapsody, embracing millions at its climax and confirming the existence of a universal spirit.

IV

Whatever a deeper acquaintance with Ranke through his letters and sayings shows him to have been, he is today invariably treated as the founder of the modern discipline of history. No man has been more clearly responsible for laying down the rules by which historians now pursue their craft, the standards by which they evaluate one another. To several generations his method of source criticism has been imperative for obtaining a final and truly correct knowledge of the past. The techniques of academic research have been refined, but basically they follow the procedures Ranke developed. At the same time, the hopes of the school he started lie largely in ruins. If we look around, it is obvious that after 150 years of effort to build the edifice of scientific history, dogmatic partisan histories flourish as never before. Ranke's outlook, though still widely honored, has itself become part of history and carries with it the aura of a world that is gone. The debate about its strength and weakness keeps its originator alive in memory, not as a leader, but as a controversial figure.

Although Ranke was hailed at the end of his career as "the greatest living historian," even from the publication of his earliest studies there had been a reaction against his works. A persistent criticism was that even a limited amount of drama was missing—a lack made worse by Ranke's rule not to relate what was already well known. Every figure and event was smoothed, every angle sanded down, every pronouncement made moderate and bland: "mutton well-cooked and plenty of carrots," was the poet Heine's remark. In an increasingly nationalistic Germany his outlook was considered too cosmopolitan; his impartiality implied a deficiency of passion and moral judgment—both of which, many feel, great histories require. The Prussian historian Droysen scoffed at the objectivity of the "eunuch." Doubt was even thrown on how thoroughly Ranke had investigated the evidence. In 1861, after having gone critically through the *History of the Popes* and his French history, a Czech scholar wrote:

> The shallowness of his studies in the latter is astonishing. Not only is he lacking in a complete knowledge of the printed literature, but he even resorts to deception, wishing to make his readers believe that he has worked through the archives. . . . His citations are mere crumbs stuck together in a chance fashion to produce the appearance of being the results of systematic study.

The root of the problem was in the nature of the man. With his serene religious faith Ranke believed not even the most exalted of mortals could fundamentally change the world's eternal destinies; hence he looked on politics past and present with aloofness. He was a conservative who (it would seem) was not fully aware until 1848 that he lived in an age of revolutions; and at that juncture his advice to Frederick William IV was to stand firm against the monarchy's liberalization. Prussia had achieved greatness by its kings and its army; and when he edited the conservative *Historico-Political Review* from 1831 to 1836—his sole excursion into active political life—he urged that each state should progress from the foundations of its past, instead of importing ideas from France, England, or the United States. Most of the time he watched the current scene with unfeigned calm and, in his last years, believed that his trust had been justified by the apparent victory of traditional forces in Europe. In the twentieth century Ranke's critics possess fresh ammunition, and none of his characteristics are now more likely to provoke attack or disbelief than his "scientific" method and his lukewarm morality.

As Ranke himself said, his objectivity was a reaction against the historians of his youth. They had sat in judgment on the past so as to serve present and future interests; in varying degrees they had pressed history into a mold of their own design. Voltaire had done this more and more as time went on; Hegel had done it from the beginning. Ranke wished instead "to show the actual past" for a purpose greater than giving facts for the sake of facts, a purpose welcomed by his contemporaries as a return to essentials. His new method was in many ways negative. It distrusted the Romantic imagination, it rejected systems, it emphasized institutions rather than people, it was eager to dissociate history from literature, and it professed not to moralize. For the responsible historian, it argued, the words "rise," "decline," and "fall," "success," and "failure" had only a limited value and were better avoided. Above all, the "science" of history was determined to get rid of philosophy. To compensate, it offered the chance of absolute certainty—which far outweighed all that was thrown away. If sources were correctly analyzed, history could be written scientifically once and for all.

Since Ranke's time, however, "total objectivity" has led to results he did not, perhaps could not, foresee. To begin with, the larger religious and spiritual vision by which he guided his own research was abandoned by professional historians, who, more sure of their skills, came to see the archives—or history itself—as the repository of supreme truth. Statements of particulars were substituted for a generality and the large view, and practitioners of historicism fragmented historical studies into meaningless portions, maintaining that it was impossible to reduce human activity to general laws. There have been great gains from their contention, but after 150 years of monographs and doctoral theses piling up, the suspicion grows that the facts will never be complete or ultimately speak for themselves. If so, perhaps something is wrong with the idea of history derived from Ranke but lacking his scope.

When a historian has a preconceived notion of history's direction, he is tempted to make his facts fit that idea. Ranke to his credit diverted attention from history's meaning and end until such time as the gaps in solid evidence had been filled. But provisional, piecemeal conclusions are hard to live with indefinitely; and one historian after another has felt compelled to try to recapture the missing half of Ranke's vision in some form which satisfied—either because studies seem to support the conclusion or out of sheer impatience. In Germany, nationalism established itself as the new faith, and more recent movements in the West have included full-scale explanations from Marxism, from the Freudians, from racist ideologies, from anthropology, from animal behavior—and from the return to religious faith in God's guidance, as shown in Toynbee. The methods of scientific history, moreover, can no longer elicit trust when the reasoning behind them is no longer held to produce entirely sufficient answers. In a less self-confident time than the nineteenth century a history that is more than the offspring of philology is desired, one that spreads open the past and present, dares to predict the future, lives vividly in the mind of the historian, speaks to the new condition of humanity, and responds to pressing contemporary questions—a history, indeed, much like the kind Ranke rejected. In a state of affairs in which a decisive change is imminent, there is no further opportunity for painstaking research, still more documentation, and eventually the long calm gaze; and it is then that Western man's thoughts on history generally revert to visionary conceptions—which shed light from quarters Ranke-inspired scholars choose to ignore.

My intention is not to judge among the rival schemes of history and select a winner. The inquiry of the historian in his specific historical setting remains the focus of my interest. It does seem, however, that the scientific and the visionary outlooks on the past—the one Greek, the other chiefly Jewish in origin—should each be regarded as helpful. Rational investigation corrects the exuberance of nebulous, often dogmatic insights; but a vision spurs and enlarges the rational enterprise. It brings vitality to the whole pursuit; without it the study of history would be tediously repetitious. Rational analysis remains Western historiography's prime distinction, and research into, for example, what caused the Renaissance should continue because that represents sanity; but that research should be redefined—perhaps radically—in light of new experiences, because that is sanity too.

Ranke's method incompletely followed has therefore led to an incredible increase in information about the past, and to the present state of historical knowledge rent by rival schools. Meanwhile history's foundations as a scientific discipline become less certain. We understand now that the facts of history are not the same as the facts of science; the historian can never be like the chemist, because he does not deal with chemicals he takes down from the shelf. The events the chemist describes occur whenever the experiment is repeated. The events the historian ˜studies have not been duplicated in the same manner, or with the same results, over the course of human affairs. If he could examine all events the historian could still only offer a set of hypothetical conclusions, since, from known experience, the next event may well disprove them. His "science" would bear little relation to reality, for most circumstances of each event would be dismissed as distracting the survey. In the end the belief that history can be made completely factual, error-free, and predictable, has turned out to be as idealized—and subjective—an approach to the past as the systems it sought to replace. It is a relic of the nineteenth century, when science itself was a wide-ranging ideology.

By making the "scientific method" synonymous with the critical examination of documents, Ranke was adopting an oversimplified theory of knowledge. He believed that if the impartial scholar immersed himself long enough in the evidence, the past would speak to him and patterns would emerge of their own accord—an essentially intuitive process. The twentieth-century historian is much more aware of complexity in interpreting phenomena and of his own relationship to his materials. He assumes his independence, and he approaches the sources with questions rather than expects answers to spring forth without previous questions. He knows the evidence in front of him embodies biases for which he must allow. The Venetian Relations do take us further in our understanding of the European past, but what they record is still only those events which happened to impress the Venetian ambassadors. Those astute gentlemen had their idiosyncrasies and blind spots, too—like the historian reading what they wrote. He has learned also what Ranke painfully discovered when the *Historico-Political Review* failed—that a presentation of the facts as they are does not guarantee their acceptance. The audience has its own opinions of what is important, and knows today from experience that historical "truth" is changeable.

To call history a science today would imply that it can claim an accuracy it does not possess; and to rely upon written evidence as much as Ranke did restricts the historian's possible modes of investigation. He needs all the resources he can assemble, all the methods he can use; and he can be hampered as well as helped by the data in front of him. Much of what he requires is missing because it has been destroyed; and of the data that remain much is suspect because it has survived by accident—which means it may be unrepresentative. Of course the historian needs to master the information he has; but the best he can do is to arrange what is available carefully, making his best estimate of the unknown quantities. Indeed, the nature and accuracy of these estimates represent one important index of a historian's skills. No longer can we say with the confidence of the trigger-happy nineteenth-century naturalist, "What's hit's history—what's missed's mystery." The working center of historical studies probably lies now in the no-man's-land in between—which makes the historian's life far more difficult than in those days when tasks and goals were more clearly defined and seemed capable of accomplishment.

Ranke's own works were not free from the stamp of personality, and, in the *History of the Popes,* he conceded that an Italian or a

Catholic historian would treat the sources in another style; but, compared to some of the more popular writers of his day, who assigned every leading figure in the world's history to heaven or hell, or elaborated the idea of progress into fantastic cosmic designs, his occasional judgments are notable for their restraint—and are all the more effective. But his decision at the start of his career to establish the facts first and then proceed to interpretation has exposed him to criticism of a graver sort; for he, and ten times more strongly his German successors, have been charged with being indifferent to higher values and showing a deplorable absence of humanity. There are occasions when withholding judgment is not enough—or may be too much.

Ranke's reluctance to commit himself in the *History of the Popes* produced a conflict between German Catholic and Protestant historians which lasted for years. When, as a conservative monarchist, he had to adjudicate between Charles I and Cromwell, he was accused of being "too fair." Perhaps no one has marshaled the case against him better than Lord Acton, an unusually cosmopolitan Englishman in close touch with the German historical movement. Much concerned with the problem of moral judgments in history, Acton disliked the strong verdicts delivered by Macaulay and Michelet; but, as his manuscript notes reveal, he was appalled that in the *History of the Popes* Ranke does not condemn the Inquisition, and that in the *History of England* he proves William III's responsibility for the Massacre of Glencoe but balks at pronouncing him guilty. Acton remarks at one point, "Ranke would say: As to religion, politics, philosophy, literature, people differ. If we wait until all differences are reconciled, we shall wait for ever. If we try to reconcile them ourselves, we shall never get to work at our real business. There are things on which men can be made to agree; that is the domain, not of thought, but of fact." This attitude was to Acton inexcusable. No cause, he agreed, was too odious to be fairly stated; but he held that people as well as their acts should be condemned and that, without falling into cheap morality, a man should be measured by the worst he had committed. "You cannot judge without the low-water mark," he jotted down to himself. In his inaugural lecture at Cambridge in 1895, Acton paid tribute to Ranke's influence, which he himself had felt: "We meet him at every step, and he has done more for us than any other man." But he could not refrain from calling the modern study of history Ranke had initiated "colorless," as well as critical and innovative. In an essay on German historians, Acton commented that Ranke "speaks of transactions and occurrences when it would be safe to speak of turpitude and crime."

There is a great deal in Ranke to justify these remarks. In his

French history he refused to commit himself on Louis XIV's revocation of the Edict of Nantes and considered it would be "a painful business" to explore the Huguenot persecutions in detail. Again, when he told of Frederick the Great's seizure of Silesia in 1740 from Maria Theresa of Austria—a crime in the eyes of all (including Prussia) who had sworn to protect her territories—he merely said "fortunately it is not the historian's task to pronounce upon the justice of the King's claims." To suppose a modern example, instead of assigning any responsibility for starting the Second World War, Ranke might choose only to report in a precise fashion what took place in the years and months preceding Hitler's invasion of Poland. In general, events which others would describe so as to make temperatures rise Ranke handles with kid gloves. To Acton, whose great plan—never started—was to write a history of liberty that would repudiate civil and religious absolutism and uphold the rights of conscience, the proper guideline was "if, in our uncertainty, we must often err, it may be sometimes better to risk excess in rigor than in indulgence."

In Ranke's defense, it must be said that what some may see as an evasion of one of the historian's duties was to him a positive requirement. If everything in history displays the hand of God, it would be presumptuous, to say the least, for a mortal to apportion blame and reward. That was reserved to God alone. Discussing Machiavelli, he argued that historical personages could hardly be judged, if only because the historian could never hope to understand their true nature or their inner feelings; he accordingly showed the author of *The Prince* as a product of his time, not as an immoralist. In another of his well-known phrases, Ranke once said that the historian could only lift the veil on a mystery; he implied that to explore further would amount to sacrilege. He may all his life have attempted "to show the actual past," but, like Augustine, he saw both good and evil as parts of God's plan and the ultimate triumph of God as assured. There was also in him an unwillingness, probably encouraged by his Lutheran religion, to question the acts of authority.

To look at history with such reverence today is likely to seem irresponsible. Abstaining from hasty judgments remains an excellent quality in a historian; but the ultimate effect of Ranke's outlook upon the practice of history in Germany was disastrous. With his faith in the unity of life in God he saw the state as an end in itself, an idea of God meant to fulfill its innate tendencies—not as an instrument for its population's welfare. The interests of the state and of the individuals in it were fundamentally the same; and the state's chief task was to adopt foreign policies which would make the state strong and independent so that this divinely appointed growth could go forward. The state therefore could not sin if it followed its own higher interests; it became the institutional embodiment of morality and its victories a vindication of its moral principles. Many German scholars after Ranke —particularly the "Prussian school"—took this position. Their view of history was not formed by Ranke alone, nor was it unanimous, but it changed little from that of the post-Napoleonic era—a view which idealized the state, judged the state by the achievement of its interests, and whose thinking was curiously inbred. A similar nationalist attitude of mind existed in other countries; but its most notorious expression occurred in Nazi Germany where this view led many scholars to define their duty as serving the state and their profession, not asking or trying to answer larger questions.

It finally took the force of arms—the conquest of the Fatherland by foreign soldiers—to change profoundly the German understanding of the historian's social responsibility. In 1945 the state had undeniably shown itself to be capable of error; and the self-assumptions of the orthodox academic view of history were thoroughly debased. The doyen of German historians, Friedrich Meinecke, called on his countrymen to rediscover the humanitarian values of Goethe and to see past societies as civilizations as Burckhardt, the nineteenth-century Renaissance historian, did; and many scholars conducting a searching reappraisal of German history have since rejected Ranke's emphasis on politics, individuals, and the state. Questioning the pervasive Rankean doctrine that the only way to understand the past is to become absorbed in the individual character of the subject-matter, they have also borrowed theories and methods from the social sciences; and they have generally approached the past with greater skepticism. Not just in Germany, but in every country, there has been an attempt to define afresh the nature of the historian's function, for twentieth-century experience has led to the demand that historians do more than busy themselves interminably in the archives at decisive moments, deciphering the sacred hieroglyphics. Taking risks for themselves as well as their reputations, they should stand up with the rest of humanity and be counted.

In view of the common acknowledgment of German intellectual distinction in the nineteenth century, the post-war German debate is important, not only wherever German methods of research have had their influence, but to any discussion of history's aims and purposes; and, as Ranke's conception of history is revised, he comes to be seen as he was and not for what his followers have made him out to be. He remains today frequently the central figure on which historiographical argument turns; but when he is set in the context of his times it becomes obvious that the world to which his ideals relate has vanished. The nineteenth century in Europe was hardly peaceful, but many features of social, political, and intellectual life persistently took on characteristics of order and permanence among the middle and upper classes. To believe that history, an inquiry indelibly marked by personal conviction, could be made secure for all time demands unusual self-assurance. Ranke possessed an inner serenity of his own, but his objective, fact-centered approach to history was the product of his age; and it was embraced by his contemporaries partly because, standing where they did, they too considered a scientific history to be within their grasp.

Ranke's political outlook was formed in the years following Napoleon's defeat, when the great powers of Europe shared the management of Europe among themselves; and, in spite of the recent revolutions, it became possible to regard European history very much in political and diplomatic terms as an endless series of bloody adjustments to maintain the European system. To Ranke there was little reason to believe the community of nations he knew—established at the beginning of the modern era—would not last in much the same way forever. Today the theater of politics is much more the world, and the twentieth century has seen the decline of Europe and the movement of power into the hands of other leaders, none of whom are wholly European. In an interdependent global society it is hard to believe any more that nations have separate destinies; and national histories in the old style are really no longer viable because a nation's causal nexus no longer determines its future to the same degree. Though the number of nation-states has multiplied, some motives for studying the nation therefore no longer exist. It has, moreover, become very difficult to think of history so exclusively as the study of politics, difficult too sometimes to see it at all as a discipline in its own right.

If Ranke's design of a unified series of national histories now seems archaic, so does his crowning effort as he conceived it—his *History of the World* portraying the steady accretion of the Western cultural heritage. There is more to world history than the history of Western civilization writ large, and it is not easy either to share the impression of such close continuity. For Ranke, however, whether the topic was universal history, European history, or German history, the theme of the past was growth and renewal according to the inner principles of the unit concerned; and he finally accepted Bismarck's Prussia because it seemed to be fulfilling its greater destiny out of its own resources when it founded the German Empire. As history demonstrated continuity in politics, so did it also in religion, and he could not bring himself to imagine a world in which Christianity would not play a vital part. No doubt this was one reason why he preferred the study of the Middle Ages to that of any other era and was reluctant to write the history of his own times, with their disturbing challenge to the religion he knew.

Clearly Ranke's starting point for the investigation of history is not our own; and he should be evaluated as much by our distance from him as by what he moved away from in his scholarship. He was of course fortunate to have his chances when he did. As Acton wrote in 1867 of Ranke's use of the Venetian Relations, "it was a new vein, and a little produce went a great way. . . . Thirty years ago, the use of a few unconnected reports, or a few casual instructions, implied a miracle of research." Acton surely underestimates Ranke's persistence in mining that vein, which Ranke's letters reveal and fifty-four volumes of collected works display; but there is some justice in his observation, "I always hold up Ranke as in many ways a model student." "The dust of archives blots out ideas," Acton also wrote, "no great man had as few as Ranke." Here again is a measure of our separation from him; for, in the ideological conflicts of today, contemporary man has come to expect his history to be interpreted in light of ideas or themes, often forcefully expressed, which involve him in a creative process. He finds something lacking when they are omitted—although, compared to Ranke's time, the meaning of history no longer seems so available for discovery.

Ranke, then, is on many counts a discredited figure, charged variously with shallowness, mysticism, impossible ideals of objectivity, an inability to judge where judgment is due, lack of color, lack of subtlety, and with being the father of specialists and the promoter of nationalism. Paradoxically, although these allegations may not be entirely deserved and are often exaggerated, there are few historians whose profiles are so evident in their works as his. He wished, he said, to extinguish himself from the history he was writing; but once we have become accustomed to his personality, and especially after we comprehend what he was trying to do, he appears indelibly present, both as an individual and as a product of the European mind at an important stage in its development. Looking beyond him few forms of history are so identifiable as the scientific. Yet, for all the criticism, something of inestimable value remains. When one recalls that Ranke was followed as professor at Berlin by Heinrich von Treitschke, the demagogic apostle of Prussian and German destiny, as the Dutch historian Pieter Geyl wrote, "suddenly you feel in Ranke's mind a breadth, a balance, a humanity, a distinction, and you realize what a precious gift was this self-restraint, this striving to understand and to enter into the past and its own sphere, different as it might be."

In such circumstances, to suspend judgment, to probe ceaselessly before committing oneself to any conclusion, to keep to the facts in so far as they are obtainable, even to risk meaninglessness, become positive qualities, not defects, and Ranke's understatement of his overall vision seems prudent and advantageous. When history is constantly thrust on us today in the form of so many competing ideologies, his open-mindedness, his striving for detachment, and his universal outlook seem frequently more desirable than ever, a priceless ingredient of Western historiography, indeed of Western civilization. It has never been more necessary to be strict in the examination of evidence; and the question "what actually happened?" remains as relevant now as it was in Ranke's day.

CHAPTER SEVEN

MARX

I

The problem whether continuity or change is more typical of history is familiar to everyone, and it has stimulated many of the most notable studies and new conceptions of the past. The two conditions of being cannot of course be entirely separated; for there is general agreement that no continuous situation can be altogether exempt from change, and that not even radical changes break completely with what they supersede. To Ranke, a conservative monarchist, continuity was the dominant theme of the European past, for history was progressive in the sense of a heritage accumulating. It could be observed from his study window, as Berlin grew from the capital of Prussia to be the center of the German Empire. But his younger contemporary Karl Heinrich Marx, who also viewed history in progressive terms, saw instead that the great constant in human affairs was change. No development was more plain or more important to grasp, none was more vital to understand properly; and "the locomotive of history" was revolution.

To Ranke the ultimate cause of historical events was the hand of God. To Marx that belief was rubbish. He rejected interpretations by way of any abstract ideas and announced that history's movement was determined by methods of production, generating new social and political relationships in a world of material reality. "The history of all hitherto existing society is the history of class struggles," was the programmatic opening of the *Manifesto of the Communist Party* which he wrote with Friedrich Engels in 1848. In turning from Ranke to Marx, we leave (but not absolutely) Romantic idealism and the conviction that history has a purpose. We enter the bustling, expanding, stock-jobbing, slum-spawning world of mid-nineteenth-century capitalism, a world where the "invisible hand" described by Adam Smith was thought to promote the common good by unleashing the enlightened self-interests of the businessman as he pursued profit. It was a world whose mechanism Marx sought to explain, and whose life as an organism he disowned.

Standing by Marx's grave his friend Engels prophesied, "His name will endure through the ages, and so also will his work!" Today the Marxist version of history is probably the most influential historical theory there is, in spite of countless attacks upon it. Engels exaggerated when he said Marx "died beloved, revered and mourned by millions of revolutionary fellow-workers—from the mines of Siberia to California, in all parts of Europe and America"; but now in China, the Soviet Union, and Eastern Europe nearly one-half of the world's population officially subscribes to his teaching, and he enjoys the prestige of being inviolable to criticism. As a militant political force, Marxist socialism has shaped twentieth-century history by inspiring the Russian, Chinese, Cuban, and Vietnamese revolutions, and it continues to affect events in Asia, Africa, and Latin America. A new group of heroes—men like Che Guevara and Frantz Fanon—have taken the place of the old, as exemplars of the New Man who is the only real hero. Marx, moreover, freed from his Soviet or Chinese context, lives a vigorous life in the West, where many scholars of integrity consider the liberal traditions of capitalist society inadequate or falsely based. They find that, among the wide variety of political doctrines, Marxism poses and answers best their most compelling queries. Indeed, so potent has Marxist theory proved to be, that one might say the overwhelming challenge confronting those historians who do not see the whole sum of human experience contained in a particular kind of economic process is to provide a respectable alternative explanation of it.

It is, however, a distortion to speak of a Marxist version of history as if it existed by itself. All views of history reach for the large issues because of the range and latent significance of human activities; but, if we take Marx's works together, we see in them an attempt at a complete system of knowledge, interlocking and displaying immense erudition, though also incoherent and hard to interpret in both its terms and its conclusions. Standing on the shoulders of the classical economists, Marx believed he had discovered a science of human society in which politics, economics, philosophy, literature—everything, including history—was related to the social structure from which it sprang. The several kinds of Marxism which have evolved offer their sectarian refinements; but the unfinished edifice on the grand scale remains Marx's creation. Like all philosophies it sets out to encompass all of human experience; like Christianity its dogma claims to be self-sufficient, and it simultaneously points to a new order. As in the case of Augustine we must necessarily confine ourselves here to Marx's conception of history—usually called historical materialism, or economic determinism; but we find, as we did with Augustine before, that it cannot really be detached from the rest of the design. Since it lies at the core of Marx's thought, as he admitted, it touches every area of his research and therefore demands to be examined in light of the whole. Marx's fixed intention to put an end to the idea that history could be studied seriously in comparative isolation is one major reason for his appeal.

Only the most devout of Marx's followers can still believe the confident deductions of *Das Kapital—Capital*, as we shall call it—are eternally flawless; but only the most ignorant or embittered anti-Marxist would deny that our understanding of the social origins of human thinking, of the effects of wealth on society, of the changes wrought by new forms of technology, and of human alienation in a world of productivity has been extended—if it was not prompted—by Marx's critical investigation. It is not desirable to shut off Marxist thought with a wall of silence or contempt; its essential mode of inquiry has frequently proved itself fruitful. It also becomes provincial to do so, for it is no longer possible to conduct our lives without reference to that part of the world where his theory is final. To be fair, Marx has taken his place as one historical thinker among the others who shape our current outlook; and, like the rest, he is a figure with particular strengths but not a few weaknesses, a man who broke new ground, but like all men who was limited by his era and his very preoccupations. The result of his labors was extravagantly set forth by Engels in the funeral oration:

> Just as Darwin discovered the law of development of organic nature, so Marx discovered the law of development of human history: the simple fact, hitherto concealed by an overgrowth of ideology, that mankind must first of all eat, drink, have shelter and clothing, before it can pursue politics, science, art, religion, etc. . . .

The essential question Marx put to the past, both academic and practical, was epitomized in the title of a pamphlet his revolutionary descendant Lenin wrote in 1903: "*What Is To Be Done?*"

II

Compared with Ranke, whom I felt obliged to introduce, Marx's name is among the world's best known. His full-bearded face gazes down from gigantic posters at May Day rallies and is reproduced endlessly in books and magazines. The *Communist Manifesto*, barely noticed when it first appeared, is now, like the Christian Gospels, available in nearly all countries at a minimal price—and for the same reasons: its publishers want its message heard by everybody. And yet there is a need to tell who Marx was and what his writings say, for he is an author whose works people usually think they have read whether they have or not. Like the other figures we have met, he is a man with several reputations; and he is still so controversial, so hypnotic a living force, that dispassionate evaluation is most difficult. To Engels—the first of his many interpreters—he was a scientist and, above all, a revolutionary; and to the ruling classes for over a century Marx has personified the specter of communism, which, in the *Manifesto*, he and Engels declared was haunting Europe. To some of a new generation in the West, however, he has recently become guide, philosopher, and friend, the humanist who tried to free mankind from economic exploitation; to their skeptical opponents his thought is a shambles, and they see his followers as barely able to hide this from themselves. Marx himself has become a prime subject for historical analysis.

Participating once in the popular Victorian parlor game of "Confessions," Marx wrote down an account of his character:

Your favorite virtue	Simplicity
Your favorite virtue in man	Strength
Your favorite virtue in woman	Weakness
Your chief characteristic	Singleness of purpose
Your idea of happiness	To fight
Your idea of misery	Submission
The vice you excuse most	Gullibility
The vice you detest most	Servility
Your aversion	Martin Tupper [a Victorian popular writer]
Favorite occupation	Book-worming
Favorite poet	Shakespeare, Aeschylus, Goethe
Favorite prose-writer	Diderot
Favorite hero	Spartacus, Kepler
Favorite heroine	Gretchen [in Goethe's *Faust*]
Favorite flower	Daphne [flowering laurel]
Favorite color	Red

Favorite name	Laura, Jenny [two of his daughters; Jenny was also his wife's name]
Favorite dish	Fish
Favorite maxim	*Nihil humani a me alienum puto* ['I consider that nothing human is alien to me.']
Favorite motto	*De omnibus dubitandum* ['You must have doubts about everything.']

The man who embodied himself in this sketch was born at Trier in the German Rhineland in 1818. Both his parents were Jewish, and both in time chose to become Protestant, his father having been baptized shortly before his son's birth in order to continue his profession as a lawyer. No part of Germany had been more affected by the French Revolution's news and institutionalization of liberty, equality, and fraternity, and the Napoleonic laws had removed many restrictions from Jews in that heavily Catholic area. But on Napoleon's defeat Trier and its large neighboring territories were ceded to Prussia, whose reactionary policies particularly affected the middle classes—those who had welcomed the spread of new ideas and the loosening of old controls. Jews were now only allowed to hold civil positions by royal dispensation.

To what extent Marx was molded by his Jewish background is hard to say. He looked upon his family tradition with a mixture of love and hate, and the difficulties inherent in being a Christianized Jew may have given a special urgency to his concept of alienation. They cannot fail to have caused him to observe society more acutely. It has been maintained that the intricacy of argument in his voluminous system can best be explained by his forebears on both sides having been rabbis, in Trier and elsewhere. More likely, the chief influence on his early years was his father, who, like some Jews of his generation, had absorbed the thinking of Voltaire and Rousseau and strongly believed in the power of human reason to understand and improve the world. What stood in the way of achieving that goal was ignorance, or the suppression of truth by authority.

If Marx's journey to Marxism began at home, it was helped by his liberal education and by his experience of growing up in a society eager to complete what the French Revolution had left unfinished. While a law student, first at Bonn, then Berlin, he wrote romantic poetry; but he found himself increasingly drawn to philosophy, which, at Berlin, was then dominated by the towering system of Georg Wilhelm Friedrich Hegel. Breaking painfully with Romantic idealism, Marx was converted to Hegelian rationalism—an intellectual step that was probably the most important he ever took. However much Marx came to criticize

Hegel for being speculative and subjective, the method of thought and argument he learned remained with him.

We have encountered Hegel before when speaking of Scott and Ranke, and we shall meet him again; but now is the time to describe him more fully, for Marx cannot be understood without some knowledge of Hegel's great scheme. No philosopher has influenced the general study of history more profoundly than Hegel, or, in several opposing ways, the course of history itself. Born in 1770, he studied theology and held a variety of teaching positions, ending his career as professor at Berlin from 1818 until his death in 1831. He first presented his system in his *Phenomenology of the Spirit*, and, briefly, it rests on the belief in an absolute mind in which all our human minds are comprised and which all mankind's culture—its religion, art, and philosophy— expresses. History is not just a record of dates and events, it is the unfolding of this world spirit in men's lives; and, since the divine Idea —the ultimate law—of the world was Reason, the events of history embody a developmental form of Reason.

That development is the emergence of freedom, each period of history reflecting a new level at which this quality of Spirit has been realized in mankind. "World history," Hegel said in his lectures, "is the progress of the consciousness of freedom." In the ancient Orient the ruler alone was free, in classical antiquity some were free, but in the modern Germanic nations—the highest stage thus far—recognition has dawned that all men are free. This progress has been achieved by the struggle of contradictories. A state of tension, Hegel argued, continually exists between any present state of affairs and its opposite; and out of this fight of thesis and antithesis a synthesis emerges gradually, this forward motion being termed "dialectic"—a debating term for the means of arriving at a higher conclusion. The process occurs endlessly. At each stage a great man with intuitive access to the reality of the Idea appears, a man able to define the will of society and accomplish it. Unknowingly, while pursuing worldly ambitions, he works in the service of Ultimate Reason, bringing together in himself the needs of the time and of the individual, and he pushes mankind forward one more step. Caesar, Hegel commented, "had to do what was necessary" when he overthrew the Roman republic; Alexander and Luther were men of this kind too, and Hegel had seen such a great man in action. In a letter of 1806, sent from Jena on the day of Napoleon's occupation, he wrote, "The Emperor—this world soul—I saw riding through the city to a review of his troops; it is indeed a wonderful feeling to see such an individual who, here concentrated in a single point, sitting on a horse, reaches out over the world and dominates it."

Such a philosophy had many attractions. Never before, Engels recalled, had all natural, historical, and spiritual aspects of the world been represented as passing through a constant transformation and development. Everything fitted in an organic totality, and there was now a logic to history and a determinism that previous ideas of progress had lacked. The events of the Napoleonic era seemed to demonstrate the dialectic at first hand; it made every problem appear capable of resolution—a further motive influencing the Prussian government to ask Hegel, a quiescent liberal, to teach at Berlin. Marx became a "Young Hegelian," influenced by a lecturer, Bruno Bauer, and earned his doctorate with a dissertation defending the liberating views of the Greek philosopher Epicurus. Disinclined to an academic career, he moved to Cologne and soon launched into journalism, first as a contributor and then, in 1842, as editor of the liberal *Rhenish Gazette*. In that position he came to see as never before the constraints under which Prussian life operated, and the economic facts behind them. In contrast to Hegel, who admired the Prussian state for its freedom under discipline, Marx found nothing ideal about it. The grievances of the Rhineland woodcutters and of Mosel winegrowers against government restrictions brought forth from him articles with socialist arguments—arguments he learned from one of the newspaper's founders, the revolutionary Moses Hess. In 1843, after Marx had urged open public debate to remedy the laws, the paper was suppressed and he became a jobless intellectual. The censors had made the last few weeks of his editorship intolerable. "In Germany I cannot start on anything fresh," he wrote; "here you are obliged to falsify yourself." He had long been in love with Jenny von Westphalen, whose father—a neighbor in Trier—had taken a special interest in his mental growth. Shortly after marrying her, he moved to Paris.

Before setting out, however, Marx read Ludwig Feuerbach's *Preliminary Theses for the Reform of Philosophy*, which impressed him greatly. He had already found religion—a connecting link between philosophy and politics—an easy target for its support of the landed class; and he knew Feuerbach's *Essence of Christianity*, published in 1841. In that work the reclusive philosopher had claimed that God had no separate existence and was merely the outward projection of various human needs. In the *Preliminary Theses*, he approached speculative philosophy with the same purpose of demolition. Hegel, Feuerbach charged, had actually strengthened religion by being engrossed with the infinite and the absolute, and by depicting freedom's evolution as guided by superhuman ends. True philosophy should begin instead with the finite, with the real—in other words with man as science shows him to be, and with what the human body wants as much as the human spirit. "Thought arises from being," he wrote, "—being does not arise from thought." Marx immediately agreed, now seeing Hegel's conceptions as far removed from everyday experience. He drew Feuerbach's conclusions into his own social and historical studies and prepared a critique by paragraphs of Hegel's political theory. The introduction he finally wrote proved to be one of his most brilliant essays. In it Marx attacked religion as man's imaginary escape from deprived circumstances. But religion could not be simply dismissed, because the comforts it offered were for millions an obstacle to material betterment:

> The basis of irreligious criticism is: *Man makes religion*, religion does not make man. And indeed religion is the self-consciousness and self-regard of man who has either not yet found or has already lost himself. But *man* is not an abstract being squatting outside the world. Man is *the world of men*, the state, society. This state and this society produce religion, which is an *inverted consciousness of the world* because they are an *inverted world*. Religion is the generalized theory of this world, its encyclopedic compendium, its logic in popular form, its spiritualistic point d'honneur, its enthusiasm, its moral sanction, its solemn complement, its general ground of consolation and justification. It is the *fantastic realization* of the *human essence* inasmuch as the human essence possesses no true reality. The struggle against religion is therefore indirectly the struggle against *that* world whose spiritual *aroma* is religion.

> *Religious* suffering is the *expression* of real suffering and at the same time the *protest* against real suffering. Religion is the sigh of the oppressed creature, the heart of a heartless world, as it is the spirit of spiritless conditions. It is the *opium* of the people.

> The abolition of religion as people's *illusory* happiness is the demand for their *real* happiness. The demand to abandon illusions about their condition is a *demand to abandon a condition which requires illusions*. The criticism of religion is thus in *embryo a criticism of the vale of tears* whose *halo* is religion.

Marx's activity with the **Rhenish Gazette** made political writing, and the necessary research, into his life's occupation; but his socialism was not yet entirely formed, and his notions of the working class—the proletariat—were still rather indistinct. The sixteen months he spent in Paris were crucial and maturing. The city that was Europe's cultural capital was the scene also of increasing political unrest. The Revolution of 1789 had failed to satisfy all expectations, particularly the hope for economic equality; and the rapid expansion of industry in the 1840s had widened the gap between rich and poor. Under the monarchy of Louis Philippe, the capitalists of the bourgeoisie—the middle classes, the industrialists, the owners of property—appeared to rule a very large working population (a great many immigrant Germans among them) wholly for its own benefit. The situation raised many social questions, and radical and socialist theories flourished.

The leading school of social reformers at the time were the so-called utopian socialists, the heirs of the Count of Saint-Simon, Charles Fourier, and others, and the followers of Auguste Comte. Saint-Simon had called for a grand reconstruction of society by industrial leaders and men of science. The industrialists would rule, the aim of this scientific reorganization being to improve the existence of all classes, including the poor. If labor were divided in a spirit of brotherhood, he argued, spontaneous social justice would result. Many of his impractical ideas were elaborated by Comte into a humanist philosophy known as Positivism. Seeing man's knowledge rising up from myth and religion to science, Comte urged society to learn from an objective analysis of social conditions and to follow the laws of sociology, a word he invented. In the new era life would be minutely regulated to promote social feeling over self-love, and everything judged on its utility. Fourier's future was even more precise. To achieve the desired form of social harmony, most of the restraints civilization had placed on the human passions should be removed. The new economic unit would be the "phalanx," containing 1,620 people. Its members would live together in a communal building or "phalanstery," and the work—mostly of an agricultural kind—would be divided according to natural inclinations. Since everyone did the task he liked, and could change it at will, all would be satisfied. Another influential utopian thinker was the Welsh industrialist Robert Owen, who had made New Lanark, where his mills were situated, into a model town.

Utopian socialists therefore planned for social change by redesigning society on a fairer basis than the free-enterprise system; but they did not develop an effective strategy. Being natural optimists, they assumed acceptance of their ideas would be guaranteed by a string of shining examples. Attempts were made to establish phalansteries, and ideal colonies were set up in the United States, like Owen's New Harmony in Indiana; but accumulated experience began to show that these communities, worked out on paper, could never be successful for long. The failures, however, merely inspired the converts to return to the drawing-board to make revisions; the thought of effecting their plans through workers' revolts in the cities never impressed them. To Marx

—fresh from his encounter with the Prussian police, his mind full of Feuerbach's insistence that the only real world was the material world —utopian socialists were hopelessly idealistic; and he quickly chose to mix with practical socialist thinkers, like Louis Blanc, Pierre-Joseph Proudhon, and Mikhail Bakunin, who knew of the working class directly and sought to overthrow capitalist society by drastic means. By the spring of 1844 he had begun to use the term "communist" to define his views. The word had formerly described a social system where all the community owned and shared in the wealth. It now began to part from "socialist" as Marx stressed his further belief that the classes were polarized and a workers' revolution was imminent.

It was in Paris that Marx met Friedrich Engels, the son of a wealthy cotton manufacturer who also had a factory in Manchester, England; and a collaboration began which lasted until Marx's death. In Manchester Engels had seen the Industrial Revolution surging forward; and he had been struck by the colossal productive forces it had created, and by the wrenching social changes it involved—degrading, he believed, both masters and workers who were bound in the system together. When he met Marx he was preparing his first book, *The Condition of the Working Class in England in 1844,* a bitter attack on what he had observed. Engels performed two indispensable functions at this moment in the evolution of Marx's thought. He drew Marx's attention to the factual evidence on social questions to be found in studies of British labor, detaching him still further from the cloudy generalizing which marked most German philosophy; and he introduced him to the classic economic theories of Adam Smith, Thomas Malthus, and David Ricardo, which had been formulated during the dawn of the Industrial Revolution. More than this, Engels, a rich man from his father's business, supported Marx and his family through all the years ahead. With little money of his own and no steady position, Marx's career would have been quite impossible without Engels's generosity.

Marx's outlook while in Paris has been preserved in manuscripts released from the Moscow archives in 1932, when the Soviet Union wished to show there was an affinity between Marx and Western liberalism. These notes on economics and philosophy, drawing on anarchist social criticism, are attractive for their humanitarian ideals. Man, according to Marx, was meant to be his own creator, to express himself in his labor; but the capitalist system, which saw value only in money and private property, had alienated him from himself and debased him. This was not a conjecture, Marx stated, but "a contemporary fact of political economy." Man therefore did not control his own destiny, since the work of his hands—which should be fulfilling and a source of pleasure—was directed and possessed by the persons or things he served; and his simple harmonious relationship to his fellow man was poisoned by the paying of wages. To regain his essential capacities and his integrity, man needed to be liberated from all the restraints suppressing him. These manuscripts arrived in the West when the older Marx, the prophetic economist, was becoming easy to refute, and, utopian and unhistorical, they provoked endless debate on Marxism's true meaning. More than any other of his writings they have led to the late twentieth-century conception of a young passionate Marx, who—as opposed to the tedious canonized Marx—was a democrat and a fighter for human freedom, who placed human dignity higher than the fetish of gold, and who feared the effect of organization and routines on the life of the all-round natural individual.

Compelled by the French government to leave Paris after Prussian complaints about some anti-Prussian articles he had written for a German periodical, Marx next settled for three years in Brussels. There he founded a Communist Correspondence Committee in which he sought, among other activities, to rid the movement of fantastic dreams and to place it on what to him was the only constructive theoretical foundation—a strictly scientific analysis of the economic structure of bourgeois society. He had already defined the main features of his materialist scheme of history, which, in 1846, he and Engels would develop further in *The German Ideology*; but he sketched some of his leading ideas in advance in his *Theses on Feuerbach*, which criticized that philosopher for being too remote. To Marx the question whether objective truth could be reached by human thinking was finally a practical matter; the truth was authentic when it had survived application to reality. The eleventh and best-known thesis runs: "The philosophers have only *interpreted* the world in various ways; the point is, to *change* it."

In 1847 Marx and Engels were commissioned by the newly founded Communist League (mainly a group of exiled Germans in more liberal countries) to write a manifesto announcing the League's doctrines. We shall return later to that famous document, which incorporated a number of current socialist ideas but bound them together with materialist philosophy and delivered its message in stirring language. But, for all its posthumous success, it was almost overlooked when it was published the following year; for, in 1848, revolutions broke out spontaneously in one European country after another, from independent causes. Hastily returning to Cologne Marx became editor of the revived *Rhenish Gazette*, called for a united democratic German republic and a war against tsarist Russia, the fortress of reaction, and told the German working class to band together and save their arms for use against the bourgeoisie. As it happened no lasting revolution occurred, the Prussian government regained control, and Marx was arrested and charged with sedition. Though acquitted at his trial he was soon expelled; and, after a brief stay in Paris, he moved to London in 1849 where he remained.

Although Marx lived and wrote for over thirty more years, it is important to see his thought as being intimately related to the challenges of the 1840s and reflecting the political and economic conditions of that period. The central event of his life was the revolutionary year of 1848, in which he played no great role but agitated energetically for the working class; but, with the triumph of custom and tradition in Germany and throughout Europe, he and Engels retired in defeat to continue the apparently hopeless struggle. The Communist League broke up into rival factions, and Marxist socialism became little known even among socialists until the 1870s. But by the year 1848, when he and Engels wrote the *Communist Manifesto*, Marx had completed his essential interpretation of history. The *Manifesto* spells out all the key concepts—the class struggle, the historical stages, the process, the vision—above all the idea that the purpose of knowing history is to change history. Some expansion and modification remained to be done —to Marxists none ever seems to be enough; but that call to arms, with other writings touching on the revolutionary episode—*The Class Struggles in France* and *The Eighteenth Brumaire of Louis Bonaparte*—are the central works for understanding Marx on history and, indeed, much of his thought in general.

The early years Marx spent in England were wretched. What financial resources he had were repeatedly exhausted, and he and his family were evicted more than once from their lodgings for nonpayment of rent. Illness affected him and his wife, and caused the deaths of three of their infant children; and there was the constant strain of loneliness and humiliation, and the bizarre discussions of refugee politics to contend with. In 1850 he and Engels considered emigrating to America. Nonetheless the family retained a maid, for his wife acted as his secretary, and only once did Marx descend to anything resembling manual work, when he applied for a job as a railway clerk—to be turned down on account of his poor handwriting. The pawnshop became indispensable, and his wife's silver, bearing the crest of the Earls of Argyll with whom there was a distant family connection, was surrendered more than a few times for cash. In 1852, Marx wrote that he had been unable to go out for a week, having pawned his coat to buy paper. A few shillings at the right moment made the whole difference between barest subsistence and total ruin. A Prussian government spy left a vivid and, it seems, an accurate description of the family's home in London's Soho district:

> As father and husband, Marx, in spite of his wild and restless character, is the gentlest and mildest of men. Marx lives in one of the worst, therefore one of the cheapest quarters of London. He occupies two rooms. The one looking out on the street is the salon, and the bedroom is at the back. In the whole apartment there is not one clean and solid piece of furniture. Everything is broken, tattered and torn, with a half inch of dust over everything and the greatest disorder everywhere. In the middle of the salon there is a large old-fashioned table covered with an oilcloth, and on it there lie manuscripts, books and newspapers, as well as the children's toys, the rags and tatters of his wife's sewing basket, several cups with broken rims, knives, forks, lamps, an inkpot, tumblers, Dutch clay pipes, tobacco ash—in a word, everything topsy-turvy, and all on the same table. A seller of second-hand goods would be ashamed to give away such a remarkable collection of odds and ends.

> When you enter Marx's room smoke and tobacco fumes make your eyes water so much that for a moment you seem to be groping about in a cavern, but gradually, as you grow accustomed to the fog, you can make out certain objects which distinguish themselves from the surrounding haze. Everything is dirty, and covered with dust, so that to sit down becomes a thoroughly dangerous business. Here is a chair with only three legs, on another chair the children are playing at cooking—this chair happens to have four legs. This is the one which is offered to the visitor, but the children's cooking has not been wiped away; and if you sit down, you risk a pair of trousers.

A new way of life nonetheless began to take shape amid the poverty. In June 1850 Marx obtained a ticket to the Reading Room of the British Museum, where he was to study so regularly and hard during the years ahead. Occasional gifts supplemented the funds that letters begging Engels for money brought in; and he was invited to write articles on current affairs for the *New York Daily Tribune* by Charles Dana, its radical editor. When political circumstances permitted, Marx made brief visits to the Continent. In 1856, helped by a small inheritance, he and his family managed to leave their miserable surroundings for a small house near Hampstead Heath, a rural area they had often reached on foot for Sunday excursions and picnics. Wilhelm Liebknecht, Marx's follower and a founder of the German Social-Democratic Workers' party, recalled those outings in which reading the papers and discussing politics alternated with games and donkey-riding, the family as it returned singing patriotic German songs and reciting Dante or Shakespeare. Marx's daughter, Eleanor, later remembered her father's gift for story telling, his infectious irresistible laugh, and his love of the novels of Fielding, Scott, and Balzac, which he read again and again.

It was not, however, until 1864 that two further legacies gave Marx enough financial security to move to a second, larger house in Hampstead, in whose pleasant study *Capital* was written. Crammed with books and papers, the room contained a desk, armchair, and sofa, and on the mantelpiece were photographs of Marx's wife and daughters, of Wilhelm Wolff (a pioneer German propagandist and agitator), and of Engels. In time further decorative touches were supplied by gifts of a bust of Zeus, thunder-hurling king of the gods, and a piece of tapestry that Leibniz, the seventeenth-century mathematician and philosoper, whom Marx greatly admired as a rationalist, had had in his study. After 1870 Engels was a close neighbor; he would meet with Marx regularly after lunch for a walk on the heath, or, if the weather was bad, for a conversation indoors, the two men wearing a track in the study carpet as they paced from corner to corner.

Soon after arriving in England, Marx already had begun to lay the foundations for a great work on economics. As the events of 1848 receded into the background, he read intensively in all fields relating to his subject, among them the writings of economists, books on monetary policies, agriculture, technology, the factory system, and accounts of the history, commerce and customs of as many civilizations as possible, from the Indian to the Inca. With so many avenues opening, his area of research expanded endlessly and projects were delayed; but his aim remained to discover the laws of mankind's development, particularly with regard to labor and wages. In proceeding toward his goal he did not rely on speculative philosophy of any kind but, like every other economist, on the firmest facts then available. For Marx, many of these were contained in the bulky volumes of reports and statistics issued by British government departments and known as Blue Books. By marshaling such solid evidence and reviewing all he could, Marx believed he could reach clear scientific conclusions; and his approach to history, especially the history of recent times, has since accelerated the trend away from literary sources, such as memoirs and letters, toward the documentation provided by public records, charters, and parish registers. He was not averse, however, in his historical works or any others, to expressing himself imaginatively and using suitable literary quotations—thereby leaving his own mark on his treatment of materials.

From a manuscript outline known as the *Grundrisse*, Marx wrote *A Critique of Political Economy* in 1859, to be followed by the first volume of *Capital* in 1867 (the final two volumes were compiled by Engels from Marx's drafts after his death). *Capital* is of course Marx's masterwork, valuable for his insights into the whole mechanism of capitalist economy, and containing his theory of surplus value—to Engels, Marx's chief "discovery" in economics; but after all the sacrifice, *Capital's* immediate public reception was almost nonexistent. The edition of one thousand took four years to be sold; the reaction among Marx's colleagues in the International Working Men's Association was summed up by one member, who on receiving the book said he felt like a man who had been given an elephant and did not know what to do with it. Nevertheless, though some have severely questioned its assumptions and conclusions, the book became the starting point for further studies that have had large implications for twentieth-century society.

That same International Working Men's Association, commonly called the First International and founded in 1864 by agreement between certain French and English trade-union leaders, gave Marx the opportunity to reenter active politics. He became its director and persuaded its general council in London to adopt his particular activist ideology in England and at international meetings; but, after the Paris Commune's defeat in 1871, he lost control of the International to the Russian anarchist, Bakunin, largely owing to his intolerant and impolitic behavior. By then the years of struggle had seriously depleted Marx's strength, and, though he wrote a notable paper taking issue with the founding program of the German Social-Democratic Workers' party in 1875, his most creative days were over. After increasing ill health, he died in 1883, intestate and stateless, thus indicating the contempt in which he held bourgeois society and national distinctions. He was buried in Highgate Cemetery in London, where a large marble block with a huge cast-iron head now commemorates his grave, a shrine bedecked with flowers by visiting Marxist socialists from all over the world. The Marxist brand of socialism had not yet gained momentum, and it was Engels, surviving for thirteen years, who saw its transformation into the revisionist, nonrevolutionary parties of Germany and France, which made it a force in European politics.

III

The materialist tradition of modern philosophy, the foundation of Marxism, has its origins in the Scientific Revolution. Philosophers have always argued over the ultimate reality underlying all phenomena, the idealist school seeing it as some form of mind, the materialist as particles of matter—the mind's opposite. In his *Discourse on Method*, Descartes set theology aside and saw matter alone as being basically quantitative, theoretically explainable in scientific laws and mathematical formulas. French philosophers of the Enlightenment, such as La Mettrie, Diderot, and d'Holbach, propounded a materialist outlook with arguments which assumed men were molded by physiology and circumstances. In Germany, philosophy after Kant was mostly idealist; but, well before the mid-nineteenth century, numerous materialist thinkers confidently denied the existence of God or of any Idea dominating the material world. They claimed that matter had primacy over all and that ideas only mirror or somehow rationalize the material world itself.

Converted to this creed by Feuerbach, Marx observed society in Germany, France, and later in England, and concluded that man's beliefs reflected his primary physical needs. Civilization was therefore rooted in economic conditions, for everything in the human world had grown from man's attempts to satisfy such needs. Hegel—who had tied ideas to facts—saw history as the rise of freedom through the Greeks, Christianity, and the French Revolution, culminating in the rational freedom he found in Prussia. While agreeing with Hegel's method of argument, Marx strongly disputed that ideas such as freedom cause social change. He was convinced from his reading and experience of the reverse, that economic and social conditions generate ideas. It is a legal fiction that society is founded on the law, he told the jury at his trial in 1849. On the contrary, he insisted, the law is founded on society, and expresses the common interests and needs of society determined by the prevailing dominant mode of production:

> The Code Napoléon, which I have in my hand, did not produce modern bourgeois society. Bourgeois society, as it arose in the eighteenth century and developed in the nineteenth, merely finds its legal expression in the Code. As soon as it no longer corresponds to social relationships, it is worth no more than the paper it is written on.

As Marx and Engels said, they found Hegel standing on his head and put him on his feet again. The dialectical movement, from thesis and antithesis to synthesis, was for them now governed by phenomena which were actual and measurable—not by the divine Idea; and history accordingly became for Marx the story of the material evolution of human society. But Marx persuaded himself that this evolution by stages still had a purpose; for mankind would progress toward a completely harmonious society, he believed, in which man's true nature would be rediscovered and fulfilled—a society he called communism. The *Communist Manifesto* presents his understanding of the historical process. The document, originally planned in the form of a political catechism, became on Engels's suggestion a historical narrative instead, with a most powerful and eloquent effect. It drew on their doctrines to that date, also from the scheme of history the two collaborators had drafted in such early works as *The Holy Family* and *The German Ideology*. But the *Manifesto*, that rapid summary, was far more than a pocket-manual of history, or of society; it was a call to action, accomplishing in itself Marx's eleventh thesis against Feuerbach—that the point is to change the world, not merely to talk about it. It thus expressed Marx's desire no less than his theory.

The *Manifesto* opens with the famous statement that the history of all society up to the present is the history of class struggles; but, like many first lines, this should perhaps best be seen as a conclusion. It rests on an argument set forth in *The German Ideology*, in which Marx and Engels supplemented Feuerbach's (and any biologist's) notion of man as a species with the concept of man as an active, social being. Since the first premise of all human history is the existence of living human individuals, they wrote, the first fact to be established is the social organization of these individuals and their consequent relationship to the rest of nature:

> All historiography must proceed from these natural bases and their modification in the course of history through the actions of men. Man can be distinguished from the animal by consciousness, religion, or anything else you please. He begins to distinguish himself from the animal the moment he begins to *produce* his means of subsistence. . . . The nature of individuals thus depends on the material conditions which determine their production.

As the modes of production and of exchange had created one form of social organization after another, the *Manifesto* said, classes with conflicting interests had fought each other uninterruptedly, as oppressors and oppressed. Each time the fight had ended "either in a revolutionary re-constitution of society at large, or in the common ruin of the contending classes."

To be exact, the era of class society is rhetorically designated by Marx as "pre-history," for it pales beside the history to come with a classless, communist society. And "history" was certainly not a force on its own account, as some German philosophers were treating it.

"*History* does *nothing*," Engels wrote in *The Holy Family*; "it 'possesses *no* colossal riches,' it 'fights *no* battles!' Rather it is *man*, actual and living man, who does all this, who possesses and fights; 'history' does not use man as a means for *its* purposes as though it were a person apart; it is *nothing* but the activity of man pursuing his ends." The first stage of "pre-history" was the primeval community, in which land was held in common and the tasks of agriculture, hunting, and fishing were shared; but as the population grew a division of labor occurred, slavery was introduced, and what Marx described as a "complicated arrangement of society into various orders, a manifold gradation of social rank" came into existence almost everywhere. This characterized the second stage, society in the form of the ancient city-state.

In ancient Rome, Marx noted, there existed patricians, knights, plebeians, and slaves. Established by agreement or conquest, this new community relied upon slave labor to supply its needs; and first movable property and then land passed into private ownership. The division of labor became far more rigid, and industry and seaborne commerce found their interests conflicting. In the end Rome's fall was not caused by the barbarian invasions or a weakening of moral fiber, but by the depopulation of Italy, the effect of landed property being concentrated in the hands of decaying families who turned it over to pasture and depended on imported corn.

Feudalism came next, a form of society based on the countryside, the ranks consisting of lords, vassals, guildmasters, journeymen, apprentices, and serfs, with subordinate gradations within each group. In the unsettled Middle Ages the feudal nobles, replacing the Roman patricians, combined to assert themselves over serfs who, like slaves, provided the necessary labor force in rural districts. The guild systems in the towns were a feudal organization of manufacture; and, responding to the needs of nobility and townsmen alike, feudal kingdoms and the trappings of medieval civilization arose. In the earliest towns (the *bourgs* in French), however, the leading citizens fought their overlords and wrested charters of liberties from them, becoming the first elements of the bourgeoisie. Private property expanded as a result of commercial and industrial enterprise, and a great stimulus was given to emerging capitalism—the investment of wealth in private business —by the discovery of America and a sea route to India. "Trade with the colonies, the increase in the means of exchange and in commodities generally, gave to commerce, to navigation, to industry, an impulse never before known, and thereby, to the revolutionary element in the tottering feudal society, a rapid development." The outcome was the arrival of the present epoch, the era of the bourgeoisie.

The present age to Marx had established in its turn new classes, new conditions of oppression, new forms of struggle in place of the old; but it was distinctive in having simplified class antagonisms. "Society as a whole," he wrote, "is more and more splitting up into two great hostile camps, into two great classes directly facing each other: Bourgeoisie and Proletariat." Taking the textile industry as his example of the general pattern, Marx noted that labor became concentrated in single workshops, markets grew to meet a rising demand for goods, and steam engines and mechanization revolutionized production. Power then moved into the hands of the industrial middle classes, the millionaires, the leaders of whole industrial armies who owned the means of production and employed wage labor. With every step forward the bourgeoisie increased its capital, trampled on every other class deriving from the Middle Ages, and advanced in political strength, so that now, to Marx, "the executive of the modern State is but a committee for managing the common affairs of the whole bourgeoisie." As in each age, the ruling ideas—religious, political, educational—were those of the ruling class.

The contemporary manner of life was both brutal and demeaning. Wherever the bourgeoisie had got the upper hand, it had "put an end to all feudal, patriarchal, idyllic relations"; it had left no other bond between man and man "than naked self-interest, than callous 'cash-payment.'" It had resolved personal worth into exchange value, it acknowledged only one freedom—free trade, exploited shamelessly without any pretence of religious or political scruples—and it had "converted the physician, the lawyer, the priest, the poet, the man of science, into its paid wage laborers." The need for a constantly growing market for its products had caused the bourgeoisie to draw the entire world into its grip.

From this point onward the *Manifesto* is an analysis of the capitalist system with occasional glimpses of historical perspective. Capitalism too was doomed, Marx and Engels argued, as mankind continued its passage from one social organization to another. "Modern bourgeois society with its relations of production, of exchange and of property, a society that has conjured up such gigantic means of production and of exchange, is like the sorcerer, who is no longer able to control the powers of the nether world whom he has called up by his spells." They noted the recurring economic crises, the epidemics of overproduction, "when society suddenly finds itself put back into a state of momentary barbarism"; and to these the capitalist answer had always been to expand and exploit more ruthlessly than ever. But in doing so, "not only has the bourgeoisie forged the weapons that bring death to itself;

it has also called into existence the men who are to wield those weapons—the modern working class—the proletarians."

Angrily sketching the debasement of work and the family under modern industrial conditions, and the descent of labor into ever-deepening pauperism, the two authors saw the proletariat as the new slave class, deprived of the wealth it had created. But, as industry had grown, the workers also had increased in numbers and strength, and they had been joined by sections of the ruling class, casualties of cutthroat free enterprise. Unlike earlier historical movements that had promoted minorities, a united proletariat stood for the interests of the huge majority, and was unable to stir "without the whole superincumbent strata of official society being sprung into the air." By creating modern industry, the bourgeoisie had therefore produced its own gravediggers. As power became concentrated in fewer and fewer hands, it became more vulnerable, and therefore the fall of capitalism and the proletariat's victory were equally assured. The worker had no nationality, for, under the present system, a German worker had more in common with a French worker than with a German nobleman or bourgeois; and the Communist party had no interests separate from those of the proletariat as a whole in all countries. Other socialists still clung to their bourgeois masters. They either tinkered with capitalism or talked pedantic nonsense. Communism alone was realistic, and the party's ends could only be achieved by the overthrow of existing society, abolishing private property, and utterly transforming the relations of production. "Let the ruling classes tremble at a Communistic revolution," the *Manifesto* concluded. "The proletarians have nothing to lose but their chains. They have a world to win. WORKING MEN OF ALL COUNTRIES, UNITE!"

The explosion of social protest from France to Hungary in 1848 required that the words of the *Communist Manifesto* be dramatic; besides, the authors were confident the literary style of their message would not impair their theory. They were sure their solution to man's problems would remain intact and defeat the ideas of their adversaries because it alone was truly scientific. The crucial human activity, Marx and Engels believed, was man wresting his livelihood from nature together with other men, so that the species might survive. If this were so—and to them it demonstrably was—then to understand history properly meant investigating how men have managed to fill their stomachs and satisfy other material needs. Research indicated how man has devised one form of society after another to serve his economic self-interest—from the primitive communal to the capitalist. But his life-or-death struggle with the natural environment never ceases, and the only genuine difference between those societies lies in how production is organized. Modes of production in fact define the categories of civilization; for, when new productive forces are acquired, the way of earning a living changes and the signs of social relations with it. "The windmill gives you society with the feudal lord," Marx wrote elsewhere, "the steam mill, society with the industrial capitalist." The whole movement of history was now perfectly rational, and no society had been more successful than capitalism in subduing nature. But economic systems and their supportive theories were ultimately justified by whether they had satisfied genuine human wants and desires; and with Marx we once again find a view of man shaping a view of history.

Most Western thinkers have believed that human nature does not vary; the schemes of Thucydides and Machiavelli are examples of that position. Marx declared, however, that human nature has both permanent and semipermanent traits. Hunger and love are obviously enduring; but other traits are caused by the social and economic formation of the time, and by the new needs and capabilities that have evolved. In large measure man determines his nature by his activity, and in 1876 Engels took this theory back to man's very origins. When apes stopped walking on all fours they had freed the hand for more specialized purposes; and, in the transition from ape to man, this was the decisive step—not just because it implied the tool and its general effect on the face of the world, but because the same hand would grow flexible enough to create Raphael's paintings and the music of Paganini. Man did not fashion tools and remain a brute; by changing his environment by his labor, he also changed himself. "All history is nothing but a continuous transformation of human nature," Marx wrote. All the signs indicated that this historical process was fixed; but, whenever man had moved from one society and from one modification of his nature to another, his passage had been marked by a series of antagonistic conflicts. Humanity might be classified in many kinds of social groups; but, of all possible human divisions, the only ones which mattered were those of "class."

The idea of history as class struggle was hardly new; a central theme of Livy's history of Rome, for instance, had been the prolonged contest between the patrician and plebeian orders. But with Marx we soon discover we are offered not only a new version of history but a vocabulary to go with it. Marx seldom gave formal definitions and analyses, partly because he was constantly reinterpreting and clarifying his own ideas; but he gave certain words a special significance, and it is vital that the reader grasp them. We have met with "bourgeois," "capitalism," and "proletariat" already; "class" for Marx did not denote social rank, but an economic and social group self-consciously bound together by a common relationship to the means of production. Throughout history the class owning the means of production of the day—the materials and tools used to produce commodities—had exploited the rest, "exploit" simply meaning for one man to make a profit from employing others. The great conflicts had primarily been fought over this ownership of the immediate material means of subsistence, not over politics or ideologies. They were therefore to be understood correctly as struggles between classes defined in economic terms.

The tensions over ownership in society had always led inexorably to revolution; but, when the next great revolution occurred, it would be the last, for a whole phase of human development would end. The working class, the proletariat, would triumph, and there would no longer be a class rising from beneath to challenge their supremacy—kings, nobles, and bourgeoisie would all be eliminated; and, if history was the story of class struggles, when no further struggles remained there could be no more history—or, rather, "pre-history" would be over, and true "history" would begin. On the ruins of capitalism a new society would arise; but the new life would resemble man's existence in the original classless world, for in essence Marx and Engels took up Rousseau's cry that civilization had destroyed the idyllic life men had shared in the primitive community. Each economic advance had shackled the majority more firmly to the interests of the privileged few; but in an equal society there would no longer be a ruling class who could cruelly cripple the nature of the ordinary man. As revolutionary change created a new environment, so a new being would emerge under the new conditions, a being who would be truly human because life would be organized around genuine human needs. Transforming the earth with his willing labor, he would correspondingly uplift himself; and he would lead a life of dignity and brotherhood and joy—each man as newly made, we may believe, as the world on the first of May.

The guillotine would not fall on the past completely, for this new society would profit from all the technology developed over the centuries to aid survival. It would only become established if the masses, having first been reduced to a propertyless condition, would see any renewal of property rights as intolerable. A "dictatorship of the proletariat" (as Lenin used the term) would first prevent the bourgeoisie from returning to power; but, when the danger of counterrevolution was over, it would yield to an absence of government, an anarchy of a most positive, perfect character. Nations and states would disappear, and the supreme social goal would be to restore the individual's integrity. Under capitalism a working function had been imposed on each man and woman; but under communism, Marx and Engels in their early writings said, "where nobody has an exclusive area of activity and each can train himself in any branch he wishes, society regulates the general production." This makes it possible, they continued, "to do one thing today and another tomorrow, to hunt in the morning, fish in the afternoon, breed cattle in the evening, criticize after dinner, just as I like, without ever becoming a huntsman, a fisherman, a herdsman, or a critic." The new society would be fair; the slogan "From each according to his ability, to each according to his needs!" should be inscribed on its banners, Marx wrote in 1875. It would be free from depressions, because, since the community owned the means of production, there would be no employees, profits, or lack of purchasing power. Nonetheless, as the *Manifesto* said, it would seek to increase the total of productive forces with utmost speed, to show in practice that the socialist system was more efficient and prosperous than the capitalist. Lenin once remarked that socialism meant electrification plus the soviets—a memorable oversimplification of this idea.

History for Marx therefore moved in linear fashion, but in the end described a grand circle—from primitive communism to communism restored. It is worth recalling that the word "revolution" had not lost its earlier common meaning of movement in an orbit or circular course, as used by Copernicus in his book *On the Revolutions of the Heavenly Bodies*. When arguing for a return to a social organization something like the original, Marx and Engels—like many other political revolutionaries—showed themselves, interestingly, to be in a sense reactionary. What passed for progress around them—the changes which had once encouraged Voltaire in England, and were articles of faith to the nineteenth-century bourgeois—was mere temporary prosperity built on very shaky foundations. The revolutions of 1848 were the result of a depression the previous year; and, though the Great Exhibition of 1851 (the "Pantheon in the modern Rome" Marx called it) symbolized a return to economic stability, further depressions should be expected. At an anniversary dinner of the *People's Paper* in 1856, Marx spoke of new forces in society bewildering the middle classes and aristocracy; but the proletariat should recognize in these its brave friend "the old mole that can work in the earth so fast, that worthy pioneer—the

Revolution." Each crisis hastened the morning; and, when Darwin's *Origin of Species* appeared in 1859, Marx immediately saw its theory of natural selection providing parallel evidence for the class struggle in history. Although he later criticized Darwin's theory as too accidental, he also asked if he might dedicate the second volume of *Capital* to the great biologist—an honor Darwin declined, believing the work was atheistic, and not wishing to discomfort his family.

But if the revolution was inevitable, why did Marx endure such hardship and work so arduously to bring it about? The problem is partly solved when we remember that for over half his life Marx was a failed revolutionary. He had a natural longing for self-justification. He was also of the opinion, his son-in-law reminisced, "that a scientist could only debase himself by giving up active participation in public life or shutting himself up in his study or laboratory like a maggot in cheese and holding aloof from the life and political struggle of his contemporaries." But there was a further reason he dismissed any thought of being an idle spectator of economic determinism: if man made his own history—instead of Hegel's mystical world spirit or absolute mind—history required human choice and action, and with it the possibility of human failure. The revolutions of 1848 had been abortive; but they were nonetheless the first workers' uprisings, and he was convinced there would be more. The great change, violent no doubt, could be accelerated; and, by better planning, the workers might be able to win the next round in their fight for victory.

History thus also gave Marx a standpoint for judging current events. When the future Napoleon III seized power in 1851, the theorist was prompted to write *The Eighteenth Brumaire of Louis Bonaparte* to demonstrate how the class struggle in France had enabled "a grotesque mediocrity to play a hero's part." Hegel had once remarked that great events and personages appear twice; Marx expanded the phrase, saying they come first as tragedy, the second time as farce. Men do make their history, he continued, but not under circumstances of their choice; "the tradition of all the dead generations weighs like a nightmare on the brain of the living." At the greatest moment of revolutionary challenge, they anxiously summon up the spirits of the past, borrowing names, battle cries, and costumes "to present the new scene of world history in this time-honored disguise and this borrowed language." Napoleon III's success, as Marx saw it, was entirely artificial. He had persuaded the bourgeoisie he could restore stability, and the workers of Paris of his concern for them, by little more than the glamor of his name; and his power in the end rested, not on any class support, but on his control of the army and bureaucracy. A new revolution was likely with the next economic crisis; the proletariat should band together and prepare for it by improved organization, realistic tactics, and education in class consciousness. In 1870, Marx expected Napoleon III's defeat in the Franco-Prussian War to provoke this further revolution in France, but the resulting Paris Commune was a failure too. Perhaps Lenin's most practical addition to Marxist socialism was to make a trained political party led by an elite of full-time revolutionaries into the spearhead of the amorphous working class.

Marx therefore abandoned Hegel's belief that there are certain men who embody human destiny—Napoleon Bonaparte being the most vividly remembered. The historical process did not need particular kings, or generals, or philosophers. When they appeared they were the crest of the wave, not the wave itself; and all causes which were not actual reflexes of the existing economic life Marx dismissed as secondary, or "epiphenomena." Society found appropriate figures to deal with each situation, but no one individual was indispensable. According to this view, if Columbus had not discovered America someone else would have, and soon, given the commercial expansion of the time; and, even if Napoleon had defeated Wellington at Waterloo, the war would have ended with a British victory in the long run, because Britain had a greater economic potential than France. Carrying this argument forward, we might say that, if Lenin had somehow managed to miss the train the German government provided for him in 1917, the outcome in Russia would still have been the same. Infant capitalism and peasant ownership of land would eventually have yielded to socialism.

Engels shared Marx's opinion. Writing on the German Reformation he saw Luther's religious experience as peripheral, and concentrated on what to him was the real event—the revolt of the German peasants led by Thomas Münzer, who advocated common ownership of the means of life. By putting history on a fully materialist basis, what remains for the Marxist are the truly important facts. In retrospect, we find Hegel's followers splitting into two camps—the "Hegelians of the Right," conservatives who revered the charismatic leader, the man on horseback establishing a strong state, but rejected the strict theory of the process of change, and "Hegelians of the Left," who kept the dialectic but saw economics governing history, and revolutions, not individuals, pushing mankind to the next stage. The resulting intellectual conflict became a major theme of European thought and politics into the twentieth century; and the two sides met finally in mortal combat amid the burning rubble of Stalingrad.

IV

Although at first only the outcasts of society followed Marx's ideas, Marxism is now a central force in world affairs. Not only is its influence on modern thought indelible, but it has had specific results. It has shaped the policies of many sorts of governments and provided a core for some of the most powerful political movements of the twentieth century. Day in, day out, the vast propaganda apparatuses of the Communist states proclaim that capitalism is doomed and urge revolution to finish it off. The divisions within Marxism strain theoretical compatibility, but acceptance of Marx, however much he is reinterpreted, still begins with the acceptance of his scheme of history. He formed his ideas in the climate of 1848; but, since they have far outgrown their original context, his impact requires some further explanation.

One major source of Marx's appeal has been the unified conception of knowledge he offers. He took all things for his subject, examined them, and sought to establish relationships between every part of them. As the harmony and plausibility of other composite theories—notably the Christian and the progressive—have weakened, his consistent materialism gives an alternative center to life where one may be wanted; and the resemblance of Marx's scheme of past, present, and future to certain themes in the Judaeo-Christian tradition becomes one of its assets. It is incorrect to call Marxism a religion, despite the fervor of some of its adherents; no one could have tried harder than Marx to prevent his thought from taking a religious direction. But his history is linear and apocalyptic, ending with a time of peace and plenty, and he saw the human story as a struggle, as several of his predecessors did. To Augustine history was a conflict between God and the devil, to Voltaire it was between reason and superstition, and to Marx it was class versus class. In these elementary respects his system may be adopted without breaking basic patterns of thinking.

Marx's work has been hailed by his adherents as a great scientific achievement as well—which means, in our present culture, granting it a special prestige. Like Voltaire, Marx aimed to discover the laws governing human history; but, to his followers, he far surpassed Voltaire in his success. His learning and his methods for conducting his detailed analysis were superior, and he chose to study man as he went about his most fundamental activity—the attempt simply to stay alive. No evidence, Marx's supporters claim, can be more definitive than that; and for them Marx proved from his investigations that mankind is advancing irreversibly toward a goal. Instead of progress depending on

the fortunate appearance of enlightened monarchs, it is clearly gen-
erated by higher technology; and, with knowledge of this deterministic
process, change becomes comprehensible, setbacks are seen as temporary,
and men can be evaluated once and for all. They are to be judged less
for what they say or do than for what they represent in the economic
structure. Finally, the shape of human destiny is understood correctly.
It will be the natural continuation of the dialectic; and thus the final
stage of communism restored becomes an accurate forecast, not a
utopian fantasy. Marx sketched no more than an outline of the new
society, and his defenders argue that it is nowhere yet fully realized; but
they, like he, are satisfied that, once the proletariat is victorious, a better
life for mankind is inevitable.

For the orthodox Marxist, therefore, the full meaning of history is
secured—a prize which still eludes Ranke's school of historians. Ranke
too was opposed to Hegel's generalizations and tried to turn history
into a science; but, by Marxist standards, his inquiries were superficial.
His feats with documentation were of a largely technical kind, and he
went no further than writing national histories, dealing with politics,
war, and diplomacy—topics which to Marx could only be made intelligible by tracing events to their economic roots. This was not a
fruitful way to explore the human past when a coherent understanding
of social causation was needed, with an emphasis on the present.
Though the Marxist finds Ranke's research useful, for him its theory
does not conform to social realism; where Ranke asks us to keep an
open mind on the larger issues, Marx greets us with his certainty.

Marx, however, did not intend his analysis of history just for
academic criticism. It was to be tested against everyday life; and the
disruptions of nineteenth-century society which he described—the headlong industrialization, the widening gulf between rich and poor, the
recurring economic crashes, and the appalling conditions in which men
and their families lived and labored—could be verified easily by any
worker from his own experience. The social injustice was obvious—and
it has been repeated when other societies have entered the race for
modernization. The governments of different European countries might
ignore it, but in the working class a natural sympathy for Marx's views
existed—and exists today—born out of anger at economic exploitation.
Though H. G. Wells was no follower in his later years (and incidentally
reduced Marx himself to an "epiphenomenon"), he once wrote:

> There would have been Marxists if Marx had never lived. When I
> was a boy of fourteen I was a complete Marxist, long before I had
> heard of Marx. I had been cut off from education, caught in a detest-

able shop, and I was being broken in to a life of mean and dreary toil. I was worked too hard and for such long hours that all thoughts of self-improvement seemed hopeless. I would have set fire to the place if I had not been convinced it was over-insured.

Marx's personality is an additional source of his movement's strength; his moral outrage—unsentimental, and unrelated to any particular system of ethics—puts a stamp on his ideas that no one else could have given them. But how adequate have Marx's methods and analyses turned out to be? Their broad impact on the study of history today is as great as Ranke's was in 1900; but we may question whether the first words of the *Manifesto* are at all a factual statement, for much of hitherto existing society shows the absence, not the presence, of class struggle (a problem Marx attempted to solve in *The Eighteenth Brumaire*). Many of Marx's critical terms, like "class" and "state," are ambiguous, and "class" is not the only valid criterion for sorting humanity. Age, sex, religion, and race are other useful means of grouping. It is no coincidence Marx came from Germany, a country where social distinctions were rigidly defined. His assumption that ideas have no effect on the material process of production—rather the process itself determines politics, religion, art, and so forth—has been hotly disputed; there is a causal interaction, as we see whenever Marx's own theories are deliberately put into practice. After Lenin and Hitler we are more aware than before how the force of one individual's character can help create an economic environment—and after Kennedy, how exceptional qualities may quicken a nation's heart and mind. In general, Marx exaggerated his claim that all history may be explained perfectly by economics. His views often seem the result more of his prejudices than close analysis, and they were restricted by the knowledge available, some of which was faulty. He took his theory for primitive social organization, for example, from Lewis Morgan, an American anthropologist now discredited. He was much more open than many of his followers to new evidence and second thoughts; but history today merits a scrutiny of greater sophistication than Marx suggested or was capable of doing.

We also have a natural interest in testing Marx's predictions. By applying his intelligence, imagination, and historical perception to the early period of global industrialization, Marx was extraordinarily right about so many tendencies of social conditions; but few of his forecasts, like most others made a century ago, have actually come true. He was correct in pointing to two vulnerable features of the capitalist system— the increase in monopolies, and the likelihood of prolonged depressions (as experienced in the 1930s); but he did not foresee that, in the advanced industrialist countries where the revolution might be first expected, class conflict would diminish. Rather than the total rejection of capitalism the mass of people have usually bargained and compromised with their employers for a greater share in the wealth produced. They have enjoyed increasing affluence and have used their voting power to obtain still more. Nor could Marx predict that the new discipline of economics would become instrumental, a matter not so much for prediction as for conscious manipulation by government. Marxists have diagnosed this practice as capitalism's death twitches, but modern Western productivity far outstrips the efforts of centrally managed economies in everything from machine tools to food—the result of the profit motive, market pricing, and far greater legally protected personal freedoms, among other factors. Industrial capitalism, which Marx and Engels once believed was at its peak in certain parts of Europe in 1848, was in fact in its infant stage and has proved to be remarkably capable of development. Concerning other areas of Marx's doctrine, nationalism has proved more enduring than he anticipated—in both world wars societies united across class lines to resist a common enemy; and religion today demands to be taken more seriously. It no longer guarantees a philosophy's acceptance to claim it is fully scientific.

Marx saw chronology in terms of steps, not dates, and he set no time limit on his forecasts. He ultimately measured the worth of each system by whether it had stimulated the changes he wanted, and the future was a preordained sequence of such change. The great workers' revolution has yet to occur and there is no absolutely sure way of demonstrating that the dialectical process will go forward to that stage; if it does, why must it end with the triumph of the proletariat and not further continue—as, according to Hegel, it should? Indeed, it appears to be continuing in Eastern Europe where, although rulers claim the workers' revolution has happened, new classes form in a supposedly classless society, and intellectuals—and workers—oppose a bureaucratic state. The thesis and antithesis emerge and clash again. There is a tension between Marx the scholar and Marx the revolutionary; it is not the least of his attractions. But on this subject, the passion of the revolutionary clearly won.

The Marxist interpretation of history has not been helped in the West by the example of Soviet historians obliged to use Marxism as their only working philosophy. It is difficult for anyone to fit modern European history into Marx's imprecise outline; but the Soviet historian of Russia, required to identify in Russian history Marx's evolving economic relations, has the added problem that the Russian Revolution is an anomaly in the dialectical process. It succeeded unexpectedly in a country which had barely reached the capitalist stage; and, rather than being followed quickly by revolutions in Western Europe, it spread instead to China, Latin America, and Africa. The conclusion that it was, not an uprising against the bourgeoisie in the most backward Western society, but a revolt against imperialism in the most advanced Eastern or colonial one often seems more credible to the non-Marxist— but Soviet Marxism repudiates this idea. The complexities of periodization are even more acute when Soviet scholars try to write histories of countries currently at still earlier stages of economic development. The wish to make history into an implement for world revolution spoils the symmetry of Marxist theory.

But these distortions are increased by others created by Soviet methods of control; nowhere, perhaps, is transmission of the past supervised so thoroughly. In the Soviet Union the chief purpose of history is to indoctrinate people to the goals of modernizing Russian society and preserving Bolshevik power; and historians are charged to show the past both as decadent and as the glorious march of progress toward communism. The state has not withered away since the "ten days that shook the world" in 1917. It is totalitarian and oppressive; and the individual scholar understands his research may be frustrated— and his career halted—if he challenges the official doctrines. The Communist Party is held to be infallible; but the sudden shifts in the party line—and the never-ending play by Marxist intellectuals with Marx's flexible concepts—put the Soviet scholar under further stress. He can use his training and knowledge to bargain for the chance to publish manuscripts, but the party's functionaries make final decisions on any changes in the prevailing Marxist version of history. Their actions make laughable Soviet claims that history is now a science. Objectivity, as the West knows it, is equated with political crime; the cults of Stalin and then of Lenin belie the minor historical role assigned to the individual; other figures are in turn eulogized, declared "nonpersons," and later perhaps rehabilitated; and whatever conflicts with the central Marxist theme is omitted. A new mythology, patriotic, uninspired, defended by infinite casuistry, has come into existence; and the immediate impression it gives is one of startling conservatism and limitation.

Two histories face each other in the world today. They are separated less by method or system than by attitude. One—the powerful official doctrine derived from Marx's theory—has set into a rigid mold. Its followers need it to support their arguments, but it is ritualistic, full of cant, and not a capable means of explanation. A different history can upset everything; and so, for them the course of history is clear and determined, and new ideas and techniques of history can only be pursued in accordance with Marxist ideology. In the West the other history hardly has a dominant agency. It is diffuse, divided against itself—but it takes man, not a "final" scientific law about him, as its principal problem for study. This tradition at its best is versatile and genuinely comprehensive; it absorbs new knowledge (including what Marxism can offer), enriches itself with old, and has a respect for truth. It is also sensitive to men's changing self-perceptions. This confrontation is in part a result of the rise of two great modern disciplines, economics and psychology. It shows the opposing effects of censorship and freedom, and in the conflict the West is ready to end its rival's challenge; for, as the study of man moves forward, the intelligent study of history moves with it.

The style of Marxist history is static, a style the West has rejected since Herodotus broke away from Homer. The genius of the Western tradition of history is its ability to ask new questions. Marxism looks at human affairs and sees man led primarily by economic forces; the non-Marxist tradition remains skeptical and holds that man is more than what he does—or eats. It finds the causes of human behavior to be complex. Man seldom acts entirely predictably in a given instance, nor does he always conform to his economic and social group. He is an individual who strives for power, desires sexual relations, fights to own property, and refuses a sentence of fatalism—from Marx or anyone else. In many ways he is quite irrational. He may assert his humanity by rebelling against his circumstances, but, as the twentieth century has proceeded, his grounds for revolt have been historical, political, spiritual—not exclusively economic. Other parts of his life receive his attention; and Marx and his methods cannot analyze and interpret them sufficiently. Events have produced a very different kind of human and social reality from that which Marx conceived, and a demand for independent and vigorous new questions.

Marx, nevertheless, brought certain definite benefits to the study of history. Although modern economic history by no means begins with his critical inquiry, he has become as much the crucial innovator in that field as Voltaire and Ranke were in theirs. His controversial methods have stimulated other theories, and together their influence has been to transform much historical research into a study of men's economic and social situations—often without resorting to any idea of progress. The merits of thus making history into one of the social sciences are arguable; but most of us would accept that every event has its economic causes, and we have learned to see too that the repercussions of new technology spread throughout society and even the globe. We are aware that the Crusades were caused by feudal land hunger, that the invention of the cotton gin helped lead to the American Civil War, that the railroad had staggering social consequences—and that, in the wake of sudden economic development, a political revolution is likely to follow. Marx's contemporaries might comment in a general way on such phenomena; it was Marx who structured their speculations and responded with statistical analyses (which did much to lessen the tendency to idealize the life of ordinary people). As Marx's works became known, many students of history found them immensely exciting. These works suddenly made history more relevant to the present; they also induced a sense of relief. Most traditional historians had brought absolute moral values to their task; Marx did not. Current opinion generally agrees that such values, like other aspects of ideology, change as society changes.

The Soviet betrayal of Marx's dream makes it difficult to associate Marx with the idea of a creative, fair, and equal society. Perhaps, like More's Utopia, his perfect community should be seen as unattainable, or even undesirable; but today, at least partly because of Marx's vision, a society, past or present, is measured not just by its political maturity or its material success, but by its concern for its less fortunate members. A triumph of humanitarian legislation is therefore as important a milestone as man landing on the moon—if not more so. All the countless variants of liberalism and socialism have had their effect on public opinion, though Marx would have denounced socialist cooperation with the capitalist system as "opportunism." His portrait of man, however, as a creature alienated from himself by meaningless, unrewarding work and by the division of labor, leading to the perversion of all values, gave many reformers a powerful impetus. His aggressive theme that man deserves no less than his integrity may prove his most enduring contribution to the study of history and society alike. One last distinction needs no elaborating. Before Marx, the price of a loaf of bread was hardly considered by most people to be historically important; after Marx, it was—and is.

We are left, then, with an intellectual achievement whose residue of insights and partial truths affects all areas of knowledge and penetrates practically the whole of modern thought—but which in many respects steps straight out of the later French Enlightenment, the world of Condorcet's ten eras of human progress and of Rousseau's paradise regained. Marx's insistence on a single law explaining universal history, his attempt at a fully scientific investigation to find it, and, finally, in an act of faith contradicting many of his facts, his belief that mankind now stands on the threshold of a better and inevitable future, all indicate an outlook which had its roots in the eighteenth century. But now Marx's historical materialism has become speculative itself; his followers have failed to turn the liberation they declared into the liberty he promised; and his sketch of man's destiny has become as much a castle in the air as the fantasies of Saint-Simon and Fourier, fantasies he despised.

The experience of twentieth-century man denies the crude evolutionary pattern of history Marx developed. Elements of Marx's approach to the past help us test and refine our general conclusions about capitalism, and further, about the human story, but it is absurd to pretend that they provide a scientific law. To all but the faithful, the conclusions Marx himself reached obstruct a frank inquiry. Marx's great continuing effect, however, is not economic and intellectual but political and revolutionary, for he still gives meaning to history for a great multitude whom other interpreters have failed to persuade. Playing that parlor game "Confessions," he said one of his heroes was Spartacus, the leader of a Roman slave uprising; and he identified himself with Prometheus, who, in Aeschylus's play, brings fire of the gods to release humanity. His message, therefore, can be sudden and dazzling. Like Lenin's speech on arrival at the Finland station in Petrograd, it has the power of conveying (as an observer of that event recalled) the truth, *new*, brusque, somewhat stunning, and undeniably right. It is not history confirmed by reflection, but rather by the roar of the crowd. It is history by acclamation.

CHAPTER EIGHT

NIETZSCHE

I

In 1851, in a palace of girders and glass covering nineteen acres of Hyde Park in London, the civilized nations of the earth united in peace at Britain's invitation to celebrate the achievements of industry and art. It was, as Macaulay exclaimed, a magnificent sight. The galleries filled with all that was useful or beautiful, the huge nave with its arched and glittering transept, the sublime idea of the whole festival—everything astounded the mind and the imagination. Planned and completed despite immense practical challenges, diehard critics, and fears of revolution, the Great Exhibition was an outstanding public success. But it was more than an elaborate trade fair, promoting manufacture and rewarding excellence; its higher purpose was to give a true test and a living picture of man's conquest over nature, and to consecrate his efforts anew to the fulfillment of that mission. No one spoke better on these goals than Prince Albert, chairman of the organizing commission. He wrote as a text for the Official Catalogue: "The progress of the human race, resulting from the common labor of all men, ought to be the final object of the exertion of each individual. In promoting this end, we are accomplishing the will of the great and blessed God."

The future seemed favorable—to Prince Albert, to Macaulay, even to Marx in his way; and events bore out the first two at any rate. The rest of the nineteenth century was an era of extraordinary advance in science, technology, and medicine, an age of material improvements, greater social mobility, gradual liberalization, and relatively durable peace. And yet in the 1880s a strange and tragic voice, speaking an outrageous language heard by almost no one but himself, proclaimed the total rejection of current beliefs. To Friedrich Wilhelm Nietzsche, striving, single-minded Europeans had built a flimsy civilization which faced catastrophe. The present generation were not the summit of mankind, they were educated mediocrities in their minds and lives; and, trusting in theories of inevitable progress, they lacked the will to shape the world differently, or even to hope a different world was possible. Science, positivist philosophy, and sham morality had blinded them to what in Nietzsche's eyes was glaringly obvious—that the governing ethics of civilization had collapsed, and that "progress" was merely agitated effort to find a substitute for a vital principle man had lost. For existence had no meaning after "the greatest recent event—that 'God is dead' ":

> *The madman.*—Have you not heard of that madman who lit a lantern in the bright morning hours, ran to the marketplace and cried incessantly: "I am looking for God! I am looking for God!"—As many of those who did not believe in God were standing together there he excited considerable laughter. Have you lost him then? said one. Did he lose his way like a child? said another. Or is he hiding? Is he afraid of us? Has he gone on a voyage? Or emigrated?—thus they shouted and laughed. The madman sprang into their midst and pierced them with his glances. "Where has God gone?" he cried. "I shall tell you. *We have killed him*—you and I. We are all his murderers. But how have we done this? How were we able to drink up the sea? Who gave us the sponge to wipe away the entire horizon? What did we do when we unchained this earth from its sun? Whither is it moving now? Whither are we moving now? Away from all suns? Are we not perpetually falling? Backward, sideward, forward, in all directions? Is there any up or down left? Are we not straying as through an infinite nothing? Do we not feel the breath of empty space? Has it not become colder? Is more and more night not coming on all the time? Must not lanterns be lit in the morning? Do we not hear anything yet of the noise of the gravediggers who are burying God? Do we not smell anything yet of God's decomposition?—gods, too, decompose. God is dead. God remains dead. And we have killed him."

One measure of Nietzsche's importance is that certain of his thoughts—like those of Marx—have since become commonplace. Both men saw themselves (perhaps incorrectly) as realists of a most ruthless kind, defying their contemporaries' assumptions that all trends in Western civilization were for the good, and that an exalted reason would increasingly oversee all departments of human affairs. But Marx developed an encyclopaedic doctrine; in contrast, Nietzsche said, "I mistrust all systematizers and avoid them." Systems of thought, to him, sacrificed integrity for an ideal unity; they showed the questioner had stopped questioning. Nietzsche instead would search for truth behind those commonly held beliefs; he would seek for the hidden assumptions.

The result was a collection of writings that are contradictory and enigmatic—tantalizingly so, because of their brilliance. Nietzsche neither treated his themes in an orthodox way nor employed any immediately obvious logic of thought; he called his abrupt style "philosophizing with a hammer." To argue his points he frequently used analogy—especially in his later works that leap from conclusion to conclusion, offering only the barest of evidence, expecting the reader to keep up with the writer in a wild paper-chase of inexhaustible suggestions. What to his admirers are scintillating, passionate sentences of truth, are to the unsympathetic a mindless torrent of mystifying words, making no concessions to the skeptic, and symptomatic of the final rash of Teutonic world-weariness and gloom. Such a rich genetic pool can produce a variety of intellectual progeny, but with unpredictable mutations.

Nietzsche's great vision was that—despite what optimistic rationalists or organizers of successful exhibitions were saying—every aspect of nineteenth-century civilization was about to break down. "Nihilism stands at the door," he wrote; when there was no firm footing on which a man could stand, all values became empty. The traditional Christian God was no longer credible. Nietzsche revealed the depth of his insight when the madman in his parable next burst out, "How shall we, the murderers of all murderers, console ourselves?" The death of God had at last freed man from superstition, backwardness, and tutelage. It was the event for which every enlightened thinker had been waiting, and that called for celebration; "whoever shall be born after us, for the sake of this deed he shall be part of a higher history than all history hitherto." But it had also involved mankind in an agonizing loss. With God gone, only scattered moral prejudices remained; and, in the post-Christian era, man's first task should be to establish a system of values without divine sanction—to find a new purpose and goal, a new definition of happiness, which would give him a reason to live.

Nietzsche's aim was to get to the roots of civilization's sickness as he discerned it, to diagnose its causes, and to prescribe the treatment for its cure. To go back for inspiration to those primary sources, Socrates and Plato, was not enough; with their sophisticated teachings, refined in debate with rival schools, they were part of the disease. But behind Socrates stretched a line of earlier Greek thinkers, whose speculations had grown out of poetry and spoke the directness of the inmost human tendencies. They were the great originals; there lay the clear spring-head. The master Nietzsche acknowledged was Heraclitus of Ephesus, an Ionian whose bold spirit and terse remarks we met when introducing Herodotus. Flourishing about 500 B.C., Heraclitus was contemptuous of mankind, and proudly ascetic. He believed in perpetual flux rather than permanent knowledge, and saw that life contains polarized elements working against each other; but there is stability in this tension, he held, and tension therefore has a positive quality. To ignore it, or to explain it by "laws," produces superficiality. Heraclitus confronted intellectual problems, not by laboriously rationalizing them, but by delivering comments of an often cryptic sort—defining, as it were, by jagged lightning flash: "The way up and the way down are one and the same." "You cannot step twice into the same river." "It is in changing that things find repose."

In thought and style Nietzsche renewed this tenuous link of Western philosophy, so different from the broad, cohesive inquiries of Plato and his successors; for him Heraclitus explored the genuine problems of life more honestly. Nietzsche proceeded to indict Western civilization in a shower of blazing random perceptions; and one reason why we consider him here is because his target was so comprehensive. The nineteenth century drew so much self-confidence from its conviction that it "possessed" the past that no evaluation of what Nietzsche called its "merely decorative culture" would have been complete without analyzing "the historical disease." Not an orthodox historian by any standard, he comes to us rather as the historian masked, delivering his historical theories through his first published work, *The Birth of Tragedy out of the Spirit of Music*, through his concept of the Superman, and through his notion of Eternal Recurrence. He also enters our survey because it would quite distort the contemporary study of history to omit him. Not only do his broad insights anticipate the climate in which much general discussion of history now takes place, but he wrote the most savage attack ever leveled against the modern historical profession—the second essay of his *Untimely Meditations*, entitled "The Use and Abuse of History." It is Nietzsche as a controversial critic of historians, and of history's place in a culture, that makes his appearance here absolutely necessary.

I shall not, like some scholars, try to make Nietzsche's teachings on history wholly consistent; for they are not, and that would impair the aim of a man who sought above all to provoke debate, not to engage in it himself. Besides, for a reader to benefit from any such scheme, he should be familiar with the wide range of Nietzsche's works and his shifting forms of expression; for Nietzsche developed and to an extent altered his ideas a good deal during his lifetime, to make his shocks more effective. As it happens, *The Birth of Tragedy* and "The Use and Abuse of History," which contain the gist of his historical viewpoint and criticism, were written with clarity; and it is in the former that the question which prompted Nietzsche's entire civilizational inquiry is casually posed: "If we could imagine an incarnation of dissonance—and what is man if not that?" To bring man to self-discovery again and to energize his lost abilities was Nietzsche's overpowering motive, no matter where he turned his gaze. But, in Sigmund Freud's opinion, Nietzsche first had a more penetrating self-knowledge than any man ever likely to live; and certainly his books reflect his intimate sense of his own discordant personality. Discovering Nietzsche himself therefore becomes the best introduction to understanding his chaotically versatile thought.

II

Nietzsche wrote his own autobiography in a sense, a masterpiece of sarcasm entitled *Ecce Homo* (Behold the Man)—the words of course with which Pilate presented Jesus to the Jews. The headings of the four main chapters tell something of its character: "Why I am So Wise," "Why I am So Clever," "Why I Write Such Excellent Books," and "Why I am a Destiny." But Nietzsche was reluctant to pursue any inquiry in factual detail, and we shall trace his life in more normal fashion. This too has difficulties, for, in the hands of his sister, who edited his works, and of the Nazi movement, he was shown to the world as an anti-Semite, the glorifier of war, famous for such phrases as "the will to power" and "blond beast." That this portrait is a travesty is easily proved from his original writings; but Nietzsche's Nazi reputation, to which we shall return, further complicates our appraisal of a man who confused his ideas deliberately, and who died after twelve years of insanity.

Nietzsche was born at Röcken in the Prussian province of Saxony in 1844, and—like Ranke—was descended from a line of Lutheran clergymen; but in 1849 his pious and apparently ineffectual father died, and his mother moved with her small son and daughter and her husband's two unmarried sisters to the home of her mother-in-law. Nietzsche thus spent his childhood in an otherwise entirely female family of strict religious principles, a background with which in time he firmly broke. The experience may have caused his notorious later remarks on women; it certainly appears to have accentuated a loneliness that became his all-pervasive mental trait. "At an absurdly early age, at the age of seven," he was to write, "I already knew that no human word would ever reach me." Like Ranke again, he attended Schulpforta, a celebrated German school, and proceeded to the University of Bonn to study theology and classical philology; but, when his admired philology professor Friedrich Ritschl moved to Leipzig the following year, Nietzsche left theology and Bonn behind and followed him. Training in textual analysis he won exceptional distinction; and even before he received his doctorate, he was recommended by Ritschl for a professorship of classical philology at Basel. Ritschl's letter, which gained him the appointment in 1869, was glowing:

> However many young talents I have seen develop under my eyes for thirty-nine years now, *never yet* have I known a young man, or tried to help one along in my field as best I could, who was so mature as early and as young as this Nietzsche. His *Museum* articles he wrote in the second and third year of his *triennium*. He is the first from whom I have ever accepted any contribution at all while he was still a student. If—God grant—he lives long enough, I prophesy that he will one day stand in the front rank of German philology. He is now twenty-four years old: strong, vigorous, healthy, courageous physically and morally, so constituted as to impress those of a similar nature. On top of that, he possesses the enviable gift of presenting ideas, talking freely, as calmly as he speaks skillfully and clearly. He is the idol and, without wishing it, the leader of the whole younger generation of philologists here in Leipzig who—and they are rather numerous— cannot wait to hear him as a lecturer. You will say, I describe a phenomenon. Well, that is just what he is—and at the same time pleasant and modest. Also a gifted musician, which is irrelevant here.

But, though Nietzsche arrived at Basel with these advantages, he made few friends there. He did gain the acquaintance of Jacob Burckhardt, the famous historian of Renaissance art and civilization; and, becoming a Swiss citizen, he started taking his perspectives on Germany from beyond its borders. At first he taught successfully; but he was (despite Ritschl's praise) fundamentally miscast for spending his life editing Greek manuscripts. His interests ranged too freely (shortly before Basel had invited him, he had considered changing his career to chemistry). Moreover, at Leipzig he had found in a second-hand bookshop Arthur Schopenhauer's barely known work, *The World as Will and Representation*, published nearly fifty years previously; and this philosopher set the pattern of all Nietzsche's later thinking as much as Hegel did for Marx. When Nietzsche made his discovery he had abandoned theological studies, was in revolt against his family's religion, and was disillusioned with the gregarious student life he had forced himself into at Bonn. He saw in Schopenhauer's thought "a mirror that reflected the world, life, and my own soul with hideous magnificence." "I understood him," he wrote on another occasion, "as though he had written for me."

We have already met philosophers who believed that ultimate reality lies in Mind, or in Matter; to Schopenhauer, the most real thing in the whole of nature was Will. Men are driven constantly to do or possess what they desire, he argued; but, because the will's needs are never satisfied, they experience frustration and defeat, and the world—which is torn by conflicting individual wills—is therefore a place of endless suffering. Life is a long desire that is never fulfilled, Schopenhauer wrote; and, since happiness is impossible, the only valid outlook to take is pessimism. How then can we come to terms with this situation, founded in the order of existence and so contrary to what the optimists around us say? The logical course would be suicide, but Schopenhauer rejected this because the will to live is too strong. What passes for knowledge was to him merely the will's projection; and the only possible way to obtain freedom from the tyranny of our wants, to be made pure, is to cease willing, or desiring, altogether. His theory of self-annihilation is reminiscent of Buddhism, and he acknowleged his debt to Hindu and Buddhist scriptures as well as to Plato and Kant. But temporary relief might be gained by contemplating works of beauty created by genius; and, of all art forms, music expresses most directly the will's passion for transfiguration.

Schopenhauer's book not only spoke to Nietzsche's melancholy, it offered a means of escape. Its notion of the universal will prompted his thinking, and he was struck by the philosopher's conception of the meaning and function of art. But where might the genius be found through whom one could attain this extraordinary freedom? Schopenhauer was dead, but in 1869, in the village of Tribschen, at no great distance from Basel, Richard Wagner had come to live. Composer, librettist, theatrical producer, and revolutionary, Wagner was a heroic figure in whom art and life seemed inseparable; and, to Nietzsche's generation, he had begun to personify the highest aesthetic ideals.

In 1868, at a concert Nietzsche attended in Leipzig, the prelude to Wagner's opera *Tristan und Isolde* and the overture to *Die Meistersinger* were played. "I cannot bring myself to keep critically cool towards this music," he wrote immediately after, "every fiber, every nerve thrills in me." Meeting Wagner in person two weeks later, he discovered to his rapture that the composer too was a follower of

Schopenhauer, and that *Tristan*, with its unearthly melodies of sublimated eroticism when the lovers renounce each other, had been written under the direct inspiration of *The World as Will and Representation*. Soon after reintroducing himself in Switzerland, Nietzsche wrote to a friend:

> I have found a man who reveals to me, as no other does, the image of what Schopenhauer called the "genius" and who is penetrated through and through by that wonderfully deep philosophy. This is no other than Richard Wagner, concerning whom you must not accept any judgment to be found in the press, in the writings of musical experts, etc. No one knows him and can judge him, for the whole world stands on a different basis and is not at home in his atmosphere. In him there rules such an unconditional ideality, such a noble seriousness of life, that near him I feel as if I were near the divine.

Perhaps Nietzsche's reverence for Wagner, who was thirty years older than he, may be partly explained by his seeking a father substitute. If so, his choice, like everything else he did, is self-revelatory. In his stormy career Wagner was often on the run from creditors or police; and, convinced of the greatness of his art, he was determined to make the world accept it. The music of the future, he maintained, must bring all the arts together; and, calling his operas "music dramas," he was responsible for every part of their production, from score to costumes. Forced by violent criticism to defend his ideas in detail, he had settled in Switzerland under the boundless patronage of King Ludwig II of Bavaria; and, accompanied by Cosima von Bülow, the daughter of Franz Liszt, he was enjoying unusual peace and security. He welcomed Nietzsche's hero-worship, seeing in him one of the first of a wave of young admirers who might be useful in propagating the Wagner movement. Nietzsche's position at Tribschen soon became established. Whenever his professional duties allowed he attached himself to Wagner's unconventional household, ecstatic at such intimacy, correcting proofs of Wagner's writings and discussing aesthetic theories while the composer worked on *Siegfried*.

Serving briefly as a medical orderly in the Franco-Prussian War, Nietzsche experienced a physical and nervous breakdown; but he recovered, and in 1872 he published his first book, an event which should have established his academic reputation. *The Birth of Tragedy out of the Spirit of Music*, however, was not what Ritschl had promised. Dedicated to Wagner—who had himself written an essay in the field— and turning a discourse on Greek tragedy into praise for Wagner's "music drama," to most readers it seemed no more than a thinly disguised polemic on one of the most divisive cultural issues of the day. Nonetheless, looking back at the work now, its fundamental idea was brilliant. When most classical philologists were producing close studies of Greek texts and Greek writers, Nietzsche took a daring new view of the whole of Greek civilization. He drew attention to the irrational, "unclassical" side of the Greek character; and he argued that it complemented the serene proportions of the Greek mind so celebrated by his contemporaries for its achievements. Greek tragedy, rising from myth and ritual, had reached its highest form while it preserved the abandon of choral dance; when rationalism triumphed, it destroyed tragedy's essential vitality. The book that then was scorned or savagely attacked by Nietzsche's colleagues is today hailed as a revolution in the modern understanding of Greek life and thought.

To the young Nietzsche, Wagner embodied the excellence of Greek nature in its neglected entirety; Nietzsche would even recollect that to relieve the unbearable pressure of second-rate German culture, he needed Wagner as one needs hashish. But, with continuing proximity to the great man, his admiration weakened. Instead of following *The Birth of Tragedy* with a work specifically on Wagner as the two had planned, he turned to writing his miscellaneous and unpopular *Untimely Meditations.* As for Wagner, he came to see his own future lying unmistakably in Bavaria—indeed how could he ignore the signs when the monarch was practically draining the country's treasury to encourage the musical and dramatic innovator whose productions held him enthralled? Neuschwanstein, Ludwig II's newly built architectural extravaganza, was a castle inspired by *Tannhäuser* and *Lohengrin,* and was only part of a larger obsessive dream to metamorphose the world into a stage under Wagner's intimate direction, where the king could travel the book of history as the mood took him. In 1872 the foundation stone of a great festival theater for the performance of Wagner's works was laid at Bayreuth; and in 1876 the doors opened for the performance of *The Ring of the Nibelungs*—the cycle of operas retelling the German legends of the struggle between men and gods, and of the trials and adventures of the human soul. Nietzsche came, prepared still to believe this was "the dawn of the combat" against cultural mediocrity, sat through the first rehearsal—and fled. In *Ecce Homo* he described what prompted this drastic action:

> Anyone who has any idea what visions had been flitting across my path even at that time can guess how I felt when I one day came to myself in Bayreuth. It was as if I had been dreaming. . . . Where was I? I recognized nothing, I hardly recognized Wagner. In vain I

scanned my memories. Tribschen—a distant isle of the blessed: not the shadow of a resemblance. The incomparable days of the foundation-stone laying, the little band of *initiates* who celebrated them and who did not lack fingers for delicate things: not the shadow of a resemblance. *What had happened?*

Nietzsche's dismay was not primarily at Wagner's art, which still combined many of the strengths of Greek drama at its most vigorous. It was caused by Wagner's showmanship, his compromise with the crowd of educated Philistines—a term Nietzsche had devised in the first of his *Untimely Meditations*—for the sake of popular success. The dream of perfect beauty created by self-immolating genius—of an incomparable national culture—was shattered, and its place taken by tricks of the theater, the composer as circus master and cult object, and a turgid mixture of religion and brash victorious imperialism. Having abandoned the aesthetic ideal, Wagner of all people came to symbolize for Nietzsche the sickness of his era, grossly materialistic, loudly pro-German, and despicably anti-Semitic. In Nietzsche's development, only the break with Wagner had equalled meeting him; henceforth he would combat decadence alone. "What had happened?" became a question transcending personal significance; it was a question staring out from every single crevice of Western civilization now, to be answered with his companion question, "What is man?" "Strange!" he commented, "I am continually possessed by this thought: that my history is not solely a personal history, that in living as I do live, forming myself and setting myself on record, I am serving the interests of many."

Rising above his desolation, above the loss of the unique friend he yet recalled as "the great benefactor of my life," Nietzsche was able to see that Wagner had in fact become an obstacle to his growth as a thinker and writer; and, when *Parsifal* was produced in 1882, his conclusions were sealed—Wagner the disciple of Schopenhauer had devised a fraudulent relief from modern suffering through medieval Christian myth. In 1879, bored with philology and wishing to follow his own inclinations free from responsibilities, he left Basel with a pension, citing grounds of illness. From that time forward he arranged his life largely to benefit his health, spending summers usually in Switzerland and winters on the French or Italian Riviera. Increasingly withdrawn, though on the fringe of that Middle European intellectual set which was to find a rough focus in the circle of Sigmund Freud, he devoted himself to his furious writings, plagued by migraine and near-sightedness, unable to cope with most practical details of life. A Viennese physician who wrote about Nietzsche in several letters described a visit to him at Nice in December 1883:

> His small room is bare and inhospitable-looking; it certainly has not been chosen with a view either to ease or comfort, but solely on account of economy. It has no stove, no carpet, and no daintiness, and when I was there it was bitterly cold. Nietzsche was exceedingly friendly. There was nothing of false pathos or of the prophet about him, although I had expected it from his last work; on the contrary, he behaved in quite a harmless and natural way, and we began a commonplace conversation about the climate and dwellings. Then he told me, but without the slightest affectation or assumption, how he had always felt that a task had been laid upon him, and that he intended to perform it to the utmost of his power, as far as his eyes would permit him. Just fancy, this man lives all alone and is half blind. In the evening he can never work at anything. There are many contradictions in Nietzsche, but he is a downright honest man, and possesses the utmost strength of will and effort. . . . He is absolutely convinced of his mission, and of his future fame; this belief gives him strength to bear all his misfortunes, his bodily sufferings, even his poverty. Of one thing I am certain, Nietzsche is chiefly a man of sentiment.

In *Human, All Too Human* (1878), Nietzsche had abandoned ordinary prose, choosing an aphoristic style so as to clear the path better for a new philosophy. He wrote *The Wanderer and His Shadow, Daybreak,* and *The Joyful Science* in this manner, treating profound problems, he said, "as I do a cold bath—quick in, quick out. That one thereby fails to get down deep enough, fails to reach the depths, is the superstition of hydrophobics, enemies of cold water; they speak without experience." For a few months in 1882 he believed he had found a companion and heiress to his gifts, the exceptionally talented and attractive Lou Salomé, a Russian half his age. He fancied that she could construct a unity from his jangling productions; but, when she deserted him for another liaison, he exploded in insults and tried to pull his thought together in a major work himself. The result was *Thus Spoke Zarathustra,* his best-known book, an extravagant prose poem full of satire, blasphemy, and frenzy, an anti-Bible parodying some of the Bible's most sacred portions (with no connection to the ancient Persian prophet named in Nietzsche's title) and ardently making known his ideas of Eternal Recurrence and of the Superman. In it he gave his philological training its freest rein, not in a scholarly fashion, but allowing his highly intuitive, penetrating mind to wrench the most out of forms of language, as a skilled musician draws nuances of sound from his instrument.

But, in spite of his ceaseless efforts to be heard, Nietzsche received, after his earliest publication, practically no immediate public response to his works. When noticed at all they were dismissed as eccentric or pathological, and the indifference which greeted *Thus Spoke Zarathustra* almost shattered him. Since he printed many of his books at his own expense, they became still further in his eyes his special offspring; and his message grew fiercer and louder. He cursed Christianity as the ultimate debasement of man's natural instincts, denying man his basic needs, and reducing values to a "slave morality." Democracy, too, he abhorred for bringing men down to an equal level. Strongly against the flow of public opinion, he demanded that superior men be elevated to form an elite class of new leaders. Driving himself without mercy, writing now chiefly for himself and sometimes including self-quotations, he produced in three years *Beyond Good and Evil*, *On the Genealogy of Morals*, *The Wagner Case*, and *Twilight of the Idols*, as well as the manuscripts of *The Anti-Christ*, *Nietzsche contra Wagner*, and *Ecce Homo*. He closed the last work with Voltaire's battlecry—*Écrasez l'infâme!*

But the pace and the strain to which he subjected himself were too great. Debilitated, demonic in his urge to expose the misconceptions on which civilization rested, and solitary, he collapsed on a street in Turin in January 1889, at the sight of a horse being flogged. Whether his peculiar existence alone brought this about, whether it was hereditary madness, the terminal effects of syphilis, or—as Freud might have seen it—a long-desired escape forcing itself through the unbearable tension, is still unsolved. At any rate his madness was a release. "Sing me a new song: the world is transfigured and all the heavens are full of joy" was the note, signed "The Crucified," he sent to Peter Gast, a composer; and he wrote other letters, even more unbalanced, to Burckhardt, Cosima Wagner, the king of Italy, and the pope, some under the signature of "Dionysus." Rescued, he was pronounced incurably insane; and, placed in the care of his mother and sister, he died at Weimar in 1900. Out of the mass of papers he left, fragments often scribbled down during lonely Alpine walks, his sister posthumously published a selection entitled *The Will to Power: An Attempt at a Revaluation of All Values*.

III

Though Nietzsche's life ended in a complete mental breakdown, it is important to say that he showed no definite sign of insanity until shortly before his collapse. There is thus no reason to discount his works, though their tone does become increasingly frantic. They are the record of his unequal struggle with the dark, godless tragedy of existence, a tragedy which for Nietzsche was also the predicament of mankind. Man, who once believed he was made in God's own image, had now become an animal, literally and without reservations. But this had been man's choice. "Ever since Copernicus," he wrote, "man has been rolling down an incline, faster and faster, away from the center— whither? Into the void? Into the 'piercing sense of his emptiness'? But has not this been precisely the most direct route to his old ideal?"—the ideal of wholly scientific knowledge? We should remember that late-nineteenth-century Germany and Austria were the leading forums of debate on the subjects of science and human nature; and Nietzsche was one of several intellectuals who wrestled with the problems of alienation and despair. In him, however, the catastrophe that faced Western civilization—the collapse of moral order—produced not only the bleakest pessimism but also the strongest urge to expose the contradictions in the modern world, which were the cause of all its troubles. He would explore man's motivations; "who before me at all among philosophers has been a *psychologist?*" he asked.

The nihilism of which Nietzsche spoke was the total separation between the facts and values of life. It was a state of affairs largely ignored by evolutionary theorists of society; it was disastrously evident, he thought, in Germany. There was no remedy to it except abandoning the wreckage of the old culture completely; but, he observed, "it can be a sign of strength." "Actually, every major growth is accompanied by a tremendous crumbling and passing away," he wrote; "suffering, the symptoms of decline, *belong* in the times of tremendous advances; every fruitful and powerful movement of humanity has also created at the same time a nihilistic movement." Only by reuniting the dissonant parts of man's nature and acquiring a new source of values, might a truly human, unrepressive, unhypocritical civilization come into being. But, like Voltaire advocating progress, Nietzsche had more than an idea to propose for the future. He stressed an actual example of his model society. For him, early classical Greece represented the almost perfect other land, and his argument in some form sustains all his books, which, as he insisted, are properly a single creation. It provides, of course, the thesis of his first work, *The Birth of Tragedy out of the Spirit of Music,* which ruined him professionally; and it is also the background to his assertion that the chief end in studying history is to enhance life in every aspect and experience. To understand Nietzsche as a critic of history, we should first look further at Nietzsche, the Wagner-struck philologist, writing on the origins of Greek culture.

Perhaps no people have ever exerted such a fascination on others as the classical Greeks did on nineteenth-century Europeans. The appeal of Greek art, encouraged by Winckelmann, Goethe, and Hegel, Byron dreaming of Greek freedom and dying for it, the stunning archaeological discoveries of Schliemann, and Benjamin Jowett's attempt to make Oxford into a training ground for society's guardians on lines suggested in Plato's *Republic*—these are just a few illustrations of an era's deep belief that Greek civilization was unsurpassable. The Greek phenomenon had been variously explained. The Enlightenment had seen Periclean Athens as the first major staging area in the advance of human reason; the Romantic poet Schiller, as Nietzsche recalled, viewed Greek artists as naive children, nurtured in the bosom of nature; but still no explanation seemed sufficient. What then was the inner secret of the Hellenic ideal, made manifest in beauty, thought, and human character? Few subjects were more intriguing than the dynamic of this divinized society.

In *The Birth of Tragedy*, Nietzsche saw two strands in Greek culture, represented by the gods Apollo and Dionysus. The Apollonian element was the one on which scholars and educators had lavished attention—rational, symmetrical, and orderly, finding its highest expression in Greek classical sculpture, architecture, and systematic philosophy. But, he believed, there had been another force equally important—the Dionysian, which broke through structural devices in floods of untamed passion, and whose deity was worshiped not liturgically in a columned temple but orgiastically in revels amid groves of trees. What was crucial to understand was that to the early Greeks both gods were equally important, and that Greek civilization had shone with its greatest brilliance when these two strands in its nature had been in harmony.

To see the Greeks solely as serious artists and philosophers with an unclouded outlook on life, Nietzsche argued, was an error and a fantasy. Their existence was a cruel one, constantly disrupted by wars and privations; and the recurring melancholy or the emotional abandon which scholars had remarked on but passed by was in fact the expression of an underlying pessimism. This was as vital a part of the Greek spirit as the motives which led to more sophisticated enterprises. Tragedy, the first form of Greek drama, had grown out of the Dionysian religion of preclassical times. It was an attempt to make existence endurable by elevating it to art—an explanation reminiscent of Schopenhauer; and it had reached its highest state in the plays of Aeschylus, when the Dionysian chorus again and again discharged itself in Apollonian images. Rapture and order were thus united. While Greek drama retained this shared character, it flourished; but Socratic rationalism soon gained the upper hand, and in the plays of Euripides polished dialogue received the central place. The chorus, which had provided such strong dramatic currents, survived only as a shadow of its former self.

Greek classical drama therefore became decadent; it would now live under the illusion "that thought, guided by the thread of causation, might plumb the farthest abysses of being and even *correct* it." Socrates, the prototype of the new "theoretical" man, was also "the first who was able not only to live under the guidance of that instinctive scientific certainty but to die by it, which is much more difficult." The implications of his rationalist thought far transcended their impact on drama.

> Once [Nietzsche continues] we have fully realized how, after Socrates, the mystagogue of science, one school of philosophers after another came upon the scene and departed; how generation after generation of inquirers, spurred by an insatiable thirst for knowledge, explored every aspect of the universe; and how by that ecumenical concern a common net of knowledge was spread over the whole globe, affording glimpses into the workings of an entire solar system—once we have realized all this, and the monumental pyramid of present-day knowledge, we cannot help viewing Socrates as the vortex and turning point of Western civilization.

But thenceforward, to "every noble and gifted man" had come the unsettling perception that there are limits to the optimism implicit in logic. "If we look about us today, with eyes refreshed and fortified by the spectacle of the Greeks, we shall see how the insatiable zest for knowledge, prefigured in Socrates, has been transformed into tragic resignation and the need for art; while, to be sure, on a lower level that same zest appears as hostile to all art and especially to the truly tragic, Dionysian art." To the young philology professor, however, his urgent need for an art uniting reason with the wisdom of Dionysian ecstasy had been met by the emergence out of German music and philosophy of a new drama and a new Aeschylus in the genius of Richard Wagner. In the tragic myth of *Tristan* one could hope for everything and forget all that was most afflicting. Like an intoxicated reveler, one could thrill in every nerve to its sublime musical dissonances, and feel impelled to dance oneself—as Nietzsche says he did on the hills overlooking Nice.

Apollo and Dionysus represented for Nietzsche the two sides to human nature, and they gave him the standards by which he evaluated history and the work of historians. In his earlier writings directly relating to history, he saw an ideal civilization as holding both elements in balance. An inferior society emphasized one at the expense of the other. Three periods of history were discernible, each identified by the highest values men had held. The first was the era of early man, who had lived by intuition alone. When he ceased to be nomadic and accepted the rules of a group, he lost his freedom to express his instinctive emotions and sublimated them; but this decisive event (though causing him self-inflicted suffering) was his gain in creative power. In the second period, the age of Greek culture, reason and instinct were each held vital to man's happiness; and the Greeks took their strong passions and directed them in a rational and artistic manner without degrading them. That was the secret of their excellence.

But in the third period, from Socrates onward, Western civilization had elevated the values ascribed to Apollo, and neglected or purposely submerged its Dionysian energies. History indeed became the descending arc of a great cycle in which these two drives repeatedly fought each other. Dionysian waves hurled themselves against Apollonian barriers and sometimes broke through; but they had always been driven back and restrained by a stronger Apollonian reaction. In this way Paul had blunted the message of Jesus, Aquinas had done the same to St. Francis, and so had Calvin to Luther, and European nationalists to Napoleon. In Renaissance Italy and the France of Louis XIV a temporary harmony had existed, but the French Revolution ended what was left of that tradition. Reason then became as much modern man's dominant characteristic as intuition was his primitive forebear's; and the disintegration of culture began in earnest.

Never before had the two forces been so far apart as in the nineteenth-century world, which crushed instinct in the name of scientific theory, systematic thought, social convention, and efficient government. Never had the Dionysian spirit been so domesticated, cheapened, and repressed. What was trumpeted as the glorious final chapter of human progress was to Nietzsche a culture at its lowest ebb, bent on oversimplifying man and checking his natural impulses. This was the formula for decadence. The Greeks at their best had understood life in all its wildness and beauty; they had seen it as a struggle, not as a rest from combat, and had thereby become a race of near-legendary beings. Nineteenth-century Europeans rejected the authentic Greek genius, however loud their admiration; proudly proclaiming their future to be limitless, they were actually closing it and barring it to the contagion of reality. Early man by comparison had been a higher type, for he was always at the edge of a great harvest of achievements.

"I hate everything that merely instructs me without increasing or directly quickening my activity." Nietzsche took Goethe's words to open his essay "The Use and Abuse of History," and to judge the worth of the historical study. He knew that his thoughts would appear unseasonable in a Germany which revered Hegel and Ranke; but, precisely because he believed history to be so necessary to life, he felt compelled to argue against their type of scholarship, which was now a costly and superfluous luxury:

> We do need history, but quite differently from the jaded idlers in the garden of knowledge, however grandly they may look down on our rude and unpicturesque requirements. In other words, we need it for life and action, not as a convenient way to avoid life and action, or to excuse a selfish life and a cowardly or base action. We would serve history only so far as it serves life; but to value its study beyond a certain point mutilates and degrades life: and this is a fact that certain marked symptoms of our time make it as necessary as it may be painful to bring to the test of experience. . . . I am trying to represent something of which the age is rightly proud—its historical culture—as a fault and a defect in our time, believing as I do that we are all suffering from a malignant historical fever and should at least recognize the fact.

To define the advantages and disadvantages of history, Nietzsche first contrasts historical awareness with its absence. The beast of the field lives unhistorically, grazing and ruminating, contentedly forgetful of any moment but the present; but man, however much he may envy the beast, can never change places with it. He is tied to the past by his memory, and, "however far or fast he runs, that chain runs with him." The weight of history is a burden constantly pressing him down, causing suffering, not pleasure. But life in any true sense is absolutely impossible without forgetfulness—in the smallest and greatest happiness, forgetting is the one thing that makes it happiness; and there is, Nietzsche argues, a degree of historical sense that injures and finally destroys a living thing, whether it is a man or a society. "We must," he writes, "know the right time to forget as well as the right time to remember, and instinctively see when it is necessary to feel historically and when unhistorically. This is the point that the reader is asked to consider: that the unhistorical and historical are equally necessary to the health of an individual, a community, and a system of culture."

A man's historical knowledge may be limited or incorrect, Nietzsche says, yet "he may stand forth in unconquerable health and vigor, to the joy of all who see him." Another man with far more judgment and learning may fail in life because he has too many perspectives on everything, and cannot shake himself free from their delicate network to commit a straightforward act of will or desire. "Man can only become man by first suppressing this unhistorical element in his thoughts, comparisons, distinctions, and conclusions, letting a clear sudden light break through these misty clouds by his power of turning the past to the uses of the present. But an excess of history makes him flag again, while without the veil of the unhistorical he would never have the courage to begin."

In spite of its blindness, ignorance, and fallibility, Nietzsche writes, "this condition, unhistorical and antihistorical throughout, is the cradle not only of unjust action, but of every just and justifiable action in the world." It causes generals to win victories, nations to gain freedom, and artists to paint great pictures. Historical men see the past supporting the present and stimulating their longing for the future. The man of action "forgets most things in order to do one . . . and only recognizes one law—the law of that which is to be." He sees no salvation in evolution; for him "the world is complete and fulfills its aim in every single moment." He recognizes the accidental nature of historical events and understands all the history of nations and individuals from within. In short, he reaches a "super-historical" standpoint of consciousness.

But, because "the historical prejudice" is such a feature of modern life, it reclaims our attention. "History, so far as it serves life, serves an unhistorical power, and thus will never become a pure science like mathematics. The question how far life needs such a service is one of the most serious questions affecting the well-being of a man, a people, and a culture." "History," Nietzsche goes on to say, "is necessary to the living man in three ways: in relation to his action and struggle, his conservatism and reverence, his suffering and his desire for deliverance. These three relations answer to the three kinds of history—so far as they can be distinguished—the *monumental*, the *antiquarian*, and the *critical*." Each of them has some disadvantage for life, each can grow into weeds; but, if they are used in the right proportions and cultivated carefully, each can confer great benefits.

"Monumental" history is the story of great men of the past, held up as models to imitate, either for what they were or for what they have come to symbolize. Its usefulness lies in the knowledge that greatness existed, was therefore possible, and so may be possible again. Modern man is heartened; but such examples for conduct are unavoidably vague.

Circumstances never repeat themselves exactly, and the same motives that mixed in one man never interact again in precisely the same way. The careers of Caesar or Columbus cannot be forced into a general principle, and monumental history as a result deceives. It lives by false analogy, enticing "the brave to rashness, and the enthusiastic to fanaticism," and making them act, whether they wish it or not, as though their motto were: "Let the dead bury the—living!" Its teaching can never be completely true, it risks being dressed up in fiction, and whole tracts of the past are forgotten or despised; "they flow away like a dark, unbroken river, with only a few gaily colored islands of fact rising above it." But if the man who will produce something great has need of the past, he will master it by means of monumental history.

An "antiquarian" approach to history, on the other hand, is found in the man who looks back to his roots with love and trust, who sees the history of himself in all that survives from former times—his ancestors' furniture, or the walls, the turreted gates, and the institutions of his town. His links with the past become intuitive, and the antiquarian spirit yields its greatest value "in the simple emotions of pleasure and content that it lends to the drab, rough, even painful circumstances of a nation's or individual's life." Yet it too has its dangers; and, surely with the Rankean school of scholarship in mind, Nietzsche graphically describes what happens when the historical sense no longer preserves life but mummifies it:

> Antiquarian history degenerates from the moment that it no longer gives a soul and inspiration to the fresh life of the present. The spring of piety is dried up, but the learned habit persists without it and revolves complacently round its own center. The horrid spectacle is seen of the mad collector raking over all the dust heaps of the past. He breathes a moldy air; the antiquarian habit may degrade a considerable talent, a real spiritual need in him, to a mere insatiable curiosity for everything old; he often sinks so low as to be satisfied with any food, and greedily devours all the scraps that fall from the bibliographical table.

Too much antiquarian history, with no sure instinct for the present, "hinders the mighty impulse to a new deed and paralyzes the doer."

As for "critical" history, it brings the past to judgment, interrogates it, and finally condemns it. It treads ancient pieties underfoot in the name of a different future. Man must have the strength to break up the past in this way, and here and there a victory is won; but, "though we condemn the errors and think we have escaped them, we cannot escape the fact that we spring from them"—which frustrates our well-intentioned efforts to set up a new existence. At best, critical history amounts to "a conflict between our innate, inherited nature and our knowledge."

All three forms of history thus have great life-giving potential; but, if we take a quick glance around us, "we fly back in astonishment." The clearness, naturalness, and purity of the connection between life and history have vanished, and an excess of history has placed man's inner and outer life in mutual opposition. He now feels by theory, and gestures by precedent; and, in this decadent state—evident most of all in Germany—he forfeits any chance of cultural distinction. Yet he imagines he can judge the past more justly than his predecessors did; and, as all bonds cease between "machines for thinking, writing, and speaking" and their historical subjects, "we see noisy little fellows measuring themselves with the Romans as though they were like them," scholars burrowing in the remains of the Greek poets as if these were bodies to be dissected, "a race of eunuchs" who are "the Eternal Objective." This empty culture is less a genuine culture than a kind of knowledge about culture. It does not look at a deed, a work of poetry or of music, for itself. It instead asks who the author was, so it can compare it to others, criticize, and offer him advice; and it ends in utter cynicism.

How can history have lost its positive value so dramatically? Why does it dominate the equally necessary unhistorical sense? The original historical note "sang of action, need, and terror"; but the overtone "lulls us into a soft dilettante sleep." "It is as though the heroic symphony had been arranged for two flutes for the use of dreaming opium smokers." For Nietzsche, this deterioration began when historians chose to serve science; for then they were obliged to recreate the past as fully and faithfully as possible, and to ignore the social impact of their work. Reciting obscure facts, unable to generalize instructively, robbing men of the illusions they need, they had steadily ruined the culture. "Everything is favored that does not rouse emotion, and the driest phrase is the correct one," Nietzsche wrote; "they go so far as to accept a man who is *not affected at all* by some particular moment in the past as the right man to describe it." The historical student, trained to be a specialist, marks out a little isolated period for sacrifice. He applies his method, masters his corner of knowledge, makes it yield results—and kills it. Modern scholars, in fact, are like hens worn out from being forced to lay too many eggs. "They are certainly not 'harmonious' natures; they can merely cackle more than before, because they lay eggs oftener; but the eggs are always smaller though their books are bigger."

"You can explain the past only by what is most powerful in the

present," Nietzsche tells his reader; only by straining your noblest qualities to their utmost will you discover what is greatest in the past, most worth knowing and preserving. "Like by like! otherwise you will draw the past to your own level." One should not believe any history that does not spring from a mind able to be both simple and profound. History therefore needs to be written by the man of experience and character; and only he who is building up the future has the right to judge the past. "Make of yourselves a mirror where the future may see itself." History should not be asked to be the means and the instrument to that future."If you want biographies . . . feast your souls on Plutarch, and dare to believe in yourselves when you believe in his heroes." "A hundred such men—educated against the fashion of today, made familiar with the heroic, and come to maturity—are enough to give an eternal quietus to the noisy sham education of this time."

With these remarks Nietzsche states his impending theme—the reconstruction of history by and for a new elite. The historical culture of the present day has created in man the habits of old age, making him passive and retrospective; and Hegel's enormous influence has doubled the danger man is in. For Hegel allows man to excuse his degeneration by making him believe, "by a neat turn of the wheel," that he is the true meaning of all past creation, the necessary result of the world-process; and every event behind him appears as the victory of logic, or of the "Idea realizing itself." But, fortunately, there have always been men "who troubled themselves very little about the 'thus it is,' in order that they might follow a 'thus it must be' with greater joy and greater pride." The future knows them as the "firstcomers." "Is our time perhaps such a 'firstcomer'?" Nietzsche asks. If there is a future culture, it will commend the present for its active historical sense at least:

> The historical imagination has never flown so far, even in a dream; for now the history of man is merely the continuation of that of animals and plants; the universal historian finds traces of himself even in the utter depths of the sea, in the living slime. He stands astounded in face of the enormous way that man has run, and his gaze quivers before the mightier wonder, the modern man who can see all this way! He stands proudly on the pyramid of the world-process; and while he lays the final stone of his knowledge, he seems to cry aloud to listening Nature: "We are at the top, we are at the top; we are the completion of Nature!"

But man's pride in his condition is full of irony. "O thou too proud European of the nineteenth century," Nietzsche counters, "art thou not mad? Thy knowledge does not complete Nature, it only kills thine own nature! Measure the height of what thou knowest by the depths of thy power to *do*." The time will come, he continued, "when we shall wisely keep away from all constructions of the world-process, or even of the history of man—a time when we shall no more look at masses but at individuals who form a sort of bridge over the wan stream of becoming. They may not perhaps continue a process, but they live out of time, as contemporaries; and, thanks to history that permits such a company, they live as the Republic of geniuses of which Schopenhauer speaks. One giant calls to another across the waste space of time, and the high spirit-talk goes on, undisturbed by the wanton, noisy dwarfs who creep among them." "The task of history," he wrote, reaching the heart of his message, "is to be the mediator between these, and even to give the motive and power to produce the great man. The aim of mankind can lie ultimately only in its highest examples."

From all aberrations of the historical sense, Nietzsche concludes, "we have the right to defend our youth"; for, "in this kingdom of youth I can cry Land! Land!" "I trust in the inspiring power that directs my vessel instead of genius," he wrote; "I trust in *youth* that has brought me on the right road in forcing from me a protest against the modern historical education, and a demand that man must learn to live, above all, and only use history in the service of the life he has learned to live." The first generation of fighters and dragon-slayers would only glimpse the happiness and beauty ahead; but, once man had let his own experience affect his studies and had regained touch with his sincere emotions, a healthy valid culture would at last be possible again. A culture can only reflect the condition of its creators, and German culture was trying wrongly to produce as its highest type the professor. But this is against nature, for it conceives the flower without the stalk; a genuine culture can only rise and bloom from life.

The antidotes to the historical disease are none other than the two poisons he named at the start of his inquiry, Nietzsche declares—the powers of the "unhistorical" and the "super-historical." Youth, with its natural instinct of health, has guessed these remedies already; but what assurance do we have that we can be cured and become men again, not mere shadows of humanity? "The Delphian god cries his oracle to you at the beginning of your wanderings: 'Know thyself,'" Nietzsche answered. "It is a hard saying, for that god 'tells nothing and conceals nothing but merely points the way,' as Heraclitus said. But whither does he point?" In certain epochs the Greeks had been in a similar danger, when their culture and religion was a chaos of foreign forms and ideas; but, by learning to organize the chaos and "thinking back to themselves, to their own true necessities, and letting all the sham necessities go," they had become their own masters again. They thus became the ancestors and models for all the cultured nations of the future; and, looking once more at their matchless example, Nietzsche brings his essay to an end.

The historical sense, Nietzsche wrote later, emerged as an actual faculty of mind—man's sixth sense—in the nineteenth century. It then became possible to grasp quickly the hierarchy of values by which a people, a community, or an individual once lived and thus to have "secret access" to all the past—and yet the nineteenth century "possessed" all centuries but its own. For, treating the past by its own standards, it no longer used history in the indispensable role of testing life for quality. The German student was being taught to follow the steps of Hegel, Ranke—or Bismarck—to success; but the heroic individual takes the work of others, grasps the salient facts, and at the right moment throws them away in a burst of creative energy which is his alone. To Nietzsche's critics, such an outlook is far too straightforward; it is likely to see the past in terms of good and evil, black and white, sensible and irrational. But to Nietzsche it distinguished not only Caesar and Napoleon, but every man who has trusted in himself and acted. No other sort of man should be permitted to teach history to the young. Greek civilization showed what the victories of such men could achieve, but Nietzsche eventually held out another prospect for the future than the life of Greece restored; for, he announced in *Thus Spoke Zarathustra*, "Behold, I teach you the Superman."

IV

More than any other of Nietzsche's ideas, the Superman has gripped popular imagination. A finer, different type of man—strong, intelligent, and just—he is clearly the heir to similar heroes in world myth and literature. The German term, "Übermensch" ("Overman"), dates from the seventeenth century, and Nietzsche seems to have taken it from Goethe; but it is now firmly linked with Nietzsche's name—though current versions of the concept are misleading. When in 1938 the Superman of the science-fiction comic strips appeared, he flew above skyscrapers, battled mad scientists, and ignited explosives with his X-ray eyes. He disguised himself as Clark Kent, a timid character who, when changed into a superior being, became every child's fantasy of power. This comic-book Superman's moral image absurdly caricatures Nietzsche's teaching, and his athletic prowess was—to say the least—hardly what Nietzsche can have intended; nor was the Superman's tragic living manifestation in the Second World War, the jack-booted

German officer striding over the prostrate slave-laborers. How Nietzsche's idea was linked to the Nazi creed of a new master race forms a disastrous episode in the growth of his reputation.

With their jumbled themes and their loose and obscure detail, Nietzsche's writings are a gift to the unscrupulous; and his ambitious sister, Elisabeth Förster-Nietzsche, the widow of a fanatical anti-Semite who had failed at founding a German colony in Paraguay, saw that she could build a new career for herself when her brother's books suddenly grew famous in the 1890s. Imperial Germany was looking for a new messiah and a new philosophy; and, establishing an archive of Nietzsche's papers at Weimar, she personally directed the publication of his remaining manuscripts and brought out new editions of his works. She revised or suppressed all that interfered with the legend she had planned, and she also wrote biographies of her brother emphasizing her role as his confidante and chosen interpreter. Not only did she further confuse the already difficult texts (she hardly understood his thought at all), but the Nietzsche she made known to the world was a man who supported and enhanced her late husband's views. The thinker adopted by the Nazi movement as an intellectual and spiritual guide was largely a creation of Elisabeth Förster-Nietzsche. He was deceptively quoted as urging ruthlessness, aggression, and German expansion; as preaching eugenics and being a violent Jew-hater; and his condemnation of Christianity and democracy also lent itself to Nazi policies. He had, moreover, praised authority and leadership; and he—and his sister— therefore stood in high regard with Hitler, who was photographed at Weimar contemplating a bust of the author of "master morality."

The scandal of Elisabeth Förster-Nietzsche's curatorship has long been revealed. Everything Nietzsche wrote needs to be read in light of his whole philosophy, in the form that he left it; and it is now plain that he was no narrow German nationalist—he was European in sympathy, took pride in the idea he was of Polish descent, and once wrote that, as an artist, a man has no home except in Paris. Nor was he anti-Semitic—he detested his brother-in-law, was disgusted with Wagner's prejudice, and saw all great cultures proceeding from mixed races. And he was certainly no proto-Nazi—he ridiculed the Germany of his time as a country of followers. But his cloudy dreams proved diabolical in the hands of the wrong dreamer; and the stigma of guilt by association began only to be erased in the 1950s, when his writings were carefully inspected.

How, then, should we view Nietzsche's controversial doctrine of the Superman, and of Eternal Recurrence, both of which connect with his notion of history? Our starting point is the madman's shout that God is dead. In Nietzsche's Europe only a madman could utter the truth that God no longer explained the world, or effectively touched men's emotions or engaged men's minds; perhaps only a madman could see that, when men fully understood this news, madness would be universal. But over the centuries Christianity had become debased. The only true Christian died on the Cross, Nietzsche said; and, by legalism and persecution, the Church had encouraged weakness in the believer. Only slaves could accept the blessedness of being peace-loving and poor in spirit, and the death of God was therefore man's opportunity. But to have lost God also meant that man's life lost any profound significance; and Nietzsche insisted that some substitute be found to give man a purpose and a definite ideal of happiness. The glory of man's predicament was that he was now summoned to choose his own goal. "Once you said 'God' when you gazed upon distant seas," spoke Zarathustra, "but now I have taught you to say 'Superman.' God is a supposition; but I want your supposing to reach no further than your creating will. Could you *create* a God? —So be silent about all gods! But you could surely create the Superman."

The Superman is man's image of himself as he could be but is not yet—what he might be if he could overcome himself. "Man is something that should be overcome," Nietzsche wrote; "What have you done to overcome him?" In man's struggle to create something above and beyond himself, he is helped by his will—the drive of his will to power over others, but also, more importantly, over himself. The aim is an exalted one. "What is good?" Nietzsche asked in *The Anti-Christ*, "—All that heightens the feeling of power, the will to power, power itself in man. What is bad?—All that proceeds from weakness. What is happiness?—The feeling that power *increases*—that a resistance is overcome." Even when dangerous to society the will to power is still good, for its great energies can still be applied to self-overcoming. The ordinary man tries to preserve the life he has. He is satisfied with the progress mankind has made; " 'We have discovered happiness,' say the Ultimate Men and blink." But the exceptional man recognizes the will to power—which is properly the will to hope and create—and gives it freedom. He raises himself above other mortals and knows that, though God is dead, his own faith in a higher existence lives on. He is now something to be accomplished, he has now become, by his strength, his own destiny.

"The Superman is the meaning of the earth," Zarathustra said to the people. "Let your will say: The Superman *shall be* the meaning of the earth." Man was in fact a bridge between the animals and Superman—not a goal in himself. "What is the ape to men? A laughing-stock or a painful embarrassment. And just so shall man be to the Superman: a laughing-stock or a painful embarrassment." The beast in man is thus left behind as he ceaselessly reaches for a higher level of consciousness, culture, and freedom. Nietzsche's papers do not show a strategy for Aryan world mastery, nor is the will to power part of the Darwinian struggle for survival of the fittest. Men are basically on the same level as animals, he believed, except for a few higher specimens; but these are the result of conscious human choice, not of natural selection. The successful man to Nietzsche was not the most adaptable but the most exotic, the rarest, the most unusually talented; and the excellence of this new nobility lay in its diversity—not in a single type. Rising above the herd, they fulfilled the great aim of mankind—to produce its highest examples. "Our way is upward, from the species across to the super-species," Nietzsche wrote; but his theory was distinctly aristocratic.

The Superman, it must be said, never really comes to life in Nietzsche's scattered references to him. He has been criticized as a piece of Romantic nonsense ("a Siegfried who knows Greek"), and as the embodiment of all that Christianity fights against—though Nietzsche's teaching has some Christian traits. But the idea is shaped from the material of history, for behind Nietzsche's abstraction stand occasional "sovereign individuals" of tremendous determination and self-mastery—Socrates, Caesar, Jesus, Michaelangelo, Cesare Borgia, Frederick the Great, Goethe—men who have willed themselves to greatness, and who have been freed from respect for tradition and conventional morality. It is partly inspired by Renaissance ideals and owes much to Hegel; and Napoleon was the then-recent great figure against whom extraordinary human powers were still measured. It was not, however, Napoleon's conquests which should be admired, Nietzsche held, but what he had made of himself. Such men became symbols of excellence—and educational models. They had possessed the wisdom of the super-historical point of view as well as of the historical and unhistorical; and in them we see the meaning of life and history. For they set forth the values men should learn; and, in their record of self-creation and self-mastery, history became a work of art.

But in fact the superior man, the real Superman, is and has not been existent anywhere. "There has never yet been a Superman," Zarathustra cried. "I have seen them both naked, the greatest and the smallest man. They are still all-too-similar to one another. Truly, I found even the greatest man—all-too-human!" Nietzsche admired Caesar more than Napoleon as the embodiment of the man who takes his strong passions and directs them. He once wrote that his ideal was "the Roman Caesar with Christ's soul." But the clearest impression of the Superman from actual life that Nietzsche gives us is Pericles making his famous funeral oration—the mightiest and worthiest man on earth, Nietzsche commented. Pericles faced his countrymen "in the beautiful rigidity and motionlessness of a marble Olympian and began to speak, calmly, wrapped in his mantle, its draperies unmoved, his countenance without change of expression, without smile, his strong voice powerfully even . . . thundering, flashing, destroying, redeeming. . . ." The fact that he exercised this self-control amid Athens's sorrow made his example all the finer. In Pericles, reason and emotion were blended so constructively that the positive and negative elements of each perfectly balanced one another. For a moment, tension rested in complete equilibrium—and the sight was of a man unbelievably poised and aloof from the masses, flawless to the point of self-extinction. Yet even then his perfection was incomplete; for, Nietzsche wrote, the Superman's hour of greatness is also the hour of his greatest self-contempt. Man's struggle for his future is never finished. He remains the believer in impossible possibilities.

But, if man's goal now was to be Superman, what future lay beyond that? An even higher goal—or a period of decline? In what process of time was the drama being played? If God was dead, Nietzsche argued, then the whole idea that history has order and direction is void, for the governing principles of other schemes are only God in disguise. We must now accept history not with an external imprint, but as it actually is— with no beginning, no final end to which men may aspire, and no stages for men to go through to reach it. It is simply random change in a universe where time is infinite. But, since space is finite, the number of changes must be limited—like combinations in a game of dice; and at some point the universe is bound to come back to conditions that are identical, not just similar, to its previous state. The monotony of this prospect, the sense that the limits of human achievement are fixed, at first horrified Nietzsche, and he saw it made man's need to affirm his new goal all the more urgent. Man was now freed from a whole set of world hypotheses; and the purpose he must choose for himself to combat the never-ending chaos and meaninglessness of existence was to make every event of his life an act of overcoming, an increase of power, and a supreme moment of joy. He must live to repeat that joy, still saying "yes" to all that life offered him. "So live that you must desire to live again," Nietzsche wrote. "Eternity is worth it." "*This* life is your eternal life."

This was Nietzsche's doctrine of Eternal Recurrence—that time in the cosmos moves in great cycles at gigantic intervals. It came to him with the force of a mystical experience, and he claimed it was his most

important teaching. It demands our interest, not least for reasons relating to current scientific discussion. As astronomers investigate theories
that the universe began with a colossal explosion, and is now expanding,
new philosophical assumptions are tentatively defined; and these affect
the larger proportions according to which history is conceived. In-
evitably all life as we know it must die; but we may still conjecture that,
in the fullness of time, the universe will contract and be reborn from a
new hyperdense state, and that other earths and other creatures will
evolve once more—and again and again.

"What is man?" asked Nietzsche in *The Birth of Tragedy*; and he
immediately replied, "an incarnation of dissonance." To resolve man's
dilemma, which he thought had then reached unbearable proportions,
became his vocation. His views should be seen in their late nineteenth-
century context, but they are an indictment of the whole scientific
tradition which has dominated Western thought since Galileo, Bacon,
and Descartes. Nietzsche exposed the separation of human values and
science so perceptively that many readers today, agreeing with him that
this separation has been disastrous for modern society, find his opinions
congenial. "What I relate is the history of the next two centuries,"
Nietzsche wrote. "I describe what is coming, what can no longer come
differently: *the advent of nihilism*. This history can be related even
now; for necessity itself is at work here. This future speaks even now in
a hundred signs, this destiny announces itself everywhere." But Marx
too declared he knew the history of the future, and Marx also has his
supporters. How should we estimate these two prophets together?

Nietzsche and Marx share a surprising amount of common ground.
Both rejected current philosophies, both revolted against bourgeois society, both approved natural human instincts, both admired action—
and both foretold catastrophe. Each shaped his theory of history in
protest against man's self-alienation—though Nietzsche had far less
sense of community than Marx. But Marx, who was proud of demol-
ishing all previous historical schemes and who extolled man obeying
his own self, put man into another system. It had the best credentials,
Marx believed, because to him it was scientifically proven; and it defined man by what Marx saw as man's fundamental activity—his attempt physically to survive. Past, present, and future now had a rational,
linear, predetermined pattern. They could be codified, and man could
make his plans with confidence.

Nietzsche fought for man's survival in a different sense—not only
as a material creature, but in all the forms that make him unique as
man. He refused to sacrifice man to Apollo yet again, and he denied
that man's history can be deduced from any philosophical scheme.

Instead Nietzsche saw man as an individual in the absence of any structure, and saw man's will—not conditions among the masses—as causing historical change. The highest and noblest men were actually the most remote from the crowd. The popular notion that mankind was fast moving to the final stage of human progress destroyed man and civilization alike. Man would not be superior when he had conquered all his adversaries; the struggle made him great, not any ending to it. Only by regaining the selfhood he had possessed in Greek antiquity could man be truly alive and see himself as the start of his future. Only after abandoning his utopian dreams could man hope to rise at all.

Nietzsche's Romantic analysis of human nature appeals to a large audience in the late twentieth century, who suspect that Western civilization is proceeding exactly as he forecast; for they believe that today's Western man has found that the great future has severe and potentially disastrous limitations. The dreams that helped him forward before—dreams so visible at the Great Exhibition of 1851—have not only failed to come true, they are actually benefiting him less. The technological revolution may well have been a short-lived phase in human history; the failings of the social and political utopia have been starkly laid bare; and some of the arts lack enterprise and vitality, as if there were no frontier left. Man lives his life no longer in a world that manifests some order to guide him, but in a world and a universe with no apparent plan or purpose. Simultaneously, events and discoveries have carried him so far beyond his old assumptions that he is unable to fit his mind back into them. He now perceives that he has an unfamiliar outlook on the world, which implies the fact of the world's disorder and meaninglessness—and the consequent lack of truths. It was Nietzsche, not Marx, who expected this situation, his defenders say; and he held that it alone is the reality in which all historical thinking must now take place.

"So far as there are laws in history, the laws are of no value and the history of no value either," Nietzsche wrote. History must meet man's needs as he tries to reorient himself in the chaos around him; it must, like Nietzsche's aphorisms, tell of the struggle within man rather than refine external knowledge about him. On the other hand, many professional scholars reply that if Nietzsche's advice is taken, much historical knowledge is sure to be lost; and history tied to any moral values is ruled by the dictates of ideology. The past is then not only lost but falsified or obscured, as we see when Trotsky is blotted out from photographs of himself with Lenin, when Alfred Rosenberg's *Myth of the Twentieth Century* becomes the official history for Germans—or when any methodology is applied to it with supreme confidence. When the historian's task excludes moral criticism he is free to seek values of genuine worth. He then ideally shows the spirit of curiosity and lack of prejudice that marks the genuine humanist. Scholars do not just write dusty monographs; their thought sometimes reveals the world in an entirely new light. To this argument Nietzsche retorts that man cannot have any truths unless he has a valid set of values to live by; therefore, only by first choosing such values can he have a valid history. To the observer there seems no way past this stalemate—men must choose one side or the other.

Nietzsche believed that he could see a new prospect for man and wrote to make others see it too. He had already lived through the whole of nihilism, to the end, he said—"leaving it behind, outside himself." As for civilization, he asks how much history do we need? To that he offers three answers. The first is all of history, because without knowledge of the past no man's knowledge of himself can be said to be complete. The second is none of it, because at times forgetting is as important as remembering—so important that it should be investigated just as carefully. And the third and clearest answer is enough to make man into a finer human being, with all the promise and the pitfalls this allows. History must serve life, not life history. You should have as much as you need—to live!

CHAPTER NINE

Du Bois

I

"I can never forget that morning in the class of the great Heinrich von Treitschke in Berlin," wrote the light-skinned American Negro William Edward Burghardt Du Bois, recollecting his studies under Ranke's "fire-eating" successor in the 1890s.

> He was a big aggressive man, with an impediment in his speech which forced him to talk rapidly lest he stutter. His classes were the only ones always on time, and an angry scraping of feet greeted a late comer. Clothed in black, big, bushy-haired, peering sharply at the class, his words rushed out in a flood: 'Mulattoes,' he thundered, 'are inferior.' I almost felt his eyes boring into me, although probably he had not noticed me. 'Sie fühlen sich niedriger!' 'Their actions show it,' he asserted. What contradiction could there be to that authoritative dictum?

Few in Europe or America at that time would have thought any contradiction possible. At the close of a century of unprecedented progress, of increased knowledge of all kinds, and of imperialist expansion—ending with a headlong scramble for Africa—white supremacy over colored races appeared a permanent fact; and, with Britain, the United States, and lately Germany in the lead, the most recent history seemed irrefutably the record of the ascending achievements of the Anglo-Saxon and Teutonic peoples. The attitude of cultural and racial superiority Du Bois encountered in Berlin, backed by scientific dogma, reminded him of a display in a museum at Harvard showing a series of skeletons arranged from a little monkey to a tall, well-developed white man, with a Negro in the middle scarcely outranking a chimpanzee. Pronounced physically and mentally inferior, he would bitterly write, the Negro had long been the clown of history, the football of anthropology, and the slave of industry; and he noted how in elementary-school textbooks Negroes, Indians, and Chinese were habitually depicted by their most uncivilized and bizarre representatives, while the whites were portrayed by some kindly and distinguished-looking philanthropist. The study of history in the West throve on the exclusion of other cultures and commemorated the exploits which had created the West's worldwide predominance. "All is race," declared Disraeli; "there is no other truth." "I would annex the planets if I could," said Cecil Rhodes.

No small part of nineteenth-century Western man's prodigious self-confidence came from the certainty that the white race was superior because it alone had a history. It was of course known that China and India possessed venerable, fascinating cultures for which a certain respect was allowable; but their history remained obscure except to the scholar or the curious and barely researched, and what little was known to the average man encouraged him in his condescension. The history of the world was the well-documented story of Europeans impinging on the world, with ever-increasing effectiveness once the age of exploration began. Voltaire's vision of China as a land of enlightenment was disbelieved long before Lord Macartney, the first British ambassador, candidly reported in 1793 on the Celestial Empire's backwardness. The prophet Muhammad seemed hardly more than a desert madman; and Indian history was largely remembered for the horrors of the Black Hole of Calcutta and the Mutiny of 1857. As one society after another capitulated to the rifle and gunboat, it was categorized as a barbaric failed experiment, additional proof of the West's preeminence. The Golden Jubilee of Queen Victoria in 1887, Du Bois recalled, "set the pattern of our thinking. The little old woman of Windsor became a magnificent symbol of Empire. Here was England with her flag draped around the world, ruling more black folk than white and leading the colored peoples of the earth to Christian baptism, civilization and eventual self-rule. Only two years before, in 1885, Stanley, the traveling reporter, became a hero and symbol of white world leadership in Africa. The wild, fierce fight of the Mahdi and the driving of the English out of the Sudan for sixteen years did not reveal its inner truth to me. I heard only of the martyrdom of the drunken Bible-reader and free-booter, Gordon."

If Chinese, Indians, and Arabs were at least credited with having reached the stage of the semicivilized in the upward journey of mankind from savagery, the African Negro was almost universally held to have dropped out altogether—if he had started the journey at all. At the apex of human perfection stood the white man, at the foot lay the Negro, deficient in body, nature, and brain size. His instincts were bestial, his intellect sluggish, and his mind, like his land, lay wide open. "We have in East Africa," wrote Britain's first high commissioner there, "the rare experience of dealing with a *tabula rasa,* an almost untouched and sparsely inhabited country where we can do as we will." Except for a few anthropologists and receptive colonial administrators, Europeans judged the signs of the African past—customs, traditions, social hierarchies—by official or racist attitudes, and often quickly dismissed them. The Negro, more than any other race, had no history, for he had no writing and he had taken no major steps forward. Africa, Hegel had said in his lectures, "is an unhistorical continent, with no movement or development of its own." It was disqualified and needed little further consideration. Hegel's verdict is still echoing.

The ethnocentric view of the past, born out of the Western conviction that the record of Christianity, science, and material progress had sealed the white man's superiority, is now easily condemned as pseudohistory, ridiculous in its efforts to construct its arguments, bigoted in its idea of history's substance, revolting and catastrophic in the prejudices it has inspired. Yet it should not be merely repudiated as the blatant teaching of the Ku Klux Klan, of the Afrikaner with his vast system of structured privilege, or of Adolf Hitler and his eugenic theorists. Western ethnocentrism must be examined in its wider scope. It has some interest in itself, and it sometimes induced a certain sense of responsibility—in Britain and the United States at any rate. The reading public there mostly admired Rudyard Kipling's verse and approved his politics; and to take up the White Man's burden and wait on "new-caught, sullen peoples, Half devil and half child" seemed the honorable path of duty and self-respect, though the task to be undertaken was without thanks or guarantee of success. For good or ill, a racist approach to history and the world was to Western taste at the turn of the last century.

To the analyst of today the indigenous vitality of other civilizations is likely to seem more striking than the European impact, which, seen in perspective, was brief and often superficial; and the "decolonization" of the old imperial historiography is now a lively part of history's field of inquiry. The importance of Du Bois lies in the fact that, when racist mythologies were at their peak, he had the boldness to discern, from

the other side, that the Western view of history was distorted and provincial, and he rewrote history accordingly. In a lifetime of scholarship
and agitation he tried to break the conspiracy of silence which kept the
Negro race in ignorance about its past, and to restore the Negro's
rightful place in mankind's narrative. Trained as a historian, he also
used his knowledge to explain the world as he saw it; and, like Voltaire
and Marx, he committed his energies in all directions to change the
world into something he believed was better. Prophetically warning in
1903 that "the problem of the twentieth century is the problem of the
color line—the relation of the darker to the lighter races of men in
Asia and Africa, in America and the islands of the sea," he encouraged
all non-white peoples to reassess their past and discard the negative
self-image their conquerors had given them. But, proud though he was
of his Negro inheritance, Du Bois saw the history of his race as something still to be made; and in that respect he was profoundly American.

   To endow millions of men and women with a history when their
lives testify to its suppression is surely the greatest challenge a historian
can face; but to black intellectuals of today there is no doubt Du Bois
succeeded in his fundamental aim. As Martin Luther King said in a
speech honoring Du Bois, he "knew that to lose one's history is to lose
one's self-understanding and with it the roots for pride. This drove him
to become a historian of Negro life and the combination of his unique
zeal and intellect rescued for all of us a heritage whose loss would have
profoundly impoverished us." Conscious that he himself was an in-
tegral part of European civilization, "and yet, much more significant,
one of its rejected parts," Du Bois essentially wrote history in an attempt
to answer the question,"Who am I?" But, as he was aware, such a
theme was too abstract and metaphysical to a Negro community daily
confronted by the threat to sanity and life in rural areas of the South,
the terrors of the urban ghetto, and the continuing hostility of the
overwhelming majority of its fellow citizens; and he gave flesh, blood,
and lasting immediacy to his basic impulse, refining it into two questions that were still personal but richer and more evocative. "Why," he
asked at the beginning of his history-making book *The Souls of Black
Folk*, "did God make me an outcast and a stranger in mine own house?"
And, in summing up his essential point he asked, "Would America
have been America without her Negro people?" Between them these
questions shaped the many forms in which he expressed his knowledge
and his sense of his people's past.

   His motivation seems deeper yet. To Nietzsche, although an
excess of history produced the pedant, complete ignorance was the
condition of beasts of the field. To strike a vital balance between the

two was the mark of full humanity. Du Bois in his way sought nothing less for his people; but he added the insight that perverted history stunted black and white men alike. His passionate wish to give black consciousness to innumerable nameless faces asserted that a greater life was possible for all. Before reviewing his career, let us look briefly at some of the interpretations of history he met that were governed by ideas of race and heredity.

II

"Race" is a notoriously difficult concept to define; in biology the term is applied to a subgroup within a species, in social and cultural studies to a group or class or caste. There probably never was a pure human "race," and all varieties of the human species are actively or potentially capable of interbreeding. Over tens of thousands of years certain physical differences have been maintained, but accumulating medical and anthropological evidence seems to prove that theories of racial superiority or inferiority are completely false; and, since no clear biological basis of intelligence has been established, differences in intelligence appear to be caused by cultural and environmental factors—though opinion on this is not unanimous. "Race" as a group of people biologically distinct from other groups does not exist; but throughout history people have thought and acted as though it did.

In 54 B.C., Cicero wrote to a friend concerning Caesar's invasion of Britain, "there is not a scrap of silver in the island, nor any hope of booty except slaves; and I do not think you can expect any of those to have had a literary or musical education." If there was no color prejudice in the ancient world, culture prejudice was certainly present. Greeks distinguished between themselves and foreigners; Caesar, while admiring the heroic virtues of the Gauls, objected to their savagery; and, though Tacitus saw the German tribes possessing the freedom and simplicity the Romans had lost, he found much in their primitive life of which he disapproved. The Roman Empire welded a diversity of peoples into a centralized political unit, but not into a single nation; and, in cities where a large Jewish colony lived, Jews were liable to be victims of violence because of their exclusiveness. In both Greece and Rome the image of a slave was not in fact related to any ethnic origin but to the chief source of slaves at the time—which shifted from Scythia, to Thrace, to Gaul, to Britain, and in medieval Europe to the Slav countries. At bottom, "slave" was a status defined not by race but by the law.

A new principle of human society was announced by the apostle

Paul: "There is neither Jew nor Greek, there is neither bond nor free, there is neither male nor female; for ye are all one in Christ Jesus." The Church rose above human divisions; it was, nonetheless, set in the temporal world, entangled in it as Augustine so clearly understood. It inherited the prejudices within the Roman Empire as well as the tradition of thought on the subject of slavery—as an institution, and as a rich metaphor of human dualism; and it propagated a biblical symbolism of color, much elaborated in the Middle Ages, in which the great contrast was drawn between white and black. White signified Christ, light, purity, goodness, the dove of the Holy Spirit; black on the other hand represented Satan and evil, hell and night. Yellow became the color of treachery, scarlet of sin. Medieval people in their restricted world made distinctions more between Christians and heathen, or between class and class, seeing the Jews as an unassimilated enemy in their midst; but this chain of visual associations created by symbolism would have a durable and pernicious effect.

As Western Europeans left their isolation and began their ascent to global hegemony, they found strange unknown people in Africa and the Americas, and in Asia densely populated empires. The conquest of Mexico and Peru was a late extension of the Crusades, indicating the strength of Western ideology and infant technology; and, when not characterized by force, the relationship of white Catholic masters to Indian serfs became one of paternalism. In Asia, where Europeans were at best admitted only as traders, their attitude might be one of interest in the civilization around them when they were not making quick fortunes; and the voyages of Bougainville and Cook in the Pacific Ocean prompted more discussion of "noble savages" and their mode of life. The rise of discrimination was therefore neither simultaneous nor uniform; but no people appeared more opposite to the European than the African Negro. His arresting blackness and European notions of his sexuality increased the impression of obvious social and cultural differences—an impression exacerbated among the English by the Puritan doctrine of election and by the suddenness of English contact. In Brazil and Cuba racial intermixture was not to be a matter for much concern; but, at the Dutch refreshment station which grew into Cape Town, the first governor planted a hedge of wild almond beyond which no Hottentot might pass—and with it the seedling of South African history's central theme. Wherever in the world white and black daily confronted one another a pattern of stereotyped conduct developed, intricate, inconsistent, an amalgam of old complexes but marked by prejudices hardly known before. In the New World especially it was assisted by emerging capitalism; and it was controlled above all by the possession of power.

Despite conspicuous individual exceptions and the generous idealism about the Negro voiced in the French Revolution, the white man at the dawn of the nineteenth century fundamentally saw black as primitive, black as ugly, black as animal, and often black as unforgivably carnal. The prevailing attitudes had of course been vastly influenced and complicated by the institution of African slavery. In the largest forced migration in history, lasting over three hundred years, perhaps more than 11 million Negroes, taken in war among African tribes and sold, or captured by traders for the purpose, were packed in prison ships to cross the Atlantic—a commercial venture well-planned in Liverpool, Bristol, or Bordeaux—and the survivors bought by planters for very likely lifelong bondage. Though Negroes in Virginia and Maryland originally had the same status as white indentured servants, after the 1660s a black skin became equatable with "slave"; and some scholars argue that American slavery was worse than any other, deprived as Negroes were there—compared to slaves in Rome, medieval Europe, the Caribbean, and Brazil—of legal or religious rights, of the protection of society, of ancestral ties (even of name), and of practically all hope of ever improving their status. Other scholars disagree, stating that on the whole American slavery was bearable and not unpleasant, and finding that slaves kept surprisingly many links with their ancestors' culture. But, however much the slave might resist his servitude, the visible fact of his condition firmly fastened the belief in white superiority on the slaveowner, and in the American South this belief became the keystone of a whole style of life. In the long uphill battle before the religious and ethical fervor of emancipators was transformed into British statute, or, in the United States, through fire and sword into constitutional amendment, slavery, its legitimacy and its enormity, was discussed almost wholly by white men and women; for, as a West Indian historian has said, slaves by and large were for wielding hoes or machetes, not pens.

As Europe in the Victorian age rapidly conquered and exploited entire continents, the world was remade to the white man's order; and, in the case of the British Empire, it was governed under the joint inspiration of utilitarian political doctrines, the profit motive, and evangelical Christianity. Discoveries in medicine ensured the survival in oppressive climates not just of white merchants and soldiers but of their families, too; as a result, social mingling between the races, which in India especially had been fairly relaxed, became a subject sometimes fraught with near hysteria—a revealing sign. In spite of the sense of accomplished destiny that swelled in a European or an American whenever he looked at the map, a basic anxiety lay just beneath the surface. Fears of the deterioration of precious racial stock, of exhaustion of the raw materials which fed the factories at home, and of eventual colored retribution were often emotionally expressed (for example, in the supposed menace of the "yellow peril"). Elevated into a call for solemn humility in Kipling's *Recessional*, the suspicion that imperial glory could after all be transient was defiantly but tacitly conceded more often than at first appears.

For the time being, however, the belief that recent history upheld white superiority was buttressed by sharper distinctions of race as a physical category. According to scriptural evidence, although man was created by God, mankind as a whole was descended from the sons of Noah; and the Negro race was interpreted as being the offspring of Ham, whose children Noah cursed to be slaves when Ham saw his father's nakedness. Theologically the human races were seen as one, Christ having died for all; but, with new scientific knowledge at hand, eighteenth-century thinkers debated with increasing boldness how man had originated, and whether the racial types of man constituted a single species or were each a species to itself. The issue far transcended the interest of biologists in its importance for politics and philosophy. Linnaeus cautiously broke with traditionalism when he classified man as one species and placed him with the quadrupeds. He stressed man's mental and spiritual eminence over the apes, but made no place in his system for angels and saw *Homo sapiens* as having four geographical varieties—European, African, Asiatic, and American Indian.

Linnaeus's French contemporary, Buffon, considered the white-skinned people in the area of the Caucasus mountains to have the finest physique and features; and therefore, to his thinking, they were the primitive human stock from which other races had diverged as a result of environment. While Voltaire also disputed old versions of human development, the search for an explanation expanded from comparing relatively advanced societies into an inquiry on how men had risen from the way of life of Hottentots or Australian aborigines, or of wild children found in European forests, to rudimentary civilization. If man's uniqueness lay in his capacity to perfect himself, either in response to chance events as Rousseau described or through evolution as others hinted, the Caucasian race by contemporary standards showed by far the greatest measure of success. In the confused thinking of the early nineteenth century, other races might still be seen as distant cousins to Europeans, remnants who had sunk into barbarism after the Fall or in the dispersion from Babel, but their fundamental difference from the white man was verifiable from their facial features and shape of skull, and self-evident from a cursory observation of their behavior. Race—of which color was the most obvious sign—was the great divider of achievement; and a more acute awareness of class and national distinctions after the French Revolution promoted further the idea of human separation, each hierarchy being sanctified as a system ordained by Providence.

It was in this context that Count Arthur de Gobineau's *Essay on the Inequality of the Human Races* appeared in 1853. The term "Aryan" or "Indo-European" by then had come to denote the early people from whom all European languages and customs were thought to have sprung; and racial scientists had identified the tall, blond, long-headed German as the purest Aryan type, physically superlative and noble of character. Gobineau's interest lay in defending the status of the French aristocracy against plebeian republicans, and he argued that his class was of unadulterated Aryan stock (he was a Norman) while the masses were the degenerate products of racial mongrelization. He himself pointed to England as the country where the superior race had survived with least corruption, but his following was soon greatest by far in Germany, where the whole nation had been led to believe itself splendidly Aryan, a view it saw confirmed by its surge to unity and European leadership. Richard Wagner acclaimed Gobineau's conclusions, and in 1899 the composer's son-in-law, the naturalized German, Houston Stewart Chamberlain, brought out his *Foundations of the Nineteenth Century*, an exhaustive paean to German cultural supremacy based more on instinct than dispassionate research. All higher civilizations bore signs of the Aryan's incomparable touch, and Dante, Columbus, and Shakespeare, as much as Luther and Beethoven, owed their genius to their Aryan blood. Interbreeding caused deterioration, and Aryan stock should be safeguarded against the degraded Jewish minority in particular. Very widely read in Germany, Chamberlain's work prepared the way for *Mein Kampf* itself, and for Alfred Rosenberg's *Myth of the Twentieth Century*—the exposition of the Nazi doctrine of the superiority of Aryan man.

But in the end perhaps the greatest force which drove racist concepts of civilization and history into widespread acceptance in the West was the evolutionary theory of Charles Darwin freely applied by others to society. Resting his conclusions on carefully compiled scientific evidence, Darwin described the human pedigree and carefully stated his belief that progress depended on the rise and spread of ever-superior breeds of man. Physical human characteristics changed through mutation and in the process nature was continually selecting for fitness. The decline or extinction of the indigenous inhabitants of Tasmania or Tierra del Fuego signified the upward advance of mankind as a whole, a process to be viewed with charity toward the unfortunate but as the inevitable triumph of higher over lower varieties of the human species. In the competitive struggle an improved humanity would go forward to even greater accomplishments of mind and technology, and, he assumed, a loftier plane of virtue. His voyage around the world had shown him clearly the position his own country at present held. "My first feeling," he noted in his *Journal* on seeing the flourishing Australian settlement of Sydney after the towns of South America, "was to congratulate myself that I was born an Englishman."

By the 1890s, for all but a significant minority, human history on the global scale had thus been convincingly reduced to the struggle of the races, in which all the advantages currently lay with the white man, and with the Anglo-Saxons in particular. To Cecil Rhodes it was actually the Anglo-Saxon's duty to seize more territories, not so much to rule their peoples as to supplant them. Seeing how prevalent, deeply rooted, widely enforced, and seemingly unanswerable Western ideas of white supremacy had become, it is no surprise to find Du Bois writing in his autobiography: ". . . in my life the chief fact has been race." What does become remarkable is the subsequent attitude he took.

III

W.E.B. Du Bois was born in 1868, not in the South but in Great Barrington, Massachusetts, a small, elm-shaded town in the Berkshires "shut in by its mountains and provincialism." He recalled that there were perhaps twenty-five, certainly not more than fifty, non-whites in a population of five thousand; and, though a color line existed, relations between the races were flexible and tolerant, animosity being directed more at the new Irish immigrants. His ancestry was French, Dutch, and Negro, and his family poor but well known, since it had been among the earliest to come to the Housatonic valley. As a boy the racial slights he received were small, but he felt them deeply when they occurred. He clearly remembered the day he first became aware of the color problem—a girl at school refused to accept a fancy visiting card from him in a game of exchange the children were playing. "Then it dawned upon me with a certain suddenness that I was different from the others; or like, mayhap, in heart and life and longing, but shut out from their world by a vast veil." He noticed too a subtle change in his acceptability when rich vacationers arrived each summer from New York. His initial reaction was to hold the white world in contempt, but he soon saw the openings he wanted were in that world, not his, and was bitterly perplexed by his exclusion.

Determined to excel, Du Bois graduated from high school with distinction and was offered a scholarship to attend Fisk University in Nashville, Tennessee, an institution established after the Civil War for the education of future Negro leaders. He welcomed the opportunity. While on a short trip through New England, at a group picnic he had attended, he had already been astonished by the Negro community's liveliness, its laughter and style, in contrast to New England reserve; he had even been moved to tears on hearing a spiritual choir for the first time. These things he recognized as somehow inherently and deeply his own, and he was glad he would mix at college with black people of his own age, education, and ambitions. At Fisk, which was white-founded and white-staffed, he increased his sense of black consciousness and pride; but he also suffered discrimination in ways he had never dreamed of, experiencing Jim Crow laws of segregation and, when teaching one summer in east Tennessee, race relations in the country districts in the South—"the real seat of slavery," he recalled. Otto von Bismarck was his chosen subject for a graduation thesis, the man who had recently forged a nation out of a mass of rival peoples. The choice was evidence of his growing political activism, and, he later said, of an outlook that was still European and imperialistic.

Receiving to his amazement a scholarship for his further education at Harvard, Du Bois returned north, and his vague ideas and emotions on social ethics were consolidated into firm intellectual positions and fierce dedication. He professed his goal was to develop his talents so as to improve the Negroes' condition. Harvard itself never became a home to him, and he sought companionship in the Boston black community; but his work under so many distinguished teachers, notably William James and George Santayana, gave him the impression he was leading his race on the frontiers of knowledge and strengthened his intentions. His studies turned from philosophy to center for a time on history, and then gradually moved into the area of economics and sociology; for his doctoral dissertation he selected the topic of the suppression of the slave trade. His graduate work ended with two years at the University of Berlin on a fellowship, an event which was a turning point in his life. There, in his economics classes, he began to see the Negro's plight in America in world perspective, linked to the problems of the peoples of Africa and Asia and to the political development of Europe. He also received friendly treatment as an equal from ordinary Europeans, and drew the conclusion that racial animosity was cultural, not hereditary or universal. With a New England sense of purpose, Du Bois pledged himself to improve his race's status and turn the history of his time in a new direction.

Returning to the United States in 1894 he taught for two uncomfortable years at Wilberforce College in Ohio, remaining throughout a misfit there with the cane and gloves of his German student days, alienated by the dominant place given to religious activity; when offered a one-year post at the University of Pennsylvania, he immediately accepted. The attraction lay in the unique chance to study the Negro in Philadelphia at a time when colored citizens were being blamed for slums and crime. "My vision was becoming clearer," he wrote in his autobiography *Dusk of Dawn.* "The Negro problem was in my mind a matter of systematic investigation and intelligent understanding. The world was thinking wrong about race, because it did not know. The ultimate evil was stupidity." With very limited funds and only a few guidelines, Du Bois completed a door-to-door survey and found the city's theory incorrect. He accused the municipal government of restricting job opportunities, chided the Negro minority for lack of ambition and cultural development, and reproached Negro businessmen in particular for lack of leadership. Overall, the situation was examined in terms of its larger background and as it bore upon the Philadelphia community as a whole, not as something sudden, insalubrious, and detachable. Speaking to the American Academy of Political and Social Sciences on his ambition to study the complete Negro problem in the United States, he insisted that, like all phenomena of society, it deserved the most careful attention. The Negro, he claimed, "is a member of the human race, and as one who, in the light of history and experience, is capable to a degree of improvement and culture, is entitled to have his interests considered according to his numbers in all conclusions as to the common weal."

Du Bois's research in Philadelphia brought him an invitation to take charge of work in sociology at Atlanta University and to direct the annual conferences on the Negro problem being inaugurated there. During his ten-year stay in Atlanta each conference investigated a specific topic on a revolving plan, served as a forum for collecting and analyzing the latest data on the Negro's condition, and published its findings in a series of authoritative, detailed papers. At the same time Du Bois began to transform himself personally from objective social scientist to propagandist. It was becoming disappointingly clear that his studies, though accurate and well regarded, were not going to change the world by themselves; moreover, as he described it, there cut across his path "a red ray which could not be ignored." When a poor Georgia Negro killed his landlord's wife, Du Bois wrote out a statement concerning the evident facts of the incident and set out to take it personally to the office of the Atlanta *Constitution*; but on the way news met him that the Negro had been burned at the stake and small pieces of his body were being hawked as souvenirs. Turning back toward home, he began to question the usefulness of what he was doing. "One could not be a calm, cool, and detached scientist," he reasoned, "while Negroes were lynched, murdered and starved." His new militancy reached out to a wider audience when in 1903 he published *The Souls of Black Folk*, a collection of personal essays on color in America. Among the essays was an explosive criticism of Booker T. Washington, the most powerful and revered Negro leader of the period.

Unlike Du Bois, who had grown up in an environment relatively free from racial tension, Washington was raised in Virginia in the midst of strong segregationist feeling. After working in a coal mine and as a house servant, he had walked hundreds of miles to attend a Negro technical and agricultural college; and in 1881 he started a college of his own, Tuskegee Institute, at Tuskegee, Alabama, in a few run-down buildings. It became an impressive industrial training school, a testimony to Washington's conviction that by working hard the Negro would merit white respect and win a recognized place in American society. Education, especially training in the skilled trades, would open up the future for his people. The idea was appealing to both black and white—to Negroes because it seemed to offer a chance within their grasp to gain dignity and a degree of wealth, to white politicians because it kept the Negro quiet and useful within the American economy. Gifted with an attractive personality and a winning way of presenting his point of view, Washington came into national prominence in 1895 after delivering a major speech in Atlanta. He was considered the undisputed leader of the entire Negro community, on a European tour had tea with Queen Victoria, and was invited to the White House by President Theodore Roosevelt. The races to him were like the five fingers of the hand, separate but working together for mutual progress. In spite of the virtual disenfranchisement of the Negro in the South, he took a moderate stand on Negro civil and political rights, saying the Negro would participate in government when he had earned the privilege.

Du Bois congratulated Washington on his speech but differed with him sharply over tactics. He advocated instead the higher education of a "Talented Tenth" who would displace white leadership for the Negro and pull their less fortunate brethren upward. The conspicuous failure of white America to honor its promises was shocking, and white society, Du Bois was convinced, would never give anything to the Negro unless the Negro fought for it himself. He attacked the endorsement by the "Tuskegee Machine" necessary for any Negro business venture to succeed, condemned the constraints of thought Washington exercised, and denounced him for in effect admitting that the Negro was inferior. Attempts to find a common program between the two men failed, and, when Washington's supporters sought to stifle questions on voting and education at a meeting in Boston in 1905, Du Bois was outraged. He proposed an immediate conference near Buffalo, New York, "to oppose firmly present methods of strangling honest criticism; to organize intelligent and honest Negroes; and to support organs of news and public opinion." Twenty-nine men from fourteen states responded, and the group met in a small hotel at Fort Erie, Canada, to launch the Niagara Movement, dedicated to full equality, free expression, and unchecked opportunity for the Negro without delay.

To further the aims of the Niagara Movement yearly conferences were held, the first in 1906 being at Harper's Ferry, the scene of John Brown's raid and martyrdom. The time had come for a more aggressive attempt to remedy Negro grievances, especially since the level and proportion of educated Negroes was increasing. On top of strong racial prejudice in regional politics, the refusal of the federal government to suppress racism was discouraging. The Supreme Court backed segregation on a separate but equal philosophy, and, when Theodore Roosevelt was asked to take a stand on the Negro question publicly, he gave an equivocal reply. Later, a campaigning Woodrow Wilson promised fair treatment, but after his election he extended segregation among Federal employees. Negroes lost faith in a system which, in spite of its lofty ideals, seemed to them characterized by lynchings, a double standard of justice, and the widespread rejection of Negroes trying to attain or use professional skills. However strenuous their exertions, they were condemned to be eternal losers in a society which greeted European immigrants with a statue of liberty, championed social mobility, and admired above all the man of wealth. In 1909, stirred by a bloody race riot in Springfield, Illinois, a hundred years after Abraham Lincoln's birth, a group of liberals (many of them white) founded a new organization, the National Association for the Advancement of Colored People (NAACP), which absorbed practically the whole membership of the Niagara Movement. With the National Urban League, it gave concrete form to a new spirit which seized chances to improve the Negro's condition in Northern cities as well as in the South and repudiated racial stereotypes and badges of inferiority. Faced with a reaction from Southern whites, Negro leaders soon became even more united.

Leaving Atlanta, Du Bois became director of publications and research for the new NAACP and, in 1910, editor of *The Crisis*, its official magazine. Given his distinct attitudes and strong independence, the magazine soon became his personal territory, and for twenty-four years he expressed his views in a literate, forceful style, writing for educated readers mostly but trying to reach all blacks. Cases of violence and lynching suffered by Negroes were relentlessly reported, and the paper was said almost to smell of burned flesh. Negro resourcefulness against white prejudice was praised and encouraged, and Negro inadequacy exposed. Indeed, Du Bois came to be himself the symbol of the new movement, and after Washington's death in 1915 his influence was at its height. In all he did—his public appearances, his writing in several areas (including some further works of history), and his constant protest—he sought to give his race a new awareness of its quality and strength; and, though his efforts were concentrated upon the American Negro problem, he strove to lead the fight of colored men everywhere against white oppression. He had attended the founding conference of the Pan-African movement in London in 1900 and, as observer for the NAACP at Versailles in 1919, he convened a Pan-African Congress during the peace deliberations—the first of its kind—so that attention might be drawn as well to the claims of Negroes everywhere. The delegates lacked any real constituency, and the effect of the congress was far smaller than Du Bois afterwards liked to say; but the action reemphasized his understanding of race as an essentially global issue, and the congress was a harbinger of the Third World organizations that have become common in the twentieth century's second half.

Du Bois's support for the United States in the First World War was ambiguous, and his militancy gained fresh vigor after the armistice, when Negroes found the promises made to them in wartime were not to be fulfilled. In the 1920s, however, he was confronted by a more complex society in America and by rivals for the leadership of the Negro cause, among them the flamboyant Marcus Garvey, who attracted a huge following for his avowed goal to liberate Africa. Du Bois in contrast seemed too cooperative with the white world, and he lacked the personal charm of a Washington to help him retain support through tact and goodwill. Sales of *The Crisis* declined, and, after he had been forced to give up editorial control, his distance from the mainstream of NAACP thinking was strikingly shown when he announced that the old plan of a segregated economy was the only way in the end to free the Negro race. Resigning in unpleasant disagreement from the organization he had practically created, he returned to Atlanta in 1934 to continue research on the American Negro. A member again after 1944, he became something of an elder statesman for the movement in international affairs, appealing to the United Nations to force the United States to change its racial policies by marshaling world public opinion.

His last years were far less productive, but they had an interesting ending—perhaps in his case a logical one. Du Bois continued to champion the ideas he had developed as a young man, but as he surveyed the postwar scene he reached the conclusion that the Soviet Union was the only great power that practiced racial equality. He had been a member of the American Socialist party since 1911, and his pronouncements now moved rapidly closer to the lines of Communist policy. At the age of eighty-three he was arrested and charged with being the agent of a foreign power by the U.S. Department of Justice, and, after his acquittal, he was feted on journeys to Russia and China. When the Supreme Court ordered school desegregation in 1954, although he applauded what to him was miraculous, his disillusionment with the United States was becoming practically complete. He had first encountered Marxism at Berlin and had always stressed the economic features of imperialism; the American Negro was now to him part of the working class of the world, and the struggle to eliminate the color bar was assuming a new, Marxist character.

But another, more ancient loyalty also called him. In 1960 he accepted the repeated personal invitation of President Kwame Nkrumah of Ghana to visit that country, attending celebrations of Ghana's becoming a republic; and a year later he was enthusiastically welcomed when he returned to live there permanently and direct the compiling of the *Encyclopedia Africana* (a long-standing project of his), which Nkrumah's government was sponsoring. From Africa, in 1961, a little before his ninety-fourth birthday, Du Bois joined the Communist party. Dying a Ghanaian citizen two years later, he received a state funeral. His burial took place at Government House, Accra—a castle rising clifflike from the ocean, built of white stone by Danish slave traders three hundred years before. It is also supposedly the only fort in all West Africa which, in that early phase of European rivalries, was once captured by a band of Africans themselves.

IV

Clearly Du Bois fulfilled his early desire to be a leader of his race in the fight to overcome discrimination. Though he saw the world as a whole, his major concern was the improvement of the Negro's condition in America, and he related all his studies to that theme, applying it to his research rather than studying to modify it. As a young social scientist he had been sure that the truth obtained from collected data was persuasive enough, but the lynching of an untried Negro in Atlanta convinced him that in a climate of rampant emotionalism his objective research was unheeded and unwanted. He became an agitator; and all his writing after that event reflected the change. Though he did not abandon his former habits of work, he believed that the truth was better grasped by being intensely partisan; and when he turned his attention to history writing, his outstanding characteristic— in one critic's opinion—was that he combined the role of philosopher and prophet, with the historian acting as clerk.

In light of his career, we approach Du Bois the historian with certain assumptions and find them warranted. With his very many concerns and commitments his histories were often hastily produced and inclined to be superficial; after his doctorate he had little opportunity to research deeply, and his last major work, *Black Reconstruction in America*, relied heavily on secondary sources. Throughout much of his writing there are touches of the orator's style and phrasing, grandiloquent and sometimes poetic, which, though detracting from plain objectivity, make several of his books notable as literature. Using history as an implement for propaganda, he repeatedly insisted on its relevance to present-day action, to some extent even in his Harvard dissertation. There is a strong independence of mind; the founder of the Niagara Movement—who like other irritated, young black intellectuals of the day had declared "I don't care a damn what Booker Washington thinks! This is what I think, and *I have a right to think*"—carried his self-assurance into his histories. Finally, there is an overwhelming positiveness about the Negro and his place in America and the world, which in fact identifies his works as part of the twentieth-century rejection of elitist history—in Du Bois's case an elite defined by race.

Perhaps his efforts in the last direction went too far, for the white elite was replaced by the Talented Tenth, of which he was one; but, in the last analysis, Du Bois the historian is more important for the incentive he gave to the further study of the history of non-white peoples than for his productions of scholarship. *The Souls of Black Folk*, a critic has said, "may be seen as fixing that moment in history when the American Negro began to reject the idea of the world's belonging to white people only, and to think of himself, in concert, as a potential force in the organization of society." Some breadth and detail may have been missing at first from this new perspective, but passion was its gain, and its power was contagious; and from that impulse there emerged in time a new and more substantial version of the past, invigorated still with echoes of a messianic dream.

Du Bois's personal faults cannot be overlooked either, for they also affected his history writing. Among his weaknesses were egotism, an appearance of personal vanity, a gift more for drafting policy statements than for practical politics, and in the end foolishness in allowing his frustrations at American failure to stop discrimination to blind him to the inhumanities of Communist totalitarianism. Like Booker T. Washington he suffered from being too often dependent on liberal whites; and he attacked both Washington and Garvey for shortcomings that can be found in his own life. He has been characterized as a classic case of a Negro humiliated by a lifetime's treatment as an inferior by those he knows to be his inferiors. But if the West is truly in decline and now must live with the rest of the world, if, taking the long view, the crucial event in recent American history is seen to be the Supreme Court's decision in *Brown* v. *Board of Education of Topeka* in 1954, then Du Bois's work and his stimulus arguably are the most important and original contribution to historiography the United States has made.

American historians may not agree—at least the majority whose field is not black studies; but the other American views of history are largely offshoots or refinements of European ideas, with a certain American quality. History is nearly always written by the conquerors, and the history of America has shared that feature, too. But Du Bois rejected traditions of interpretation which were almost supreme, and offered as an alternative a history born out of the most brutal American experience. He defied the prejudices of dominant white history and took up the Negro's cause; but he also pointed out that the roots of whites and blacks could not be separated. This was a view which subscribed to certain American ideals, even enhanced them; and, when subject peoples in Africa and Asia fought their white masters for independence, the American story as told by Du Bois became a model to copy themselves. It is a linear view of history which begins in prison and ends in freedom, and its climax comes when the prison door swings open.

Du Bois's view has proved its adaptability, for one after another American minority emerging into social and political consciousness has applied that basic message to itself. The historic struggle of the Negro has become the prototype for the rest, and every minority pressing for its rights—women, Hispanics, Indians, sexual minorities—owes something to Du Bois. His influence has mostly been general; but he was among the few historians of his time to include and identify women in his books. He sketched a history of American Negro women, and he once wrote "the uplift of women is, next to the problem of the color line and the peace movement, our greatest modern cause." Throughout his career he challenged his audiences to change their ideas by redefining their sense of their humanity. If history is the story of man, he argued, then all races must be in it—and, by extension, we may say every group or category of person. In this version of the past, history is not about kings or presidents or economic forces. It has at its center the moral issues; it is primarily about how one human being can treat another, and it looks toward a greater mutual understanding.

In his life of active protest it is hard to think of any historian more different from Ranke, secluded in the archives, than Du Bois. The two men illustrate conflicting opinions of the historian's role in society; and the contrast between them is epitomized in their special uses of the word "veil" when defining their intent. To Ranke, all the historian was permitted to do was lift the veil on a mystery. The mystery itself, from which curiosity should be restrained, was the affair of God. The veil was the historian's province, the outward history of man to be critically examined. To Du Bois, however, the veil was the partition shutting him off from the larger world to which he too had fair entitle-ment—something he could see through but not pass beyond. The effect was smothering—he described *The Souls of Black Folk* as "a cry at midnight thick within the veil." But he knew, as a black man living in a country arranged on the white man's terms, that he and his people were forced to see themselves habitually from the other side. The resulting distortion, he wrote, was the essence and tragedy of the Negro's dilemma in America; and the veil had to go. There was no sacred mystery in white supremacy.

> After the Egyptian and Indian, the Greek and Roman, the Teuton and Mongolian, the Negro is a sort of seventh son, born with a veil, and gifted with second sight in this American world,—a world which yields him no true self-consciousness, but only lets him see himself through the revelation of the other world. It is a peculiar sensation, this double-consciousness, this sense of always looking at one's self through the eyes of others, of measuring one's soul by the tape of a world that looks on in amused contempt and pity. One ever feels his twoness,—an American, a Negro; two souls, two thoughts, two un-reconciled strivings; two warring ideals in one dark body, whose dogged strength alone keeps it from being torn asunder.

> The history of the American Negro is the history of this strife,—this longing to attain self-conscious manhood, to merge his double self into a better and truer self. In this merging he wishes neither of the older selves to be lost. He would not Africanize America, for America has too much to teach the world and Africa. He would not bleach his Negro soul in a flood of white Americanism, for he knows that Negro blood has a message for the world. He simply wishes to make it possi-

ble for a man to be both a Negro and an American, without being
cursed and spit upon by his fellows, without having the doors of
Opportunity closed roughly in his face.

A stranger in his own house, Du Bois saw in the writing of history
a means of bringing Negroes to new self-understanding, of demonstrating that they had made progress, of fairly explaining Negro failures,
and of giving his race pride in themselves among the world's peoples.
His first work, *The Suppression of the African Slave-Trade to the
United States of America, 1638–1870*, was also in a professional sense
his best. A well-researched dissertation, it became an indispensable
source on the subject for many years and, in 1898, was chosen to launch
the series of Harvard Historical Studies. Academic though its contents
were, concentrating on legislation and slave-trade cases, a practical turn
was not lacking. The history surveyed, Du Bois wrote, "would seem to
warn any nation from allowing, through carelessness and moral coward-
ice, any social evil to grow"; and, with the Civil War a recent memory,
"it behooves nations as well as men to do things at the very moment
when they ought to be done."

Leaving aside *The Philadelphia Negro: A Social Study* and his work
as editor of the *Atlanta University Studies* as properly a chapter in his
career as a sociologist, his next venture into the area of history was *The
Souls of Black Folk*. Asked by a publishing firm for a manuscript,
Du Bois had submitted an outline of what he hoped to make his life's
work, a broad and exhaustive study of the Negro problem in the United
States. Back came a request, however, for something more limited and
popular, and he complied by assembling some of his published and un-
published essays and adding a few new ones. The resulting small volume
would be by far his best-known writing, reaching a larger public than his
original project could ever have done; and its effect upon the American
Negro has been described as perhaps being greater than that of any
book published in the United States since *Uncle Tom's Cabin*.

The Souls of Black Folk has the power of a literary classic. Its
essays are rhetorical meditations on the Negro experience, each being
introduced by a few bars from a spiritual; and like that music they are
intimate, simple, and emotionally stirring. Sometimes they relate to
contemporary problems, as in the collection's most famous piece, "On
Mr. Booker T. Washington and Others," and in an essay on the Freed-
men's Bureau; but mostly they are personal sketches of life in the South,
in a critic's words "expressing the soul of one people in a time of great
stress." Here, the author says, are the three gifts the Negro race has
brought America—a gift of story and song, the gift of sweat and brawn,

and a gift of the Spirit—all given in blood-brotherhood. "Would America have been America without her Negro people?" he asks. The essay on Washington is also a review of the Negro's fight for freedom, a litany of black nationalism, recalling the names of Crispus Attucks, killed in the Boston Massacre, Toussaint L' Ouverture of Haiti, Nat Turner of Virginia and leaders of other slave revolts, John Brown, and the great leader before and after the Civil War, Frederick Douglass—an alternative version of the American past. The book is a blend of American sociology and German cultural nationalism; and its importance for Negro history lies most of all in its ability to convey ideas and emotions about this elusive Negro world to Negroes. Negro readers recognized that here was a deeply suggestive work to which they alone had full access, written by one of themselves who had created from his "double-consciousness" a clear self-image which they somehow almost knew already, to be worn in strength as naturally as the gifts had been offered. Here was the starting point from which a new self-understanding could be made.

After this success Du Bois was invited to contribute to a series of biographies relating to the Civil War, and, though thinking he might write on Nat Turner and the Negro view of slavery, he agreed in the end to prepare a study of the white abolitionist John Brown. The subject was not a neglected one of course; Brown, the fanatic and the dignified martyr, was both controversial and legendary. Du Bois's contention, however, was that Brown's place among Negro Americans had never been emphasized, and without it any knowledge of him was incomplete. "John Brown worked not simply for Black Men," he argued, "—he worked with them; and he was a companion of their daily life, knew their faults and virtues, and felt, as few white Americans have felt, the bitter tragedy of their lot." Brown was "the man who of all Americans has perhaps come nearest to touching the real souls of black folk." Materials for the book were few, but Du Bois used them with license; and when the book appeared in 1909 the broad lines of its argument were unmistakable. Brown had understood the discontent among the slaves exceptionally well, had seen the practical cost of slavery to the nation, and had acted heroically. "The cost of liberty is less than the price of repression, even though that cost be blood," Du Bois wrote, urging his example; "John Brown taught us that the cheapest price to pay for liberty is its cost today."

The Gift of Black Folk: The Negroes in the Making of America was published in 1924 as one of a series commissioned by the Knights of Columbus on racial contributions to the United States. For some time Du Bois had been interested in popularizing Negro history, and he had produced pageants, notably one to commemorate the tercenten-nial of the arrival of the first slaves at Jamestown, Virginia, in 1619. He also included short biographical sketches of famous Negroes in a chil-dren's magazine he edited for a few years, seeking to make his young readers familiar with the story and successes of their race as part of his overall purpose of teaching that being black is a normal and beautiful thing. *The Gift of Black Folk* follows in this stream; and, though its author admitted afterward it was too hurriedly done and contained several mistakes, it is the most comprehensive survey of the Negro's place in American history that he set down.

Too often, Du Bois began, the coming of the Negroes, compared to the Germans and Scandinavians, the Irish, the Jews, and others, had been regarded as "an unmitigated error and a national liability." It was high time this course of thinking should be changed. America "repre-sents peculiarly a coming together of the peoples of the world."

> My thesis [he continued] is that despite slavery, war and caste, and despite our present Negro problem, the American Negro is and has been a distinct asset to this country and has brought a contribution without which America could not have been; and that perhaps the essence of our so-called Negro problem is the failure to recognize this fact and to continue to act as though the Negro was what we once imagined and wanted to imagine him—a representative of a subhuman species fitted only for subordination.

Full of details of the Negro's contribution to American nationality as slave, freedman, and citizen, named and nameless, Du Bois's study described the areas of achievement one by one and used his evidence to prove his points. Negroes had accompanied Cortes, Pizarro, Lewis and Clark, and Fremont on their explorations, and in the twentieth century a black man, Matthew Henson, had stood at the North Pole with Robert E. Peary. Black muscle reduced the American wilderness, estab-lished modern world commerce, and, by producing cotton cheaply on a large scale, played an important part in the Industrial Revolution; and, besides being valued as personal servants, many Negroes gained reputa-tions as skilled craftsmen, mechanics, and inventors. The white man brought to America the habit of regular continuous work as a moral duty, but the Negro brought the idea of toil as a necessary evil minis-tering to the pleasures of life. "While the gift of the white laborer made America rich, or at least made many Americans rich," Du Bois wrote, "it will take the psychology of the black man to make it happy." In spite of his double motive in American wars—the desire to oppose the so-called enemy of his country along with his fellow white citizens, and the desire to obtain justice for his race—the American Negro from colonial times to the First World War had honorably served with valor and distinction, completely refuting the claim often-voiced during the Civil War that he would not really fight. In fact, Du Bois showed, without the active participation of Negro troops the Union would not have been saved, or slavery destroyed.

By incessantly struggling to be free by insurrection, by escape, by the Underground Railroad, or by organized emigration to Africa, the Negro had forced white Americans to define their own notion of freedom more clearly, Du Bois maintained. Confronted by the utter incongruity between their beliefs and their practice, white Americans had finally accepted that a true democracy must include men of all colors. After the Civil War, however, the North virtually set the Negro the task of trying to free himself; and he had done this to a surprising degree in spite of many obstacles, and had failed not because he was Negro but because he was in a minority. Negro women, like Harriet Tubman, had also led revolt, and the Negro woman in America had united the black and white races in her children of mixed blood. Culturally, the Negro had produced the only American folk music, and his spiritual quality—despite superstition and passion—had "breathed the soul of humility and forgiveness into the formalism and cant of American religion." As for writing, apart from that produced by Negroes themselves, "it would be inconceivable to have an American literature, even that written by white men, and not have the Negro as a subject." The portrayal was the story of Negro history itself:

In the days of Shakespeare and Southerne the black man of fiction was a man, a brave, fine, if withal over-trustful and impulsive, hero. In science he was different but equal, cunning in unusual but mighty possibilities. Then with the slave trade he suddenly became a clown and dropped from sight. He emerged slowly beginning about 1830 as a dull stupid but contented slave, capable of doglike devotion, superstitious and incapable of education. Then, in the abolition controversy he became a victim, a man of sorrows, a fugitive traced by bloodhounds, a beautiful raped octoroon, a crucified Uncle Tom, but a lay figure, objectively pitiable but seldom subjectively conceived. Suddenly a change came after Reconstruction. The black man was either a faithful "Befoh de wah" darky worshipping lordly white folk, or a frolicking ape, or a villain, a sullen scoundrel, a violator of womanhood, a low thief and misbirthed monster. He was sub-normal and congenitally incapable. He was represented as an unfit survival of Darwinian natural selection. Philanthropy and religion stood powerless before his pigmy brain and undeveloped morals. In a "thousands years"? Perhaps. But at present, an upper beast. Out of this today he is slowly but tentatively, almost apologetically rising—a somewhat deserving, often poignant, but hopeless figure; a man whose only proper end is dramatic suicide physically and morally. His trouble is natural and inborn inferiority, slight by scientific measurement but sufficient to make absolute limits to his possibilities, save in exceptional cases.

"Dramatically," Du Bois wrote elsewhere, "the Negro is the central thread of American history. The whole story turns on him." The Negro also had the peculiar spiritual role of being a sort of living, breathing test of America's ideals; and his monument lay everywhere. The 1920s, when *The Gift of Black Folk* appeared, were a period of increased lynchings, of a powerful Ku Klux Klan, and of the resurgence of racist practices and myths. Current attitudes were also reflected in the immigration laws of the time, which steeply reduced the annual quota from southern and eastern Europe, whose inhabitants were also considered by some to be racially inferior. Against these powerful obscurantist forces, Du Bois argued from the record that America as it now was could not have done without the Negro; and, perhaps as important in the long run, he sought in his history writing to show numerous black people as individual human beings.

Black Reconstruction in America, published in 1935, was his most ambitious historical work, and much more. The *New York Herald Tribune* described it as "a solid history of the period, an economic treatise, a philosophical discussion, a poem, a work of art all rolled into one." Preparing it, Du Bois tried to match the professional scholarship of his Harvard dissertation, and to apply loose concepts of Marxist ideology to his subject while also making a generally fervent presentation of his case; but, though he took great care with its writing, the massive book in the end was an intensified mixture of his merits and his faults, and not altogether satisfactory. It was still recognized immediately as important, a strong corrective to the usual assumptions of Negro dishonesty and incompetence in the years following the Civil War, and to the claim that only the restoration of white authority in the South had prevented that civilization's complete collapse. Du Bois reminded his readers that Reconstruction was the only period in which democracy had existed in the South, showed that the economy had recovered remarkably, and illustrated how the Negro—despite many hindrances—strode forward. If the Negro's rights had not been taken away by imperialist reactionaries, there was every indication he would have advanced further. The dismissal or neglect of this evidence by white historians, from the South especially, was "one of the most stupendous efforts the world ever saw to discredit human beings, an effort involving universities, history, science, social life and religion."

In his writing on the American past, Du Bois told white and black alike of the positive role the Negro had played, and held up to Negroes an explanation of their contemporary dilemma and a picture of themselves—in part. It was incomplete because, as he had written in *The Souls of Black Folk*, the American Negro in truth wished neither of his older selves to be lost. Yet the American experience gave to the Negro knowledge of only half that person. The other half lay in the land of his ancestors, and to understand adequately why he was a stranger in his own house his more distant and elemental origins needed to be traced. Broadly interested in the general history of the non-white peoples of the world, Du Bois found himself turning with a special sense of mission to uncovering and spreading word of the history of Africa.

His pioneer venture in that direction, *The Negro*, appeared in 1915, and was intended for a broad public. Citing a long list of authorities—among them Herodotus, who had described the Egyptians as black with curly hair, the famous Arab traveler Ibn Batuta, and the scholarly reports of recent European explorers—Du Bois sought to dispel the notion that Africa alone of all the continents had no past. The history of Egypt, well known from archaeological research and abundant in written records, predated by far that of the Greeks and Romans and was extraordinarily rich in personalities and cultural distinction; and the history of the Ethiopians, another people Du Bois considered Negroid, had been the story of heroic independence from remote antiquity. But what was completely new to most of his readers was his account of the medieval black empires and kingdoms of West Africa— of the thousand-year empire of Songhay, which at its peak stretched from Lake Chad to the Atlantic, of Ghana, whose rulers lived in glass-windowed palaces adorned with sculpture, and of Mali, whose king, on a visit to Mecca in 1324, was said to have taken with him eighty camel-loads of gold dust and an entourage of sixty thousand persons. The size of these empires, their wealth, their organization, and their technical and artistic skills in brass and bronze exploded the notion that black Africans were savages, devoid of any memorable past.

The testimony of white merchants confirmed the Arab and native information. When the Portuguese reached Guinea and the Congo in the fifteenth century, they found flourishing kingdoms which they recognized were at least equal to the states of Europe. The East African coast—the region described in the late nineteenth century as a *tabula rasa*—was reported as having thriving cities, whose richer inhabitants dressed in gorgeous robes of silk and velvet. All had fallen under the devastating impact of the slave trade conducted first by Arabs, then by European Christians. The book increased what American Negroes knew of their African past a hundredfold and convinced them they had a heritage as rich and famous as that of Europeans. Finding that current events were creating new interest in what he had written, Du Bois proceeded to revise and expand his treatment of African history in two further works, *Black Folk Then and Now* (1939) and *The World and Africa* (1947). The scope of his knowledge was reflected too in his leadership of the Pan-African movement and his appointment to be editor of the *Encyclopedia Africana*—a reference work intended to give the full truth about Africa, its history and culture. Through his labors black Americans began to glimpse themselves more totally and to identify with the world community of color, leading them, after the Second World War, to demand rights equal to those their African kinsmen were winning.

To look at Du Bois's African histories today is to see how far African studies have since come. On occasion the contents of Du Bois's books seem more fanciful than real, and their author more characterized by earnestness than by a critical spirit. But, in a society which saw the African past solely in relation to European contacts and wrote only about what little seemed deserving to be known from a Western point of view, Du Bois's works, crude though they now seem, stood out almost uniquely in subject matter and perspective. The African histories inspired others to investigate further, not least by drawing attention to the many sources their author had used, and they stimulated the study of Africa from within. The obtrusive question cannot, however, be ignored. Does Africa now have a history, or do several decades of intensified research in archaeology, demography, oral tradition, and (where Islamic civilization is found) written records only prove Hegel right after all?

Hegel, we remember, saw history as the emergence of freedom from Athens to the Prussian state; and, on the terms by which he evaluated the past, Africa—if we can still talk of it so broadly—undoubtedly shows less purposeful movement or development than Europe, or for that matter China or India. Until the twentieth century, perhaps, it has also lacked figures whose deeds seem to bring its history together—and thus make its past come to life for Europeans and Americans; nor has it anything of its own resembling the sophisticated methods of modern Western historical scholarship. We should remind ourselves, of course, that history as conceived in the West is not one of the more primitive forms of knowledge but one of the most complex, invented during the great Greek attempt to apply intelligence to man's measurement and comprehension.

It is, however, ridiculous to dismiss the story of Africa, as the Regius Professor of History at Oxford did not many years ago, as "only the unrewarding gyrations of barbarous tribes in picturesque but irrelevant corners of the globe." The vastly increased information about the beliefs, customs, and life of African peoples has led to broad acceptance of Africa's wealth of cultural and social history, also of the political intricacy of many native societies. This knowledge takes on a special importance as African history is rewritten in the post-colonial period, and the questions tend to be, for instance, not why the British took a certain line of policy in Kenya, but why the Kikuyu people—the more durable entity there—reacted in a certain way to conquest by Britain. But African history's larger importance today lies, not so much in correcting distorted Western impressions about it, or even in explaining Africa to Africans in African terms, but in contributing to a new perspective of human history as a whole. As the only commonly agreed feature of the historical process is now change—change not necessarily involving progress—Africa and its parts have come to be seen as vital components in the interplay between the several areas and civilizations of the world; and the continent itself is not regarded as strictly separable into its Mediterranean and sub-Saharan sections, or definable by its inhabitants' race and color.

But, we may further ask, should African history only be served by Western techniques of research and Western criteria? Each human society chooses the kind of historical tradition best suited to its needs; and in pre-literate Africa all that was important was preserved and transmitted orally (often with the utmost care) to apply as a whole to present situations. Africa's past may thus have to be interpreted partly on Africa's conditions, and Western concepts of movement, development, and one event causing another are therefore alien—and so are terms like "state," "class," or "world historical figure." The Western mind tends to see the whole in any cultural expression as the sum of its parts. The African, as native sculpture clearly shows, sees the whole as the whole, its spirit exuding through every detail. Indeed, this was the way in which Petrarch first saw Rome; and we may react the same when we hear American history epitomized in the Gettysburg Address. Like many returning American Negroes before and since, Du Bois wrote of his deep sensations of this sort after first setting foot on African soil; the history was clear in its entirety. Western historiography is distinguished by its commitment to rational inquiry, but it may not ignore other social and personal wants from the past when they occur—in the culture of Africa or elsewhere. For these are some of the roots from which the Western idea of history itself once sprang; and to grasp African history at all fully we must sometimes return to them.

The achievement of Du Bois, however, is more precise. Refusing a past explained by the theme of race, convinced early of the economic and social injustices of imperialism, dedicated to the removal of Negro oppression in America, he saw history as a tool for making history anew. It was to be used in keeping with the ringing words of Frederick Douglass, whose portrait hung over the living room mantel in Du Bois's home in Brooklyn: "A blow struck for freedom anywhere is a blow for freedom everywhere." As Du Bois's own impact grew, aided by the efforts of others, an interpretation of the world's history different from that commonly given by the white race began to emerge, in which Columbus's landfall becomes the death-knell for the red man, the Indian Mutiny a thwarted war of independence, and the sufferings in the Black Hole of Calcutta insignificant compared to the parade of misery at the slave market in New Orleans. Instead of Henry Morton Stanley, General Gordon, and Cecil Rhodes, the heroes are Nat Turner, John Brown, Sitting Bull, or Mahatma Gandhi. American history appears no longer as the preeminent Anglo-Saxon success story, but as the account of national plurality and at times a tale of horror. This version of the past can have strong connections with Marxist ideology, as Du Bois himself came to believe. In this form it crowds into the Mexican murals of Diego Rivera, sustains Fanon's call to violent retaliation, and was lived in action by Che Guevara. It was caught in the sight of Nikita Khrushchev, the son of freed serfs, bowing to the memorial statue of Lincoln "the great emancipator" in Washington.

"Lions have no historians," Du Bois once wrote, "and therefore lion hunts are thrilling and satisfactory human reading." Negroes, too, were supposed to have no history, which made it necessary for them to find their story themselves and tell it from their side. The twentieth century is often said to have no use for history; but the ardent search for a hold on their past by all disinherited peoples, colored and white, female and male, proves the exact opposite. To have no history is seen as a mark of defeat, of subhumanity; with a history a people stakes out a claim, and acquires in its own eyes and those of its neighbors a greater human potential. Limited and too personal in style though critics consider him to have been—even essentially unhistorical in the case of the African studies—Du Bois tried to meet this need of the neglected part of mankind. But his works stand too in the Western heritage of history as hope and promise, a theme Martin Luther King made even more plain; and there perhaps lies the secret of their greatest appeal. For, in the words that closed *The Souls of Black Folk*, in time "America shall rend the Veil and the prisoned shall go free. . . . And the traveler girds himself, and sets his face toward the Morning, and goes his way."

CHAPTER TEN

TOYNBEE

I

The historians we have encountered demonstrate how much history as an idea bears the imprint of the historian's mind and of the world in which he finds himself. He constructs his variant of the idea from his knowledge, of course, and his audience will judge it in part by his fidelity to the record of past events; but it receives its form from the questions he asks, and its thrust from the emotions with which he contemplates the experience of life around him. The great Western schemes of history, each rejecting largely accepted versions of the human story and each to some degree supplanting them, all reproduce the hopes, fears, strengths, and weaknesses of their authors and of the age they satisfied. Seldom is this characteristic more obvious than when a historian believes he lives at the end of an epoch. When the ground heaves and the temples built for eternity shake, a society's self-conceptions—once defined with confidence—are reexamined radically; and the meaning of history, a problem which shortly before had been peripheral to daily living, becomes a vital issue to be settled once again.

But it is precisely then that historical knowledge often seems most available. Hegel once said, speaking of the goddess of wisdom and her emblem, "the owl of Minerva spreads its wings only with the falling of the dusk"; and it is when an age appears to be speeding toward its conclusion that information looks most complete, insight most keen, and the details of the past come clear within a unitary system. The historian himself is no longer detached from the whole process. He is bound up in it with the rest of humanity; and, if he touches a common nerve, he is sure of their attention. These were the conditions in which Thucydides grappled with Greek history and Augustine with Roman. Theirs were books of the moment—though they were "done to last forever"; and likewise, the twentieth-century English historian Arnold Joseph Toynbee made his era's outstanding attempt to create a new total vision of man's past, present, and future when he set himself to explain the four years of horror and catastrophe that marked the First World War.

The first sentence in Toynbee's monumental work, A *Study of History*, shows his awareness of this relativity of historical thought. "In any age of any society," he wrote, "the study of history, like other social activities, is governed by the dominant tendencies of the time and place." In several autobiographical notes strewn through his publications, he placed himself squarely in his context as he saw it—one of "the last generation of middle-class English people who had finished their education and had started on a professional career before August 1914 overtook us." The violence of the shock when the war occurred was all the greater for the lack of psychological preparation. For nearly a hundred years Britain had engaged in no major conflicts, only minor hostilities which had affected the population superficially; and the middle-class English congratulated themselves on the permanent happiness they had achieved in a scientific age. History was now rather less an implement to serve the present than an accessory to a future that was certain. Recalling that as an excited boy he had watched the splendid parade of troops at Queen Victoria's Diamond Jubilee, Toynbee commented that the English crowd in 1897 "saw their sun standing at its zenith and assumed that it was there to stay." History, for them, was over.

Fifty years later, Toynbee went on to remark, this unconscious English attitude of being outside history altogether seemed sheer lunacy. The twentieth century had proved itself to be, not benign, but in every sense revolutionary; "in less than one lifetime the face of the World has changed almost out of recognition, and the West's position in the World has undergone the greatest change of all." Du Bois's contradictory view of the Queen's jubilee—that it marked the triumph of English economic aggression around the globe—no longer startles us and no longer can be dismissed. The disastrous close of what today seems a brief, anomalous pause in the world's story came in 1914; it was then that a European diplomatic system with a record of precarious successes failed to restrain the policies of its member-states; and its breakdown unleashed the accumulated forces of forty years' economic and social change, and of advances in technology and production that could be applied unsparingly to military goals. But perhaps the extent of the consequent devastation and the abyss of the human spirit it laid bare were not fully comprehended until the battles of Verdun and of the Somme in 1916, when the British suffered 400,000 casualties, the French 550,000, and the Germans 830,000. The three-month offensive at the Somme, fought in a morass of cratered mud and hideously mangled bodies, under an incessant bombardment of artillery and soft clouds of lethal gas, won the allies a maximum advance of seven miles. "Tell me, when was the war over?" asked the Antarctic explorer, Sir Ernest Shackleton, reaching the island of South Georgia after two years' isolation. "The war is not over," came the reply. "Millions are being killed. Europe is mad. The world is mad."

When at last the guns stopped firing, the largest pile of battlefield corpses in history was surmounted by the war's chief victim, the nineteenth century's belief in progress and the perfectibility of man. "Was it for this the clay grew tall?" asked Wilfred Owen, killed in France just before the Armistice, "—O what made fatuous sunbeams toil To break earth's sleep at all?" Well before the end the proud trumpet of history became a lamenting bugle, no longer blowing out over the rich dead as another English poet Rupert Brooke had it, but, in Owen's phrase, calling for them from sad shires. The mourning moved beyond personal tragedy and grieved for the undone years, the stuff dreams are made of. "Whatever hope is yours, Was my life also," Owen wrote; and, to a generation spiritually, if not bodily, scarred and shocked, history as the celebration of scientific achievement, or of race, or of conventional Christianity seemed tenable no more. It was an elegy to be written by the survivors, those fate had omitted from lists of dead friends in school cloisters and from mile upon mile of small white crosses. In 1918, to do all that was humanly possible to prevent another war ever happening again, to kindle new hope from the ashes, and to build a lasting peace were the overpowering desires of practically all men and women. The greatest dereliction was to forget.

Any proper understanding of Toynbee today and of his exposition of history must recognize him first as a man who came to maturity during the First World War and in the early years of the League of Nations; all the other roles he assumed must be subordinated to that prime influence—the ardent philhellenist, the maddeningly imprecise and inconsistent philosopher–historian–lay-theologian, the prophet, the incorrigible mystic. The early Toynbee is crucial to distinguish and must with an effort be kept in mind, for the later Toynbee evokes the living image. The world-traveling luminary, delivering his wisdom to one campus audience after another, constantly and often repetitively writing, always ready to deliver his opinions in popular magazines on current events, was from the 1950s to his death the most discussed, very probably the most learned, and sometimes the most ridiculed historian in the West. With his death, however, the man begins to be seen differently, and the forces which shaped his beliefs become more interesting and important than his latest controversial pronouncement. Toynbee's ideas are still refuted or defended, his professed humanitarian motives lie open to suspicion, his eclectic religion is perhaps more "Mish-Mash" than the oncoming wave of the future, and his multiform career can be viewed either as the chief aid or the chief hindrance to his efforts to be a serious historian. But, in the midst of continuing debate about Toynbee, nothing is more certain or plain than his obsession throughout his very many productive years with mankind's necessary choice between self-subordination and self-extinction. In that grim light, the insistence with which he eventually championed a global federation—inspired by a blending of the world's higher religions—as mankind's one remaining hope ceases to be an eccentricity; it becomes in large measure explicable. His own words, written in 1968, leave no doubt at all of war's lasting impact upon him:

> Before the end of the First World War, half my contemporaries had been killed; but I was not an eyewitness of their deaths, and it is what one has seen with one's own eyes that impresses one's imagination the most deeply and haunts one's memory the most persistently. Accordingly, the two visual memories that stand out in my mind the most vividly whenever I think of war are not the faces of my dead friends; they are the faces of three people who were strangers to me.

> In 1915, soon after I had left Oxford for London to do war-work there, I was sent on some errand to the War Office in Whitehall. As I was entering, I saw, facing me, a notice-board on which there was posted a list of officers recently reported killed, and, at the same moment, two women passed me. They had just read on the board the announcement of a death. One of the two was weeping bitterly; the other was talking rapidly and emphatically—as if her hurrying words could overtake and perhaps retrieve the cruel loss that had been suffered by her companion. I can see those two poor women's faces as clearly today in my mind's eye as, on that day, I saw them in the life. While I still have life and strength, I must work for the abolition of the wicked institution that was the cause of that terrible sorrow.

> My second visual memory is of the dead body of a young Greek soldier, killed in March 1921 at the second battle of Inönü. The body

was rigid; the face was waxen; the tiny perforation-mark in the fore-head seemed too insignificant a cause to have extinguished a life instantaneously. The dead boy was lying a few yards below the Turkish trenches on the crown of the ridge which the boy's unit had been storming. In the trenches there were the bodies of Turkish peasants—brave "embattled farmers"—that had been horribly mutilated by Greek shell-fire. These young men, Greek and Turkish, had all been brought into the World by the birth-pangs of mothers; they had been nurtured with love; and now they had been taken to be slaughtered on the threshold of manhood. I must work for the abolition of the wicked institution that was the cause of this criminal destruction of the most precious thing on Earth.

In 1954, when A *Study of History* was finally completed Toynbee looked back at the events of his lifetime and, strange as it might seem, counted himself lucky, for he had been born "into a Time of Troubles that was, by definition, an historian's golden age." Unimagined conditions had made nonsense of every common verdict on the past, and new questions crowded on the heels of the historian's most elemental one, "How has this come out of that?" First and foremost, he asked, how had it happened that he had lived to see the apparently reasonable hopes of his parents' generation so rudely disappointed, ending with the advent of Antichrist instead of a secularized version of the Kingdom of God? Why had the perpetual peace confidently forecast at the Great Exhibition of 1851 been shattered in 1914, and again in 1939? How had the twentieth century of the Christian Era come to see the eighteenth century's "laws of civilized warfare" thrown to the winds and the perpetration of atrocities instead? How through the welter of crime and blood had the eight great powers of the West been reduced to the Soviet Union and the United States, both located outside western Europe? How had the Ottoman, Hapsburg, and Indian empires been replaced by a litter of successor states, and Europe itself been dwarfed by an outer ring of new countries it had conjured into life? "How had distance come, for human purposes, to be annihilated by the invention of the art of flying? And how had Mankind's conquest of the Air come to be enslaved to the service of a subsequently invented atomic weapon which threatened to annihilate the Western Civilization and perhaps Life itself on this planet?"

Any of these questions, Toynbee recognized, would tax the time and genius of the greatest historian. Confronted by them, more than a few historians of the day sought refuge in smaller, narrower subjects; others, persuading themselves that history was still the science of progress, tried to pick up familiar pieces of their research. Some scholars even sought to sweep the contradictions aside in an all-embracing theme of apocalypse, like the Swiss theologian Karl Barth, who began to preach the unaccustomed news that man had built a second Tower of Babel in the modern state and was reaping the consequences of his pride. It is to Toynbee's lasting credit that, whether successful or not, he was at least bold enough to engage energetically all the questions flung at him by current events. His classical education, however, gave him what he described as a "binocular view of History"; and his stock version of the elemental question invariably became, "How has this come out of that state of affairs in Western as well as in Hellenic history?" Making more wide-ranging comparisons, he found ultimately he could no longer ignore a supreme question his initial thoughts on Greece and the modern West had already threatened to raise: "What was this 'door of Death' through which sixteen out of twenty-six civilizations within a twentieth-century Western historian's ken had disappeared already?" Living as he did in the sudden twilight of his own culture, in a nation struck down at the height of its power, no question seemed more pressing or timely.

II

Toynbee's attraction for us still lies in the answers he found to his supreme question and the methods he employed to reach them; for ever since the First World War the twentieth century's need to explain the turbulence of history in large but exact terms has increased, especially as the signs of Britain's eclipse and then of the West's decline have been steadily confirmed. By the erudition and industry which he brought to bear upon the problem of historical change, by his flashes of jolting insight and his hotly disputed conclusions, he continues to draw widespread attention—not least because he constantly freshened his essential thesis with the breezes of fashionable new public concerns. Though the multivolume *Study of History*, like its author, is now seen as basically a product of the 1920s, its later argument was haunted by the atomic bomb. Toynbee's writings of the 1960s reflected the urban crisis, and his last work showed his fears of man's imminent destruction of his environment. The basic message, however, remained the same throughout, a message of doom.

An intellectual edifice with scarcely an equal, *A Study of History* demands to be judged as a single entity by appropriate critical standards; but, when its idiosyncratic and impassioned creator tells us he saw himself first as the Thucydides, then as the Augustine of his age, the two resemblances he claims and the tension implicit in him quicken our own curiosity. In Toynbee's case, the information we seek is not to be gleaned from here and there; it is always at hand, and positively thrust upon us. "One of my aims in A *Study of History*," he wrote when the task was done, "has been to try out the scientific approach to human affairs and to test how far it will carry us"; but the reader is always aware of Toynbee intruding into his work by the oddities of opinion, vocabulary, and style, and by the often strange habits of selection the research displays. Self-disclosures enliven the weightiest discussions; and the *Study* ends with intimate acknowledgments of thanks to all the things which went into the making of him as an historian—books and teachers that set him thinking, conversations with relatives, emotions remembered, travel undertaken, and particular benefactors. Its ten volumes are not only a revelation of the historical process but of the author's mind in action as well—clearly a very talented mind, very conscious too of its learning and of the superior ease with which it could analyze the whole of mankind's diffuse story. Naturally, Toynbee has been criticized almost as much for the man he seems to be in his great work as he has for the theory of history it contains. When a book and its author's personality are so closely bound together, the need for knowledge of how and why the book came to be written becomes more urgent than usual.

From beginning to end Toynbee's outlook was governed by the twin influences of classical scholarship and liberal evangelical Christianity, first imparted in a Victorian atmosphere secure in the prestigious authority of its two-thousand-year-old cultural inheritance. He was born in 1889 in London, into a family distinguished for its learning and philanthropic activities. His grandfather, a noted surgeon, was well known for his efforts to improve the conditions of working-class life; his father was a social worker; and an uncle—also named Arnold Toynbee—popularized the phrase "Industrial Revolution" in a series of brilliant lectures. Toynbee's mother was no less remarkable, for she had won a first-class honors degree in history at Cambridge when very few women indeed received a university education. It was she, he recalled in gratitude, who awakened in him an interest in history, and so stood at the origins of his great book. A great-uncle, retired from the sea, told him of life aboard the full-rigged sailing ships and reminisced of India and China; and the Albert Memorial in London's Kensington Gardens "peopled my world for me, while I was still in the perambulator, with continents, quadrupeds, poets, artists, sculptors, philosophers, and men of science." The fountains at the head of the Serpentine lake nearby became, and remained, the symbolic center of Toynbee's world—as Delphi was the earth's navel for the Greeks, he says.

The family was not particularly wealthy, but it was close-knit and stimulating. Bookshelves in the home were filled with classics and general literature to be taken down and read; by his account, Toynbee at the age of eight discovered *Paradise Lost* and finished it in three days. The language of the Bible entered into his being, giving him "an intimation of the divine presence informing our fragment of a mysterious Universe." His life took a decisive turn, however, when he won a scholarship to Winchester school and began to advance on his own up the ladder into the English intellectual establishment. He rebelled against the "primitive tribal institutions" of an English public school, though he made many lasting friendships; but to have free run of the splendid library was an education in itself, and, above all, he received superb instruction in the Greek and Latin languages and literature. "At Winchester in the first decade of the twentieth century," he wrote, "we were still being given the complete humanist education of the fifteenth-century Italian Renaissance," its objective being a withdrawal from the contemporary world to regain the lost earthly paradise of antiquity. Accordingly, Toynbee as a schoolboy became proficient in translating Burke's speeches into the Latin of Cicero and Emerson's essays into Greek; and he reached the desired summit when he created original compositions in the two classical languages.

Toynbee was aware of the permanent effect that this immersion in classical studies had had upon his character, his forms of expression, and his view of history, and he willingly talked about it. Ever since he was first captivated by the classical languages, he tells us, he had felt an alienation from his mother tongue, and, when under emotional stress or wishing to write poetry, he would find himself releasing his feelings in Greek or Latin, not English. *A Study of History*, it is often remarked, reads especially in its later volumes like a pedantic translation, its sentences struggling with long dependent clauses, distorted with strange adjectives, and interspersed with Latin and Greek words which to Toynbee—though not to the average person—conveyed best the sense of what he wished to say. A few critics have approved the grand archaism of Toynbee's metaphoric style, saying it suits *A Study of History* since all the ages of mankind are summoned forth in it. Most reviewers, however, wish Toynbee's writing had more of the simplicity of classical Greek and less of the luxuriance we associate with Alexandria. It stands as an impressive performance, but an unrepeatable one, like the kind of education which produced it.

But to Toynbee the advantages of his education, begun at Win-

chester and continued at Oxford—perhaps the best the world could
then offer—were never in question; for Greek and Latin, he wrote, gave
him the key to understand history as a whole:

> For any would-be historian—and especially for one born into these
> times—a classical education is, in my belief, a priceless boon. As a
> training ground, the history of the Graeco-Roman world has its con-
> spicuous merits. In the first place, Graeco-Roman history is visible to
> us in perspective and can be seen by us as a whole, because it is over—
> in contrast to the history of our own Western world, which is a still-
> unfinished play. . . .

> In the second place, the field of Graeco-Roman history is not en-
> cumbered and obscured by a surfeit of information, and so we can
> see the wood—thanks to a drastic thinning of the trees during the
> interregnum between the dissolution of the Graeco-Roman society
> and the emergence of our own. Moreover, the conveniently manage-
> able amount of evidence that has survived is not overweighted by the
> state papers of parochial principalities, like those which, in our West-
> ern world, have accumulated, ton upon ton, during the dozen cen-
> turies of its pre-atomic-bomb age. The surviving materials for a study
> of Graeco-Roman history are not only manageable in quantity and
> select in quality; they are also well-balanced in their character. Statues,
> poems, and works of philosophy count here for more than the texts
> of laws and treaties; and this breeds a sense of proportion in the mind
> of a historian nursed on Graeco-Roman history; for—as we can see
> in the perspective given by lapse of time more easily than we can see
> it in the life of our own generation—the works of artists and men
> of letters outlive the deeds of business men, soldiers, and statesmen.
> The poets and the philosophers outrange the historians; while the
> prophets and the saints overtop and outlast them all. . . .

> The third, and perhaps greatest, merit of Graeco-Roman history is
> that its outlook is oecumenical rather than parochial. Athens may have
> eclipsed Sparta and Rome Samnium, yet Athens in her youth made
> herself the education of all Hellas, while Rome in her old age made
> the whole Graeco-Roman world into a single commonwealth. In
> Graeco-Roman history, surveyed from beginning to end, unity is the
> dominant note; and, when once I had heard this great symphony, I
> was no longer in danger of being hypnotized by the lone and outlandish
> music of the parochial history of my own country. . . .

Toynbee's classical studies at Oxford led to his appointment to a
tutorial fellowship at Balliol College in 1912; but, having the opportunity to spend a year abroad first, he went to Greece, spending the time

at the British School of Archaeology at Athens and making long walking journeys over the Greek countryside, delighting in scenes he had known only in his mind till then. Flourishing in a larger world he began to feel his education had nonetheless been cramping; and he saw that, golden though Edwardian Oxford might be, it was also small, narrow, and self-congratulating, a rut in which he was voluntarily preparing to confine himself. He began to doubt, too, the stability that his English contemporaries assumed had come to stay. He discovered the philosophy of Henri Bergson, which stressed the constancy—and the essential creativity—of growth and change. We cannot know the future because we cannot predict the element of novelty, Bergson stated; and Toynbee found supportive evidence for this theory when traveling in Crete, in the spectacle of a ruined baroque palace, confidently built by a seventeenth-century Venetian nobleman just before Crete fell to the Turks after 450 years of Venetian occupation. The inference was inescapable; "if the Venetian Empire had perished, the British Empire could not be immortal."

A severe attack of dysentery caught through drinking from a country stream made him return to England sooner than he had planned; but by a twist of fate, his sickness would save his life by making him unfit for military service. Home again, he began to absorb the impact of his journeys. His moment of insight on Crete remained vivid, and in Greece and the Balkans he had also observed the effect of international affairs on individual men and women (himself included) and on life at village level. A subject with which he had been mostly unconcerned now took on direct and personal importance:

> Yet, even then, [he wrote] I did not realize that we too were still in history after all. . . . The general war of 1914 overtook me expounding Thucydides to Balliol undergraduates reading for *Literae Humaniores*, and then suddenly my understanding was illuminated. The experience that we were having in our world now had been experienced by Thucydides in his world already. I was re-reading him now with a new perception—perceiving meanings in his words, and feelings behind his phrases, to which I had been insensible until I, in my turn, had run into that historical crisis that had inspired him to write his work. Thucydides, it now appeared, had been over this ground before. He and his generation had been ahead of me and mine in the stage of historical experience that we had respectively reached; in fact, his present had been my future. But this made nonsense of the chronological notation which registered my world as "modern" and Thucydides' world as "ancient." Whatever chronology might say, Thucydides' world and my world had now proved to be philosophically contemporary. And,

if this were the true relation between the Graeco-Roman and the Western civilizations, might not the relation between all the civilizations known to us turn out to be the same?

During the First World War Toynbee worked for the Political Intelligence Department of the Foreign Office, and to his later regret wrote several propaganda pamphlets on alleged German atrocities in France, Belgium, and Poland. He also produced two books, *Nationality and the War* and *The New Europe*, in which he looked toward a European federation, enriched, as he then saw it, by a diversity of national cultures. In 1919 he attended the Paris Peace Conference as an adviser on the Middle East to the British delegation. The casualties and the whole catastrophe of the war had increased his sense of the West's hastening demise, and in that same year an essay he read by the French writer Paul Valéry strengthened his conviction. Valéry likened countless brilliant civilizations with names such as Nineveh and Babylon to oceanliners sailing across the vastness of history, all ending in shipwreck. Because such disasters seemed far off, the modern world had dismissed them; but France, England, and Russia were also the names of fine vessels—like the *Lusitania*—and man now knew that the ocean depths held equal peril for all. "We feel that a civilization is as fragile as a life," wrote Valéry. "Circumstances which would send the works of Keats and Baudelaire to rejoin the works of Menander are no more at all inconceivable; they are in the newspapers."

His war work coming to an end, Toynbee at the age of thirty accepted a newly created professorship in Byzantine and Modern Greek language at the University of London, an appointment gained for his first-hand knowledge of current Greek and Turkish affairs as well as for his linguistic competence. It provided him with the chance to break away from the prospect of ever-narrowing specialization within the bounds of Greek and Roman history at Oxford, a career he had rejected in his mind several years before; but, as it happened, he was taking a major step, for he was setting out to study human affairs in general and turning away from the strict methods and limited goals that had become traditional among professional historians. Obtaining a leave of absence in 1921, he accompanied the Greek armies on their advance into Asia Minor and recorded his observations on the hostilities in *The Western Question in Greece and Turkey*—an inquiry into the breakdown of the peace settlement and into the shock of modern Western civilization on both parties. Foreshadowing his future writings, he noted the collapse of old cultures under the Western challenge and made a plea for mutual understanding.

Conscious of living in Thucydidean times, also a witness to cultures clashing across the Aegean Sea as Herodotus had once described, Toynbee found he was not alone in his intense interest in the parallel courses of civilizations when Oswald Spengler's *The Decline of the West* was placed in his hands. In this massive book, published in July 1918 and much discussed in defeated Germany after the war, Spengler had taken the great civilizations like the Egyptian and the classical as units for study—as Toynbee had begun to do himself—and compared them to biological organisms. Following birth, each separate civilization passed through its youth and achieved at its maturity a culture; but, like every living thing, within each was a clock which must run out, and its lifespan was irrevocably set. At the end lay old age and inevitable dissolution. Spengler therefore saw history in cyclical terms, not linear, and he abandoned the view which held that all events seemed to revolve around Western Europe. That self-centered concept was "Ptolemaic"; his discovery was "Copernican," expanding history into the "morphology of world history."

Spengler believed that, since all civilizations went through the same life process, we can predict the form our civilization will take by identifying the phase we are in. Though the clues are superficially different, they are universal throughout time and are always symbols of a cyclical progression. As gills in a fish and lungs in an animal are similar developments, so too are pyramids "contemporary" with Gothic cathedrals. Spengler offered many imaginative suggestions of this sort, but he was better at finding symptoms than causes. He did not attempt to explain why civilizations were born or why they died, stating only that in each case they had obeyed the laws of nature; and men could not halt the inexorable movement, however hard they tried. European civilization, he argued, was now in the final stages before death. Toynbee was intrigued by Spengler's analogies and insights, but he refused to accept his fatalistic, mechanistic conclusion; and he resolved to let the practical English approach explore the problem in directions that German philosophy had been unwilling to go.

All these ideas, impressions, and emotions jostled in Toynbee's head as he made an attempt in 1920 to set down his thoughts on the contemporaneity of civilizations in the form of a commentary on the second chorus of Sophocles's *Antigone*. A year later, however, he had sketched out the essential scheme of *A Study of History*; and he has left a retrospective description of the way it happened:

On Saturday, 17 September, 1921, I was travelling with my school-fellow and life-long friend Theodore Wade-Gery in the Orient Express *en route* from Constantinople to England. Before dawn we had been awakened by the rumbling of our train as it crossed the bridge over the Maritsa, below Adrianople, and, for the rest of that day, we were travelling on westward up the valley of a river that had once been famous as the Hebrus. As I stood, hour after hour, at the corridor window, watching the stream glide by, with an endless fringe of willows and poplars marking out, as they slid past, the curves of the gently flowing waters' course, my mind began to dream of historical and legendary events of which an Hellenic Thrace and an Ottoman Rumuli had been the theater: the legendary violent death of the Prophet Orpheus; the historic violent deaths of the Emperors Valens and Nicephorus; the entrenchment of the Ottoman Power on the European side of the Straits in the reign of Sultan Murad I. When a group of inquisitive Bulgarian peasants clustered round the door of our coach as the train lingered in a wayside station, my eye was caught by the fox-skin cap that one of these Thracian contemporaries of mine was wearing; for this was the headgear in which Herodotus (in Book VII, chap. 75) had paraded the Asiatic Thracian contingent of Xerxes' expeditionary force, and a picture of a Thracian fighting-man in just such a cap, which I had copied into my drawing-book eighteen years ago, had left its imprint on my memory. These stimulating sights and reminiscences must have released some psychic well-spring at a subconscious level. That evening I was still standing at the window, overwhelmed by the beauty of the Bela Palanka Gorge in the light of a full moon, as our train bore down upon Nish. If I had been crossexamined on my activities during that day, I should have sworn that my attention had been wholly absorbed by the entrancing scenes that were passing continually before my outward eye. Yet, before I went to sleep that night, I found that I had put down on half a sheet of notepaper a list of topics which, in its contents and in their order, was substantially identical with the plan of this book as it now stands printed in volumes i, iv, and vii. The path that had thus unexpectedly— and, as it might seem, casually—opened at last before my feet was to carry me farther than I then foresaw on a journey that was to take nearly thirty years to complete; but, once open, the path went on unfolding itself before me till today I find myself at this long journey's end.

Toynbee was not able to start writing A *Study of History* until 1927, but he soon began preparing to realize the project he had so fleetingly captured. His career at London University did not last much longer, as the Greeks who financed his position objected to pro-Turkish sentiments in his report and forced his resignation. In 1925, however, he was appointed director of studies for the Royal Institute of International Affairs, and the central episode in his life opened. Instead of dispersing his energies, his new duties proved indispensable to him.

The Institute had been founded toward the end of the Paris Peace Conference at a meeting, which Toynbee attended, of temporary officials in the American and British delegations. Its purpose was to make as accurate a study as possible of international developments. Independent of government, like its American counterpart, the Council on Foreign Relations, it sought to avoid a repetition of the First World War by providing expert analyses of the international scene, which it hoped would form the basis for statesmanlike action. Located at Chatham House in London, the Institute early saw that publishing objective reviews of current events should be a major part of its activities; and, after producing *The History of the Peace Conference in Paris*, it decided that annual sequels were needed in light of the outcome of Versailles and other treaties. The *Survey of International Affairs* was born, and from 1923 to 1954—two years before his retirement from Chatham House—Toynbee was personally associated with it, writing the early volumes himself and, after 1928, editing and contributing to them. They quickly won for the Institute, and for him, a lasting reputation in that field; for, besides being well documented, they were highly readable, bearing the stamp of a single mind. Current affairs were seen in terms of broad developments such as the conflict of civilizations and the emergence of new policies, and were viewed in the larger context of history from which Toynbee drew frequent analogies. The competence and intelligence of the yearbooks made them influential; and in 1936 Hitler sent for Toynbee, who was visiting Berlin, and gave him a two-and-a-half-hour private lecture in the hope that the *Survey* would be better disposed to Germany's aims and the Nazi leader.

The *Survey*, even to Toynbee's critics, has remained proof of his outstanding ability to be a first-rate historian of a Thucydidean kind—scientific in his methods, thorough in his investigations, detached in his conclusions; and they consider it a misfortune that after 1927 he chose to devote half his time to *A Study of History*, which was the supreme goal of his life. But, in his own words, "I could not, I believe, have done either piece of work if I had not been doing the other at the same time. A survey of current affairs on a world-wide scale can be made only against a background of world-history; and a study of world-history would have no life in it if it left out the history of the writer's own lifetime, for one's contemporaries are the only people whom one can ever catch alive. An historian in our generation must study Gandhi and

Lenin and Atatürk and F. D. Roosevelt if he is to have any hope of bringing Hammurabi and Ikhnaton and Amos and the Buddha back to life for himself and for his readers." From November to June each year he would compile the *Survey* in London; then he would leave to work in the country on the *Study*. His tasks, though well organized, were incredibly demanding as he tried to attain the standards of achievement he had set himself; and his first marriage collapsed, affecting him deeply. But the whole intellectual enterprise seemed absolutely worthwhile to him. He often reminded himself of the lines from Aeschylus he had learnt at school, that learning comes through suffering and that this is a law ordained by God, for individuals as well as mankind. In fact the tremendous load he imposed on himself liberated his creative powers; and he retained throughout his labors a sense that what had been represented in those few lines he had jotted down in 1921 was in some way inspired.

Besides being a scholar and an observer of international affairs, Toynbee was, as he always would be, a traveler. On foot in Greece he believed he had seen and learnt almost as much as Odysseus did, and to the end of his life the eastern Mediterranean was the area he knew best and which most fascinated him. His work for the Institute necessitated travel as far as America and China, and he would often finance such journeys by writing newspaper articles. He used these opportunities to see as much of the world as possible, not only meeting leaders like Chiang Kai-Shek but also constantly gaining new insights into mankind's past with his own eyes. Extraordinarily sensitive to the visual evidence and the symbolism contained in the remains of old civilizations, their tracks and temples half-devoured by sand or jungle, he regretted the habit in his later years of traveling by airplane, for it insulated him from the unfolding sights and sounds beneath. "If you do have to travel by plane and are given a choice of makes (you seldom are)," he wrote in his autobiographical *Experiences*, "be sure to choose a Cessna. Even in a Cessna you will see less than you would have seen on foot, but you will see almost as much as you would have seen on muleback." There was really no substitute for intimate contact with the earth itself for the historian.

The first three volumes of A *Study of History* were published in 1934, and the second three in 1939. We shall examine the contents and argument of the whole ten-volume series shortly; but when they appeared, the early volumes matched the public mood as perhaps no large-scale work had done since Macaulay's *History of England* a century before. A new world history was wanted intensely. To begin with, a hundred years of documentary research by Rankean scholars had brought results. There was now an enormous amount of verified material waiting to be sifted. In most major areas, the events of the past were by and large sufficiently established to offer a universal historian a secure basis for his work. This was a novel situation; and, as Toynbee saw, abundant new historical material had also been obtained through archaeology. The Minoan, Hittite, and Indus civilizations had been dug up from the grave, and knowledge of the cultures of Sumeria, ancient Egypt, and the New World had been transformed by sensational discoveries. But the present provided the chief incentive. The course of events since 1914 had raised an inquest into where history—and that of the West in particular—was heading, and a complete reappraisal of all the human past was demanded. History was simultaneously more accurate, vaster in time and range, and more disturbing, it seemed, than ever before.

Toynbee's audacity in trying to bring the whole record together, in asking the broadest of questions which yet were every man's questions, won him an enthusiastic following. He described his book as "one person's impression of history in the new light in which we can now see it"; but a large public welcomed that impression, whether reading it in its complete form or in an abridged version of the *Study* expertly created by D. C. Somervell. Toynbee emerged with largely pessimistic answers, but he did give Western man a more frank idea, perhaps, of his place in the historical process. "Work . . . while it is day" ran the text from the Gospel of John reprinted on the *Study*'s title page in 1934, to which were added lines from the Anglo-Saxon poem *The Lay of the Battle of Maldon*: "Thought shall be the harder, Heart the keener, Mood shall be the more, As our might lessens." From his full inquiry, he believed there was still a prospect of retrieving Western civilization and avoiding a total breakdown.

By 1939, however—with the League of Nations clearly proving inadequate to prevent the near certainty of another war—Toynbee's hopes for any future progress had weakened. There had been moments, he wrote, "when it almost seemed like tempting Fate and wasting effort to go on writing a book that must be the work of many years, when a catastrophe might overtake the writer's world within the next few weeks or days"; but he had fortified his will by humbly calling to mind the example of Augustine writing the *City of God*, a work that would inform and inspire generations to come, as a civilization fell around him, too. In the circumstances Toynbee's own thought had turned from the agnosticism he had favored at Oxford to a more religious form and expression, and the new text on the title page was a quotation from the Psalms: "Except the Lord build the house, their labor is but lost that build it. Except the Lord keep the city, the watchman waketh but in vain." Western civilization could only avert its doom by a return to the religious sources which had created it and nourished its early stages. Like Christian in *The Pilgrim's Progress*, Western man had the choice of perishing in the City of Destruction or beginning to run—"and run on crying 'Life! Life! Eternal Life!'—with his eye set on a shining light and his feet bound for a distant wicket-gate." "We may and must pray," Toynbee continued, "that a reprieve which God has granted to our society once will not be refused if we ask for it again in a contrite spirit and with a broken heart."

The last four volumes of *A Study of History*, more sprawling and hastily written than the rest, did not appear until 1954. Toynbee had placed his notes for them in New York for safekeeping during the Second World War, while he worked again for the British Foreign Office; and, when the war was over, he attempted to recover his resolution and recollect his thoughts in a Western world dominated by the memory of Belsen and Hiroshima and by fears of militant communism. He found that his view of history's pattern had changed still further, and his belief that religion was the center of history had grown:

> Yet, [he wrote] I have not returned to the religious outlook in which I was brought up. I was brought up to believe that Christianity was a unique revelation of the whole truth. I have now come to believe that all the historic religions and philosophies are partial revelations of the truth in one or other of its aspects. In particular, I believe that Buddhism and Hinduism have a lesson to teach to Christianity, Islam, and Judaism in the "one world" into which we are now being carried by "the annihilation of distance." Unlike the Judaic religions, the Indian religions are not exclusive. They allow for the possibility that there may be alternative approaches to the mystery of Existence; and this seems to me more likely to be the truth than the rival claims of Judaism, Christianity, and Islam to be unique and final revelations. This Indian standpoint is the one from which these last four volumes of my book have been written.

The publicity given to the completion of his project, and the controversy which immediately surrounded the final message of *A Study of History*—that mankind's choice lay between a nuclear holocaust and a new global civilization animated by a syncretized religion—gave Toynbee unique prominence in the public eye. During the early years of the United Nations he entered with zest upon the last phase of his career, popularizing his central themes in *Civilization on Trial, The World and the West,* and other short works (which were often collections of his lectures), writing a defense against his critics entitled *Retractations* as Augustine had done fifteen hundred years before, and speculating further on what the future held. His later miscellaneous writings show his unflagging diligence, but most of them added little to his stature. *An Historian's Approach to Religion* (1956) considered the attitude of the twentieth-century West to Christianity, and in 1964 he completed a large book on Hannibal which he had had in mind since 1913; but *Cities on the Move* (1970), predicting the emergence of "Ecumenopolis," the coming world-city, was the work of an erratic and overconfident amateur. His essential mission, though, did not change— to warn mankind of the disasters about to overtake it unless it changed its ways. When extinction threatened, he argued, any price was worth paying for the abolition of the institution of war; and in his final publication, *Mankind and Mother Earth,* he made a last attempt to communicate the message of *A Study of History* to a less responsive world. Modern science, however, not war, was now the villain, sending man to his doom by destruction of natural resources and by environmental pollution; and Toynbee looked toward a revival of spiritual values which would bring scientific development and economic rapacity to a halt. Without spiritual self-control—the more important part of civilization—man would put an end to himself.

A masterly one-volume summary of world history as he saw it, from the discovery of fire to the first moon landing, *Mankind and Mother Earth* thus struck a familiar note; and the insistence with which Toynbee pressed the new features of his argument and marshaled his vast learning behind it, though sometimes rather loosely, made the book a fitting postscript to *A Study of History.* It updated his great history as the *Survey of International Affairs* had kept abreast of developments following the First World War. In 1975, before this last work appeared, Toynbee died at York, a city whose Roman and Danish landmarks he remembered with affection. Seeing them had been his first glimpse of an England not shrouded in an artificial insularity (a view so alien, he wrote, from the spirit of Bede, the father of English history), and they had placed the country in the context of a greater civilized world. Without lessening the importance of other influences on him, his whole life could be said to have followed the path of that early experience; for man's proven ability to rise above the narrow and parochial and find knowledge, meaning, and refuge in an all-encompassing unity gave Toynbee his idea of the pattern for human action in the future.

III

A *Study of History*, begun on board the Orient Express in 1921, was completed according to Toynbee's precise statement at 6:25 P.M. on June 15, 1951, in London. He had spent the hours before in the National Gallery, looking at a favorite picture by Fra Angelico of the angels, patriarchs, prophets, saints, and martyrs worshipping Christ in His glory in their midst. The *Study* had grown during those thirty years from the merest sketch on a scrap of paper into ten thick volumes; and it would be followed by an eleventh containing maps, and a twelfth, the *Retractations*. Opening it, the reader is liable to undergo an acute feeling of dislocation, for this is no conventional history book. Quite apart from its overpowering flood of learning, it follows no chronological plan. It treats disproportionately ancient empires and cultures that few but specialists know once existed, and it takes scant notice of the West since 1500; unfamiliar heroes like Ikhnaton, Babur, Hammurabi, and Ibn Khaldun move through its pages; and there are plenty of unexpected terms—dominant minority, internal proletariat, pre-da Gaman, Zealots and Herodians, the Greek word *Oikoumene* (meaning the civilized world), and many others. Long footnotes abound, and "annexes" explore byways too important to be neglected. It is "macrohistory," an extraordinary endeavor to make sense of the total past, and to investigate "*sub specie temporis*, the mystery of the universe."

The panorama is accordingly enormous, and is presented on a scale matching that of the new cinematic screen; but it is not observed from an armchair. Toynbee's post is rather the shipwrecked flotsam described by Paul Valéry, who, Toynbee wrote, saw in imagination what Thor Heyerdahl and his companions experienced as they peered down into the awesome depths of the Pacific Ocean through the logs of their raft, *Kon-Tiki*. The author's involvement thus makes A *Study of History* more than an academic inquiry packed with proofs for theories. Its driving purpose had remained to define that "door of Death" through which all civilizations, including his own, seemed fated to go. Toynbee's spirit, however, contradicted Spengler's cold determinism. He assumed there was a design to history, but he believed that human initiative could alter it; and, by handing Western civilization a chart of what lay ahead, he hoped he might warn it to draw back from that door in time.

A *Study of History* begins with an apology, reflecting how much historical thought had been the victim of the scientific outlook and the national state. History had been "industrialized" in the West, and the chief function of scholars was to produce an abundant supply of raw materials so great compound studies like the *Cambridge Modern History* could be engineered. The historian had become the slave of the sources waiting to be examined in his field; and, when H. G. Wells's ambitious one-man project, *The Outline of History*, had appeared, Toynbee recalled that the critics had seized on its small mistakes. But the historian, like the successful industrialist, could still decide to be his own master and follow his natural impulse to see history as a whole. The task was beyond normal human ability, but it was worth trying— indeed, present circumstances left no choice. Nationalism had been equally damaging. No country was a "universe" on its own, even in the case of France or Britain; both were clearly interdependent parts of the society of Western Christendom. "Societies," not states, were the social atoms with which students of history have to deal; and he proceeded to identify them.

Toynbee defined a society—or civilization—by its territorial base, its political institutions, and especially by its distinctive religion. He established these tests from his perceptions of the Graeco-Roman or Hellenic civilization; and, noting its course, he saw a pattern there which he came to believe was generally applicable, too. Beginning in Greece, a brilliant culture had grown until it had suffered a breakdown in the Peloponnesian War. A "time of troubles" lasting four hundred years had then developed, briefly halted by the empire of Alexander, but culminating in the civil wars that destroyed the Roman republic. Under Augustus a single faction had won and had provided peace and a universal state; but this relief was temporary, and what to Gibbon had been the happiest period mankind had known was only a stage in a relentless decline. The years after the Antonine emperors saw the rising strength of the proletariat—in Toynbee's usage people who were in but not of the society—being alienated from the dominant minority's government. The internal proletariat, ruined by political and economic upheavals, embraced a higher religion, while the external—barbarians once under Rome's cultural influence—ravaged the empire by its migrations and revolts. After Diocletian's attempt to restore order, Hellenic civilization had fallen apart; but out of its residue had sprung the new affiliated civilizations of Western and Orthodox Christianity.

With this system as a guide, Toynbee examined all societies, living and dead. He found that, as Western Christian and Orthodox Christian had derived from a common Hellenic parent, so Arabic and Iranic were traceable to an extinct Syriac civilization. There were six original civilizations—Sinic, Sumeric, Minoan, Mayan, Egyptiac, and Andean— of which the last two had left no successors. Sinic society gave birth to Far Eastern civilization, Minoan to Hellenic, Sumeric to Hittite and

Babylonic, and Mayan to Mexic and Yucatec. Hindu civilization was an offspring of Indic society, which bore a relation to Sumeric. To these could be added two more, Russian Orthodox society as an offshoot of Orthodox Christian, and Japanese-Korean as a form of Sinic. In Toynbee's view, these twenty-one civilizations (their number in later volumes varied) met his standards of definition; and, though widely separated by time and distance, they were all sufficiently different from primitive societies to be classed together. To believe Western culture was the only genuine civilization was absurd; it was simply one among the rest. The earliest civilizations began no more than six thousand years ago, he thought; and he proposed to treat them all in the manner in which he had suddenly seen the Athens of Thucydides in 1914— philosophically contemporaneous members of a single species.

In a striking metaphor Toynbee saw primitive societies as "people lying torpid upon a ledge on a mountain-side, with a precipice below and a precipice above." Civilizations, he wrote, may be likened to companions of these Sleepers of Ephesus "who have just risen to their feet and have started to climb on up the face of the cliff; while we, for our part, may liken ourselves to observers whose field of vision is limited to the ledge and to the foot of the upper precipice and who have come upon the scene at the moment when the different members of the party happen to be in these respective postures and positions." The climbers, once they have started, must reach the ledge above or fall; and the majority have succumbed to defeat. Their bodies lie broken below, or, in a few cases, paralyzed at their place of last movement. Hardly any had ever risen to attempt a ledge higher than that which Western Christian civilization had achieved.

But what spurs some peoples to climb and not others? Seeing an interplay of the forces described by the Chinese terms of "Yin" (static) and "Yang" (dynamic), Toynbee concluded the last six thousand years had seen the dynamic in the ascendant. He rejected as fraudulent the view that civilizations were built by superior races such as the Nordic; and he dismissed the idea that God was directly responsible. A favorable natural environment was not by itself an entirely satisfactory cause, and he ruled out a series of accidents. The answer, he thought, must lie elsewhere. "Let us shut our eyes, for the moment, to the formulae of Science," he wrote, "in order to open our eyes to the language of Mythology"; and he discovered in the prologue of Goethe's *Faust* the reason he was seeking. In Goethe's great poem, God, who has made a perfect world, finds He has no further scope for His creative powers. To combat this, He allows Mephistopheles, the devil, to try to spoil what He has done; and, by responding to the challenge the devil offers, God wins the opportunity to carry forward His work of creation. Challenge-and-response—here was the clue to the rise of civilization in history.

Applying this insight, Toynbee detected civilizations being born wherever men had been faced with difficulties which roused them to unprecedented effort. The challenge could be in physical terms: the Egyptian society had begun from the struggle to establish life in the valley of the Nile, the Sinic likewise on the banks of the Yellow River. The Mayan was an act of defiance against the tropical forest, the Minoan an answer to the sea. The examples of Easter Island, Petra, Palmyra, Venice, and Holland also demonstrated adversity's bracing effect; and countries with stern living conditions gathered more distinguished records than their comfortable neighbors—as witness Scotland versus England, Prussia and the Rhineland, New England and the South. The challenge could be a human one: new land to be tilled, a frontier location, a crushing defeat, penalization of a class or a race (for instance, of the Christians in the Roman era, or of the Jews)—all had repeatedly provoked energetic action. Challenges, however, could be too hard, as the Vikings found when they colonized Iceland successfully but failed in Greenland; and, where life was too easy, in lotus-lands, there was no stimulus to invent, build, compose, or philosophize. Enough adversity, but not too much, was the decisive ingredient. One discernible group of civilizations—raising the total number to twenty-six—had met their particular physical or human challenge, but the effort of these five to stay at the level they had reached was all-consuming. They were the Eskimos, the Polynesians, the Nomads, the Spartans, and the Ottoman Turks.

If civilizations come out of challenge-and-response, how do they grow? In a partial explanation, Toynbee quoted Walt Whitman: "It is provided in the essence of things that from any fruition of success, no matter what, shall come forth something to make a greater struggle necessary." Successful responses bred new challenges; but Toynbee refused to see in geographical expansion and technological progress the evidence of growth. Actual growth lay in a society's spiritual life, a summarizing of self-knowledge and a capacity for self-determination. Growth of this kind originated with creative individuals—Jesus, Paul, St. Benedict, founder of Western monasticism, Muhammad, Machiavelli —or with creative minorities, all of whom had undergone the experience of a withdrawal from the society around them and a return. The Greek myth of the hero Prometheus, who stole fire from Zeus and benefited mankind, embodied the lesson of how an infant civilization advanced; and the growth became firm when a creative minority was imitated by an uncreative majority.

It was a grim fact, however, that, of the twenty-six civilizations, the great majority were now either dead, arrested, or surviving only in living fossils such as the Jews and the Parsees. Of the five remaining in the modern world—Western Christian, Orthodox Christian, Arabic, Hindu, and Far Eastern—all but the Western Christian were beyond repair; and the Western Christian itself seemed well into its "time of troubles." Discarding ideas of racial degeneration or cosmic senescence as well as Spengler's view that societies are organisms that live and die, Toynbee saw the cause of decay as a clear failure to respond to fresh challenges— which constitutes suicide. Like Alexander the Great, civilization thrived on new worlds to conquer; when a creative minority became a fully secure ruling class and no longer had the will to confront and solve new problems, a society's days were numbered. It had lost its life-giving spark. While the dominant minority idolized old self-images, the majority withdrew allegiance to it and ceased paying it the compliment of imitation. Institutions that once had worked could no longer accommodate new forces. The very talents which had made a civilization great turned into its disadvantages, and sometimes a society fell by the path it rose—militarism, for instance—often bringing about its own destruction.

Instead of changing its style drastically, a declining civilization tried to expand its territory. It became larger than was appropriate for it, which produced further challenges, met more and more by improvisation. Its existence deteriorated into a series of civil wars and class struggles. The disaffected citizenry and those groups outside the society breaking through the defenses—the internal and external proletariats— would assault the dominant minority of the time. The battle would ebb and flow, the normal rhythm (from Graeco-Roman history) seeming to be rout-rally-rout-rally-rout-rally-rout. Substitutes for the old energy would be sought, and, amid constant social experimentation, individuals would come forward, each with a solution—the new creative genius, the savior with the sword, the savior with the time machine, the philosopher masked by the king, and (to Toynbee, the one successful figure) the God incarnate in a man who promises eternal life. Meanwhile, at a certain point, the genuinely creative minority would withdraw from the conflict; on the civilization's final dissolution, it would reemerge to build a new society.

As he reviewed Western Christian civilization in 1939—the one civilization which could still avert its fate—Toynbee believed it had been first disrupted by the Wars of Religion. It had rallied momentarily in the Enlightenment, but then had plunged steeply in the modern Wars of Nationalism and it had yet to reach the universal state, the mark of the second rally. It was no more invulnerable than the civilizations of the Inca and the Hittites and could only stop its slide to oblivion if it faced its problems squarely and saw them as the ultimate challenge. To regain its creative spirit it most needed leaders who would retrieve its Christian faith—the source of its original strength. After the Second World War, however, having traced the pattern of rise and fall, Toynbee applied himself to a still larger problem—the place of civilizations in the whole historical process. Did their growth and decay show any movement toward a discoverable destiny? He now contended that civilizations could only be understood by their interactions, and he noted that old institutions do not entirely vanish. The Roman Empire reappeared as a ghost in the Holy Roman Empire of medieval Christendom, and old laws, languages, calendars, and communications were used for new purposes.

But, of greater significance to his thesis, when the creative minority finally struck out in a new direction, it transformed the most vital parts of the old civilization into the religion of the new. The best example of this was the development of the Roman Catholic Church. The new religious message the Church nurtured during the Roman era was the nucleus of the next civilizational stage; but, as the Church grew, it also took over the forms and organization of the Roman empire and gave them a new lease of life. The Pope had adopted imperial claims and titles, the bishops had assumed the role of governors of provinces, and St. Benedict in his cell was a throwback to the disciplined beginnings of the Roman republic. Christianity, however, was superior to paganism; and the history of mankind, Toynbee concluded, was fundamentally the history of progress in religion—"the serious business of the human race." Despite the periodic rise and fall of individual civilizations, religion was like a chariot mounting a single continuous incline, away from superstition and toward a more purely ethical faith, as civilizations periodically fell. Since a universal church as well as a universal state was a feature of the final phase, Toynbee expected a similar phenomenon would occur in a twentieth-century world federation; but, he argued in 1954, the new religion, now protected like a chrysalis, would not be exclusively Christian. It would come from an encounter between the four main higher religions—Christianity, Islam, Hinduism, and Buddhism—and would have finer spiritual qualities than any of them. It would take the next civilization a little nearer to fulfilling history's ultimate purpose—a closer union between man and God. Meanwhile, the proletariat would produce little of cultural value except heroic myths and sagas.

Civilizations might connect in other ways as well; and Toynbee described with many illustrations the physical contacts the modern West in particular had made with other cultures. The true turning points of history were not marked by such dates as 1066, 1789, or even 1914. The Battle of Hastings and the French Revolution were local and internal affairs compared to those crises when civilizations hitherto separate collided for the first time—Vasco da Gama's arrival in India, the Spanish conquest of Mexico and Peru, Peter the Great's westernization of Russia, Napoleon's landing in Egypt, and the defeat of the Russian navy by Japan in 1905. Taking Hellenistic and Roman aggression against the Jewish state as a model of forced confrontation, he saw such situations giving rise to "Zealots," who habitually react desperately to a loss of cultural and political autonomy, and "Herodians" who bend and adapt. Civilizations might also be joined artificially, as in the revival of learning under Charlemagne and in the celebrated Renaissance in Italy; but these were signs of a failure of nerve, not of sudden new strengths. A growing, confident civilization had no need to borrow from a predecessor.

Looking back on his whole inquiry, Toynbee claimed his analysis had shown that history was governed by a certain regularity under the law of God. Since God has given man a degree of freedom, man can react as he chooses to the challenges facing him; and, as the breakdown of so many civilizations demonstrates, it is part of God's bargain with the devil that God does not always win. But, late though it was, Western man still had time to choose the life with God that had once made his civilization great, and thereby conceivably avoid the fate that lay in store. He could even demonstrate that the six-thousand years of human civilization so far had been merely an experimental period of man's existence. Abruptly assuming a liberal-progressive, even a racist outlook, Toynbee announced that there was another reason why the modern West might break with precedents. The British and North European peoples had enlarged the civilized world—the *Oikoumene*—by their technology, and bound it together with their communications. Western culture had in fact become truly universal—something none of the other twenty-five had managed; and freedom from war offered it extraordinary opportunities. But, as the second half of the twentieth century opened, mankind seemed to Toynbee like the crew of the *Kon-Tiki* as their raft was swept toward the jagged reef that could tear it, and them, to pieces. The reef in question was the use of atomic weapons to settle the new rivalry in the world between America and Russia—a prospect of final catastrophe. The spirit of *Kon-Tiki*'s crew as they worked and met danger together gave Toynbee some hope, but all too often in the past hope had risen and flickered away; and, with

Fra Angelico's picture of the Beatific Vision radiant in his mind, Toynbee finished his *Study* with the Te Deum and a prayer of intercession to the blessed company who symbolized to him the new world religion:

> *Christe, audi nos.*
> Christ Tammuz, Christ Adonis, Christ Osiris, Christ Balder,
> hear us, by whatsoever name we bless Thee for suffering
> death for our salvation.
>
> *Christe Jesu, exaudi nos.*
> Buddha Gautama, show us the path that will lead us out
> of our afflictions.
>
> *Sancta Dei Genetrix, intercede pro nobis.*
> Mother Mary, Mother Isis, Mother Cybele, Mother Ishtar,
> Mother Kwanyin, have compassion on us, by whatsoever
> name we bless thee for bringing Our Savior into the
> World.

On the prayer goes, drawing in Mithras, "all ye devoted bodhisattvas," Lucretius, Zarathustra, Peter and Paul, John Wesley, Socrates, Ashoka, Augustine, and many more, ending with the figure who, for Toynbee, was Western Christian civilization's finest representative: "Blessed Francis, who for Christ's sake didst renounce the pride of life, help us to follow Christ by following thee." But the prayer's last line, "to Him return ye every one," was from the Koran, the sacred book of the youngest of the world's great religions. Taking the chariot one stage higher than Christianity, more ethically conscious and endowed with much more vitality, Islam, Toynbee once wrote, might be moved to play her historic role again, if a Westernized world revolted against Western domination and cried out for anti-Western leadership.

IV

Written with a strong evangelical purpose, *A Study of History* surveyed mankind at large over an immense stretch of time and tried heroically to explain the fluctuations in the human story. After marking the door where one civilization after another had met its end, Toynbee returned to the single specimen whose fate was undecided—the West. Three goals had to be met, he insisted, to win the present battle for the West's survival. "In politics, establish a constitutional cooperative system of world government. In economics, find working compromises (varying according to the practical requirements of different places and times) between free enterprise and socialism. In the life of the spirit, put the secular superstructure back onto religious foundations." The first two, abolishing war and class, were the more urgent; the third was in the long run the most important. All were ambitious undertakings, to say the least; but our future, he wrote, largely depends upon ourselves. "We are not just at the mercy of an inexorable fate."

But is this great interpretation of the nature and working of history, unparalleled in the modern age, entirely credible or sufficiently profound for Toynbee's recent audience? Western man has become accustomed during the last two or three hundred years to see his history as the story of progress, of man becoming his own master, his actions judged according to standards pressed by Voltaire. This scheme has its flaws; but Toynbee asks us to admire its opposite. He hardly looks at recent history, the era supposedly of man's finest attainments; instead, he sees the world of the modern West as a rather discreditable tailpiece to a civilization whose apogee was the thirteenth century. For, if an increasingly spiritual life is the sign of man's growth, it follows that the peak of a civilization should be when its life is imbued with creative religion more than at any time before or since.

The thirteenth century was the age when the cathedrals reached perhaps their supreme form as works of art and engineering. It was also the time when St. Thomas Aquinas fused Christian teaching and Aristotelian philosophy into a system which remains one of the marvels of the human intellect. It was the age of Toynbee's hero, St. Francis, the essence of charity, who gave his clothes to the poor and lived in sweet harmony with nature; and over the whole culture presided the Papacy, whose political power under Innocent III was never surpassed. But, simultaneously, at the heart of the ripened fruit lurked the canker —the Holy Roman Emperor Frederick II, "the wonder of the world," brilliant, unconventional, and able, a patron of science and astrology, the first of the Renaissance princes. It was he who encouraged men to divert their talent into secular activities and into building the modern state; and it was he who thereby started the downfall. To Toynbee, all that had happened after—the printing press, America's discovery, the Reformation (the Church had been still flexible enough to adapt to Francis, but not to Luther), Michaelangelo, Louis XIV, Newton, Watt, inoculation, Napoleon, the abolition of slavery, Darwin, the inventions of the telegraph and radio, the Wright brothers, the conquest of space —were symptoms of a culture that had fundamentally lost its way; and, if Western Christian society had taken a thousand years to rise, it could also take another thousand to fall. On the surface this view seems unbelievable.

A Study of History is essentially a twentieth-century condemnation of the idea of progress and of the historians who produced it—especially of Gibbon, who celebrated the Enlightenment's new freedom from the barbarism and religion which had destroyed a splendid classical past. Inverting Gibbon's landmarks, Toynbee saw the darkness following Rome's fall as the vital period of creative growth, elevated the Middle Ages from a chasm to a lofty plateau, and thought the Scientific Revolution (and the American, French, and Russian revolutions) scarcely worth a mention. If the historian's elemental question was "How has this come out of that?" for Toynbee recent historians had disastrously altered it to "How on Earth has this come out of that?" The modern world was now both dying and experiencing the pangs of a new birth, and he did not believe this process was wholly subject to scientific laws. It leads us, he wrote, "back towards the Biblical view of history which was accepted in the West from the fourth century till the end of the seventeenth."

By reintroducing the "supra-mundane dimension of Reality," Toynbee thus picked up history's religious theme where Bishop Bossuet had left it in 1681, in his *Discourse on Universal History*. *A Study of History*, however, is also a work of romantic imagination, like several other contemporary efforts to bring knowledge together in scientific form. The scale of the inquiry, and Toynbee's use of myth, recall Sir James Frazer's *Golden Bough*; and, when discussing the individual in society, Toynbee drew heavily upon the holistic philosophy of Jan Christiaan Smuts, the South African statesman and soldier. If Toynbee's manner of tackling and presenting the huge problem he set himself was original, it came, like Whitman's self-conscious style, from a deeply felt need to write out of a new experience. His monument is, above all, the product of a highly subjective mind, in which his own nature has the last word. But perhaps his *Study* had little chance to be a proper scientific work in the first place; for, hundreds of specimens, it has been said—not twenty-six—would be needed to formulate statistically respectable conclusions.

A debate on *A Study of History* quickly divides, as may be imagined, in one or all of several ways: into an argument between historians who consider a universal history to be warranted and feasible and those who reject it in preference for "microhistory," such as scrutinizing the accounts of a fifteenth-century bishop's household; into a conflict between parties who defend Toynbee's religious premises and those who see his beliefs as an anachronism; or into a battle over the erratic personality of Toynbee himself. Specific attacks have been as many and as clamorous as the questions he found thronging upon him when writing his *Study*. For example, some charge he is irrationally attached to Greece and Rome as his civilizational model, that his choice is far more the result of his lauded classical education than of any detached analysis. The Greeks do not seem as ideal today as they did to the nineteenth century; and the view that Graeco-Roman civilization went through a clear sequence of routs and rallies is also open to objection. Toynbee shamefully depreciates science—another frequent effect of his narrow type of training—and, indeed, appears curiously estranged today from the culture around him. Experts on Russian and Chinese history regard his treatment of those areas haphazard and often laughably elementary. He has little interest in the state, even less in the nation-state, which he considers a latecomer on the scene. Marxists find Toynbee's methods insufficient and his message reactionary, liberals find him too vague, and conservatives find him too soft on communism; and Jews are incensed at his opinion that they represent a living fossil. Toynbee predicted that Israel (a late product of nineteenth-century nationalism) was doomed to be crushed by the Arabs, like the kingdoms of the Crusaders. To Jews, their history is an outstanding record of challenges overcome.

Toynbee's procedure is also sharply criticized by an army of opponents. He recklessly draws analogies, they say, blurs differences within religions, and uses isolated examples like Holland and Switzerland to fit his theories. His inquiry quickly founders when his large abstract questions call for rigorous philosophical method. There is also a creeping determinism in *A Study of History*'s argument. "Challenge-and-response," at the beginning a hypothesis, has become a law by the end. Writing for the English educated class, he offers an elitist view of the past, explaining movement by select individuals or minorities. Apart from a few gifted individuals with whom he claims kinship, it seems he does not like the human race at all, seeing most of it as destructive and depraved. His definition of "civilization" remains vague and unfair to primitive societies whose modes of life are now more commonly recognized. Lastly, can we accept any longer his idea that religion is man's "serious business"? Can we believe, correspondingly, that modern history's achievements are only to be the tourist attractions of a future race? The West, we may countercharge, has never been more vigorous than in its current phase, as it devises solutions to problems demanding its utmost will and commitment. Can we write off any civilization until it is finally over? Perhaps *A Study of History* is no more than a colossal folly, another Maginot Line, a complete guide to saving mankind by a masterpiece of obsolete strategy.

In the noise of attack Toynbee's merits are often overlooked. He wrenched Western man's idea of history away from the complacent "Europacentric" or national view, as shown at Victoria's jubilee, and helped make it cosmopolitan; he united the small segments of the past into a six-thousand-year phenomenon of human enterprise; and, by denying the primacy of politics in history, he encouraged inquiry into the other forms of civilization—notably religion. While most English historians were pursuing the limited (though not necessarily less ambitious) aims set by Ranke, as if straightening the record alone were their proper business, he drew attention back to the nature of the historical process itself. Fundamentally, he started new thought by rejecting the old answers; and, in spite of his errors and incoherencies, he could see at his death some of the best and liveliest minds of the age at grips with the issues he raised. It is in this way, as much as through the discovery of new evidence, that our understanding of history moves forward.

Toynbee, moreover, provided an interested public—far larger than many historians believed existed—with an interpretation of history that recognized certain realities of twentieth-century experience. Gibbon had reasoned that no civilized people would ever fall back into barbarism "unless the face of nature is changed"; but in the First World War the face of nature had changed, and in the least expected quarter. The West had reverted to savagery, and life, both individually and collectively, suffered an almost complete loss of meaning as a result. Spengler had seen social organisms living and dying in isolation, but Toynbee gave his audiences a ray of hope: though their old civilization might fail, in some way beyond their total comprehension the world might be unfolding into something conceivably better. Some of his forecasts are surely coming true, as airports are now visibly microcosms of the global village, and Eastern sects proselytize in the streets of North America. He also seems to be correct that, if the world survives, its appearance will be largely Western, nonetheless.

In his *Retractations* Toynbee did not alter any of his central propositions or conclusions; and he still offers plenty of easy targets for his critics. His syncretized religion—a triumph of liberal Christianity at its extreme—is more like an exotic mystery cult from Asia Minor than a faith to fire a millennium. Religions in any case are greatly assisted in taking root by having a charismatic leader; and Toynbee exposed himself foolishly to charges of self-idolatry and messianic pretensions—witness his many tales of personal revelations, and the long entries on himself and his relatives in the *Study*'s index. The course of events does not always bear him out; movements for religious unity have faltered, and, in politics, nationalism has revived. Small societies now appear to have some definite advantages over large federations, which no longer seem automatically more desirable. Most damaging of all, Toynbee's system of history plays into the hands of all who seek to bring Western civilization down. In a scathing essay, written with the Second World War a recent memory, the English historian Hugh Trevor-Roper lashed out at Toynbee and defended the modern West for outstanding advances in social life and humanitarianism as well as in science and technology. There was every indication, Trevor-Roper insisted, that this astonishing vitality would continue if this best of all civilizations were constantly defended. Peace was not to be had at any price; and the future must not be abandoned to a conjectural cyclic process leading backward to religious obscurantism—or turned over to gangsters who can hasten such a destiny.

Toynbee once said that he would be content if even a quarter of his work were not forgotten. At the moment acceptance of his analysis of history rests to no small extent on the reader's temperament. The stakes are high in any revaluation of history in the current "ecumenical anarchy," however; and, if a universal state with a syncretized religion does emerge from the turmoil, Toynbee will be placed among the immortals as a prophet, or even as something of a savior after all. But, viewed in more ordinary terms, does *A Study of History* have within itself the awesomely simple strengths which could undergird the next civilization, and which were so powerfully present in the *City of God*— perhaps its closest equivalent? Probably not, for it strays from one method of inquiry to another, tries to pass as science and cannot, is hardly outstanding literature—and it conspicuously changes its message halfway through. A history does not have to be consistent to be good, and allowance must be made for an author's growth while writing— especially in a work of this scale; but it is desirable for it to avoid major internal contradictions. *A Study of History* has, in fact, already slipped into history itself; and, daunting though the task is, it is bound to be replaced eventually by a new generation's effort to see from its own situation the sum of human experience. Besides, Toynbee's character imparts less fullness and charm than Augustine's, which helped make the *City of God* so influential.

But perhaps we should judge Toynbee's work for what it really is, instead of for what we think it ought to be. *A Study of History* may reasonably be thought a strange failure by modern secular culture; but some of its faults may become its virtues, for it is an extraordinary response of the heart to history, and in that area if anywhere lies its best chance to gain an enduring power. A reading of Toynbee's many tributes to the influences on his life shows that invariably the impact of a book, a place, or a person was made most forcefully not on his mind but at the source of his whole being. Despite his scientific protestations, *A Study of History* should be seen positively as a great work of universal myth, standing in a very English literary tradition—the allegory beginning and ending in a dream. No matter that this example is huge and cumbersome, or that it starts on the Orient Express and ends in the National Gallery, Trafalgar Square. Its ascription of allegorical significance to historical figures and events makes its descent from the medieval vision of Piers the plowman, who fell asleep on the Malvern Hills and saw a fair field of folk working and wandering—and from Bunyan's dream in Bedford jail of a man clothed in rags, a book in his hand, and a great burden on his back, crying "What shall I do?" Its strength lies in Toynbee's near-superhuman attempt to reawaken in the historical form the contents of the collective unconsciousness of the past, as Jung, whom he called his "navigator psychopompus"—conductor of souls to the place of the dead—had taught him.

To Toynbee insights into the great historical process were not only to be found from university libraries or daily work at Chatham House. They were also gained from spending a summer's afternoon lying with his dog on one of the Stone Age barrows on Slingsby Moor in Yorkshire —and from many other scenes. There, he wrote in his eccentric style, his sixth sense could catch "still unspent reverberations of waves of psychic events that had been breaking upon this fringe of the *Oikoumene* since the unrecorded time at which this barrow had been heaped over the ashes of the unknown man whose presence was still brooding here in my day." In the end his most lasting contribution to historical studies may not be his jarring system or his prophecies. More likely he will be credited with having taken Jung's discovery of psychological types and primordial images and having introduced them broadly to a new creative phase of civilization. He thus encouraged recognition that patterns of behavior have been with man always and are enshrined in myth and legend; and that, in the sweep of history, universal psychic forces eternally exist which in experience we can only begin to touch.

CHAPTER ELEVEN

WELLS

I

For a historian to write directly of the future seems at first sight a plain
contradiction in terms, a denial that history by definition relates to the
past. Yet often in the West some vision of tomorrow has been
deliberately used as a device to give cohesion to the human record,
attracting and polarizing the evidence like a powerful magnet, and
enticing, too, the ordinary reader as it is sketched in outline or detail.
As we have seen, even a most objective scholar like Ranke cannot
wholly forget the future when he writes—he produced his national
histories in the belief that the European power structure would continue.
And for some men the future has been the essence of the enterprise.
Remove things hoped for, and the great impetus sustaining the work of
Augustine, Petrarch, Voltaire, and Marx subsides; Thucydides and
Toynbee might be unknown without their fear of recurring catastrophe.
Conceived in this way the past may become little more than a
background on which to project a perfect or an alarming scene, at
worst a structure nailed together to support a slogan flashing from the
roof. But, whenever the future seems to have been reliably sighted,
it changes the arrangement of the historical picture and redistributes
light, shade, scale. It becomes the new means of elucidating the past,
and may well make that past more genuine to us in the present; for
by ancient tradition, which affects history writing too, the storyteller's
leap into the fantastic must start from a ground of the most solid
reality.

The historian who tries to forecast the future has been likened to a tracker anxiously peering at a muddy road to see the footprints of the next person who is going to pass that way. History repeats itself only superficially; there are no permanent historical laws, and the future remains largely conjectural. But this has not deterred predictions, and perhaps the most beguiling light gleaming on the West's horizon has been the idea of a utopian society. Usually an historically based criticism of the existing system, utopias have often been seen as the goal toward which all history has been accumulating and from which all history may be prematurely interpreted. The reign of righteousness and peace foretold by the second Isaiah, Plato's ideal republic, Augustine's heavenly city, Utopia itself—the land of nowhere—satirized by More, the Puritan community of saints attempted in seventeenth-century England and in Massachusetts Bay, all are variations on this theme; and, with the new confidence inspired by the Scientific Revolution, the concept was freshly minted as a secular proposition. England and Pennsylvania indicated its form and attainability, *Robinson Crusoe* and reports of noble Tahitians portrayed the alternative excellence of life freed of its inessentials; and, when the shock of the French Revolution had subsided, the nineteenth century seemed to fulfill the eighteenth century's expectations. Technologically proficient, increasingly democratic and peaceful, healthier than before, and holding himself to be anatomically superior too, Western man looked back to note his progress and looked forward to calculate with assurance his closeness to the future fast approaching his grasp. In the late-nineteenth-century world transformed by his mastery, his characteristic mood was assertive and optimistic, supported by a record of human and physical challenges he had overcome with the stubborn tenacity of salmon swimming upstream.

But in the midst of this popular celebration men of science, whose efforts largely brought it about, simultaneously warned that there was absolutely no guarantee man would move continuously along the path to which he had become accustomed. Darwin had soberly stressed that existence rested on struggle, ruthless natural selection ensuring the survival of species which were better equipped to face new challenges; and his public defender Thomas Henry Huxley saw the whole cosmic process as hostile to the attainment of perfection, desirable though that goal might be. Only by developing their ethical sense, Huxley believed, might men combat and check the natural order of things. The competition might just possibly arise from beyond this planet, and it was even speculated that man might discover at some moment he was not after all the master and possessor of nature but the aboriginal

Tasmanian or Tierra del Fuegian of the universe, marked down to be victim of more advanced creatures in a new civilizational encounter. Moreover, the recently formulated second law of thermodynamics stated that, during any process, the greater the entropy of a system the less available the energy in terms of heat; and, consequently, at a date not so distant by new chronological conceptions as to be entirely incredible, the earth would become cold and life extinct. Beneath the hope and plans lay a disturbing pessimism, added to fears and insecurities of other kinds, which was based on the clear recognition that history's end was likely to be, not a perpetual British Empire—and still less the imminent return of Christ—but the unavoidable doom of an eternal silence, the temporary evolutionary accident known as man having vanished unnoticed into the night.

The problem of sheer survival—surely the ultimate issue in the late twentieth century—thus starkly emerged in modern form when belief in progress was strongest; and, in their dilemma, men looked to those figures who had explored beyond the normal limits of experience and returned—as they once did to a North African bishop, a Renaissance scholar, a French exile in England, and certain Venetian ambassadors—and they listened to their reports and new perceptions. With this in mind, we break our previously chronological sequence and approach H. G. Wells, who, early in an age of mass literacy, became celebrated for going beyond the present in his imagination and writing of things to come. His forecasts of human posterity's fate, given not just in futurist stories but in the most popular work of history ever written, excited a huge audience and still reflect our continuing hopes and fears. In other ways, too, Wells frequently seems our contemporary, although he precedes Toynbee by a generation. Political growth, cultural development, and social conflict remain as some substantial themes for reducing the whole of history to comprehension; but the closing illustration in most surveys of history today is seldom the usual political map of the world on Mercator's projection. We now find instead Wells's picture of the little speck of cosmic dust on which all mankind is travelling, the earth as photographed from space—"a morning star of hope," he called it, "our own warmer planet, green with vegetation and grey with water, with a cloudy atmosphere eloquent of fertility, with glimpses through its drifting cloud-wisps of broad stretches of populous country and narrow, navy-crowded seas." Wells's chosen viewpoint on the human epic has already become in large measure ours, and it seems almost certain to be our children's; for that reason alone, he is a very important historian for the late twentieth century.

To Wells the composite question (phrased by the astronomer

Kepler) with which he introduced his novel, *The War of the Worlds* —"But who shall dwell in these worlds if they be inhabited? . . . Are we or they Lords of the World? . . . And how are all things made for man?"—offered both an intriguing start of an imaginative tale and a valid perspective on human history. For whom had the earth finally been made—for men, or perhaps for Martians? Proudest throughout his public career to call himself a scientist, he saw man as part of the physical universe and man's story understandable largely in relation to the conclusions the biological evidence showed. Nonetheless he discerned that more immediately a worse fate than extinction could be in store— a bartering by man of humanity and individuality for the sake of order and peace. A society of this kind, which he described most explicitly in *The First Men in the Moon*, with its utterly cerebral ruler and its degenerate population bred to perform certain specialized tasks—a society where thought was controlled, the past forgotten, and all was subordinated to technology and communal needs—was unmistakably anti-utopian. Utopia achieved, it seemed, could well be not the perfect life envisioned by some, but a nightmare. Twentieth-century experience would make such nightmares easier to project, most notably in Aldous Huxley's *Brave New World* and George Orwell's *Nineteen Eighty-Four*.

This alarming prospect led Wells to take a new stance which gave him the appearance of being an optimist, a one man brain trust who surveyed the chief forces for social and political change and pressed hard for global reconstruction. Recalling his first venture into public affairs in 1900 with *Anticipations*, he wrote that he had reviewed the pretensions of democracy and stated the widely unspoken thought of the late Victorians: "This will not work." He had then considered existing governments and ruling influences, and said as plainly: "These do not work," at a time when most active people were saying, "They will work well enough for a few years more." "And so," he went on, "through circumstances and simplicity rather than through any exceptional intelligence, I arrived ahead of everyone at the naked essential question, which everyone about me was putting off for to-morrow, 'What, then, will work?' And the attempt to answer that has been the cardinal reality of my thought and writing ever since."

But this acute modern dilemma between human fate and human striving, which calls progress into doubt far more seriously than the dispute between Voltaire and Rousseau ever did—and, by the vastness of the issues it admits, can more effectively reduce the whole Baconian enterprise to a nullity than any insight Toynbee apprehended—this dilemma was not to be resolved for Wells permanently with such simple positivism. "Are all things made for man?" "What, then, will work?"

There is no point in delaying his own final answer, which came after
he had written more than a hundred books. It comes visually in a set
of panels Wells painted himself in the last year of his life on a wall
behind his London house, a house adorned with statues of the Muses.
Depicting the story of evolution, it ended with the appearance of
horned devils, and beneath the figure of Man he wrote the words
"Time to Go."

II

For the moment we must not be tempted to see Wells from the
vantage point of a Texas manned-spacecraft center or of some other
future-oriented organization. We must rediscover him as a man who
grew up in a now distant era when, in his words, history seemed to
have slowed down to a jog-trot. But, as he once said with a measure of
truth, "Queen Victoria was like a great paper-weight that for half a
century sat upon men's minds, and when she was removed their ideas
began to blow about all over the place haphazardly." His career spanned
the transition from nineteenth-century complacency to twentieth-
century rebellion at conformity and tradition; and he died at the dawn
of the atomic age. Before looking at Wells the voyager on new oceans,
let us see what kind of a human being this was who educated most of
his generation, and who, by the thrust of his questions in and out of
his *Outline of History*, lives on to argue with us how we read the human
story.

Herbert George Wells was born in 1866 in a room over the dingy
china shop where his parents made a precarious living in Bromley, on
the southern edge of London. His mother, whose fixed ambition was to
see Wells and his two older brothers settled in a respectable draper's
business, had been a lady's maid, his father a gardener who was always
ready to escape from the faltering business to earn extra income as a
traveling cricketer. Domestic life was strained, and the poorly built
home—named Atlas House, after a figure set in a window—was squalid.
In his *Experiment in Autobiography*, Wells described the shoddy
material world in which his "very ordinary brain" acquired its first
perceptions—battered furniture, vermin-infested rooms with stock lying
everywhere, an outdoor privy, and a small garbage-cluttered yard which
was his first playground. Both parents, however, were unusually literate
for their class, and, while his mother clung to religion, work, and duty
to give her life some stability, his father's restless mind wandered far
beyond his depressed circumstances. "When I was a young man of
your age," he casually told his son some twenty years later as they were

rambling on the Kentish downs, "I used to come out here and lie oh! half the night, just looking at the stars."

Wells's starts in life were many, and he early acquired the reading habit at home, gaining from books a picturesque geography and history. His formal education began at seven years old, when he was sent to Mr. Morley's academy a few doors away. The academy's chief purpose was virtually to produce good clerks, but to Mrs. Wells this separated it in every desirable way from the recently started state schools, whose mass education would incidentally provide her son by the century's end with a large part of his audience. The headmaster's views, however, were inclined toward radicalism and republicanism, and these left their own stamp on the boy. In 1880, when the family fell apart, Mrs. Wells returned to her former employers at Up Park, a seventeenth-century mansion not far away, and Wells, like his brothers, became a draper's apprentice. Bored, inattentive, reading on the side whenever he could, he was discharged before long, and briefly became a pupil-teacher in a distant relative's village school; but, when that situation collapsed, he returned to his mother to stay for a few weeks in the servants' quarters at the country house. It was at Up Park, during periodic interludes, that his education began in earnest. He found in an attic volumes of engravings by Raphael and Michaelangelo, also a box full of mysterious brass objects that clearly might be fitted together. By trial and error he made a telescope from them, and he describes how his mother discovered him in the small hours, "my bedroom window wide open, inspecting the craters of the moon." Allowed by the proprietors to roam the library stocked by their freethinking predecessor, he took interesting books away to his room and eagerly read some of Voltaire's works, Johnson's *Rasselas*—the tale of an Abyssinian prince's search for happiness amid the delusion of worldly enjoyments—Tom Paine's pamphlet of the American Revolution, *Common Sense*, and Swift's *Gulliver's Travels*. Plato's *Republic* in particular released his mind from sordidness and a growing habit of mockery with "the amazing and heartening suggestion that the whole fabric of law, custom and worship, which seemed so invincibly established, might be cast into the melting pot and made anew."

But, after a few weeks assisting a pharmacist and a short but precious opportunity at Mr. Byatt's grammar school at Midhurst to discipline his insatiable reading, Wells entered the bleakest period of his life—two further years in a drapery store under new terms arranged by his mother. Desperate to escape from what to him was permanent alienation from his real talents, he finally walked off the job and managed by hard insistence to persuade his parents to accept Mr.

Byatt's offer to take him back as a promising student. There was a price to pay that assaulted his conscience—Anglican confirmation, required by the school for teaching assistants; but, settling into lodgings, he placed on the wall two mottoes, "Knowledge is Power," and "What man has done man can do," and crammed furiously, especially in physics and biology. Along the way he reread Plato with a more critical eye on current social inequities and was struck by a contemporary best seller, Henry George's *Progress and Poverty*, which advocated a new management of national wealth in the public interest. Byatt gave him special attention, and their joint struggle was rewarded when, in 1884, Wells won a scholarship to train as a teacher at the Normal School of Science, South Kensington. "I had come," he would write, "from beginnings of an elementary sort to the fountainhead of knowledge."

The Normal School, now the Imperial College of Science and Technology and part of the University of London, was an offspring of the Great Exhibition of 1851. An effort to modernize British education and meet the threat to Britain's industrial leadership mounted by certain other nations in the halls of the Crystal Palace, it was dedicated to practical knowledge; and it quickly became a stronghold of evolutionary doctrine, for its dean and founding force was T. H. Huxley himself, in whose introductory biology class Wells was enrolled. Less vigorous than when the Darwinian controversy was raging, Huxley had a firm reputation as a brilliant scientist, an agnostic thinker, and a skillful popularizer, whose public lectures "On Coral and Coral Reefs," "On a Piece of Chalk," and "Yeast" were masterpieces of their kind. Listening in awe to his famous teacher's analysis of the structure, embryology, and succession of vertebrate forms, dissecting and researching at first hand, Wells was to consider the year spent in Huxley's class as beyond all doubt the most educational time of his life. Though practically no direct contact existed between them, Huxley remained for him "the greatest man I was ever likely to meet." In the red-brick building which belief in progress had built, Wells paradoxically learned from Huxley of the fatalism inherent in any impartial forecast of man's future; during this period he also energetically tested his own primary ideas in the debating society and participated in socialist student politics. In his second year, however, his courses failed to attract him. Poor and underfed, he fell behind, and, barely making a passing grade, had to abandon his dream of a career of research. Grand schemes still fascinated him nonetheless, and in a "picshua"—one of the many he drew throughout his life—he caricatured himself meditating on his prospects surrounded by a litter of papers bearing titles like "Secret of the

Kosmos," "Key to Politics," "Wells' Design for a New Framework for Society," "All about God," "How I Could Save the Nation."

At the end of Wells's college career his situation was one of panic, a sad reversal from all the high hopes of three years before. "I had no outlook," he wrote, "no qualifications, no resources, no self-discipline, and no physique." His life was complicated too by a romantic attachment with his cousin, whom he bored with his daring ideas on republicanism, atheism, and free love. He found an unsatisfactory teaching post in Wales, then suffered a breakdown, and slowly recuperated at Up Park—where he ransacked the library, expanding his interests into fiction and poetry. Still a semiinvalid, he returned to London and began to earn a few shillings for short scientific notes in cheap weekly papers. In time he gained a science degree by correspondence from London University, allowing him to teach at a tutorial college, where he produced his first book, *A Text Book of Biology*. With a steady position at last, he married his cousin, but quickly found her daily company confining; and soon he eloped with one of his students—another instance of his customary resorts to flight. Slowly gaining a regular market for his occasional writings, some chance remarks in a story by J. M. Barrie made him see that the reason why publishers rejected his work was often because he treated his topics too seriously. Instead, "all I had to do," he realized, "was to lower my aim —and hit." His free-lance journalism immediately became more successful; and he made his breakthrough in 1895 when *The Time Machine* was published in installments in the *Pall Mall Gazette* and critics called him a man of genius.

The Time Machine suited many preoccupations of the age, an age sensing decadence beneath the strident noise of progress, addicted to tales of mystery and horror by Poe, Stevenson, or Conan Doyle, and intrigued by Verne's remarkable forecasts. The mood has been commonly called *fin de siècle*; and, through his story, Wells himself obtained instant historical significance. The concept of a fourth dimension was an old theme of his, dating back to his years at South Kensington, but never satisfactorily used in his constant search for saleable topics; now, however, in some respects at the height of his powers, he created in *The Time Machine* a work of fiction which rested its appeal not entirely on an extraordinary invention but, within its fanciful plot, on the elements of a new intellectual system. Presented ingeniously through the mixture of scientific fact, satire, and romance Wells had by then developed, illuminated with iridescent similes and convincing impressionistic glimpses, the story gripped its readers and bore them almost effortlessly over the crucial gap between reality and the realm of fantasy. It was, moreover, Wells's special and lasting ability to write of scientific things as an ordinary man, catching at the edge of potent new ideas as they spilled into the common store; and he could guide his readers—eventually numbering millions—to a grasp of barely imaginable implications in language of often wonderful quality. The newly literate masses struggling upwards like himself were just then sharing in a general way his own experience at Byatt's grammar school, when he had suddenly woken up "to the existence of a vast and growing world of thought and knowledge outside my ordinary circle of ideas altogether." The ultimate force behind the story came straight from Huxley—who, in an age of unequalled optimism had been tempted to suppose the worst, not the best, and, as the frontiers of chronology were extended millions of years, to predict that future degeneration was more likely than utopia. Slowly but consciously, at the common level old bounds of history were being upset by scientific evidence; and, though fictional in form, *The Time Machine* borrowed Huxley's broad conclusion to the problem of likely human destiny and handed it to the much-anticipated infant about to be born, the new man of the twentieth century, for his amusement and edification.

Well-known though *The Time Machine* is, it is worth summarizing for its intense drama as well as for the history it infers. Comfortable in the atmosphere of an after-dinner conversation, a group of London gentlemen are led by their host to admit the feasibility of a fourth dimension—time—and are shown the vehicle he has constructed from nickel, ivory, and crystal to journey into the past or future. The host proposes to travel upon it, to show what he says can be done, and promises to return to the spot a week later with proof of his journey. On the appointed day, dirty and bloodstained, he suddenly reappears to join his friends and tell them of a visit to the year A.D. 802,701, "such days as no human being ever lived before."

After a hair-raising ride across the changing surface of the earth, the Traveler had stopped in a gardenlike landscape scattered with huge neoclassical buildings, and he had suddenly questioned what sort of welcome might lie in store. "What might not have happened to men?" he wondered. "What if cruelty had grown into a common passion? What if in this interval the race had lost its manliness, and had developed into something inhuman, unsympathetic, and overwhelmingly powerful? I might seem some old-world savage animal, only the more dreadful and disgusting for our common likeness—a foul creature to be incontinently slain." He met instead the Eloi—graceful and beautiful but frail, about four feet tall, and with the intellectual level of small children. Garlanded with flowers, he was led to the ruined palace that was their communal home to share in their charmingly playful but indolent life. Reflecting later upon a hill overlooking the Thames, he found himself giving an unexpected interpretation to the apparent course of events:

> It seemed to me that I had happened upon humanity upon the wane. The ruddy sunset set me thinking of the sunset of mankind. For the first time I began to realize an odd consequence of the social effort in which we are at present engaged. And yet, come to think, it is a logical consequence enough. Strength is the outcome of need: security sets a premium upon feebleness. The work of ameliorating the conditions of life—the true civilizing process that makes life more and more secure—had gone steadily on to a climax. One triumph of a united humanity over Nature had followed another. Things that are now mere dreams had become projects deliberately put in hand and carried forward. And the harvest was what I saw!

The Traveler reasoned that the scientific balancing of animal and vegetable life to suit human needs had been done well in the centuries across which his machine had leaped, and that a social paradise had been achieved; for fruit grew everywhere, brilliant butterflies flew hither and thither, and no economic struggle, disease, or surplus population was obvious. But after the battle comes the calm, and with it men had reacted to the new and altered conditions. Restless energy, once a source of strength, had no place in a life without challenges; and the artistic impulse too had almost died, as the Eloi demonstrated. "To adorn themselves with flowers, to dance, to sing in the sunlight; so much was left of the artistic spirit, and no more. Even that would fade in the end into a contented inactivity. We are kept keen on the grindstone of pain and necessity, and, it seemed to me, that here was that hateful grindstone broken at last!" Standing there in the gathering dark, the Traveler thought that he had mastered the problem of the world.

But his discovery was only a half-truth, for, in a series of adventures resulting from his vehicle's mysterious loss, he was confronted by the Morlocks. These apelike figures, who by day tended great engines in underground caverns ventilated by huge well-shafts—suggested it seems by the service-rooms at Up Park—came at night to the surface to prey on the ineffectual Eloi as their food. Man, he was forced to conclude, had become two species, the evolutionary result of the nineteenth-century difference between the capitalist and the laborer. The gulf had widened between what Wells called the "haves," above ground, carefree, and thought-free, and the "have-nots," the workers below continually adapting to their tasks in factory or mine. The separation had grown permanent, though curiously the Morlocks still made clothes for the Eloi and maintained them in their habitual needs although the ape-men had turned against their former masters. The extent of civilization's degeneracy was especially borne out to the Traveler when, accompanied by an Eloi girl he had rescued from drowning, he managed to reach a distant palace of green porcelain, "the ruins of some latter-day South Kensington." In this once splendid museum the dust was thick, the fossil skeletons broken to pieces or threaded in strings upon reeds, the machines corroded, and the place very silent, the library a wilderness of rotting paper signifying the enormous waste of labor. Everything testified to decay instead of preserving the past that man had moved beyond. The discovery of a crowbar and a box of usable matches gave him, however, the means of protection against Morlock attacks; for fire dazzled them and made them easy to strike down.

To his astonishment he came upon his vehicle where he had left it; but the Morlocks, who had stolen it, had now set it up as a trap, and only after a desperate struggle was he able to scramble onto the seat and pull the vital lever. Off he flew again into the grey light and tumult he had experienced before, ultimately stopping more than thirty million years into the future in a world of ghastly desolation. Alighting by a sea shore the Traveler watched the scarlet sky turning to night in an eclipse of the enormous sun; and the beach seemed lifeless except for lichens, the grotesque crabs he had noticed previously having vanished. Apart from the moan of the biting wind and the ripple of icy waves, the earth was still; "all the sounds of man, the bleating of sheep, the cries of birds, the hum of insects, the stir that makes the background of our lives—all that was over." But, as gusts of snowflakes blew down, something moving on a sandbank caught his attention. "It was a round thing, the size of a football perhaps, or, it may be, bigger, and tentacles trailed down from it; it seemed black against the weltering blood-red water, and it was hopping fitfully about." Nearly fainting at the sight of what could only be the last animal organism to survive a process of reversed evolution, he clambered back on his machine and returned to describe his incredible adventure—though not for long; for he soon took flight once more, and after three years, "as everyone knows now, he has never returned."

The Time Machine gained its great popular success by abandoning conventional utopias—linear progressive, benevolent Darwinian, Marxist, and Christian (for God and the hope of salvation were absent)—and rejecting the very concept, painting instead a series of horrifying situations. The accolade spurred Wells forward to profit from his peculiar gift for symbolic scientific romance; and for the next six years he rapidly wrote one best seller after another, unrelated stories of a comparable type which would inexplicably come by taking almost anything as a starting-point and letting his thoughts dreamily play around with it. He began to move in literary circles, and, using his sudden wealth, he built a house of modern design on the coast in Kent, a retreat for himself, his new wife, and their two sons. All through his life, from Atlas House to his last London home, and in his novels, places of dwelling to him were powerful influences fashioning their occupants' state of mind; and they had a significant impact upon his schemes for society. Among his many imaginative stories *The Island of Dr. Moreau*, *The War of the Worlds*, and Wells's own favorite, *The First Men in the Moon*, are, in ways resembling *The Time Machine*, works of historical analysis; and, like that first stupendous tale, they are heavy with prophetic pessimism.

The Island of Dr. Moreau (1896) took the hope that man might subdue the beast within him by ethical improvement and showed by physiological illustration the appalling cruelty that could be inflicted if the evolutionary process was artificially broken. Robinson Crusoe had once seemed to personify the history of the world, a man intelligently building civilization out of wilderness; but, on Wells's deserted island, a vivisectionist used perverted surgical skills to form strange composite creatures—swine-men, a bear tainted with dog and ox, bandaged brutes with saberlike canines and slitlike pupils, small pink homunculi—and forcibly suppressed their animal instincts to make indisputable human beings. Darwinian theory had blunted the difference between men and beasts at a distance, and Kipling's *Jungle Book* was a popular example of this two years before, wolves and the boy Mowgli living and hunting together. The cost of slow humanization in Wells's story, however, was repeated grafting and reshaping of body and brain; and some bestial traits seemed ineradicable. "But," said Dr. Moreau, "I will conquer yet. Each time I dip a living creature into the bath of burning pain, I say: this time I will burn out all the animal, this time I will make a rational creature of my own. After all, what is ten years? Man has been a hundred thousand in the making."

Swaying, and chanting, the beast-people were required to recite this litany:

Not to go on all-Fours; *that* is the Law. Are we not Men?
Not to suck up Drink; *that* is the Law. Are we not Men?

Not to eat Flesh or Fish; *that* is the Law. Are we not Men?
Not to claw Bark of Trees; *that* is the Law. Are we not Men?
Not to chase other Men; *that* is the Law. Are we not Men?

Through a long list of prohibitions they went, ending with worship of
Moreau and his infernal laboratory, the beast-people reminding themselves pathetically of the promise that some day they would emerge
fully human; but to the scientist-visitor (a student of Huxley's in fact)
they were travesties, humanity at its most debased, diabolical warnings
that man's vile emotions are ever poised to triumph. Moreau himself
confides after a pause, "as soon as my hand is taken from them the
beast begins to creep back, begins to assert itself again," and his
manufactured specimens all regress to their wholly animal habits,
killing their tormentor in a spectacular scene. Escaping from the island
terror, the visitor flees in turn from the common people he encounters
on London streets, fearing they too may suddenly shed their orderly
conduct if flimsy safeguards are removed. When history was seen as
progress, men had tried to impose rationality on the dualism of the
human character; but the logic of nature's laws governed man inexorably, and manipulation in humanity's name could only produce added
frightening episodes along the nightmarish path to his extinction.

Serialized during Victoria's jubilee year, *The War of the Worlds*
has practically passed into folk legend. Wells's setting now was the
England of the day, and the work is after a fashion a piece of contemporary history writing, reminiscent of Defoe's journal of the great
plague of 1665, with a distant echo of Thucydides. "The chances against
anything man-like on Mars are a million to one," scoffs a well-known
astronomer, at a time when the red planet was intensively studied; but
in man's "great disillusionment," leathery squid-like creatures abandoning their exhausted home descend to the earth, and stride high on
cowled metallic tripods across the southern countryside, ruthlessly
wiping out every obstacle with heat rays and suffocating black smoke.
The species *Homo sapiens* had unknowingly been watched by an
unsympathetic intelligence greater than its own, and man had been
deemed disposable. Church, army, government, and law—the boasted
evidences of English superiority—all topple into total ruin, and earthly
science is exposed as rudimentary; "never before in the history of warfare
had destruction been so indiscriminate and so universal." Here Wells
describes how, in a roaring wave of fear, the population of the world's
largest city takes to instant flight:

If one could have hung that June morning in a balloon in the blazing
blue above London every northward and eastward road running out

of the tangled maze of streets would have seemed stippled black with the streaming fugitives, each dot a human agony of terror and physical distress. . . . And this was no disciplined march; it was a stampede— a stampede gigantic and terrible—without order and without a goal, six million people, unarmed and unprovisioned, driving headlong. It was the beginning of the rout of civilization, of the massacre of mankind.

From the landing of the first Martian cylinder, through scenes uncannily projecting twentieth-century devastation, to the howling of the last Martian stricken by bacteria, the theme of *The War of the Worlds* is apocalypse and judgment. At the end, although the fabric of organized life is repaired, the old spirit has gone; for the broadening and alteration of men's views could hardly be exaggerated. "We have learned now," wrote the survivor, "that we cannot regard this planet as being fenced in and a secure abiding-place for Man; we can never anticipate the unseen good or evil that may come upon us suddenly out of space. It may be that in the larger design of the universe this invasion from Mars is not without its ultimate benefit for men; it has robbed us of that serene confidence in the future which is the most fruitful source of decadence, the gifts to human science it has brought are enormous, and it has done much to promote the conception of the commonweal of mankind." The inhabitants of Mars might have learned a lesson from the fate of their pioneers; but, "it may be, on the other hand, that the destruction of the Martians is only a reprieve. To them, and not to us, perhaps, is the future ordained."

In *The First Men in the Moon* (1901), Wells used a time-honored satirical device—a journey to earth's smaller, therefore cooler, satellite— to caricature current ambitions for a wholly rational and technological society. Lifted in a sphere by a new gravity-defying substance, Cavor, a pure scientist, and Bedford, an imperialistic businessman, land in an atmosphere-filled crater and witness the amazingly swift warming effects of the lunar sunrise. Honeycombed with caverns to the sea at its core, the moon they discover is populated by Selenites—large, twittering ant-like creatures, many with hypertrophied brains—who live in a totally organized society. Having noticed gold for the picking up, Bedford escapes with some and returns alone to earth expecting to become infinitely powerful; yet the whole enterprise for him remains a perplexing riddle:

> What is this spirit in man that urges him for ever to depart from happiness and security, to toil, to place himself in danger, even to risk a reasonable certainty of death? It dawned upon me up there in the

moon as a thing I ought always to have known, that man is not made simply to go about being safe and comfortable and well fed and amused. Against his interest, against his happiness he is constantly being driven to do unreasonable things. Some force not himself impels him and go he must. But why? Why? . . . I lost myself at last in bottomless speculation.

Cavor, however, is captured; but he manages to send back telegraphic accounts of the life he sees in the gigantic anthill. On the moon the insect is the inheritor; but, in place of the worker, soldier, winged male, queen, and slave ants observable on earth, the Selenites are differentiated in hundreds of forms, each with its fine gradations and every individual subordinate to the species. "In the moon every citizen knows his place. He is born to that place, and the elaborate discipline of training and education and surgery he undergoes fits him at last so completely to it that he has neither ideas nor organs for any purpose beyond it." A destined mathematician, for example, has the bias of his faculties stimulated at the expense of all else until "his limbs shrivel, his heart and digestive organs diminish, his insect face is hidden under its bulging contours. His voice becomes a mere squeak for the stating of formulae; he seems deaf to all but properly enunciated problems. The faculty of laughter, save for the sudden discovery of some paradox, is lost to him; his deepest emotion is the evolution of a novel computation. And so he attains his end."

Each a perfect unit in a world machine, the Selenites exhibit the results of complete and utter specialization, and perform with happiness the duty which justifies their being. Carefully trained shepherds tend the mooncalves—giant aphids—which browse by day on lunar pastures; glassblowers are almost entirely lung; and Cavor is shown young Selenites confined in jars from which only the forelimbs protrude, disfigured to become machine minders of a highly skilled sort. The swollen brains of profounder scholars render their bodies incapable of self-movement, and they are carried in sedan-tubs, wobbling jellies of knowledge, preceded by news-disseminators shouting their fame. Finally Cavor is brought before the Grand Lunar, an almost faceless mass resting on an exalted throne, whose braincase many yards in diameter is constantly sprayed and massaged by attendants.

Questioning the first human he has seen, the insect-monarch is surprised by man's readiness to come to the moon and yet remain ignorant of his own planet's interior. He is incredulous at the inefficiency of democracy and of the earthly organization of labor, at the inconvenience of diverse languages, and at the wastefulness and glorification of war. Bravely Cavor declares "our States and Empires are still the rawest sketches of what order will some day be"; but for the present the differ-ence from the moon was marked in every area. "With knowledge the Selenites grew and changed; mankind stored their knowledge about them and remained brutes—equipped." And yet the moon's pure reason, for all its triumphs, could not stifle in Cavor a disagreeable impression. Though assured that the educational techniques were benign, "that wretched-looking hand sticking out of its jar seemed to appeal for lost possibilities; it haunts me still." But he recovered quickly and reminded himself "of course, it is really in the end a far more humane proceeding than our earthly method of leaving children to grow into human beings, and then making machines of them." Cavor's messages suddenly cease, and Wells's ultimate verdict on the ambiguous lunar utopia is also left unclear.

Taken in total, however, his compellingly believable tales had thrown doubt on every dream of progress, and seen fateful cold eternity rounding off all of them; but in fact Wells had himself begun a search to fill the void with a practical answer. In *The War of the Worlds* he raised the idea of an elite group combating the invader; but his new and increasingly defiant note sprang from the grain of hope implanted at the bleak ending of *The Time Machine*. The Time Traveler had "thought but cheerlessly of the Advancement of Mankind, and saw in the growing pile of civilization only a foolish heaping that must in-evitably fall back upon and destroy its makers in the end." "If that is so," Wells continued, "it remains for us to live as though it were not so." "Suppose, after all," said Theodore Roosevelt a few years later, talk-ing with Wells in the White House garden, ". . . it all ends in your butterflies and morlocks. *That doesn't matter now.* The effort's real. It's worth going on with. It's worth it. It's worth it—even so." All things could not be man's for ever, but man could still live strenuously mean-while. The moon-traveler Bedford, describing his return, had felt "the pull of the earth upon my being, drawing me back again to the life that is real for men"; and Wells's thoughts too moved down toward the ground. With the remarkable success of his scientific romances behind him, and with his rising fame as a novelist of social comedy, he began to plan to put the globe in order and the closer meaning of its history, too.

III

"I have come to believe in certain other things, in the coherency and purpose in the world and in the greatness of human destiny," Wells announced in a lecture, "The Discovery of the Future," to the Royal

Institution in 1902. "Worlds may freeze and suns may perish, but I believe there stirs something within us now that can never die again." Off to another start the new Wells was more a preacher than a writer, and in the bright dawn of the new century his thoughts leapt up to affirm the bold ideas he had absorbed as a boy from Plato. In a society partial to self-analysis and increasingly obsessed with prediction, he asked loudly by what right the present order existed, assumed that structures and social arrangements were not inflexible, and two years before he had put forward his own prospectus for humanity. *Anticipations of the Reaction of Mechanical and Scientific Progress upon Human Life and Thought* was its full title, and with its success he later recalled "I became my own first disciple." The change in direction would turn him eventually into an historian, for *The Outline of History* is properly but one in a stream of manifestoes, inaugurated by *Anticipations*, that Wells wrote constantly until his death. All were part of a larger effort to create "a world-wide 'Open Conspiracy' to rescue human society from the net of tradition in which it is entangled and to reconstruct it upon planetary lines." The question for Wells had definitely become "What, then, will work?" His radical answer was what he termed "the New Republic."

Continuing the curves instead of the tangents of history—and thus looking back as well as forward—*Anticipations* was, Wells claimed, the first attempt to forecast the human future as a whole by extrapolating contemporary trends. Coal supplies and population growth had been estimated, works of propaganda, satire, and fantasy had been written, but here, he believed, was the first sober chart of future conditions, with the added advantage of coming from an independent source. Its essential point, "too obvious a thing to be a discovery," was that improved communications were fundamentally altering the scale of human relationships and enterprises. Though skeptical then of submarines and airplanes, Wells foresaw the highways, urban congestion, and suburban growth the new automobile would bring, and showed how these and other changes were fast destroying the long-established social and political order. In the confusion, however, an informal freemasonry of scientifically trained, public-spirited people would discover with a sort of surprise that they shared a common aim. Inevitably or by concentrated effort—and on this Wells was variable—its members would wrest power from politicians and shareholders and govern "in the cause of the higher sanity." The New Republic would emerge, "a world-state with a common language and a common rule," whose population would be regulated eugenically. All that was fine, efficient, and beautiful in the human body and mind would be encouraged; and, under the benevolent dictatorship of an austere elite, open with proper safeguards to everybody, which Wells named afterwards the Order of the Samurai, the world would be shaped better than in any dreams. It would become, as he soon called it, a modern utopia.

As controversial optimist Wells caught his readers' imagination afresh. His audacious visions, elaborated in tracts and novels, sprang partly from the heated socialism of his youth and grew by contact with the Fabian Society. That group of socialist intellectuals, which included George Bernard Shaw among their number, sought to change English life and government by the strength of arguments from solid evidence, not by revolution; but Wells, famous now, and notorious for his private life, was hardly cut out to become a major political theorist or patient reformer. He was more practical and demanding, and he identified most with the new generation, restless like himself to escape from stifling conventions and middle-class, middle-aged morality; and he wrote from his experience. In *Kipps* (1905) the struggles of a draper's apprentice illustrated the plight of the genteel poor; and in the scandalous *Ann Veronica* (1908) he relived his own elopement, upheld woman's right to sexual freedom, and with no apology gave the story a happy ending. Asking flagrantly open questions, exploring options candidly, and sketching real possibilities, he deplored wasted human potential and urged a planned global society. Today Wells's crusading protest adds another factor to his modernity. To idealistic agitators, suffragettes, and pacifists in the Edwardian years, his voice heralded genuine liberation.

The alternative to utopia in Wells's opinion was world chaos and ruin; but man could reach that end through complacency alone, and Wells challenged his vast audience to change their comfortable belief in inevitable progress before it was too late. The prospect of a general armed conflict and its dreadful aftermath had inspired many of his stories, nonetheless, including one, *The War in the Air* (1908), which started with a German attack on New York; and, when the First World War began, the catastrophe seemed to him somehow partly his own responsibility. Instantaneously, though, he was also ready to recognize in it the one event likely to bring humanity back to a sense of its true interests. On the hot evening of August 4, 1914, he quickly wrote a newspaper article whose title epitomized his view and became a powerful slogan—"The War That Will End War"; and in 1918, as the victory bells pealed out ecstatically, he spoke out strongly for a League of Nations to ensure eternal peace, an idea his prospectus had held out in its many versions. Now if ever was the time for a new world to be built. But utopia's chances of survival, he saw, would depend on a new harmony among peoples, an outlook freed from the " 'King and Country' stuff" that had divided men into armed camps and nearly wrecked civilization. Ultimately, Wells thought, the war had been caused by "an educational breakdown," and planetary salvation now depended on mankind agreeing on a new history for all and teaching it. History would thus no longer be an implement for war; it would become a plowshare. "There can be no common peace and prosperity," he wrote, "without common historical ideas."

A book presenting history to the ordinary citizen had been in Wells's mind ever since his first year at South Kensington; but the task now seemed urgent, and it had his emotional commitment. His auto-biography tells how he came to ponder the plan and decided to go ahead. Whenever a League of Nations had been discussed,

> . . . everyone seemed to have read a different piece of history or no history at all, and . . . consequently our ideas of the methods and possibilities of human association varied in the wildest manner. The curious fact dawned upon me that because I was not a "scholar" and had never been put under a pedant to study a "period" intensely and prematurely, and because I had a student's knowledge of biology and of the archaeological record, I had a much broader grasp of historical reality than most of my associates.

Professional historians, he believed, could not or would not undertake to produce a plain history of mankind. "They lived in an atmosphere of mutual restraint. They would not dare to do anything so large, for fear of incidental slips and errors. They were unused to any effective co-operation and their disposition would be all towards binding together a lot of little histories by different hands, and calling the binding a synthesis; and even if they could be persuaded to do anything of the sort it would certainly be years before it became available." The thought that he might write a broad but compact history himself, describing how the present situation had come about, grew increasingly attractive. Wells decided he could afford a year on the project ("although it might bring in very little"), and set to work "with the *Encyclopaedia Britannica* at my elbow."

He pillaged other books too, for points of fact and for substructures to basic arguments; a team of willing experts checked for errors in the draft manuscript; and Wells digested the great mass of material into his individual kind of vivid prose at a cracking pace. "Here we come over the High Pamirs—and mix with the Aryan peoples" he was heard to chant one day after a morning's fanatical toil in his study. When *The Outline of History,* over one-thousand-pages long, appeared in

1919, it was hailed as an incredible feat, and proved to be his greatest best seller; and, with a copy in almost every English-speaking home (often the only historical work) and translations far and wide, it gave him immediate respectability. Here was the vast and scattered past of all mankind marvelously caught in a single glance; here was history as science, clear, useful, and easily accessible; here was hope rising from the ashes with a blueprint for the future; and here emphatically was a story, gripping and memorable, without footnotes or references, its words plain enough to have been written on a standard typewriter. These credentials and Wells's special talents ensured the *Outline*'s astonishing reception, which swamped all criticisms of detail or interpretation, and charges of plagiarism; and it is doubtful that any history book before or since has had such a triumphant impact.

Wells had chosen the *Outline*'s theme long before. Ever since his schooldays at Mr. Morley's academy he had disliked mere dates, pedigrees, and enactments. He had outgrown history as the ascent of the white—or English—race with his adolescence; and Marxism seemed to him a mental epidemic of spite hindering truly creative revolution. Great men were only interruptions in the broad onward movement of human affairs; and, as for Christianity, he had, for example, spent a whole episode in *The War of the Worlds* showing how ineffectual it was. The great and obvious alternative—already the basis of his manifestoes—was history as progress, tied, as Huxley had trained him to see it, to a biological foundation. The *Outline* started with the origins of the globe itself, the record of the rocks, and the momentous movement of the first living things from water to dry land. "We do not know how life began upon the earth," Wells confessed, but he described with scientific imagination the great ages of plants, reptiles, and mammals, the climatic shifts, and the harsh process of natural selection. Evidence pointed to man's appearance about 600,000 B.C., when history in the strict sense could be said to begin; but man owed his heredity to the millions of years beforehand and remained subject to laws of nature operating since creation. What occurred in geological time was vital for a correct understanding of mankind's past and prospects. Enduring patterns of behavior had been set, including the habit of association, and there for Wells lay the force uniting history. Ever since reptiles had sheltered their eggs and protected their offspring, animal communities had increased their interdependence; and history had become one story of ever-expanding relationships, culminating in the airplane- and radio-linked human world of his day.

The future Wells looked forward to was the federation of mankind, and he noted every stage in human sociability. A surprisingly large and very readable part of the *Outline* describes the life of primitive man—the little Neanderthal tribes hammering flints and preparing skins at squatting places, the larger-brained Cro-Magnon race hunting, painting, perhaps taming the horse, and the beginnings of settled agriculture by Neolithic peoples who reached the highest form of political association till then in their Swiss-lake villages. "What was man thinking about himself and about the world in those remote days?" Wells asked. Probably, he wrote, the first true men "took day and night, sun and stars, trees and mountains, as being in the nature of things—as a child takes its meal times and its nursery staircase for granted." But gradually a primitive religion of fears and propitiations emerged, and, with speech, a tribal mind came into existence whose monstrous ideas seem oddly far more savage than the simplicity and directness typical of the rock painters. "Hitherto a social consciousness had been asleep and not even dreaming in human history. Before it awakened it produced nightmares." Progress was also conceived by Wells as the growth of knowledge and the spread of enlightenment; and in man's upward march shameful practices had to be eliminated:

> Away beyond the dawn of history, 3,000 or 4,000 years ago, one thinks of the Wiltshire uplands in the twilight of a midsummer day's morning. The torches pale in the growing light. One has a dim apprehension of a procession through the avenue of stone, of priests, perhaps fantastically dressed with skins and horns and horrible painted masks—not the robed and bearded dignitaries our artists represent the Druids to have been—of chiefs in skins adorned with necklaces of teeth and bearing spears and axes, their great heads of hair held up with pins of bone, of women in skins or flaxen robes, of a great peering crowd of shock-headed men and naked children. They have assembled from many distant places; the ground between the avenues and Silbury Hill is dotted with their encampments. A certain festive cheerfulness prevails. And amidst the throng march the appointed human victims, submissive, helpless, staring towards the distant smoking altar at which they are to die—that the harvests may be good and the tribe increase. . . . To that had life progressed 3,000 or 4,000 years ago from its starting-place in the slime of the tidal beaches.

"Half the duration of human civilization and the keys to all its chief institutions," Wells wrote, "are to be found *before* Sargon I," whose conquest of Sumeria he placed at 2750 B.C.; but the circumscribed vision of early, separated cultures contrasted sharply with modern man's. "We know more today, indeed, of the world of 600 B.C. than any single living being knew at that time," he commented—far more than even the remarkable Herodotus. "We map it out, see it as a whole in relation to past and future. We begin to learn precisely what was going on at the same time in Egypt and Spain and Media and India and China." In our mind's eye we could share the wonder both of Carthaginian sailors voyaging down the West African coast and of Negroes who lit warning beacons on the shore; and perhaps eventually all men would understand all the past together. Trade, navigation, and money were all notable developments, but none surpassed writing—an invention of whose powers Wells was particularly aware. Writing had made intellectual growth possible, and given men accurate knowledge in common. For the first time, therefore, they had the chance to see their story as a worldwide human adventure.

The world today, however, was still only at the beginning of knowledge; but near the close of the pre-Christian era immense constructive ideas had emerged, in Greece and Palestine especially, and a crucially significant phenomenon had occurred. Mankind, Wells thought, had started to grow up from a predominantly barbaric past and reach out responsibly to greater and broader purposes. "The last twenty-three centuries of history are like the efforts of some impulsive, hasty immortal to think clearly and live rightly. Blunder follows blunder; promising beginnings end in grotesque disappointments; streams of living water are poisoned by the cup that conveys them to the thirsty lips of mankind. But the hope of men rises again at last after every disaster." The first experiment, Alexander's empire, was glorious but futile, but it revealed the oneness of human affairs and the practicability of a world law and organization; and, at the beginning of the third century B.C., the general result of the transformation in the ancient Mediterranean was that three of the great structural ideas that rule the modern mind had arisen—science, universal righteousness, and a human commonwealth. "The rest of the history of mankind," Wells wrote (and the view was irresistible to his ordinary readers), "is very largely the history of those three ideas . . . spreading out from the minds of the rare and exceptional persons and peoples in which they first originated, into the general consciousness of the race, and giving first a new color, then a new spirit, and then a new direction to human affairs."

From that point onward Wells defined progress as the further stages of these three ideas in action, and men were judged according to the help they had given. Authentic heroes were few in the crowded cast, villains numerous, and plain failures many for varying reasons. In the exercise of free intelligence Herodotus, Socrates, Plato, the boldly speculative friar Roger Bacon, Voltaire, Darwin, and of course Huxley, were among those who gained top marks; at the bottom, indeed outside the running, were the pedants of the Alexandrian library, the court of the Inquisition, and ecclesiastical opponents of the evolutionary theory. Wells admired Christ but not Christianity, despised Muhammad but approved Islam, and had mixed feelings for the Buddhist life of withdrawal; but all world religions complemented by inspiration and insight what history and science displayed—that men formed one universal brotherhood and shared "a common human destiny upon this little planet amidst the stars." In politics idols from David and Solomon to Bismarck were thrown down; but the greatest scoundrels were men who had held world dominion in their grasp but had used their power for selfish ends—Caesar (an "elderly sensualist"), Charlemagne (restless, self-confident, "rather suggestive of William II, the ex-German Emperor"), Louis XIV (exceptionally capable, "but his prevailing occupation was splendor"), and, blackest of all, Napoleon:

> Now surely here was opportunity such as never came to man before. Here was a position in which a man might well bow himself in fear of himself, and search his heart and serve God and man to the utmost. The old order of things was dead or dying; strange new forces drove through the world seeking form and direction; the promise of a world republic and an enduring world peace whispered in a multitude of startled minds. Had this man any profundity of vision, any power of creative imagination, had he been accessible to any disinterested ambition, he might have done work for mankind that would have made him the very sun of history. All Europe and America, stirred by the first promise of a new age, was waiting for him. Not France alone. France was in his hand, his instrument, to do with as he pleased, willing for peace, but tempered for war like an exquisite sword. There lacked nothing to this great occasion but a noble imagination. And failing that, Napoleon could do no more than strut upon the crest of this great mountain of opportunity like a cockerel on a dunghill. The figure he makes in history is one of almost incredible self-conceit, of vanity, greed, and cunning, of callous contempt and disregard of all who trusted him, and of a grandiose aping of Caesar, Alexander, and Charlemagne which would be purely comic if it were not caked over with human blood.

The great benefactors, on the other hand, were enlightened men who had worked sanely and all too briefly to meet authentic human needs—the Indian monarchs Ashoka and Akbar, Genghis Khan who established religious toleration across the breadth of Asia, the utopian socialist Robert Owen, and Abraham Lincoln. The primitive type of the new world society was Rome, as always scanned for guidance and now as interesting to the political student "as a carboniferous amphibian or an *archaeopteryx* to the student of zoological development"; but, though Rome in her time was advanced in form, she had been "Neanderthal" in spirit. The popes failed to organize a united world, and the Holy Roman Empire was "a claim and an argument rather than a necessary reality." In a momentous break with the past, however, the United States entered the scene in the eighteenth century. "It was like something coming out of an egg," Wells wrote, a form of government European in heritage but an unprecedented clean start, a new community built on "the bare and stripped fundamentals of human association." Four million thinly scattered people set out to perform what Athenian philosophers had done in imagination and theory over two thousand years before. "It was a new method becoming practical in human affairs." The modern states of Europe had evolved slowly and planlessly out of preceding things; "the United States were planned and made."

The actual makers of history in the nineteenth century, "the people whose consequences will be determining life a century ahead," were those who had struggled to develop and apply positive sciences of economics, politics, and education. By comparison the foreign ministers and "statesmen" had been no more than "troublesome and occasionally incendiary schoolboys," playing pranks on the construction site of a great building whose nature they did not understand. Scientific discovery, a mechanical revolution, and rapid industrial growth brought universal change, and after 1848 they caused men to try to adopt mentally and politically to the new conditions; but the curse of the new age was nationalism. The frame of reference within which men saw their lives had been shifting from heaven to earth ever since the Renaissance, but now "men were brought to feel that they were as improper without a nationality as without their clothes in a crowded assembly." New tribal gods, dim vast deities like Britannia, Germania, and France with her liberty cap, ruled Europe and, by extension, the world; and empire was the crown of national success. "All human history," Wells wrote, "is fundamentally a history of ideas." It was the source of great tragedy that "nation" and "empire" were "plausible and dangerously unsound working ideas," representing nothing innate or unchangeable in human nature, only a failure to face new opportunities. Since men and women lacked a broad historical outlook and had lost the charity of a world religion, these exaggerated abstractions were accepted; "their danger to all the routines of ordinary life was not realized until it was too late."

The American lesson taught that peace and unity of action had been unreachable until the people of Virginia, Massachusetts, and the other colonies had seen themselves as people of the United States; but in Europe international rivalries were perpetuated, and when the First World War came it surpassed all fears. In 1918 a world hungry for peace, but without any will-power to gain it, welcomed President Wilson's Fourteen Points with rapture. Wilson, however, was one of Wells's failures, an impractical egotist, and the League of Nations by its very title was tailored to precedent. Instead of man ruling the earth at last, the war had produced in the League a "homunculus in a bottle." But, as the epic story of man's adventure, indeed of life itself, rose to a crisis amid prodigious questioning, Wells affirmed, "we are in the dawn of a great constructive effort." What, then, would work? Wells's answer, to which he believed all history had been moving (he had proved it) and human necessities pointed categorically, was a Federal World State. "Nationalism as a God must follow the tribal gods to limbo. Our true nationality is mankind." As the drama entered the present, he summoned all men to an "immense task of adjustment."

As a biologist Wells knew the survival of any species depended on its flexibility in new situations, and so far man had somehow managed to endure. With talk of even greater havoc in another war, the absolute condition for survival now was a world law under a world government. The price of adaptation was small compared to the prospect this offered, for the abandonment of warfare and the establishment of social justice would mean an unparalleled release of creative energy into other fields and the true beginning of human adventure. As man left his old ways behind, his ancient restlessness would not let him treat any problem as intractable; and, in the course of a few generations, Wells wrote euphorically, "every little country town could become an Athens, every human being could be gentle in breeding and healthy in body and mind, the whole solid earth man's mine and its uttermost regions his playground." The characteristics of the new utopia would be a common world religion, simple and natural; a world state sustained by universal, lifelong education; no armies, navies, or unemployed; world organization of scientific research, which "compared with that of today will be like an ocean liner beside the dug-out canoe of some early heliolithic wanderer"; freedom of thought; and economic organization for the public good. In the present distress the dream seemed as distant as a life of civilized pleasures to a child born and bred in a slum; but, to realize it, nothing was needed but collective effort and a sense of extreme urgency. "Human history"—and Wells's words were widely quoted— "becomes more and more a race between education and catastrophe." Yet it was just five hundred years since the Aztec empire, like the Druids before, believed that its continuing existence needed repeated human sacrifices; and the day might be close "when we shall no longer tear out the hearts of men, even for the sake of our national gods." On the larger time-scale the miseries of the current era could be seen as transitory. History had never gone forward easily, but it had always progressed; and Wells's closing mood was one of fervent optimism.

In certain respects *The Outline of History* complements Toynbee's great *Study*, and *vice versa*, both being born out of the First World War, both reacting to historical impoverishment, and both intensely anxious for the human race. Wells's work, on the other hand, was a whirlwind achievement aimed at a general audience, Toynbee's a most elaborate and learned inquiry; and Wells was a biologist, largely self-taught, Toynbee a highly educated classical scholar. For a shrunken globe Wells advocated an essentially political and social solution, the outcome he thought of natural forces; Toynbee came to see man's salvation lying in a higher religion, sketched exotically. In seeking to bring everything together and lift it to a higher level, the *Outline* vaguely descends from Humboldt's encyclopaedic *Cosmology* which had influenced Wells as a boy; but its greatest resemblance is surely to the writings of Voltaire in its claims to be scientific, its interpretation of the past as progress, in the size (and often similarity) of its prejudices, and in its insistence that history is for building a better life. "Human Ecology," Wells would call it, the working out of biological, intellectual, and social consequences, and he wished it to displace conventional historical studies, which to him were limited or trivial. Such an enlarged and purposeful form of analysis, basically uncomfortable with the past, naturally clashes with customary academic interests. Wells's disapproval of politics may be justly questioned, he neglected the arts, and social and economic developments are hard to fit into an evolutionary pattern. But these points on the whole were mostly missed by Wells's public, who were engrossed by the future too.

Undeniably the *Outline* had and continues to have great strengths—artistic merit as a whole, a powerful storyline holding it together, and, most of all, a central place in the vast drama for the common man, not as a silent multitude but personified in absorbing generalizations. To Wells, and to his young readers at the turn of the century, the common man was history's true hero—as he invariably was in Wells's novels. His labor had supported society, his talents had repeatedly burst through restrictions of priests and rulers, and, though his were the corpses strewn on battlefields while diplomats danced, a better future would be built through his good sense. Progress occurred through his initiative (a confidence Voltaire did not have) and was measured by improvement in his status. To be straightforward, the hero of the *Outline* was actually Wells himself, reliving his own breakthrough from dirty china shop to well-run country house—the last the most delightful setting of life to him, and providing him with his nostalgic model for a world of universal, cultivated gentlefolk. He greeted few parts of the future more than the elimination of drudgery. Memories of his mother ceaselessly scrubbing the floor of their home, or of himself, undernourished and angry, lifting heavy bales of cloth up and down at a customer's whim, were never lost. His sympathies stayed with the class he had left, and he called that great majority of mankind to enter a new world, too, where they could use their talents to the full and breathe fresh air. His ordinariness, he claimed, was proof that anyone could rise above his origins and change. Why not, therefore, the human race? Designed for all the world's peoples, the *Outline* succeeded in being the only kind of total history most people can easily remember, with its down-to-earth statements, its novellike form, and its final illustration the future reference for all the human past—a map with "The United States of the World" scrawled across it in bold letters. Its content risked being superficial, but at last, it seemed, here was the heart of the matter called history, quite simply the real story; and to a secular age Wells's book appeared as an alternative to the Bible.

IV

The tragedy of the remainder of Wells's hurrying career was that events did not bear him out; for, though mankind was impressed by the future he described, it did not change then and there to make it happen. People read his books and heard him lecture in his high-pitched voice, but on the whole they argued or compromised with his idealism; and professional educators spurned the *Outline*. At the height of his fame in the 1920s, Wells cast himself as an energetic Samurai, a founding member of the international intelligentsia, a social engineer who talked with Lenin and Henry Ford and tried to bring the world's leaders into unison, an antimonarchist, and a man of the future who had his son learn Russian instead of Latin. The work of President Franklin Roosevelt and the White House "Brains Trust" encouraged him that a new type of ruling class was coming, and Wells praised the New Deal; Soviet communism he considered inefficient, doctrinaire, and contemptuous of human dignity, especially after a three-hour conversation with Stalin. Large popular surveys of science and economics followed *The Outline of History*, Huxley's grandson Julian serving as a collaborator; and Wells became rich, though never secure. But his talents began to decline, his message became too familiar, and finally his utopian vision grew stale. Audiences forsook him for new writers and other excitements, the Depression produced other ideologies, and another war ceased to be unthinkable.

As reason had failed to persuade perhaps fear could try again, and in 1933 Wells pulled his tired imagination together and wrote *The Shape of Things to Come*. With uncanny accuracy he described the next war breaking out in 1940 over the Polish Corridor, followed by a twenty-year conflict, largely fought in the air, which halved the world's population and reduced the stricken remnant to a primitive condition. But a flicker of hope remained. This time the airmen, internationalists controlling communications, would band together in an "ultimate revolution"; and, by 2036, a new elite would have mastered genetics, altered the earth's landscape and climate, and, in Wells's film version, sent a man and a woman to the moon. By also showing air raids and the use of poison gas on massed civilians, the film may have helped create a mood of appeasement, though its regimented utopia was unattractive. The lack of a more vigorous public response convinced Wells that catastrophe was well on its way.

Never ceasing to make known his worsening fears, though often erratically, Wells reverted in the end to the Huxleyan pessimism of his first books and became certain that man as a species was doomed. In *The Fate of Homo Sapiens*, published on the eve of the Second World War, he wrote:

> Adapt or perish, that is and always has been the implacable law of life for all its children. Either the human imagination and the human will to live rises to the plain necessity of our case, and a renascent *Homo sapiens* struggles on to a new, a harder and a happier world dominion, or he blunders down the slopes of failure through a series of unhappy phases, in the wake of all the monster reptiles and beasts that have flourished and lorded it on the earth before him, to his ultimate extinction. Either life is just beginning for him or it is drawing very rapidly to its close.

The record of biology showed that no dominant species had ever been continuously succeeded by its descendants, and the human brain examined coldly was just another organic aid, not an all-powerful instrument. Man had failed to develop ethically and pass the current test for his survival; therefore nature was casting him off. The whole evolutionary experiment which had produced him was coming to a summary and disastrous conclusion and would have to begin once more along different lines. When the war began Wells endured the London blitz. The war's ending with atomic fission (which he had forecast in 1913) and the bombing of Hiroshima was absolute proof to him of man's desperate situation. Science, the means to improve the quality of life in so many of his books, was now turning against man and overpowering him. In *Mind at the End of its Tether*, appearing just before his death in 1946, Wells distilled his anger and frustration and saw the world devoid of recuperative power. In the past he had liked to think "that Man could pull out of his entanglements and start a new creative phase of human living. In the past two years, in the face of our universal inadequacy, that optimism has given place to a stoical cynicism. The old men behave for the most part meanly and disgustingly and the young are spasmodic, foolish and all too easily misled. Man must go steeply up or down and the odds seem to be all in favor of his going down and out." In 1913, atomic warfare had been, as so often in his books, the traumatic prelude to a golden age. In the darkness of 1945 the only hope Wells could express was a faint echo of *The Time Machine*'s resolute last paragraph, a faith in "that small minority which will succeed in seeing life out to its inevitable end." His own epitaph, he said, would be quite short: "God damn you all: I told you so."

In retrospect—and at odds with his general reputation—Wells's optimistic years were surely his most untypical; and his pessimism was perhaps well founded, not just from our knowledge of evolutionary laws but from the growing deterioration of civilized life. At least that would be one conclusion to reach today. While the planet's resources are plundered or spoilt, its problems await a concerted solution; and its population meanwhile often seems ready to follow suicidal slogans like those Orwell parodied in *Nineteen Eighty-Four*—"War is Peace," "Freedom is Slavery," "Ignorance is Strength"—instead of the mottoes of self-help Wells placed in his student lodgings, or the immediate steps he urged for the rebirth of society. It was Orwell, though, who remarked that Wells was too sane to understand the modern world. In the *Outline* Wells had concentrated on the growth of science, enlightenment, and liberty, and had refused to see the past as the record of greed and conflict that it really was—both major and apparently permanent features of human activity. A glance back over the centuries shows that men have hardly ever acted in their best interests, and that there is little likelihood they will suddenly start behaving differently. War and violence, respected scientists say, are in our genes.

But, by telling mankind in effect to study history to forget history, Wells conformed to a dominant streak in his character. His own reaction to difficulty was invariably to try a new start; and the theme of escape, of a flight in imagination to something conceivable but so far unreached (unlike the inventions in Verne's stories), is a very common one too in his novels. Seen in this light, *The Outline of History* is an account of man escaping by degrees from ignorance and bondage—and a plan for the greatest escape of all; and *The Shape of Things to Come* ends with a new start for the human race on the moon. The final crisis for Wells's idealism came when he saw no route from reality left. "The door closes upon us for evermore," he wrote in 1945. "There is no way out or round or through."

Western man in the late twentieth century is surely skeptical of easy escapes, more aware of the earth's uniqueness, and sees new challenges arising out of a sense of resignation. On the whole he is inclined to think utopias monotonous, and he has yet to be fully persuaded that Wells's eventual ideas for the human race as a result of genetic control are more perceptive than the moral of *The Island of Dr. Moreau*. Constantly at the crossroads of opportunity we understand more than before that the possibility of good is always the possibility of evil, and the same in reverse. But, though blunders have continued, hope has never been entirely lost; and the other permissible conclusion today is an opposing one—that Wells's new society is clearly emerging, and that his best assessments and aims have proved remarkably gifted in foresight and profitable to follow. His dreams have not all come true—but neither so far has his prophecy of extinction; in fact *The World Set Free*, his story in 1913 about atomic warfare, told of a lasting peace being secured through absolute fear of a repeated conflict. A world law under a world government has not yet arrived, but it sometimes appears attainable. Nationalism is relatively subdued within a network of international ties and obligations; and surely never has the human race been better fed, housed, or had more opportunities for education. We are assured by other scientific authorities that there is nothing in our genes that commits us to aggression.

Other forces of course have been at work, but, from this perspective, Wells's *Outline* has been another case of a history making history. In up-to-date, popular form his survey enthusiastically taught the world once more that history was progress, and thereby it stimulated further movement onward. Its designation of man as part of nature prepared for the new historical interests of an age conscious of man's place in the environment. And, finally, without Wells's imaginative vision of the human story extending into space and time, marked by unprecedented ventures, late-twentieth-century man might not have been quite as audacious and his spirit would have been far poorer. "That's one small step for a man, one giant leap for mankind" were the first words spoken on the moon, and they epitomized Wells's idea of the exhilarating upward course of human destiny to which Western thoughts habitually revert at times of high achievement. The epic may finish in silence;

but, whenever a new "advancement of mankind" seems under sail, the Wells remembered is likely to be the Wells who wrote:

> For MAN no rest and no ending. He must go on—conquest beyond conquest. This little planet and its winds and ways, and all the laws of mind and matter that restrain him. Then the planets about him, and at last out across immensity to the stars. And when he has conquered all the deeps of space and all the mysteries of time—still he will be but beginning.

The speaker in *The Shape of Things to Come* did not close the film with these words, however. He stated man's urgent dilemma yet again. Is it the stars—or death, he asked; all the universe—or nothing? Which shall it be? "WHICH SHALL IT BE?" He was left waiting for the audience's answer.

THE
AMERICAN
FRONTIER

I

From Herodotus to Wells to the present, history as an idea has remained as the first great Western historian defined it—an inquiry. History in its other form, man's story, begins with an event; but, as man's commentary on man, history always begins with a question, and, indeed, historians often choose opening events chiefly with reference to their answers. Each answer, however, has exposed in time a further problem which prompts a further question, though old questions keep some validity and are never entirely lost; rather, they are built into the ongoing enterprise of analysis. The questions we have reviewed are a sample of what we might have explored, but they exemplify the leading questions nonetheless. Drawn together, they and their variants embody the central issues of Western historiography:

What caused Greeks to fight Persians—or men to fight other men? Why is Europe (or the West, for that matter) different from Asia? What exactly brought the Athenian state to ruin and defeat? What lessons can history teach? Why did Rome fall, and civilization with it? What is God's purpose and plan for man? "What else, then, is all history, if not the praise of Rome?" "Who can doubt that Rome would rise up again if she but began to know herself?" How do you gain power and keep it? "Has the restoration of the arts and sciences done more to corrupt civilized life or improve it?" How can a bridge be built between the new Scotland and the old—or between any new civilization and its predecessor? What actually happened—or, can the past be shown *wie es eigentlich gewesen? What Is To Be Done?* "If we could imagine an incarnation of dissonance—and what is man if not that?" How much history do we need? "Why did God make me an outcast and a stranger in mine own house?" "Would America have been America without her Negro people?" "How has this come out of that?"—meaning, how did hopes of progress and perpetual peace end in barbarous warfare, the demolition of empires, the belittlement of Europe, and finally the threat to Life itself on this planet? What is the "door of Death" through which most civilizations have already disappeared? "Are all things made for man?" "What, then, will work?"

Most of the history now available to us is the sum of answers to these questions or their variants. The changing questions suggest the limits of each version of the past. They also reflect Western man's persistence in adapting his past to serve his life, and history, as an implement designed to serve the present, is therefore constantly experimental. The "superhistorians" we have met represent in effect Western civilization at its major times of self-assessment. All ultimately asked the question that is history's real starting point—"Who am I?"—and the success of each encouraged other men to explore their questions further, improve them, and find answers for themselves insofar as the past confers identity. Man in time still defies total comprehension; but the heritage of these inquiries is obvious in the extent and diversity of historical studies today.

It is, looking back, a heritage of information, though its growth has been irregular. Our factual knowledge of the past rests on the work of countless scholars collecting, testing, and coordinating evidence. With the profuse results of Rankean scholarship so readily at hand, we easily forget that every name, place, and date in the past once had to be verified; we then marvel that Herodotus and Thucydides could ever aim at such precision with their limited resources. But it is also a heritage of innovation, since it includes the work of another type of historian who brings a different talent to the enterprise. He asks a radical question, and finds an unimagined answer in evidence till then unrelated to it. Every great historian possesses something of this talent; but, for all the merits of steady, systematic research, historical knowledge seems often to leap forward when a man finds received and accepted historical explanations incompatible with reality, and thinks instead in new categories. In this light the history of history is a tale of new beginnings and new blood, of daring improvisations that have their counterparts in other fields. The effects of such developments can hardly be overestimated. The Western idea of history itself began with questions asked well beyond the normal limit.

The ability to make this leap is the chief mark of the "superhistorian." He is often a perceptive amateur, who, trusting in the knowledge he has and in the validity of his own intuitions, puts a broad, simple question to the past in order to make sense of his historical situation. Though his question may be shared by others, he tends to ask it in isolation, isolation or adversity breeding insight. Quite plainly nothing seems to stimulate his thought more than a crisis; and his thoughts on events, individually and collectively, are colored by his primary opinions. For instance, if he takes a cyclical view, his idea of history will probably be pessimistic and stoical, and strict chronology will have little importance to him; for he sees certain circumstances repeating themselves, with largely predictable results. But, if his outlook on time is linear, his history will be optimistic and activist and will emphasize chronology, since he holds that particular events can only be understood through the events preceding them. Discerning change or continuity in men's affairs, he speculates on human destiny and historical laws; no decision, however, determines his thought—or any historian's thought—more fully than his assessment of human nature. Though the "superhistorian" may claim he is impartial, a bias is crucial to his whole endeavor, and he closes off certain lines of inquiry while opening others. His innovating attitude may cause him to use distinctive language, images, metaphors, as Herodotus, Scott, Marx, and Toynbee did. He rarely changes his central message; in extreme cases he sees his own role in giving a new history to the world as indispensable.

In the modern West the only positive innovators are commonly thought to be those who aided the growth of "scientific" history. This conclusion is partly correct, since every successful innovator supports his argument with evidence which other men can test and verify for themselves. But the truth is not so narrow. Innovators' questions, by their nature, stir controversy and curiosity of all kinds about man's past, and alter the methods, purpose, and whole arrangement of historical studies. They also connect with questions in other disciplines, and prompt philosophers to discuss the principles and province of historical knowledge more abstractly than we have here—a debate requisite to the whole modern historical enterprise. No innovator gains universal acceptance because each view of history has its own limitations, being a personal view set down at a particular time (though some have been more comprehensive or vocal than others). The innovator's basic question, however, arises from life in the present; and though his answer is

preceded by internal reflection, it receives its form by broad externaliza-
tion, speaking to everybody—the discipline of history's best claim to
its future survival. His critics may deny his answer, but, when it relaxes
the weight of the past by solving an urgent problem, it releases men for
action. In short, the innovator's insights complement and in time re-
direct the scholar's techniques. Western man's capacity for original
inquiry into his past is one of the glories of his civilization.

The late twentieth century is heir to all the achievements of
scholarship and innovation; but, while historical information expands
in fascinating detail, there is no direction to Western historical thinking, nothing which gives the study of history a plan or character, not
yet (despite Wells and mass education) common historical ideas or
even a universal calendar, only the wreckage of apparently faulty systems and schemes. Simultaneously, the course of current events, the
emotions they inspire, and energetic debate on man, his nature, and
his institutions, have all produced an increased conflict of opinions
about the past, in which questions, answers, and old questions and
answers rediscovered, are scarcely savored before being overlaid by new
knowledge and new preoccupations. "Here are the facts which will tell
you the truth," writes the scientific historian. "Here is the truth which
will set you free," speaks the visionary. The public caught between them
finds it harder than ever to accept the traditional versions of the past
more than superficially. Some people prefer such confusion; to others
the meaninglessness is perplexing, leading them to suspect that the
history of man is unintelligible.

When old versions of the past cease to serve the present, for men
to repeat old questions and old techniques and decline to fashion a
new history is not wholly defensible as a sign of prudence or piety. It
constitutes rejection of the most creative impulse in the Western historical tradition. To ask fundamental questions, and make history purposely into present thought about the past, was the feat of each of the
"superhistorians"—not least of Ranke, the "father of historical science."
As Nietzsche observed, a question which combines historical consciousness with life and experience is a sign of cultural health and vitality. The
old questions, valuable though they are, come down to us from vanished
worlds. We in our world today should renew the grand inquiry, and
study the past again to find our own distinctive answer.

But, though the whole Western tradition of historical inquiry is
our background, our idea of history is ordinarily formed in a national
context. National traditions of historical writing are the first and often
the strongest we encounter; and we have already seen how new his-

torical questions relate to the local style and effectiveness of old questions and answers. The historiography of any one country would be
appropriate to exemplify a new history's possible point of departure.
Let us illustrate the nature of a national heritage of inquiry by selecting
the history of history in the United States.

II

"In the beginning all the world was America," wrote the English
philosopher John Locke nearly two centuries after Columbus's landfall.
The enormously varied Indian tribes had their own histories, which they
searched to explain the Europeans' arrival; but history conceived as an
inquiry in America starts with Western man's attempt to describe his
first sight of the new continent, so striking to him in his cultural isolation. The early Spanish reports spread the news of islands different
from anything in Europe, luxuriant, extraordinarily rich in exotic animals, plants, and minerals. The simple life of the inhabitants, however,
recalled to Europeans the life of a golden age which Latin poets had
portrayed. Western man was enamored with classical antiquity when
he discovered America, and he used antiquity's metaphor of a pastoral
paradise to interpret his experience. His first response to the New
World, which still affects the reality, was one of wonder.

When the Spanish, French, and English settled in the continent's
northern half, they brought their European heritage with them; since
the English colonial experiment was ultimately the most successful in
forming the United States, the English origins of an American national
historiography hold our attention. The first account of English settlement was John Smith's *A True Relation* . . . (1608), chronicling the
first year of the Virginia Company's plantation, a brief work he later
expanded into *The Generall Historie of Virginia*. Smith wrote in the
spirit of Richard Hakluyt, whose famous Elizabethan history of English
geographical discovery, vivid and painstakingly accurate, also told of the
heroic exploits of Hawkins, Drake, and other English seamen seeking
America's wealth and fighting Catholic Spain. Smith frankly recorded
the settlers' difficulties, their starvation and their hostile encounters
with Indians—though the story of how his life was saved by Pocahontas
may be a fabrication; but he ended both his books on a note of mer-
cantile optimism. His works thereby anticipated numerous similar tracts,
written by Englishmen and published in England, arguing from the
record why a particular colony offered most chance of gain to its in-
vestors. These promotional histories spoke of majestic forests, abundant

wildlife, and large navigable rivers, a land waiting for industrious people. "Heaven and earth never agreed better to frame a place for man's habitation," Smith maintained.

Though America does not have Europe's depth of historical background, it has a rich heritage of its own thought on leading historical issues. The Puritans of Plymouth and Massachusetts Bay, convinced that God had sent them on an errand into the wilderness, self-consciously justified their emigration in light of biblical teaching and the events of the Reformation. Their mission to plant a "city of God" would further reveal God's guidance of His elect, they believed. New England's history was therefore of unique importance to the world's history in this religious scheme, in small ways as well as large, not least regarding the settlers' conflicts with the Indians; and, when the original Puritan faith declined, remembrance of its acts served to uphold the orthodox ministry. But when governors and divines like William Bradford and Cotton Mather wrote the history of their colony, they valued history for reasons of Renaissance humanism besides those of Augustinian Christianity. They read and followed the models of Thucydides, Plutarch, and Sir Walter Raleigh's *History of the World*, as well as John Foxe's *Acts and Monuments of the Christian Martyrs*. The same blend of secular learning and Puritan purpose is found in most early histories of Virginia, though less emphatically. The confidence in New England's special nature which Puritan historians possessed, and their relatively numerous and authoritative works compared to those produced in other colonies, soon, however, placed New England at the center of the American historical stage. Far from being a relic of Europe, Puritan historical thought, with its respect for accuracy and learning, with its capacity for self-analysis and public defense, with its sense of a large argument, gave future American historical writing some of its finest qualities.

The Enlightenment came to the American colonies both from Europe and from the colonies' own resources, when, as in Franklin's case, Puritan religion was shed but certain Puritan habits and humanistic attributes were kept. American historians began to apply rationalist standards to their studies; but, whereas Voltaire urged men to select from the past to build a better future, American society—as Voltaire himself observed of Pennsylvania—had already through design or circumstances abandoned many evils which the *philosophes* attacked. Free of aristocracy, feudalism, bishops, and luxury—free, indeed, of the dark European past—Americans visibly lived in an immense, wild Eden, mastering nature and prospering. When the Revolution occurred, some of the ablest historians were Tories (conspicuously Thomas Hutchinson), being respectful of tradition; but the leading American patriots conceived the Revolution to be a moral and political struggle in Enlightenment terms as well as a legal and cultural search for identity. When it succeeded, it provided clear proof of the power of man's agency in human affairs, and of secular progress. "We can no longer say there is nothing new under the sun," wrote Jefferson. "For this whole chapter in the history of man is new." In 1782, Hector St. John de Crèvecoeur, a French surveyor who once settled in New York State, a self-described "farmer of feelings," posed the question which in spirit has governed American national historical inquiry ever since: "What then is the American, this new man?"

The attempts of American historians to answer this question begin after the Revolution with the topic of the Revolution itself. The war with England had united most colonists more than any previous event, and patriots now urged that the Revolution's heroic memory should be preserved to instruct the public and to forge a lasting bond among the people of the United States. Americans had as yet no national history told by themselves, only local histories in which colonies pressed their claims against England and sometimes against each other. Biographies of leading revolutionaries, especially George Washington, partly met this need, and "Parson" Weems's imaginative anecdotes, notably the cherry-tree story, taught virtues appropriate to republican citizens. But the greater want, the surviving Founding Fathers lamented, was for a large-scale record and analysis of the Revolution as a whole, explaining its origins, course, and significance for mankind. The sources for such a work were scattered throughout the thirteen states; many were naturally in England. We cannot name more than a few major figures of American historiography in this brief sketch; but the gathering and publication of indispensable documents slowly proceeded, assisted by the growing national spirit after the War of 1812. The ambitions and labor finally bore fruit when the first volume of George Bancroft's *History of the United States* appeared in 1834.

Born in Massachusetts in 1800, the son of a Unitarian clergyman, Bancroft had studied at German universities after Harvard, and encountered there Herder's and Hegel's philosophies and the new scientific methods of German historians. Returning to America he was briefly an educator; but, becoming a Jacksonian Democrat, he embarked on a long, distinguished career in public life, which included serving as minister to London and later Berlin (where he enjoyed Macaulay's and Ranke's friendship). Universally acknowledged in his lifetime as America's greatest historian, he died in 1891. His twelve-volume *History*, which finally reached from America's discovery to the adoption of the

Constitution, owes much to German thought. History taught that freedom was unfolding in the world under divine guidance, Bancroft idealistically believed; the vanguard of this movement, however, could not be Prussia—as Hegel had indicated—but was clearly the United States, where all men enjoyed liberty under a democratic government and the voice of the people was acknowledged as the voice of God. Taking Herder's idea that nations developed organically, Bancroft saw the seeds of the American genius lying in Germany and continuously growing by way of England, and New England. "The spirit of the colonies demanded freedom from the beginning," he wrote. Bancroft's success rested on the current wish to keep the Revolution a powerful memory, his strong moral positions (in which he differed from Ranke), his Romantic characterization and portrayal of people, his own self-assurance—and on his work's solidity. He researched with tremendous industry, employed assistants in America and England at his own great expense, and stressed the importance of original authorities (though he did not always follow them scrupulously). He oversimplified the colonial story too, and indulged in flights of language; but, despite his faults, by introducing both German techniques of study and nationalist concepts to the United States he brought order and life to the Revolution's widespread records. He also gave Americans a confidence that their history, though brief compared to Europe's, was nonetheless unparalleled, and a firm sense of foreordained destiny.

Francis Parkman, who lived from 1823 to 1893, developed parts of Bancroft's central theme. A Bostonian—like many nineteenth-century American historians—he early planned to take the conflict between France and England for the mastery of North America as his subject, "or, in other words, the history of the American forest." He set two aims before him, he said: "One was to paint the forest and its tenants in true and vivid colors; the other was to realize a certain ideal of manhood, a little medieval, but nevertheless good." Courting physical hardship and seeking first-hand atmosphere, he traveled West as a young man and lived among the Sioux, an experience on which he drew for his first two books, *The Oregon Trail* and *The Conspiracy of Pontiac*. In 1865 he began to publish his seven-volume study of his chosen topic, in which he ranged the absolutism of New France against the liberty of New England. Parkman's research was extremely thorough despite his half-blindness and persistent ill health, and his works remain expert. His literary style of writing owes much to Scott and James Fenimore Cooper in its character portrayal and descriptive passages, of which the account of La Salle's expedition down the Mississippi is an outstanding example. Parkman saw his whole story as a struggle between titanic forces, in which heroic individuals (not the common man) controlled each colony's destiny—a view for which he had most scope for expression in *Montcalm and Wolfe*. The Indian was no noble savage to him, and the French—feudal, monarchist, and Catholic—were inferior to the Protestant Anglo-Saxons, though Parkman admired individual Frenchmen, notably Champlain and Frontenac, and the Jesuit missionaries. "A happier calamity never befell a people than the conquest of Canada by British arms," he wrote. His characterization of the pioneer American, virile, living a life of action in the open air, in contrast to Boston's "Brahmin" class, living in comfort on inherited wealth, won many admirers, among them Theodore Roosevelt.

Parkman's distrust of the common man and his call for a reinvigorated elite illustrate that a problem existed—which American historians still share—in assessing America's advance. How could the commonly accepted signs of modern progress—the vigorous democracy, the railroads, the North's industrialization, the furious growth of new cities in the West—be reconciled with Jefferson's firm belief that the community of yeoman farmers with which the United States began represented conditions close to perfection? The ideas of nineteenth-century American historians were faced with yet a further challenge. The Civil War was both a breakdown of America's "perfect" political system, and, with its four years of bloodshed and devastation, a blow to Americans' faith in progress. American history appeared more complex than the Romantic nationalist historians had imagined. In the years before the war, local historians, especially Southerners, had reacted against the broad national history Bancroft and others devised, and had defended the interests of their states and regions against the federal government and New England's claim to superiority; and now the war itself, and the period of Reconstruction afterwards, were strong incentives to historical thinking in North and South alike, raising issues of causation, politics, morality, and the authentic theme of the American story. The Civil War is still the leading topic of American historiography, demonstrating like perhaps no other event the discord between national ideals and realities. In the North it produced the conviction that American history's continuity in the form of the Union had been saved, in the South a historical heritage rooted in the experience of failure and defeat.

The same problem of possible national decline intrigued Henry Adams (1838–1918). Born into a family which had given the United States two presidents, he studied at Harvard and briefly at Berlin; and he acted as his father's secretary while his father was minister to England during the Civil War. After teaching at Harvard for seven years, he then moved to Washington and lived independently, writing and traveling. Adams's most ambitious work, his nine-volume *History of the United States During the Administrations of Thomas Jefferson and James Madison,* was mainly chronological, but it began and ended by stressing the American national character as the key to interpreting American political history. He imagined a traveler in the wilderness that was Washington in 1800, musing "among the unraised columns of the Capitol" upon the destiny of the idealistic new nation. Adams, however, could look back from 1889, and the evidence suggested to him that between 1800 and 1815 the essential American character had become fixed. This character was both visionary and practical, libertarian, secular, and progressive, "a new variety of man"; and history's chief interest in the United States thenceforward was "to know what kind of people these millions were to be."

Adams later decided he could explore a society's traits more fully by studying medieval Europe; but even in his concern to understand American history, he proposed an exact science of history in which the rise of the American empire and the fall of Rome could equally be explained by stages of progress analogous to physical laws. Since all energy reaches a peak and declines, Adams argued that "social energy" must adhere to this scheme. Man had been fired in different eras by different sources of force, but by 1815 the pattern of America's future growth seemed established. But, if the national character should ever become sluggish, "the inertia of several hundred million people, all formed in a similar social mould, was as likely to stifle energy as to stimulate evolution." Americans in fact had varied prospects before them.

> They were intelligent, but what paths would their intelligence select? They were quick, but what solution of insoluble problems would quickness hurry? They were scientific, and what control would their science exercise over their destiny? They were mild, but what corruptions would their relaxations bring? They were peaceful, but by what machinery were their corruptions to be purged? What interests were to vivify a society so vast and uniform? What ideals were to ennoble it? What object, besides physical content, must a democratic continent aspire to attain? For the treatment of such questions, history required another century of experience.

To some extent Henry Adams provides a link between two types of American historian; for the figures we have reviewed so far have all primarily been amateurs—magistrates, clergymen, politicians, or wealthy patricians—and they have all come from the East. In the late nineteenth century, however, the amateur historian in America lost prestige, as he did in Europe, to the university-based historian who had been professionally trained. These new men were critical of the Romantic nationalists' broad view and novelistic treatment of the American past, though they did not completely discard their predecessors' beliefs, some of which were now reinforced for them by the Darwinian theory of evolution. Instead, they sought limited topics, not sweeping subjects; and, by producing detailed monographs referring to all available materials, they claimed that they worked according to the principles of scientific research. Their combined studies, they believed, would enable historians to generalize accurately about the nation. One school, for example, sought a new understanding of colonial history through a minute inspection of records of the colonies' laws and trade within the context of the British Empire as a whole, an approach which closer ties between the United States and Britain also made congenial to them. The influence of German scholars dominated the rise of "scientific" history in America, nowhere more than at Johns Hopkins University. It was there that Herbert Baxter Adams, founding secretary of the American Historical Association in 1884, had inaugurated Ranke's seminar method of teaching graduate students.

Herbert Baxter Adams also led American historical thinking on the subject of the American character's uniqueness. Studying institutions comparatively like a philologist studying languages, he analyzed the government of selected New England towns; and he concluded from his research that the "germs" of American democracy lay in the councils of Germanic tribes once described by the Roman historian Tacitus. Out of these primitive councils in forests had evolved the parliamentary system, religious reformation, and the popular revolutions distinctive of all Anglo-Saxon peoples, "the ideas which have formed Germany and Holland, England and New England, the *United States*." "It is just as improbable that free local institutions should spring up without a germ along American shores," wrote Adams, "as that English wheat should have grown here without planting." To Adams, therefore, the influence of Europe and of the Eastern seaboard upon America's development was supreme. In 1893, however, his "germ theory" was radically challenged by a young historian, Frederick Jackson Turner, who proposed instead a "frontier hypothesis."

Turner was born in 1861 in Portage, Wisconsin, the son of a journalist. Describing his boyhood there, he wrote: "I have poled down the Wisconsin [River] in a dugout with Indian guides . . . through virgin forests of balsam firs, seeing deer in the river,—antlered beauties who watched us come down with curious eyes and then broke for the tall timber,—hearing the squaws in their village on the high bank talk their low treble to the bass of the Indian polesman,—feeling that I belonged to it all." He also once saw a lynched man hanging from a tree, and witnessed gangs of Irish raftsmen taking over the town on wild sprees. These memories of Portage as a place where pioneers and Indians mingled on the edge of the wilderness stayed with him. "The frontier in that sense, you see, was real to me," he told a correspondent, "and when I studied history I did not keep my personal experience in a water tight compartment away from my studies." After his undergraduate work at the University of Wisconsin, Turner, who aimed to be a professional historian, went to Johns Hopkins for graduate training. Encountering the "germ theory" from Adams himself, he soon rejected the belief that democracy was carried to America by immigrants; it conflicted with what he knew from his own life in the Midwest. "The Frontier theory was pretty much a *reaction* from that due to my indignation," he later admitted; but he admired his economics instructor, Richard T. Ely, who taught him that society developed in well-defined stages—hunting and fishing, pastoral, agricultural, trading and commerce, and industrial—and that the concentration of settlement decided a variety of economic and social factors. Returning to the University of Wisconsin in 1890 with a doctorate, having chosen the frontier as his field of special study, Turner began to express his ideas in his teaching. Two early papers reveal the direction of his thought; but neither was as provocative as his paper, "The Significance of the Frontier in American History," which he delivered before the American Historical Association at the World's Columbian Exposition in Chicago in 1893.

"Up to our own day American history has been in a large degree the history of the colonization of the Great West," Turner wrote. "The existence of an area of free land, its continuous recession, and the advance of American settlement westward, explain American development." In the East familiar institutions had evolved in a limited area; but on the continually advancing frontier line, American social development continually began over again. "This perennial rebirth, this fluidity of American life, this expansion westward with its new opportunities, its continuous touch with the simplicity of primitive society, furnish the forces dominating American character. The true point of view in the history of this nation is not the Atlantic coast, it is the Great West." "The frontier is the line of most rapid and effective Americanization," he stated. "The wilderness masters the colonist":

It finds him a European in dress, industries, tools, modes of travel, and thought. It takes him from the railroad car and puts him in the birch canoe. It strips off the garments of civilization and arrays him in the hunting shirt and the moccasin. It puts him in the log cabin of the Cherokee and Iroquois and runs an Indian palisade around him. Before long he has gone to planting Indian corn and plowing with a sharp stick; he shouts the war cry and takes the scalp in orthodox Indian fashion. In short, at the frontier the environment is at first too strong for the man. He must accept the conditions which it furnishes, or perish, and so he fits himself into the Indian clearings and follows the Indian trails. Little by little he transforms the wilderness, but the outcome is not the old Europe, not simply the development of Germanic germs, any more than the first phenomenon was a case of reversion to the Germanic mark. The fact is, that here is a new product that is American.

As the frontier moved from the Atlantic to the Blue Ridge, to the Mississippi valley, to the Rockies, to the Pacific, social and political life had grown less complex and more distinctly American. The evidence even, perhaps, illustrated the course of universal history. "The United States lies like a huge page in the history of society," Turner said. "Line by line as we read this continental page from West to East we find the record of social evolution." "Stand at Cumberland Gap," he went on, "and watch the procession of civilization, marching single file—the buffalo following the trail to the salt springs, the Indian, the fur-trader and hunter, the cattle-raiser, the pioneer farmer—and the frontier has passed by. Stand at South Pass in the Rockies a century later and see the same procession with wider intervals between." There were actually several frontiers in each area—the trader's, the rancher's, or the miner's—and each line of settlement was affected by different attractions—geological conditions, the Indian trade, good cattle ranges, army posts, or good soils. "Sections" rather than states came into existence from the relations between the several geographic regions. The society within each section adapted to the particular physical and social environment, and the interacting sections created the American national spirit.

And what, Turner asked, was the impact of the frontier on the East and on the Old World? The frontier promoted the formation of a composite American nationality; it was a melting pot where immigrants were Americanized, liberated, and fused into a mixed race, "English in neither nationality nor characteristics." The frontier's advance also decreased America's dependence on England for supplies; and, after the Revolution, "the legislation which most developed the powers of the national government, and played the largest part in its activity, was conditioned on the frontier." The Louisiana Purchase, and most national political action regarding land, tariff, and other internal improvements, resulted from frontier needs and demands; "the frontier worked against the sectionalism of the coast." The frontier made the American population as a whole more mobile, altering life in the East and even the Old World. The most important effect of the frontier, however, was the furtherance of democracy in America and in Europe.

Turner concluded by arguing that the American intellect's most striking features were produced by frontier life:

> That coarseness and strength combined with acuteness and inquisitiveness; that practical, inventive turn of mind, quick to find expedients; that masterful grasp of material things, lacking in the artistic but powerful to effect great ends; that restless, nervous energy; that dominant individualism, working for good and for evil, and withal that buoyancy and exuberance which comes with freedom—these are traits of the frontier, or traits called out elsewhere because of the existence of the frontier. Since the days when the fleet of Columbus sailed into the waters of the New World, America has been another name for opportunity, and the people of the United States have taken their tone from the incessant expansion which has not only been open but has even been forced upon them.

"He would be a rash prophet who should assert that the expansive character of American life has now entirely ceased," Turner wrote. "Movement has been its dominant fact, and, unless this training has no effect upon a people, the American energy will continually demand a wider field for its exercise. But never again will such gifts of free land offer themselves." The ever-retreating frontier had been to the United States and more remotely to Europe what the Mediterranean Sea once was to the Greeks, offering new experiences and calling out new institutions and activities. "And now, four centuries from the discovery of America, at the end of a hundred years of life under the Constitution, the frontier has gone, and with its going has closed the first period of American history."

Turner's paper at first received scant attention; but by 1900, after he and his students had propagated its theme, the "frontier hypothesis" had defeated the "germ theory" to become the prevailing view of American history until Turner's death in 1932. During his career at Wisconsin and Harvard he never refined adequately his conception of the process at work in Western development. Perhaps the tragic deaths of two of his children checked his growth as a scholar; certainly he lavished time on his students instead of writing books; in any case he was a perfectionist, whose greater talent was for methodically assembling data than for setting down the results. The frontier eventually interested him less than the geographic sections of America, on which he wrote another paper, "The Significance of the Section in American History," in 1925. The "frontier hypothesis," however, captured the American public's imagination as well as the historical profession's. As Turner observed, the United States Census of 1890 no longer recognized the frontier's existence; and the movement West, noted by Franklin and Tocqueville, celebrated by Bancroft, Parkman, and countless other writers as the tide of history, was becoming a nostalgic topic in both West and East, preserving the dream of a simpler, more natural way of life. Turner further included the whole country in his thesis; by seeing the West as the place where North and South met and mingled into a nation, he assisted a sense of American unity and optimism as the memory of the Civil War receded. His paper still can seem immediately persuasive. It also exploited the newly developing social sciences in an unprecedented fashion in American historiography, and raised appealing problems for more research.

Turner's thesis, often overstated by his disciples, has had many critics since the 1930s. His poetic language and loose terminology obscure his argument, the very words "frontier" and "West" never being made explicit, and statistical evidence shows that the land was not free for most settlers; they bought it from speculators. Turner ignored the coastal frontier, the procession through Cumberland Gap was less orderly than he believed, and the pioneer's life was more social. Cities attracted population too, from Europe and from within America, and in times of economic depression the frontier did not act as the discontented population's "safety valve"; migration to it demonstrably decreased. Eastern influence on the West remained strong in matters of government, religion, and cultural and educational ideals; in fact, the frontier encouraged some of the American character's less attractive features, such as lawlessness, wastefulness, careless self-confidence, and ruthlessness toward nature and other peoples. And, if the frontier formed the settler so much, as Turner claimed, why did not an identical way of life develop on other frontiers—in Canada, Australia, Siberia, or South Africa? Turner's critics have charged him with seeing the frontier as the sole cause of the American identity, though he himself insisted that it was only one aspect of the truth. The Depression reduced the glamor of individualism for many Americans; to Marxist historians, Turner ignores the class struggle and the growth of industries and towns. Perhaps the "frontier hypothesis" is rooted in Turner's personal ideology. In its crudest form it perpetuates myths of the West, and reduces American history to the story of cowboys and Indians. But, despite these and other objections, it is widely assumed today to be correct in its major assumption—that free land has defined the American experience; and it has proved to be by far the most fertile explanation of the history of the United States.

It is interesting to recall that Turner and Du Bois were contemporaries, and that both saw American history as the story of freedom. Turner saw freedom in terms of the land and its opportunities. Du Bois is so important a historian because he intensely perceived that freedom was still an unfulfilled ideal for Americans—indeed, for mankind—and described the American experience accordingly. Turner, though conservative in spirit, was nonetheless one of the "Progressive" historians, who, like the broad Progressive movement in contemporary politics, viewed the American experience in the tradition of democratic reform. Charles Beard, however, whose reputation rose as Turner's fell, was a left-wing Progressive, an activist, and a prolific and versatile author. Beard, born in Indiana in 1874, was impressed in youth by Populist doctrines, and, while studying at Oxford, he lectured on the Industrial Revolution to workingmen. Appointed to the faculty of Columbia University in 1904, he taught both history and politics, and announced with a colleague, James Harvey Robinson, a fresh approach to history which they called "the new history." A response to the rapid rise of the social sciences, it sought to cover all aspects of human affairs and make history pragmatically useful. Beard's interpretation of American history was not as original as Turner's, but it has been almost as influential. The chief purpose of his research and writing was to relate economic interests and politics, taking as his guide James Madison's theory of party conflict stated in the tenth of the *Federalist Papers*; and, dismissing other historical schools, Beard proposed the "theory of economic determinism" as a new means of understanding American history.

During his career Beard applied this theory in non-Marxist form to four important historical events. In his first, most hotly debated book, *An Economic Interpretation of the Constitution of the United States* (1913), he statistically reviewed the amount and the geographical distribution of money and public securities held by members of the Constitutional Convention. He found that the Convention was composed of leading property holders, not selfless patriots, who had excluded from their meeting representatives of the propertyless mass of the American population. The resulting Constitution was "an economic document drawn with superb skill by men whose property interests were immediately at stake; and as such it appealed directly and unerringly to identical interests in the country at large." In 1915, Beard published *Economic Origins of Jeffersonian Democracy*, and argued that political parties in the United States arose from the contest between the capitalist and the democratic pioneer.

After resigning from Columbia in 1917 in defense of academic freedom, Beard coauthored *The Rise of American Civilization* (1927) with his wife Mary, and reached a large popular audience. Taking a comprehensive view of the American past up to the present, the Beards reinterpreted it largely in terms of America's economic growth and the interests of specific groups. England's search for trade and profits had laid the structural base, the colonists had started their own business enterprises, and an energetic minority of merchants had planned and accomplished the Revolution. The hinge of American history, though, was not the winning of independence but the mid-nineteenth-century transition from an agricultural to an industrial society, a deep-running change which culminated in the Civil War. The war, really a class struggle between Northern merchants and industrialists and the Southern planting aristocracy, was "a Second American Revolution and in a strict sense, the First," a genuine social revolution in which "the fighting was a fleeting incident." Northern capitalism triumphed, only to be challenged in the opening twentieth century by new forces making for social democracy. Finally, Beard's concern in his later years to link foreign affairs and domestic policies led to his writing *President Roosevelt and the Coming of the War, 1941* (which appeared just before his death in 1948). In this controversial work, Beard, an isolationist, accused Roosevelt of deliberately leading the United States into war in pursuit of his personal power. Beard's books, bold though sometimes erratic, appealed to readers of the New Deal era who respected economic explanations. Though Beard's findings have since been largely disproved (sometimes from information unavailable to him), his insights stimulated a new generation of scholars to explore and quantify the social and economic evidence of the American past. *The Rise of American Civilization* is also the last major attempt to give all American history a coherent theme or direction.

Surveying American historiography, we see certain familiar questions of Western historiography being asked in an American context, and familiar answers delivered in localized form. Both questions and answers, however, are distinct enough to create an individual historical tradition. We also see some "superhistorians" on a national scale, like

Bancroft and Turner, who illustrate that the national historical inquiry primarily examines the American character. Other concepts interpreting that character include the absence of a medieval heritage, the abundance of exploitable natural resources, the population's mobility. Crèvecoeur's question of 1782 still awaits a unanimous answer. But Americans have seldom been deeply attached to the past, despite its importance to the Puritans and the Founding Fathers. Many immigrated to flee from their own history, and most have charted their lives by the future, partly because, in Emerson's phrase (which Turner copied), "America is another word for Opportunity." Failure for one man often proved to be opportunity for another, and new opportunities still constantly unfold. Nevertheless, in twentieth-century America—and in the Western world—the breadth and freedom of opportunity has narrowed, the effect, according to the American historian Walter Prescott Webb, of the closing of the "Great Frontier."

Writing in 1952, Webb argued that the American frontier Turner described was only a fragment of the vast vacant lands in North and South America, South Africa, Australia, and New Zealand which began opening up to the European "Metropolis" about the year 1500. Western man, half-starved, practically penniless, with very little freedom, and with almost no means of escape, grasped the miraculous gifts of land and treasure the explorers offered him, and vigorously exploited them. The first impact on Europe was mainly economic—a sudden excess of land and capital for division among a relatively fixed number of people. The spectacular business boom which followed favored those institutions and ideas adapted to a dynamic and prosperous society; and, especially on the frontier itself, society recrystallized under new conditions which gave the individual a time of maximum freedom. The advance of European settlement should explain much of Western civilization's modern development, Webb believed, just as the American advance explains American development. The waves of new wealth in succession led Western man to consider the boom the normal state; but about 1900 the "Great Frontier" closed down across the globe, the magnificent windfall ended, and, because the boom was a "frontier boom," it is unrepeatable. Any new, comparable boom will be quite different in form and consequences, and as yet none of the so-called "new frontiers" has materialized. No Columbus has come in from one of these voyages bringing continents and oceans, gold or silver, or grass or forest to the common man. The specialized institutions and methods of living Western man devised to function in a society dominated largely by frontier forces are meanwhile under severe strain. "If the frontier is gone," Webb concluded, "we should have the courage and honesty to recognize the fact, cease to cry for what we have lost, and devote our energy to finding solutions to the problems that now face a frontierless society."

This, I suggest, is the context in which American history, Western history, the Western idea of history itself, should now be reassessed. In the United States the physical frontier ended in 1890, but the old sense of human possibility it fostered lasted until about 1970; and then the end came in agony. It quickly followed the Kennedy years, when many Americans had welcomed a young President's call to be new pioneers on a "New Frontier" of unfulfilled hopes. History's theme then stood forth as advancing reason and liberty, its contents to be analyzed with detached intelligence; but the unfolding Vietnam War, a war abroad but also a rending of American society, produced instead a sharp sense of human limits. It denied Americans their expected "Great Society"; and it shook their faith in their country's fundamental innocence, their trust in its energy, and their hope that, alone among nations, the United States would escape a tragic fate. The war's diverse events revealed that, although the American story had often been told, the true perspective on that story was uncertain.

Such crises herald new histories to replace the old, unsettled views. They force new questions while events are still vivid; and current American questions converge once more upon the "new man's" actual nature. The historian who seeks to solve the new form of that problem performs his chief social function—and, if his answer appeals to his audience, he secures history's acceptance as a vital intellectual venture. But he must, in his argument, confront the new realities. To avoid these he may try to preserve illusions; then he deprives ongoing society of knowledge in some way able to strengthen it, thereby rejecting the main Western historical tradition. The next major American history may at first appear to be an experiment, but its scope will be total and its theme receptive to more technical inquiries. It will also look ahead; and, until it arrives, Americans will have no modern idea of their whole history, only the ideas previous generations gave them. A new American history, however, affects the world. In some degree all nations share each other's histories, selecting from all man's experience to serve their present needs. When any historic nation reinterprets itself, the result therefore affects the rest; and as we have seen, sometimes a national experience can help explain the history of mankind. Eighteenth-century Europe, in its expanding circumstances, challenged the historian to sustain "progressive" man. As the approaching twenty-first century brings the world more knowledge and different human possibilities, its challenge—and its disputed prize—is man's redefinition in another light.

III

It would be extraordinary if, in an age outstanding for its intellectual activity, the idea of history remained largely untouched. Western man has found it expedient to adopt new conceptions of the past before, notably in the eras of Augustine and Voltaire; and the conditions for a major elemental change are again clearly present in the late twentieth century. New discoveries, not least about man's place in the universe, have led to Western man's general uncertainty of mind; in most fields of knowledge, and in many areas of social life, he finds the traditional answers no longer appear to fit his circumstances. Never has historical study been so diverse in its interests, so lively, so readily possible, yet so unsure of the resulting information's meaning; and the public finds the past largely isolated from daily living. In short, Western man is now as remote from his past as Francis Bacon in Elizabethan England believed his own civilization to be, changed by printing, gunpowder, and the compass. Bacon's goal was new knowledge in place of old knowledge made obsolete, and Western man has now reached the same alarming but disturbingly promising moment in self-analysis from which were born in their time the modern idea of progress, the Christian view of history, even the very idea of history. For he too wonders who he is; and one road of inquiry points backward.

We have seen in this book a "superhistorian" emerging when a man, struggling with a pressing contemporary problem, turns to the past and finds an answer by combining research and insight. He stands out from other historians because, by an original perception, he solves the large historical problem of his day (which is also a human problem); simultaneously, he seems to point future historiography in a profitable new direction. A "superhistorian" also takes materials closest to him, and risks letting his personality enter his story. The great, difficult, historical issues shrink in size when tied to the immediate. No such resulting work of history is likely to last unless it accords with the evidence; but it only gains importance as a cultural force if it asks and answers a question acutely significant for both the seeker and his audience. It attests the circumstances which produced it. But, as we have seen, the questions of "superhistorians" always start as attempts to answer the fundamental, all-encompassing question, "Who am I?" Whenever men go back to asking this basic human question, it seems that the study of history returns to its original purpose of serving the present, and renews its powers of instruction. We are not wholly what we were, nor will we remain what we are; but to ignore a connection between past and present is to deny ourselves a vital part of knowledge of ourselves as human beings, the growth of which is the study of history's chief merit. The real heroes of history are therefore not the usual actors, but the "superhistorians" who have advanced human self-knowledge through their insights and their skills.

There are, of course, difficulties in creating a new history. History is a large and cumbersome discipline, covering the whole range of human experience. It also has immense cultural implications; and men guard the history they know jealously, almost superstitiously, in spite of outward indifference to it and regardless of evidence or logic. In this respect modern man is still very like primitive man; and the authorities over him, with a vested interest in preconceived versions, have an age-old conflict with intellectual leadership. But, once man has been changed by new experience, his mind cannot be adjusted to its earlier form; once an ambitious mariner had sailed the Atlantic, he could not be entirely satisfied with sailing the Mediterranean, for he would see it differently; and Western man, too, should now admit the growth he has made, and take a new perspective on himself. When Western man devises a new history, he will be encouraged by the example of his predecessors in all ages who took the same initiative to give the human past order and meaning. Instead of seeing them as discredited scholars, he may find in them his intellectual peers, perhaps his superiors in creative thought; and he will recognize that his goal and theirs are shared— a new story of man which answers the searchings of the age, and a new place for the memory in human consciousness.

Why should we believe that the list of "superhistorians" is finished? The present age is no different in its sense of disorientation from the ages which produced Herodotus, Augustine, Voltaire, and Ranke; and the prize today is a new history not just for America, or for any nation, but for the world. "Each age writes the history of the past anew with reference to the conditions uppermost in its own times," wrote Turner; and our heirs will belittle us if they cannot count a new comprehensive version of man's past among our many achievements. Though current historical study may seem lively to us, later generations may consider it only an aimless prelude to another of historiography's unpredictable beginnings. Christian historians unexpectedly supplanted Greek and Roman; Voltaire did not anticipate Scott; nor did Scott foresee Ranke, nor Ranke the influence of Marx or Toynbee. No new answer is likely to be complete, and, we must surely conclude, historical truth lies in a multiplicity of views; for any new history, like all its precedents, will be the reflection of its age. Yet, as past time ends for the moment with ourselves, we in turn can assess it by asking our own questions from life in the present; and our questions are as legitimate as the old questions first were, whose insolubility is a spur to further asking. The idea of history is a repeated act of human intelligence. The story of man's past is still waiting to be written.

BIBLIOGRAPHY

GENERAL READING

CARR, EDWARD HALLETT, *What Is History?*, Alfred A. Knopf, New York, 1962.

COLLINGWOOD, R. G., *The Idea of History*, 1946; reprint, Oxford Univ. Press, New York, 1956.

HIGHAM, JOHN, et al., *History*, Prentice-Hall, Englewood Cliffs, N.J., 1965.

HUGHES, H. STUART, *History as Art and as Science: Twin Vistas on the Past*, Harper and Row, New York, 1964.

KAMMEN, MICHAEL, ed., *The Past Before Us: Contemporary Historical Writing in the United States*, Cornell Univ. Press, Ithaca, N.Y., 1980.

PLUMB, J. H., *The Death of the Past*, Macmillan, London, 1969.

POPPER, KARL, *The Poverty of Historicism*, Harper and Row, New York, 1964.

STRAYER, JOSEPH R., ed., *The Interpretation of History*, Peter Smith, New York, 1950.

Chapter One
HERODOTUS AND THUCYDIDES

COCHRANE, C. N., *Thucydides and the Science of History*, 1929; reprint, Russell and Russell, New York, 1965.

CORNFORD, F. M., *Thucydides Mythistoricus*, 1907; reprint, Univ. of Pennsylvania Press, Philadelphia, 1971.

GRANT, MICHAEL, *The Ancient Historians*, Charles Scribner's Sons, New York, 1970.

HERODOTUS, *The Histories*, trans. A. de Selincourt, rev. A. R. Burn, Penguin Books, London, 1972.

MYRES, J. L., *Herodotus: Father of History*, Clarendon Press, Oxford, 1953.

DE SELINCOURT, AUBREY, *The World of Herodotus*, Little, Brown, Boston, 1962.

THUCYDIDES, *The Peloponnesian War*, trans. Rex Warner, Penguin Books, London, 1954.

WOODHEAD, A. GEOFFREY, *Thucydides on the Nature of Power*, Harvard University Press, Cambridge, Mass., 1970.

Chapter Two
AUGUSTINE

AUGUSTINE, *The City of God*, trans. John Healey, 2 vols., E. P. Dutton, New York, 1957.

———, *The Confessions*, trans. R. S. Pine-Coffin, Penguin Books, London, 1961.

BEDE, *A History of the English Church and People*, trans. Leo Sherley-Price, Penguin Books, London, 1955.

BROWN, PETER, *Augustine of Hippo: A Biography*, Univ. of California Press, Berkeley and Los Angeles, 1967.

BUTTERFIELD, HERBERT, *Christianity and History*, Charles Scribner's Sons, New York, 1950.

COCHRANE, C. N., *Christianity and Classical Culture: A Study of Thought and Action from Augustus to Augustine*, 1940; reprint, Oxford Univ. Press, New York, 1957.

MC INTIRE, C. T., ed., *God, History, and Historians: Modern Christian Views of History*, Oxford Univ. Press, New York, 1977.

MILBURN, R. L. P., *Early Christian Interpretations of History*, 1954; reprint, Greenwood Press, New York, 1980.

Chapter Three
PETRARCH AND MACHIAVELLI

BISHOP, MORRIS, *Petrarch and his World*, Univ. of Indiana Press, Bloomington, 1963.

GILBERT, FELIX, *Machiavelli and Guicciardini: Politics and History in Sixteenth-Century Florence*, Princeton Univ. Press, 1965.

MACHIAVELLI, NICCOLO, *The Discourses*, trans. L. J. Walker, Penguin Books, London, 1970.

———, *History of Florence and of the Affairs of Italy*, Harper and Row, New York, 1960.

———, *The Prince*, trans. George Bull, Penguin Books, London, 1961.

MOMMSEN, THEODOR H., "Petrarch's Conception of the Dark Ages," *Speculum*, XVII (1942), 226–242.

RIDOLFI, ROBERTO, *The Life of Niccolo Machiavelli*, trans. Cecil Grayson, Univ. of Chicago Press, 1964.

WHITFIELD, J. H., *Petrarch and the Renascence*, 1943; reprint, Russell and Russell, New York, 1965.

Chapter Four
VOLTAIRE

BECKER, CARL, *The Heavenly City of the Eighteenth-Century Philosophers*, Yale Univ. Press, New Haven, 1932.

BESTERMAN, THEODORE, *Voltaire*, 3rd edition, Univ. of Chicago Press, 1977.

BRUMFITT, J. H., *Voltaire: Historian*, Oxford Univ. Press, 1958.

MACAULAY, THOMAS BABINGTON, *Selected Writings*, ed. J. Clive and T. Pinney, Univ. of Chicago Press, 1972.

NISBET, ROBERT, *History of the Idea of Progress*, Basic Books, New York, 1980.

SWAIN, J. W., *Edward Gibbon the Historian*, Macmillan, London, 1966.

VOLTAIRE, F. M. AROUET DE, *The Age of Louis XIV*, trans. M. P. Pollack, J. M. Dent and Sons, London, 1961.

———, *Letters on England*, trans. Leonard Tancock, Penguin Books, London, 1980.

Chapter Five
SCOTT

COCKSHUT, A. O. J., *The Achievement of Walter Scott*, New York Univ. Press, 1969.

GORDON, ROBERT C., *Under Which King?: A Study of the Scottish Waverley Novels*, Oliver and Boyd, Edinburgh, 1969.

JOHNSON, EDGAR, *Sir Walter Scott: The Great Unknown*, 2 vols., Hamish Hamilton, London, 1970.

LUKACS, GEORGE, *The Historical Novel*, 1962; reprint, Humanities Press, Atlantic Highlands, N.J., 1978.

MICHELET, JULES, *The People*, ed. J. P. McKay, Univ. of Illinois Press, Urbana, 1973.

SCOTT, WALTER, *Redgauntlet*, 1824; reprint, E. P. Dutton, New York, 1957.

———, *Waverley*, 1814; reprint, E. P. Dutton, New York, 1969.

TREVOR-ROPER, H. R., *The Romantic Movement and the Study of History*, Athlone Press, London, 1969.

Chapter Six
RANKE

BUTTERFIELD, HERBERT, *Man on His Past: The Study of the History of Historical Scholarship*, Beacon Press, Boston, 1960.

GEYL, PIETER, *Debates with Historians,* ch. 1, "Ranke in Light of the Catastrophe," World Publishing Co., Cleveland, 1958.

GOOCH, GEORGE PEABODY, *History and Historians in the Nineteenth Century,* Beacon Press, Boston, 1959.

IGGERS, GEORG G., *The German Conception of History: The National Conception of Historical Thought from Herder to the Present,* Wesleyan Univ. Press, Middletown, Conn., 1968.

———, "The Image of Ranke in American and German Historical Thought," *History and Theory,* II (1961), 17–40.

VON LAUE, THEODORE H., *Leopold Ranke: The Formative Years,* Princeton Univ. Press, 1950.

VON RANKE, LEOPOLD, *History of the Latin and Teutonic Nations (1495–1514),* trans. G. R. Dennis, G. Bell and Sons, London, 1909.

———, *The Theory and Practice of History,* ed. G. G. Iggers and K. von Moltke, Bobbs-Merrill, Indianapolis, 1973.

Chapter Seven
MARX

HEER, NANCY W., *Politics and History in the Soviet Union,* M.I.T. Press, Cambridge, Mass., 1971.

HEGEL, G. W. F., *Lectures on the Philosophy of World History,* ed. D. Forbes, Cambridge Univ. Press, 1975.

MCLELLAN, DAVID, *Karl Marx: His Life and Thought,* Harper and Row, New York, 1974.

MARX, KARL, *Writings of the Young Marx on Philosophy and Society,* ed. L. D. Easton and K. H. Guddat, Doubleday, Garden City, N.Y., 1967.

MARX, KARL, and ENGELS, FRIEDRICH, *Basic Writings on Philosophy and Society,* Doubleday, Garden City, N.Y., 1959.

———, *The Communist Manifesto,* ed. A. J. P. Taylor, Penguin Books, London, 1967.

RADER, MELVIN M., *Marx's Interpretation of History,* Oxford Univ. Press, 1979.

WILSON, EDMUND, *To the Finland Station,* Doubleday, Garden City, N.Y., 1953.

Chapter Eight
NIETZSCHE

DANTO, ARTHUR C., *Nietzsche as Philosopher,* Macmillan, New York, 1965.

HAYMAN, RONALD, *Nietzsche: A Critical Life,* Weidenfeld and Nicolson, London, 1980.

KAUFMANN, WALTER A., *Nietzsche: Philosopher, Psychologist, Antichrist,* World Publishing Co., Cleveland, 1964.

LEA, FRANK A., *The Tragic Philosopher: A Study of Friedrich Nietzsche*, Methuen, London, 1957.

NIETZSCHE, FRIEDRICH, *The Birth of Tragedy, and the Genealogy of Morals*, trans. Francis Golffing, Doubleday, Garden City, N.Y., 1956.

————, *Thus Spoke Zarathustra*, trans. R. J. Hollingdale, Penguin Books, London, 1969.

————, *The Use and Abuse of History*, trans. Adrian Collins, Bobbs-Merrill, Indianapolis, 1957.

SOLOMON, ROBERT C., ed., *Nietzsche: A Collection of Critical Essays*, Doubleday, Garden City, N.Y., 1973.

Chapter Nine
DU BOIS

BARZUN, JACQUES, *Race: A Study in Superstition*, Harper and Row, New York, 1965.

BRODERICK, FRANCIS L., *W. E. B. Du Bois: Negro Leader in a Time of Crisis*, Stanford Univ. Press, Palo Alto, 1959.

CLARKE, JOHN HENRIK, et al., *Black Titan: W. E. B. Du Bois*, Beacon Press, Boston, 1970.

DU BOIS, W. E. B., *Dusk of Dawn: An Essay toward an Autobiography of a Race Concept*, Schocken Books, New York, 1968.

————, *The Gift of Black Folk*, The Stratford Co., Boston, 1924.

————, *The Negro*, 1915; reprint, Kraus-Thomson Org., Millwood, N.Y., 1975.

————, *The Souls of Black Folk*, introduction Saunders Redding, Fawcett Publications, Greenwich, Conn., 1976.

FAGE, J. D., ed., *Africa Discovers Her Past*, Oxford Univ. Press, 1970.

Chapter Ten
TOYNBEE

DRAY, WILLIAM H., "Toynbee's Search for Historical Laws," *History and Theory*, I (1960), 32–54.

HUGHES, H. STUART, *Oswald Spengler: A Critical Estimate*, Charles Scribner's Sons, New York, 1962.

MONTAGU, M. F. ASHLEY, ed., *Toynbee and History: Critical Essays and Reviews*, Porter Sargent, Boston, 1956.

TOYNBEE, ARNOLD J., *Civilization on Trial, and The World and The West*, Oxford Univ. Press, New York, 1948.

————, *Experiences*, Oxford Univ. Press, New York, 1969.

————, *Mankind and Mother Earth*, Oxford Univ. Press, New York, 1976.

————, *A Study of History*, abridged, D. C. Somervell, 2 vols., Oxford Univ. Press, New York, 1947–57.

TREVOR-ROPER, H. R., "Arnold Toynbee's Millennium," *Encounters*, ed. Stephen Spender et al., Basic Books, New York, 1963, 131–151.

Chapter Eleven
WELLS

BERGONZI, BERNARD, *The Early H. G. Wells: A Study of the Scientific Romances*, Univ. of Toronto Press, 1961.
——, ed., *H. G. Wells: A Collection of Critical Essays*, Prentice-Hall, Englewood Cliffs, N.J., 1976.
HILLEGAS, MARK R., *The Future as Nightmare: H. G. Wells and the Anti-Utopians*, Oxford Univ. Press, New York, 1967.
MACKENZIE, NORMAN, and MACKENZIE, JEANNE, *The Time Traveller: The Life of H. G. Wells*, Weidenfeld and Nicolson, London, 1973.
WELLS, H. G., *Experiment in Autobiography*, Macmillan, New York, 1934.
——, *The Fate of Homo Sapiens*, Secker and Warburg, London, 1939.
——, *The Outline of History*, 3rd edition, Macmillan, New York, 1921.
——, *Seven Science Fiction Novels*, Dover Publications, New York, 1934.

Epilogue
THE AMERICAN FRONTIER

BILLINGTON, RAY ALLEN, *Frederick Jackson Turner: Historian, Scholar, Teacher*, Oxford Univ. Press, New York, 1973.
CUNLIFFE, MARCUS, and WINKS, ROBIN, eds., *Pastmasters: Some Essays on American Historians*, Harper and Row, New York, 1969.
DOUGHTY, HOWARD, *Francis Parkman*, Macmillan, New York, 1962.
FITZGERALD, FRANCES, *America Revised*, Atlantic-Little, Brown, Boston, 1979.
HOFSTADTER, RICHARD, *The Progressive Historians*, Alfred A. Knopf, New York, 1968.
NYE, RUSSEL B., *George Bancroft: Brahmin Rebel*, Alfred A. Knopf, New York, 1945.
POTTER, DAVID, *People of Plenty: Economic Abundance and the American Character*, Univ. of Chicago Press, 1954.
SAMUELS, ERNEST, *Henry Adams: The Middle Years*, Harvard Univ. Press, Cambridge, Mass., 1958.
TAYLOR, GEORGE R., ed., *The Turner Thesis Concerning the Role of the Frontier in American History*, D. C. Heath and Co., Boston, 1956.
WEBB, WALTER PRESCOTT, *The Great Frontier*, Univ. of Texas Press, Austin, 1952.
WISH, HARVEY, *The American Historian*, Oxford Univ. Press, New York, 1960.

INDEX